Contino Publishers

Philosophy

1

I Edition by Contino Publishers Ltd.

May 2014

ISBN : 978-88-99049-03-4

Friedrich Nietzsche

Beyond Good and Evil

with the original
German text in appendix

Translated from German
by Helen Zimmern

Dorking, UK

Preface

SUPPOSING that Truth is a woman—what then? Is there not ground for suspecting that all philosophers, in so far as they have been dogmatists, have failed to understand women—that the terrible seriousness and clumsy importunity with which they have usually paid their addresses to Truth, have been unskilled and unseemly methods for winning a woman? Certainly she has never allowed herself to be won; and at present every kind of dogma stands with sad and discouraged mien—IF, indeed, it stands at all! For there are scoffers who maintain that it has fallen, that all dogma lies on the ground—nay more, that it is at its last gasp. But to speak seriously, there are good grounds for hoping that all dogmatizing in philosophy, whatever solemn, whatever conclusive and decided airs it has assumed, may have been only a noble puerilism and tyronism; and probably the time is at hand when it will be once and again understood WHAT has actually sufficed for the basis of such imposing and absolute philosophical edifices as the dogmatists have hitherto reared: perhaps some popular superstition of immemorial time (such as the soul-superstition, which, in the form of subject- and ego-superstition, has not yet ceased doing mischief): perhaps some play upon words, a deception on the part of grammar, or an audacious generalization of very restricted, very personal, very human—all-too-human facts. The philosophy of the dogmatists, it is to be hoped, was only a promise for thousands of years afterwards, as was astrology in still earlier times, in the service of which probably more labour, gold, acuteness, and patience have been spent than on any actual science hitherto: we owe to it, and to its "super-terrestrial" pretensions in Asia and Egypt, the grand style of architecture. It seems that in order to inscribe themselves upon the heart of humanity with everlasting claims, all great things have first to wander about the earth as enormous and awe-inspiring caricatures: dogmatic philosophy has been a caricature of this kind—for instance, the Vedanta doctrine in Asia, and Platonism in Europe. Let us not be ungrateful to it, although it must certainly be confessed that the worst, the most tiresome, and the most dangerous of errors hitherto has been a dogmatist error—namely, Plato's invention of Pure Spirit and the Good in Itself. But now when it has been surmounted, when Europe, rid of this nightmare, can again draw breath freely and at least enjoy a healthier—sleep, we, WHOSE DUTY IS WAKEFULNESS ITSELF, are the heirs of all the strength which the struggle against this error has fostered. It amounted to the very inversion of truth, and the denial of the PERSPECTIVE—the fundamental condition—of life, to speak of Spirit and the Good as Plato spoke of them; indeed one might ask, as a physician: "How did such a malady attack that finest product of antiquity, Plato? Had the wicked Socrates really corrupted him? Was Socrates after all a corrupter of youths, and deserved his hemlock?" But the struggle against Plato, or—to speak plainer, and for the "people"—the struggle against the ecclesiastical oppression of millenniums of Christianity (FOR CHRISTIANITY IS PLATONISM FOR THE "PEOPLE"), produced in Europe a magnificent tension of soul, such as had not existed anywhere previously; with such a tensely strained bow one can now aim at the furthest goals. As a matter of fact, the European feels this tension as a state of distress, and twice attempts have been made in grand style to unbend the bow: once by means of Jesuitism, and the second time by means of democratic enlightenment—which, with the aid of liberty of the press and newspaper-reading, might, in fact, bring it about that the spirit would not so easily find itself in "distress"! (The Germans invented gunpowder—all credit to them! but they again made things square—they invented printing.) But we, who are neither Jesuits, nor democrats, nor even sufficiently Germans, we GOOD EUROPEANS, and free, VERY free spirits—we have it still, all the distress of spirit and all the tension of its bow! And perhaps also the arrow, the duty, and, who knows? THE GOAL TO AIM AT....

Sils Maria Upper Engadine, JUNE, 1885.

Chapter I

Prejudices of the philosophers

1. The Will to Truth, which is to tempt us to many a hazardous enterprise, the famous Truthfulness of which all philosophers have hitherto spoken with respect, what questions has this Will to Truth not laid before us! What strange, perplexing, questionable questions! It is already a long story; yet it seems as if it were hardly commenced. Is it any wonder if we at last grow distrustful, lose patience, and turn impatiently away? That this Sphinx teaches us at last to ask questions ourselves? WHO is it really that puts questions to us here? WHAT really is this "Will to Truth" in us? In fact we made a long halt at the question as to the origin of this Will—until at last we came to an absolute standstill before a yet more fundamental question. We inquired about the VALUE of this Will. Granted that we want the truth: WHY NOT RATHER untruth? And uncertainty? Even ignorance? The problem of the value of truth presented itself before us—or was it we who presented ourselves before the problem? Which of us is the Oedipus here? Which the Sphinx? It would seem to be a rendezvous of questions and notes of interrogation. And could it be believed that it at last seems to us as if the problem had never been propounded before, as if we were the first to discern it, get a sight of it, and

RISK RAISING it? For there is risk in raising it, perhaps there is no greater risk.

2. "HOW COULD anything originate out of its opposite? For example, truth out of error? or the Will to Truth out of the will to deception? or the generous deed out of selfishness? or the pure sun-bright vision of the wise man out of covetousness? Such genesis is impossible; whoever dreams of it is a fool, nay, worse than a fool; things of the highest value must have a different origin, an origin of THEIR own—in this transitory, seductive, illusory, paltry world, in this turmoil of delusion and cupidity, they cannot have their source. But rather in the lap of Being, in the transitory, in the concealed God, in the 'Thing-in-itself—THERE must be their source, and nowhere else!"—This mode of reasoning discloses the typical prejudice by which metaphysicians of all times can be recognized, this mode of valuation is at the back of all their logical procedure; through this "belief" of theirs, they exert themselves for their "knowledge," for something that is in the end solemnly christened "the Truth." The fundamental belief of metaphysicians is THE BELIEF IN ANTITHESES OF VALUES. It never occurred even to the wariest of them to doubt here on the very threshold (where doubt, however, was most necessary); though they had made a solemn vow, "DE OMNIBUS DUBITANDUM." For it may be doubted, firstly, whether antitheses exist at all; and secondly, whether

the popular valuations and antitheses of value upon which metaphysicians have set their seal, are not perhaps merely superficial estimates, merely provisional perspectives, besides being probably made from some corner, perhaps from below—"frog perspectives," as it were, to borrow an expression current among painters. In spite of all the value which may belong to the true, the positive, and the unselfish, it might be possible that a higher and more fundamental value for life generally should be assigned to pretence, to the will to delusion, to selfishness, and cupidity. It might even be possible that WHAT constitutes the value of those good and respected things, consists precisely in their being insidiously related, knotted, and crocheted to these evil and apparently opposed things— perhaps even in being essentially identical with them. Perhaps! But who wishes to concern himself with such dangerous "Perhaps"! For that investigation one must await the advent of a new order of philosophers, such as will have other tastes and inclinations, the reverse of those hitherto prevalent—philosophers of the dangerous "Perhaps" in every sense of the term. And to speak in all seriousness, I see such new philosophers beginning to appear.

3. Having kept a sharp eye on philosophers, and having read between their lines long enough, I now say to myself that the greater part of conscious thinking must be counted among the instinctive functions, and it

is so even in the case of philosophical thinking; one has here to learn anew, as one learned anew about heredity and "innateness." As little as the act of birth comes into consideration in the whole process and procedure of heredity, just as little is "being-conscious" OPPOSED to the instinctive in any decisive sense; the greater part of the conscious thinking of a philosopher is secretly influenced by his instincts, and forced into definite channels. And behind all logic and its seeming sovereignty of movement, there are valuations, or to speak more plainly, physiological demands, for the maintenance of a definite mode of life For example, that the certain is worth more than the uncertain, that illusion is less valuable than "truth" such valuations, in spite of their regulative importance for US, might notwithstanding be only superficial valuations, special kinds of *niaiserie*, such as may be necessary for the maintenance of beings such as ourselves. Supposing, in effect, that man is not just the "measure of things."

4. The falseness of an opinion is not for us any objection to it: it is here, perhaps, that our new language sounds most strangely. The question is, how far an opinion is life-furthering, life-preserving, species-preserving, perhaps species-rearing, and we are fundamentally inclined to maintain that the falsest opinions (to which the synthetic judgments a priori belong), are the most indispensable to us, that without a recognition of logical fictions, without a comparison of

reality with the purely IMAGINED world of the absolute and immutable, without a constant counterfeiting of the world by means of numbers, man could not live—that the renunciation of false opinions would be a renunciation of life, a negation of life. TO RECOGNISE UNTRUTH AS A CONDITION OF LIFE; that is certainly to impugn the traditional ideas of value in a dangerous manner, and a philosophy which ventures to do so, has thereby alone placed itself beyond good and evil.

5. That which causes philosophers to be regarded half-distrustfully and half-mockingly, is not the oft-repeated discovery how innocent they are—how often and easily they make mistakes and lose their way, in short, how childish and childlike they are,—but that there is not enough honest dealing with them, whereas they all raise a loud and virtuous outcry when the problem of truthfulness is even hinted at in the remotest manner. They all pose as though their real opinions had been discovered and attained through the self-evolving of a cold, pure, divinely indifferent dialectic (in contrast to all sorts of mystics, who, fairer and foolisher, talk of "inspiration"), whereas, in fact, a prejudiced proposition, idea, or "suggestion," which is generally their heart's desire abstracted and refined, is defended by them with arguments sought out after the event. They are all advocates who do not wish to be regarded as such, generally astute defenders, also, of their

prejudices, which they dub "truths,"—and VERY far from having the conscience which bravely admits this to itself, very far from having the good taste of the courage which goes so far as to let this be understood, perhaps to warn friend or foe, or in cheerful confidence and self-ridicule. The spectacle of the Tartuffery of old Kant, equally stiff and decent, with which he entices us into the dialectic by-ways that lead (more correctly mislead) to his "categorical imperative"—makes us fastidious ones smile, we who find no small amusement in spying out the subtle tricks of old moralists and ethical preachers. Or, still more so, the hocus-pocus in mathematical form, by means of which Spinoza has, as it were, clad his philosophy in mail and mask—in fact, the "love of HIS wisdom," to translate the term fairly and squarely—in order thereby to strike terror at once into the heart of the assailant who should dare to cast a glance on that invincible maiden, that Pallas Athene:—how much of personal timidity and vulnerability does this masquerade of a sickly recluse betray!

6. It has gradually become clear to me what every great philosophy up till now has consisted of—namely, the confession of its originator, and a species of involuntary and unconscious auto-biography; and moreover that the moral (or immoral) purpose in every philosophy has constituted the true vital germ out of which the entire plant has always grown. Indeed, to understand how the abstrusest metaphysical assertions

of a philosopher have been arrived at, it is always well (and wise) to first ask oneself: "What morality do they (or does he) aim at?" Accordingly, I do not believe that an "impulse to knowledge" is the father of philosophy; but that another impulse, here as elsewhere, has only made use of knowledge (and mistaken knowledge!) as an instrument. But whoever considers the fundamental impulses of man with a view to determining how far they may have here acted as INSPIRING GENII (or as demons and cobolds), will find that they have all practiced philosophy at one time or another, and that each one of them would have been only too glad to look upon itself as the ultimate end of existence and the legitimate LORD over all the other impulses. For every impulse is imperious, and as SUCH, attempts to philosophize. To be sure, in the case of scholars, in the case of really scientific men, it may be otherwise—"better," if you will; there there may really be such a thing as an "impulse to knowledge," some kind of small, independent clock-work, which, when well wound up, works away industriously to that end, WITHOUT the rest of the scholarly impulses taking any material part therein. The actual "interests" of the scholar, therefore, are generally in quite another direction—in the family, perhaps, or in money-making, or in politics; it is, in fact, almost indifferent at what point of research his little machine is placed, and whether the hopeful young worker becomes a good philologist, a mushroom specialist, or a chemist; he is not CHARACTERISED by becoming this or that. In the philosopher, on the contrary, there is absolutely nothing impersonal; and above all, his morality furnishes a decided and decisive testimony as to WHO HE IS,—that is to say, in what order the deepest impulses of his nature stand to each other.

7. How malicious philosophers can be! I know of nothing more stinging than the joke Epicurus took the liberty of making on Plato and the Platonists; he called them Dionysiokolakes. In its original sense, and on the face of it, the word signifies "Flatterers of Dionysius"—consequently, tyrants' accessories and lick-spittles; besides this, however, it is as much as to say, "They are all ACTORS, there is nothing genuine about them" (for Dionysiokolax was a popular name for an actor). And the latter is really the malignant reproach that Epicurus cast upon Plato: he was annoyed by the grandiose manner, the mise en scene style of which Plato and his scholars were masters—of which Epicurus was not a master! He, the old school-teacher of Samos, who sat concealed in his little garden at Athens, and wrote three hundred books, perhaps out of rage and ambitious envy of Plato, who knows! Greece took a hundred years to find out who the garden-god Epicurus really was. Did she ever find out?

8. There is a point in every philosophy at which the "conviction" of the philosopher appears on the scene; or, to put it in the words of an ancient mystery:

Adventavit asinus, Pulcher et fortissimus.

9. You desire to LIVE "according to Nature"? Oh, you noble Stoics, what fraud of words! Imagine to yourselves a being like Nature, boundlessly extravagant, boundlessly indifferent, without purpose or consideration, without pity or justice, at once fruitful and barren and uncertain: imagine to yourselves INDIFFERENCE as a power—how COULD you live in accordance with such indifference? To live—is not that just endeavouring to be otherwise than this Nature? Is not living valuing, preferring, being unjust, being limited, endeavouring to be different? And granted that your imperative, "living according to Nature," means actually the same as "living according to life"—how could you do DIFFERENTLY? Why should you make a principle out of what you yourselves are, and must be? In reality, however, it is quite otherwise with you: while you pretend to read with rapture the canon of your law in Nature, you want something quite the contrary, you extraordinary stage-players and self-deluders! In your pride you wish to dictate your morals and ideals to Nature, to Nature herself, and to incorporate them therein; you insist that it shall be Nature "according to the Stoa," and would like

everything to be made after your own image, as a vast, eternal glorification and generalism of Stoicism! With all your love for truth, you have forced yourselves so long, so persistently, and with such hypnotic rigidity to see Nature FALSELY, that is to say, Stoically, that you are no longer able to see it otherwise—and to crown all, some unfathomable superciliousness gives you the Bedlamite hope that BECAUSE you are able to tyrannize over yourselves—Stoicism is self-tyranny—Nature will also allow herself to be tyrannized over: is not the Stoic a PART of Nature?... But this is an old and everlasting story: what happened in old times with the Stoics still happens today, as soon as ever a philosophy begins to believe in itself. It always creates the world in its own image; it cannot do otherwise; philosophy is this tyrannical impulse itself, the most spiritual Will to Power, the will to "creation of the world," the will to the causa prima.

10. The eagerness and subtlety, I should even say craftiness, with which the problem of "the real and the apparent world" is dealt with at present throughout Europe, furnishes food for thought and attention; and he who hears only a "Will to Truth" in the background, and nothing else, cannot certainly boast of the sharpest ears. In rare and isolated cases, it may really have happened that such a Will to Truth—a certain extravagant and adventurous pluck, a metaphysician's ambition of the forlorn hope—has participated therein:

that which in the end always prefers a handful of "certainty" to a whole cartload of beautiful possibilities; there may even be puritanical fanatics of conscience, who prefer to put their last trust in a sure nothing, rather than in an uncertain something. But that is Nihilism, and the sign of a despairing, mortally wearied soul, notwithstanding the courageous bearing such a virtue may display. It seems, however, to be otherwise with stronger and livelier thinkers who are still eager for life. In that they side AGAINST appearance, and speak superciliously of "perspective," in that they rank the credibility of their own bodies about as low as the credibility of the ocular evidence that "the earth stands still," and thus, apparently, allowing with complacency their securest possession to escape (for what does one at present believe in more firmly than in one's body?),—who knows if they are not really trying to win back something which was formerly an even securer possession, something of the old domain of the faith of former times, perhaps the "immortal soul," perhaps "the old God," in short, ideas by which they could live better, that is to say, more vigorously and more joyously, than by "modern ideas"? There is DISTRUST of these modern ideas in this mode of looking at things, a disbelief in all that has been constructed yesterday and today; there is perhaps some slight admixture of satiety and scorn, which can no longer endure the BRIC-A-BRAC of ideas of the most varied origin, such as so-called Positivism at present throws on the market;

a disgust of the more refined taste at the village-fair motleyness and patchiness of all these reality-philosophasters, in whom there is nothing either new or true, except this motleyness. Therein it seems to me that we should agree with those skeptical anti-realists and knowledge-microscopists of the present day; their instinct, which repels them from MODERN reality, is unrefuted... what do their retrograde by-paths concern us! The main thing about them is NOT that they wish to go "back," but that they wish to get AWAY therefrom. A little MORE strength, swing, courage, and artistic power, and they would be OFF—and not back!

11. It seems to me that there is everywhere an attempt at present to divert attention from the actual influence which Kant exercised on German philosophy, and especially to ignore prudently the value which he set upon himself. Kant was first and foremost proud of his Table of Categories; with it in his hand he said: "This is the most difficult thing that could ever be undertaken on behalf of metaphysics." Let us only understand this "could be"! He was proud of having DISCOVERED a new faculty in man, the faculty of synthetic judgment a priori. Granting that he deceived himself in this matter; the development and rapid flourishing of German philosophy depended nevertheless on his pride, and on the eager rivalry of the younger generation to discover if possible something—at all events "new faculties"—of which to be still prouder!—But let us reflect for a

moment—it is high time to do so. "How are synthetic judgments a priori POSSIBLE?" Kant asks himself—and what is really his answer? "BY MEANS OF A MEANS (faculty)"—but unfortunately not in five words, but so circumstantially, imposingly, and with such display of German profundity and verbal flourishes, that one altogether loses sight of the comical niaiserie allemande involved in such an answer. People were beside themselves with delight over this new faculty, and the jubilation reached its climax when Kant further discovered a moral faculty in man—for at that time Germans were still moral, not yet dabbling in the "Politics of hard fact." Then came the honeymoon of German philosophy. All the young theologians of the Tubingen institution went immediately into the groves—all seeking for "faculties." And what did they not find—in that innocent, rich, and still youthful period of the German spirit, to which Romanticism, the malicious fairy, piped and sang, when one could not yet distinguish between "finding" and "inventing"! Above all a faculty for the "transcendental"; Schelling christened it, intellectual intuition, and thereby gratified the most earnest longings of the naturally pious-inclined Germans. One can do no greater wrong to the whole of this exuberant and eccentric movement (which was really youthfulness, notwithstanding that it disguised itself so boldly, in hoary and senile conceptions), than to take it seriously, or even treat it with moral indignation. Enough, however—the world grew older, and the dream vanished. A time came when people rubbed their foreheads, and they still rub them today. People had been dreaming, and first and foremost—old Kant. "By means of a means (faculty)"—he had said, or at least meant to say. But, is that—an answer? An explanation? Or is it not rather merely a repetition of the question? How does opium induce sleep? "By means of a means (faculty)," namely the virtus dormitiva, replies the doctor in Moliere,

> *Quia est in eo virtus dormitiva,*
> *Cujus est natura sensus assoupire.*

But such replies belong to the realm of comedy, and it is high time to replace the Kantian question, "How are synthetic judgments a PRIORI possible?" by another question, "Why is belief in such judgments necessary?"—in effect, it is high time that we should understand that such judgments must be believed to be true, for the sake of the preservation of creatures like ourselves; though they still might naturally be false judgments! Or, more plainly spoken, and roughly and readily—synthetic judgments a priori should not "be possible" at all; we have no right to them; in our mouths they are nothing but false judgments. Only, of course, the belief in their truth is necessary, as plausible belief and ocular evidence belonging to the perspective view of life. And finally, to call to mind the enormous influence which "German philosophy"—I hope you understand its right to inverted commas (goosefeet)?—has exercised throughout the whole of Europe, there is no doubt that a certain VIRTUS DORMITIVA had a share in it; thanks to German philosophy, it was a delight to the noble idlers, the virtuous, the mystics, the artiste, the three-fourths Christians, and the political obscurantists of all nations, to find an antidote to the still overwhelming sensualism which overflowed from the last century into this, in short—"sensus assoupire."...

12. As regards materialistic atomism, it is one of the best-refuted theories that have been advanced, and in Europe there is now perhaps no one in the learned world so unscholarly as to attach serious signification to it, except for convenient everyday use (as an abbreviation of the means of expression)—thanks chiefly to the Pole Boscovich: he and the Pole Copernicus have hitherto been the greatest and most successful opponents of ocular evidence. For while Copernicus has persuaded us to believe, contrary to all the senses, that the earth does NOT stand fast, Boscovich has taught us to abjure the belief in the last thing that "stood fast" of the earth—the belief in "substance," in "matter," in the earth-residuum, and particle-atom: it is the greatest triumph over the senses that has hitherto been gained on earth. One must, however, go still further, and also declare war, relentless war to the knife, against the "atomistic

requirements" which still lead a dangerous after-life in places where no one suspects them, like the more celebrated "metaphysical requirements": one must also above all give the finishing stroke to that other and more portentous atomism which Christianity has taught best and longest, the SOUL-ATOMISM. Let it be permitted to designate by this expression the belief which regards the soul as something indestructible, eternal, indivisible, as a monad, as an atomon: this belief ought to be expelled from science! Between ourselves, it is not at all necessary to get rid of "the soul" thereby, and thus renounce one of the oldest and most venerated hypotheses—as happens frequently to the clumsiness of naturalists, who can hardly touch on the soul without immediately losing it. But the way is open for new acceptations and refinements of the soul-hypothesis; and such conceptions as "mortal soul," and "soul of subjective multiplicity," and "soul as social structure of the instincts and passions," want henceforth to have legitimate rights in science. In that the NEW psychologist is about to put an end to the superstitions which have hitherto flourished with almost tropical luxuriance around the idea of the soul, he is really, as it were, thrusting himself into a new desert and a new distrust—it is possible that the older psychologists had a merrier and more comfortable time of it; eventually, however, he finds that precisely thereby he is also condemned to INVENT—and, who knows? perhaps to DISCOVER the new.

13. Psychologists should bethink themselves before putting down the instinct of self-preservation as the cardinal instinct of an organic being. A living thing seeks above all to DISCHARGE its strength—life itself is WILL TO POWER; self-preservation is only one of the indirect and most frequent RESULTS thereof. In short, here, as everywhere else, let us beware of SUPERFLUOUS teleological principles!—one of which is the instinct of self-preservation (we owe it to Spinoza's inconsistency). It is thus, in effect, that method ordains, which must be essentially economy of principles.

14. It is perhaps just dawning on five or six minds that natural philosophy is only a world-exposition and world-arrangement (according to us, if I may say so!) and NOT a world-explanation; but in so far as it is based on belief in the senses, it is regarded as more, and for a long time to come must be regarded as more—namely, as an explanation. It has eyes and fingers of its own, it has ocular evidence and palpableness of its own: this operates fascinatingly, persuasively, and CONVINCINGLY upon an age with fundamentally plebeian tastes—in fact, it follows instinctively the canon of truth of eternal popular sensualism. What is clear, what is "explained"? Only that which can be seen and felt—one must pursue every problem thus far. Obversely, however, the charm of the Platonic mode of

thought, which was an ARISTOCRATIC mode, consisted precisely in RESISTANCE to obvious sense-evidence—perhaps among men who enjoyed even stronger and more fastidious senses than our contemporaries, but who knew how to find a higher triumph in remaining masters of them: and this by means of pale, cold, grey conceptional networks which they threw over the motley whirl of the senses—the mob of the senses, as Plato said. In this overcoming of the world, and interpreting of the world in the manner of Plato, there was an ENJOYMENT different from that which the physicists of today offer us—and likewise the Darwinists and anti-teleologists among the physiological workers, with their principle of the "smallest possible effort," and the greatest possible blunder. "Where there is nothing more to see or to grasp, there is also nothing more for men to do"—that is certainly an imperative different from the Platonic one, but it may notwithstanding be the right imperative for a hardy, laborious race of machinists and bridge-builders of the future, who have nothing but ROUGH work to perform.

15. To study physiology with a clear conscience, one must insist on the fact that the sense-organs are not phenomena in the sense of the idealistic philosophy; as such they certainly could not be causes! Sensualism, therefore, at least as regulative hypothesis, if not as heuristic principle. What? And others say even that the

external world is the work of our organs? But then our body, as a part of this external world, would be the work of our organs! But then our organs themselves would be the work of our organs! It seems to me that this is a complete REDUCTIO AD ABSURDUM, if the conception CAUSA SUI is something fundamentally absurd. Consequently, the external world is NOT the work of our organs—?

16. There are still harmless self-observers who believe that there are "immediate certainties"; for instance, "I think," or as the superstition of Schopenhauer puts it, "I will"; as though cognition here got hold of its object purely and simply as "the thing in itself," without any falsification taking place either on the part of the subject or the object. I would repeat it, however, a hundred times, that "immediate certainty," as well as "absolute knowledge" and the "thing in itself," involve a CONTRADICTIO IN ADJECTO; we really ought to free ourselves from the misleading significance of words! The people on their part may think that cognition is knowing all about things, but the philosopher must say to himself: "When I analyze the process that is expressed in the sentence, 'I think,' I find a whole series of daring assertions, the argumentative proof of which would be difficult, perhaps impossible: for instance, that it is *I* who think, that there must necessarily be something that thinks, that thinking is an activity and operation on the part of a being who is

thought of as a cause, that there is an 'ego,' and finally, that it is already determined what is to be designated by thinking—that I KNOW what thinking is. For if I had not already decided within myself what it is, by what standard could I determine whether that which is just happening is not perhaps 'willing' or 'feeling'? In short, the assertion 'I think,' assumes that I COMPARE my state at the present moment with other states of myself which I know, in order to determine what it is; on account of this retrospective connection with further 'knowledge,' it has, at any rate, no immediate certainty for me."—In place of the "immediate certainty" in which the people may believe in the special case, the philosopher thus finds a series of metaphysical questions presented to him, veritable conscience questions of the intellect, to wit: "Whence did I get the notion of 'thinking'? Why do I believe in cause and effect? What gives me the right to speak of an 'ego,' and even of an 'ego' as cause, and finally of an 'ego' as cause of thought?" He who ventures to answer these metaphysical questions at once by an appeal to a sort of INTUITIVE perception, like the person who says, "I think, and know that this, at least, is true, actual, and certain"—will encounter a smile and two notes of interrogation in a philosopher nowadays. "Sir," the philosopher will perhaps give him to understand, "it is improbable that you are not mistaken, but why should it be the truth?"

17. With regard to the superstitions of logicians, I shall never tire of emphasizing a small, terse fact, which is unwillingly recognized by these credulous minds—namely, that a thought comes when "it" wishes, and not when "I" wish; so that it is a PERVERSION of the facts of the case to say that the subject "I" is the condition of the predicate "think." ONE thinks; but that this "one" is precisely the famous old "ego," is, to put it mildly, only a supposition, an assertion, and assuredly not an "immediate certainty." After all, one has even gone too far with this "one thinks"—even the "one" contains an INTERPRETATION of the process, and does not belong to the process itself. One infers here according to the usual grammatical formula—"To think is an activity; every activity requires an agency that is active; consequently"... It was pretty much on the same lines that the older atomism sought, besides the operating "power," the material particle wherein it resides and out of which it operates—the atom. More rigorous minds, however, learnt at last to get along without this "earth-residuum," and perhaps some day we shall accustom ourselves, even from the logician's point of view, to get along without the little "one" (to which the worthy old "ego" has refined itself).

18. It is certainly not the least charm of a theory that it is refutable; it is precisely thereby that it attracts the more subtle minds. It seems that the hundred-times-

refuted theory of the "free will" owes its persistence to this charm alone; some one is always appearing who feels himself strong enough to refute it.

19. Philosophers are accustomed to speak of the will as though it were the best-known thing in the world; indeed, Schopenhauer has given us to understand that the will alone is really known to us, absolutely and completely known, without deduction or addition. But it again and again seems to me that in this case Schopenhauer also only did what philosophers are in the habit of doing—he seems to have adopted a POPULAR PREJUDICE and exaggerated it. Willing seems to me to be above all something COMPLICATED, something that is a unity only in name—and it is precisely in a name that popular prejudice lurks, which has got the mastery over the inadequate precautions of philosophers in all ages. So let us for once be more cautious, let us be "unphilosophical": let us say that in all willing there is firstly a plurality of sensations, namely, the sensation of the condition "AWAY FROM WHICH we go," the sensation of the condition "TOWARDS WHICH we go," the sensation of this "FROM" and "TOWARDS" itself, and then besides, an accompanying muscular sensation, which, even without our putting in motion "arms and legs," commences its action by force of habit, directly we "will" anything. Therefore, just as sensations (and indeed many kinds of sensations) are to

be recognized as ingredients of the will, so, in the second place, thinking is also to be recognized; in every act of the will there is a ruling thought;—and let us not imagine it possible to sever this thought from the "willing," as if the will would then remain over! In the third place, the will is not only a complex of sensation and thinking, but it is above all an EMOTION, and in fact the emotion of the command. That which is termed "freedom of the will" is essentially the emotion of supremacy in respect to him who must obey: "I am free, 'he' must obey"—this consciousness is inherent in every will; and equally so the straining of the attention, the straight look which fixes itself exclusively on one thing, the unconditional judgment that "this and nothing else is necessary now," the inward certainty that obedience will be rendered—and whatever else pertains to the position of the commander. A man who WILLS commands something within himself which renders obedience, or which he believes renders obedience. But now let us notice what is the strangest thing about the will,—this affair so extremely complex, for which the people have only one name. Inasmuch as in the given circumstances we are at the same time the commanding AND the obeying parties, and as the obeying party we know the sensations of constraint, impulsion, pressure, resistance, and motion, which usually commence immediately after the act of will; inasmuch as, on the other hand, we are accustomed to disregard this duality, and to deceive ourselves about it by means of the synthetic term "I": a whole series of erroneous conclusions, and consequently of false judgments about the will itself, has become attached to the act of willing—to such a degree that he who wills believes firmly that willing SUFFICES for action. Since in the majority of cases there has only been exercise of will when the effect of the command—consequently obedience, and therefore action—was to be EXPECTED, the APPEARANCE has translated itself into the sentiment, as if there were a NECESSITY OF EFFECT; in a word, he who wills believes with a fair amount of certainty that will and action are somehow one; he ascribes the success, the carrying out of the willing, to the will itself, and thereby enjoys an increase of the sensation of power which accompanies all success. "Freedom of Will"—that is the expression for the complex state of delight of the person exercising volition, who commands and at the same time identifies himself with the executor of the order—who, as such, enjoys also the triumph over obstacles, but thinks within himself that it was really his own will that overcame them. In this way the person exercising volition adds the feelings of delight of his successful executive instruments, the useful "underwills" or under-souls—indeed, our body is but a social structure composed of many souls—to his feelings of delight as commander. L'EFFET C'EST MOI. what happens here is what happens in every well-constructed and happy commonwealth, namely, that the governing class identifies itself with the successes of the commonwealth. In all willing it is absolutely a question of commanding and obeying, on the basis, as already said, of a social structure composed of many "souls", on which account a philosopher should claim the right to include willing-as-such within the sphere of morals—regarded as the doctrine of the relations of supremacy under which the phenomenon of "life" manifests itself.

20. That the separate philosophical ideas are not anything optional or autonomously evolving, but grow up in connection and relationship with each other, that, however suddenly and arbitrarily they seem to appear in the history of thought, they nevertheless belong just as much to a system as the collective members of the fauna of a Continent—is betrayed in the end by the circumstance: how unfailingly the most diverse philosophers always fill in again a definite fundamental scheme of POSSIBLE philosophies. Under an invisible spell, they always revolve once more in the same orbit, however independent of each other they may feel themselves with their critical or systematic wills, something within them leads them, something impels them in definite order the one after the other—to wit, the innate methodology and relationship of their ideas. Their thinking is, in fact, far less a discovery than a re-recognizing, a remembering, a return and a home-coming to a far-off, ancient common-household of the

soul, out of which those ideas formerly grew: philosophizing is so far a kind of atavism of the highest order. The wonderful family resemblance of all Indian, Greek, and German philosophizing is easily enough explained. In fact, where there is affinity of language, owing to the common philosophy of grammar—I mean owing to the unconscious domination and guidance of similar grammatical functions—it cannot but be that everything is prepared at the outset for a similar development and succession of philosophical systems, just as the way seems barred against certain other possibilities of world-interpretation. It is highly probable that philosophers within the domain of the Ural-Altaic languages (where the conception of the subject is least developed) look otherwise "into the world," and will be found on paths of thought different from those of the Indo-Germans and Mussulmans, the spell of certain grammatical functions is ultimately also the spell of PHYSIOLOGICAL valuations and racial conditions.—So much by way of rejecting Locke's superficiality with regard to the origin of ideas.

21. The CAUSA SUI is the best self-contradiction that has yet been conceived, it is a sort of logical violation and unnaturalness; but the extravagant pride of man has managed to entangle itself profoundly and frightfully with this very folly. The desire for "freedom of will" in the superlative, metaphysical sense, such as still holds sway, unfortunately, in the minds of the half-

educated, the desire to bear the entire and ultimate responsibility for one's actions oneself, and to absolve God, the world, ancestors, chance, and society therefrom, involves nothing less than to be precisely this CAUSA SUI, and, with more than Munchausen daring, to pull oneself up into existence by the hair, out of the slough of nothingness. If any one should find out in this manner the crass stupidity of the celebrated conception of "free will" and put it out of his head altogether, I beg of him to carry his "enlightenment" a step further, and also put out of his head the contrary of this monstrous conception of "free will": I mean "non-free will," which is tantamount to a misuse of cause and effect. One should not wrongly MATERIALISE "cause" and "effect," as the natural philosophers do (and whoever like them naturalize in thinking at present), according to the prevailing mechanical doltishness which makes the cause press and push until it "effects" its end; one should use "cause" and "effect" only as pure CONCEPTIONS, that is to say, as conventional fictions for the purpose of designation and mutual understanding,—NOT for explanation. In "being-in-itself" there is nothing of "casual-connection," of "necessity," or of "psychological non-freedom"; there the effect does NOT follow the cause, there "law" does not obtain. It is WE alone who have devised cause, sequence, reciprocity, relativity, constraint, number, law, freedom, motive, and purpose; and when we interpret and intermix this symbol-world, as "being-in-itself," with things, we act once more as we have always acted—MYTHOLOGICALLY. The "non-free will" is mythology; in real life it is only a question of STRONG and WEAK wills.—It is almost always a symptom of what is lacking in himself, when a thinker, in every "causal-connection" and "psychological necessity," manifests something of compulsion, indigence, obsequiousness, oppression, and non-freedom; it is suspicious to have such feelings—the person betrays himself. And in general, if I have observed correctly, the "non-freedom of the will" is regarded as a problem from two entirely opposite standpoints, but always in a profoundly PERSONAL manner: some will not give up their "responsibility," their belief in THEMSELVES, the personal right to THEIR merits, at any price (the vain races belong to this class); others on the contrary, do not wish to be answerable for anything, or blamed for anything, and owing to an inward self-contempt, seek to GET OUT OF THE BUSINESS, no matter how. The latter, when they write books, are in the habit at present of taking the side of criminals; a sort of socialistic sympathy is their favourite disguise. And as a matter of fact, the fatalism of the weak-willed embellishes itself surprisingly when it can pose as "la religion de la souffrance humaine"; that is ITS "good taste."

22. Let me be pardoned, as an old philologist who cannot desist from the mischief of putting his finger on

bad modes of interpretation, but "Nature's conformity to law," of which you physicists talk so proudly, as though—why, it exists only owing to your interpretation and bad "philology." It is no matter of fact, no "text," but rather just a naively humanitarian adjustment and perversion of meaning, with which you make abundant concessions to the democratic instincts of the modern soul! "Everywhere equality before the law—Nature is not different in that respect, nor better than we": a fine instance of secret motive, in which the vulgar antagonism to everything privileged and autocratic—likewise a second and more refined atheism—is once more disguised. "Ni dieu, ni maitre"—that, also, is what you want; and therefore "Cheers for natural law!"—is it not so? But, as has been said, that is interpretation, not text; and somebody might come along, who, with opposite intentions and modes of interpretation, could read out of the same "Nature," and with regard to the same phenomena, just the tyrannically inconsiderate and relentless enforcement of the claims of power—an interpreter who should so place the unexceptionalness and unconditionalness of all "Will to Power" before your eyes, that almost every word, and the word "tyranny" itself, would eventually seem unsuitable, or like a weakening and softening metaphor—as being too human; and who should, nevertheless, end by asserting the same about this world as you do, namely, that it has a "necessary" and "calculable" course, NOT, however, because laws obtain in it, but because they are absolutely LACKING, and every power effects its ultimate consequences every moment. Granted that this also is only interpretation—and you will be eager enough to make this objection?—well, so much the better.

23. All psychology hitherto has run aground on moral prejudices and timidities, it has not dared to launch out into the depths. In so far as it is allowable to recognize in that which has hitherto been written, evidence of that which has hitherto been kept silent, it seems as if nobody had yet harboured the notion of psychology as the Morphology and DEVELOPMENT-DOCTRINE OF THE WILL TO POWER, as I conceive of it. The power of moral prejudices has penetrated deeply into the most intellectual world, the world apparently most indifferent and unprejudiced, and has obviously operated in an injurious, obstructive, blinding, and distorting manner. A proper physio-psychology has to contend with unconscious antagonism in the heart of the investigator, it has "the heart" against it even a doctrine of the reciprocal conditionalness of the "good" and the "bad" impulses, causes (as refined immorality) distress and aversion in a still strong and manly conscience—still more so, a doctrine of the derivation of all good impulses from bad ones. If, however, a person should regard even the emotions of hatred, envy, covetousness, and imperiousness as life-conditioning emotions, as factors which must be present,

fundamentally and essentially, in the general economy of life (which must, therefore, be further developed if life is to be further developed), he will suffer from such a view of things as from sea-sickness. And yet this hypothesis is far from being the strangest and most painful in this immense and almost new domain of dangerous knowledge, and there are in fact a hundred good reasons why every one should keep away from it who CAN do so! On the other hand, if one has once drifted hither with one's bark, well! very good! now let us set our teeth firmly! let us open our eyes and keep our hand fast on the helm! We sail away right OVER morality, we crush out, we destroy perhaps the remains of our own morality by daring to make our voyage thither—but what do WE matter. Never yet did a PROFOUNDER world of insight reveal itself to daring travelers and adventurers, and the psychologist who thus "makes a sacrifice"—it is not the sacrifizio dell' intelletto, on the contrary!—will at least be entitled to demand in return that psychology shall once more be recognized as the queen of the sciences, for whose service and equipment the other sciences exist. For psychology is once more the path to the fundamental problems.

Chapter II

The free spirit

24. O sancta simplicitas! In what strange simplification and falsification man lives! One can never cease wondering when once one has got eyes for beholding this marvel! How we have made everything around us clear and free and easy and simple! how we have been able to give our senses a passport to everything superficial, our thoughts a godlike desire for wanton pranks and wrong inferences!—how from the beginning, we have contrived to retain our ignorance in order to enjoy an almost inconceivable freedom, thoughtlessness, imprudence, heartiness, and gaiety—in order to enjoy life! And only on this solidified, granite-like foundation of ignorance could knowledge rear itself hitherto, the will to knowledge on the foundation

of a far more powerful will, the will to ignorance, to the uncertain, to the untrue! Not as its opposite, but—as its refinement! It is to be hoped, indeed, that LANGUAGE, here as elsewhere, will not get over its awkwardness, and that it will continue to talk of opposites where there are only degrees and many refinements of gradation; it is equally to be hoped that the incarnated Tartuffery of morals, which now belongs to our unconquerable "flesh and blood," will turn the words round in the mouths of us discerning ones. Here and there we understand it, and laugh at the way in which precisely the best knowledge seeks most to retain us in this SIMPLIFIED, thoroughly artificial, suitably imagined, and suitably falsified world: at the way in which, whether it will or not, it loves error, because, as living itself, it loves life!

25. After such a cheerful commencement, a serious word would fain be heard; it appeals to the most serious minds. Take care, ye philosophers and friends of knowledge, and beware of martyrdom! Of suffering "for the truth's sake"! even in your own defense! It spoils all the innocence and fine neutrality of your conscience; it makes you headstrong against objections and red rags; it stupefies, animalizes, and brutalizes, when in the struggle with danger, slander, suspicion, expulsion, and even worse consequences of enmity, ye have at last to play your last card as protectors of truth upon earth—as though "the Truth" were such an

innocent and incompetent creature as to require protectors! and you of all people, ye knights of the sorrowful countenance, Messrs Loafers and Cobweb-spinners of the spirit! Finally, ye know sufficiently well that it cannot be of any consequence if YE just carry your point; ye know that hitherto no philosopher has carried his point, and that there might be a more laudable truthfulness in every little interrogative mark which you place after your special words and favourite doctrines (and occasionally after yourselves) than in all the solemn pantomime and trumping games before accusers and law-courts! Rather go out of the way! Flee into concealment! And have your masks and your ruses, that ye may be mistaken for what you are, or somewhat feared! And pray, don't forget the garden, the garden with golden trellis-work! And have people around you who are as a garden—or as music on the waters at eventide, when already the day becomes a memory. Choose the GOOD solitude, the free, wanton, lightsome solitude, which also gives you the right still to remain good in any sense whatsoever! How poisonous, how crafty, how bad, does every long war make one, which cannot be waged openly by means of force! How PERSONAL does a long fear make one, a long watching of enemies, of possible enemies! These pariahs of society, these long-pursued, badly-persecuted ones—also the compulsory recluses, the Spinozas or Giordano Brunos—always become in the end, even under the most intellectual masquerade, and perhaps without being themselves aware of it, refined vengeance-seekers and poison-Brewers (just lay bare the foundation of Spinoza's ethics and theology!), not to speak of the stupidity of moral indignation, which is the unfailing sign in a philosopher that the sense of philosophical humour has left him. The martyrdom of the philosopher, his "sacrifice for the sake of truth," forces into the light whatever of the agitator and actor lurks in him; and if one has hitherto contemplated him only with artistic curiosity, with regard to many a philosopher it is easy to understand the dangerous desire to see him also in his deterioration (deteriorated into a "martyr," into a stage-and-tribune-bawler). Only, that it is necessary with such a desire to be clear WHAT spectacle one will see in any case—merely a satyric play, merely an epilogue farce, merely the continued proof that the long, real tragedy IS AT AN END, supposing that every philosophy has been a long tragedy in its origin.

26. Every select man strives instinctively for a citadel and a privacy, where he is FREE from the crowd, the many, the majority—where he may forget "men who are the rule," as their exception;—exclusive only of the case in which he is pushed straight to such men by a still stronger instinct, as a discerner in the great and exceptional sense. Whoever, in intercourse with men, does not occasionally glisten in all the green and grey colours of distress, owing to disgust, satiety, sympathy,

gloominess, and solitariness, is assuredly not a man of elevated tastes; supposing, however, that he does not voluntarily take all this burden and disgust upon himself, that he persistently avoids it, and remains, as I said, quietly and proudly hidden in his citadel, one thing is then certain: he was not made, he was not predestined for knowledge. For as such, he would one day have to say to himself: "The devil take my good taste! but 'the rule' is more interesting than the exception—than myself, the exception!" And he would go DOWN, and above all, he would go "inside." The long and serious study of the AVERAGE man—and consequently much disguise, self-overcoming, familiarity, and bad intercourse (all intercourse is bad intercourse except with one's equals):—that constitutes a necessary part of the life-history of every philosopher; perhaps the most disagreeable, odious, and disappointing part. If he is fortunate, however, as a favourite child of knowledge should be, he will meet with suitable auxiliaries who will shorten and lighten his task; I mean so-called cynics, those who simply recognize the animal, the commonplace and "the rule" in themselves, and at the same time have so much spirituality and ticklishness as to make them talk of themselves and their like BEFORE WITNESSES—sometimes they wallow, even in books, as on their own dung-hill. Cynicism is the only form in which base souls approach what is called honesty; and the higher man must open his ears to all the coarser or finer cynicism, and congratulate himself when the clown becomes shameless right before him, or the scientific satyr speaks out. There are even cases where enchantment mixes with the disgust—namely, where by a freak of nature, genius is bound to some such indiscreet billy-goat and ape, as in the case of the Abbe Galiani, the profoundest, acutest, and perhaps also filthiest man of his century—he was far profounder than Voltaire, and consequently also, a good deal more silent. It happens more frequently, as has been hinted, that a scientific head is placed on an ape's body, a fine exceptional understanding in a base soul, an occurrence by no means rare, especially among doctors and moral physiologists. And whenever anyone speaks without bitterness, or rather quite innocently, of man as a belly with two requirements, and a head with one; whenever any one sees, seeks, and WANTS to see only hunger, sexual instinct, and vanity as the real and only motives of human actions; in short, when any one speaks "badly"—and not even "ill"—of man, then ought the lover of knowledge to hearken attentively and diligently; he ought, in general, to have an open ear wherever there is talk without indignation. For the indignant man, and he who perpetually tears and lacerates himself with his own teeth (or, in place of himself, the world, God, or society), may indeed, morally speaking, stand higher than the laughing and self-satisfied satyr, but in every other sense he is the more ordinary, more indifferent, and less instructive case. And no one is such a LIAR as the indignant man.

27. It is difficult to be understood, especially when one thinks and lives gangasrotogati [Footnote: Like the river Ganges: presto.] among those only who think and live otherwise—namely, kurmagati [Footnote: Like the tortoise: lento.], or at best "froglike," mandeikagati [Footnote: Like the frog: staccato.] (I do everything to be "difficultly understood" myself!)—and one should be heartily grateful for the good will to some refinement of interpretation. As regards "the good friends," however, who are always too easy-going, and think that as friends they have a right to ease, one does well at the very first to grant them a play-ground and romping-place for misunderstanding—one can thus laugh still; or get rid of them altogether, these good friends—and laugh then also!

28. What is most difficult to render from one language into another is the TEMPO of its style, which has its basis in the character of the race, or to speak more physiologically, in the average TEMPO of the assimilation of its nutriment. There are honestly meant translations, which, as involuntary vulgarizations, are almost falsifications of the original, merely because its lively and merry TEMPO (which overleaps and obviates all dangers in word and expression) could not also be rendered. A German is almost incapacitated for

PRESTO in his language; consequently also, as may be reasonably inferred, for many of the most delightful and daring NUANCES of free, free-spirited thought. And just as the buffoon and satyr are foreign to him in body and conscience, so Aristophanes and Petronius are untranslatable for him. Everything ponderous, viscous, and pompously clumsy, all long-winded and wearying species of style, are developed in profuse variety among Germans—pardon me for stating the fact that even Goethe's prose, in its mixture of stiffness and elegance, is no exception, as a reflection of the "good old time" to which it belongs, and as an expression of German taste at a time when there was still a "German taste," which was a rococo-taste in moribus et artibus. Lessing is an exception, owing to his histrionic nature, which understood much, and was versed in many things; he who was not the translator of Bayle to no purpose, who took refuge willingly in the shadow of Diderot and Voltaire, and still more willingly among the Roman comedy-writers—Lessing loved also free-spiritism in the TEMPO, and flight out of Germany. But how could the German language, even in the prose of Lessing, imitate the TEMPO of Machiavelli, who in his "Principe" makes us breathe the dry, fine air of Florence, and cannot help presenting the most serious events in a boisterous allegrissimo, perhaps not without a malicious artistic sense of the contrast he ventures to present—long, heavy, difficult, dangerous thoughts, and a TEMPO of the gallop, and of the best, wantonest humour? Finally, who would venture on a German translation of Petronius, who, more than any great musician hitherto, was a master of PRESTO in invention, ideas, and words? What matter in the end about the swamps of the sick, evil world, or of the "ancient world," when like him, one has the feet of a wind, the rush, the breath, the emancipating scorn of a wind, which makes everything healthy, by making everything RUN! And with regard to Aristophanes—that transfiguring, complementary genius, for whose sake one PARDONS all Hellenism for having existed, provided one has understood in its full profundity ALL that there requires pardon and transfiguration; there is nothing that has caused me to meditate more on PLATO'S secrecy and sphinx-like nature, than the happily preserved petit fait that under the pillow of his death-bed there was found no "Bible," nor anything Egyptian, Pythagorean, or Platonic—but a book of Aristophanes. How could even Plato have endured life—a Greek life which he repudiated—without an Aristophanes!

29. It is the business of the very few to be independent; it is a privilege of the strong. And whoever attempts it, even with the best right, but without being OBLIGED to do so, proves that he is probably not only strong, but also daring beyond measure. He enters into a labyrinth, he multiplies a thousandfold the dangers which life in itself already

brings with it; not the least of which is that no one can see how and where he loses his way, becomes isolated, and is torn piecemeal by some minotaur of conscience. Supposing such a one comes to grief, it is so far from the comprehension of men that they neither feel it, nor sympathize with it. And he cannot any longer go back! He cannot even go back again to the sympathy of men!

30. Our deepest insights must—and should—appear as follies, and under certain circumstances as crimes, when they come unauthorizedly to the ears of those who are not disposed and predestined for them. The exoteric and the esoteric, as they were formerly distinguished by philosophers—among the Indians, as among the Greeks, Persians, and Mussulmans, in short, wherever people believed in gradations of rank and NOT in equality and equal rights—are not so much in contradistinction to one another in respect to the exoteric class, standing without, and viewing, estimating, measuring, and judging from the outside, and not from the inside; the more essential distinction is that the class in question views things from below upwards—while the esoteric class views things FROM ABOVE DOWNWARDS. There are heights of the soul from which tragedy itself no longer appears to operate tragically; and if all the woe in the world were taken together, who would dare to decide whether the sight of it would NECESSARILY seduce and constrain to sympathy, and thus to a doubling of the woe?... That

which serves the higher class of men for nourishment or refreshment, must be almost poison to an entirely different and lower order of human beings. The virtues of the common man would perhaps mean vice and weakness in a philosopher; it might be possible for a highly developed man, supposing him to degenerate and go to ruin, to acquire qualities thereby alone, for the sake of which he would have to be honored as a saint in the lower world into which he had sunk. There are books which have an inverse value for the soul and the health according as the inferior soul and the lower vitality, or the higher and more powerful, make use of them. In the former case they are dangerous, disturbing, unsettling books, in the latter case they are herald-calls which summon the bravest to THEIR bravery. Books for the general reader are always ill-smelling books; the odor of paltry people clings to them. Where the populace eat and drink, and even where they reverence, it is accustomed to stink. One should not go into churches if one wishes to breathe PURE air.

31. In our youthful years we still venerate and despise without the art of NUANCE, which is the best gain of life, and we have rightly to do hard penance for having fallen upon men and things with Yea and Nay. Everything is so arranged that the worst of all tastes, THE TASTE FOR THE UNCONDITIONAL, is cruelly befooled and abused, until a man learns to introduce a little art into his sentiments, and prefers to

try conclusions with the artificial, as do the real artists of life. The angry and reverent spirit peculiar to youth appears to allow itself no peace, until it has suitably falsified men and things, to be able to vent its passion upon them: youth in itself even, is something falsifying and deceptive. Later on, when the young soul, tortured by continual disillusions, finally turns suspiciously against itself—still ardent and savage even in its suspicion and remorse of conscience: how it upbraids itself, how impatiently it tears itself, how it revenges itself for its long self-blinding, as though it had been a voluntary blindness! In this transition one punishes oneself by distrust of one's sentiments; one tortures one's enthusiasm with doubt, one feels even the good conscience to be a danger, as if it were the self-concealment and lassitude of a more refined uprightness; and above all, one espouses upon principle the cause AGAINST "youth."—A decade later, and one comprehends that all this was also still—youth!

32. Throughout the longest period of human history—one calls it the prehistoric period—the value or non-value of an action was inferred from its CONSEQUENCES; the action in itself was not taken into consideration, any more than its origin; but pretty much as in China at present, where the distinction or disgrace of a child redounds to its parents, the retro-operating power of success or failure was what induced men to think well or ill of an action. Let us call this

period the PRE-MORAL period of mankind; the imperative, "Know thyself!" was then still unknown.—In the last ten thousand years, on the other hand, on certain large portions of the earth, one has gradually got so far, that one no longer lets the consequences of an action, but its origin, decide with regard to its worth: a great achievement as a whole, an important refinement of vision and of criterion, the unconscious effect of the supremacy of aristocratic values and of the belief in "origin," the mark of a period which may be designated in the narrower sense as the MORAL one: the first attempt at self-knowledge is thereby made. Instead of the consequences, the origin—what an inversion of perspective! And assuredly an inversion affected only after long struggle and wavering! To be sure, an ominous new superstition, a peculiar narrowness of interpretation, attained supremacy precisely thereby: the origin of an action was interpreted in the most definite sense possible, as origin out of an INTENTION; people were agreed in the belief that the value of an action lay in the value of its intention. The intention as the sole origin and antecedent history of an action: under the influence of this prejudice moral praise and blame have been bestowed, and men have judged and even philosophized almost up to the present day.—Is it not possible, however, that the necessity may now have arisen of again making up our minds with regard to the reversing and fundamental shifting of values, owing to a new self-consciousness and acuteness in man—is it not possible that we may be standing on the threshold of a period which to begin with, would be distinguished negatively as ULTRA-MORAL: nowadays when, at least among us immoralists, the suspicion arises that the decisive value of an action lies precisely in that which is NOT INTENTIONAL, and that all its intentionalness, all that is seen, sensible, or "sensed" in it, belongs to its surface or skin—which, like every skin, betrays something, but CONCEALS still more? In short, we believe that the intention is only a sign or symptom, which first requires an explanation—a sign, moreover, which has too many interpretations, and consequently hardly any meaning in itself alone: that morality, in the sense in which it has been understood hitherto, as intention-morality, has been a prejudice, perhaps a prematureness or preliminariness, probably something of the same rank as astrology and alchemy, but in any case something which must be surmounted. The surmounting of morality, in a certain sense even the self-mounting of morality—let that be the name for the long-secret labour which has been reserved for the most refined, the most upright, and also the most wicked consciences of today, as the living touchstones of the soul.

33. It cannot be helped: the sentiment of surrender, of sacrifice for one's neighbour, and all self-renunciation-morality, must be mercilessly called to account, and

brought to judgment; just as the aesthetics of "disinterested contemplation," under which the emasculation of art nowadays seeks insidiously enough to create itself a good conscience. There is far too much witchery and sugar in the sentiments "for others" and "NOT for myself," for one not needing to be doubly distrustful here, and for one asking promptly: "Are they not perhaps—DECEPTIONS?"—That they PLEASE—him who has them, and him who enjoys their fruit, and also the mere spectator—that is still no argument in their FAVOUR, but just calls for caution. Let us therefore be cautious!

34. At whatever standpoint of philosophy one may place oneself nowadays, seen from every position, the ERRONEOUSNESS of the world in which we think we live is the surest and most certain thing our eyes can light upon: we find proof after proof thereof, which would fain allure us into surmises concerning a deceptive principle in the "nature of things." He, however, who makes thinking itself, and consequently "the spirit," responsible for the falseness of the world—an honourable exit, which every conscious or unconscious advocatus dei avails himself of—he who regards this world, including space, time, form, and movement, as falsely DEDUCED, would have at least good reason in the end to become distrustful also of all thinking; has it not hitherto been playing upon us the worst of scurvy tricks? and what guarantee would it

give that it would not continue to do what it has always been doing? In all seriousness, the innocence of thinkers has something touching and respect-inspiring in it, which even nowadays permits them to wait upon consciousness with the request that it will give them HONEST answers: for example, whether it be "real" or not, and why it keeps the outer world so resolutely at a distance, and other questions of the same description. The belief in "immediate certainties" is a MORAL NAIVETE which does honour to us philosophers; but—we have now to cease being "MERELY moral" men! Apart from morality, such belief is a folly which does little honour to us! If in middle-class life an ever-ready distrust is regarded as the sign of a "bad character," and consequently as an imprudence, here among us, beyond the middle-class world and its Yeas and Nays, what should prevent our being imprudent and saying: the philosopher has at length a RIGHT to "bad character," as the being who has hitherto been most befooled on earth—he is now under OBLIGATION to distrustfulness, to the wickedest squinting out of every abyss of suspicion.—Forgive me the joke of this gloomy grimace and turn of expression; for I myself have long ago learned to think and estimate differently with regard to deceiving and being deceived, and I keep at least a couple of pokes in the ribs ready for the blind rage with which philosophers struggle against being deceived. Why NOT? It is nothing more than a moral prejudice that truth is worth more than semblance; it is, in fact, the worst proved supposition in the world. So much must be conceded: there could have been no life at all except upon the basis of perspective estimates and semblances; and if, with the virtuous enthusiasm and stupidity of many philosophers, one wished to do away altogether with the "seeming world"—well, granted that YOU could do that,—at least nothing of your "truth" would thereby remain! Indeed, what is it that forces us in general to the supposition that there is an essential opposition of "true" and "false"? Is it not enough to suppose degrees of seemingness, and as it were lighter and darker shades and tones of semblance—different valeurs, as the painters say? Why might not the world WHICH CONCERNS US—be a fiction? And to any one who suggested: "But to a fiction belongs an originator?"—might it not be bluntly replied: WHY? May not this "belong" also belong to the fiction? Is it not at length permitted to be a little ironical towards the subject, just as towards the predicate and object? Might not the philosopher elevate himself above faith in grammar? All respect to governesses, but is it not time that philosophy should renounce governess-faith?

35. O Voltaire! O humanity! O idiocy! There is something ticklish in "the truth," and in the SEARCH for the truth; and if man goes about it too humanely—"il ne cherche le vrai que pour faire le bien"—I wager he finds nothing!

36. Supposing that nothing else is "given" as real but our world of desires and passions, that we cannot sink or rise to any other "reality" but just that of our impulses—for thinking is only a relation of these impulses to one another:—are we not permitted to make the attempt and to ask the question whether this which is "given" does not SUFFICE, by means of our counterparts, for the understanding even of the so-called mechanical (or "material") world? I do not mean as an illusion, a "semblance," a "representation" (in the Berkeleyan and Schopenhauerian sense), but as possessing the same degree of reality as our emotions themselves—as a more primitive form of the world of emotions, in which everything still lies locked in a mighty unity, which afterwards branches off and develops itself in organic processes (naturally also, refines and debilitates)—as a kind of instinctive life in which all organic functions, including self-regulation, assimilation, nutrition, secretion, and change of matter, are still synthetically united with one another—as a PRIMARY FORM of life?—In the end, it is not only permitted to make this attempt, it is commanded by the conscience of LOGICAL METHOD. Not to assume several kinds of causality, so long as the attempt to get along with a single one has not been pushed to its furthest extent (to absurdity, if I may be allowed to say so): that is a morality of method which one may not repudiate nowadays—it follows "from its definition,"

as mathematicians say. The question is ultimately whether we really recognize the will as OPERATING, whether we believe in the causality of the will; if we do so—and fundamentally our belief IN THIS is just our belief in causality itself—we MUST make the attempt to posit hypothetically the causality of the will as the only causality. "Will" can naturally only operate on "will"—and not on "matter" (not on "nerves," for instance): in short, the hypothesis must be hazarded, whether will does not operate on will wherever "effects" are recognized—and whether all mechanical action, inasmuch as a power operates therein, is not just the power of will, the effect of will. Granted, finally, that we succeeded in explaining our entire instinctive life as the development and ramification of one fundamental form of will—namely, the Will to Power, as my thesis puts it; granted that all organic functions could be traced back to this Will to Power, and that the solution of the problem of generation and nutrition—it is one problem—could also be found therein: one would thus have acquired the right to define ALL active force unequivocally as WILL TO POWER. The world seen from within, the world defined and designated according to its "intelligible character"—it would simply be "Will to Power," and nothing else.

37. "What? Does not that mean in popular language: God is disproved, but not the devil?"—On the contrary!

On the contrary, my friends! And who the devil also compels you to speak popularly!

38. As happened finally in all the enlightenment of modern times with the French Revolution (that terrible farce, quite superfluous when judged close at hand, into which, however, the noble and visionary spectators of all Europe have interpreted from a distance their own indignation and enthusiasm so long and passionately, UNTIL THE TEXT HAS DISAPPEARED UNDER THE INTERPRETATION), so a noble posterity might once more misunderstand the whole of the past, and perhaps only thereby make ITS aspect endurable.—Or rather, has not this already happened? Have not we ourselves been—that "noble posterity"? And, in so far as we now comprehend this, is it not—thereby already past?

39. Nobody will very readily regard a doctrine as true merely because it makes people happy or virtuous— excepting, perhaps, the amiable "Idealists," who are enthusiastic about the good, true, and beautiful, and let all kinds of motley, coarse, and good-natured desirabilities swim about promiscuously in their pond. Happiness and virtue are no arguments. It is willingly forgotten, however, even on the part of thoughtful minds, that to make unhappy and to make bad are just as little counter-arguments. A thing could be TRUE, although it were in the highest degree injurious and dangerous; indeed, the fundamental constitution of

existence might be such that one succumbed by a full knowledge of it—so that the strength of a mind might be measured by the amount of "truth" it could endure—or to speak more plainly, by the extent to which it REQUIRED truth attenuated, veiled, sweetened, damped, and falsified. But there is no doubt that for the discovery of certain PORTIONS of truth the wicked and unfortunate are more favourably situated and have a greater likelihood of success; not to speak of the wicked who are happy—a species about whom moralists are silent. Perhaps severity and craft are more favourable conditions for the development of strong, independent spirits and philosophers than the gentle, refined, yielding good-nature, and habit of taking things easily, which are prized, and rightly prized in a learned man. Presupposing always, to begin with, that the term "philosopher" be not confined to the philosopher who writes books, or even introduces HIS philosophy into books!—Stendhal furnishes a last feature of the portrait of the free-spirited philosopher, which for the sake of German taste I will not omit to underline—for it is OPPOSED to German taste. "Pour etre bon philosophe," says this last great psychologist, "il faut etre sec, clair, sans illusion. Un banquier, qui a fait fortune, a une partie du caractere requis pour faire des decouvertes en philosophie, c'est-a-dire pour voir clair dans ce qui est."

40. Everything that is profound loves the mask: the profoundest things have a hatred even of figure and likeness. Should not the CONTRARY only be the right disguise for the shame of a God to go about in? A question worth asking!—it would be strange if some mystic has not already ventured on the same kind of thing. There are proceedings of such a delicate nature that it is well to overwhelm them with coarseness and make them unrecognizable; there are actions of love and of an extravagant magnanimity after which nothing can be wiser than to take a stick and thrash the witness soundly: one thereby obscures his recollection. Many a one is able to obscure and abuse his own memory, in order at least to have vengeance on this sole party in the secret: shame is inventive. They are not the worst things of which one is most ashamed: there is not only deceit behind a mask—there is so much goodness in craft. I could imagine that a man with something costly and fragile to conceal, would roll through life clumsily and rotundly like an old, green, heavily-hooped wine-cask: the refinement of his shame requiring it to be so. A man who has depths in his shame meets his destiny and his delicate decisions upon paths which few ever reach, and with regard to the existence of which his nearest and most intimate friends may be ignorant; his mortal danger conceals itself from their eyes, and equally so his regained security. Such a hidden nature, which instinctively employs speech for silence and concealment, and is inexhaustible in evasion of

communication, DESIRES and insists that a mask of himself shall occupy his place in the hearts and heads of his friends; and supposing he does not desire it, his eyes will some day be opened to the fact that there is nevertheless a mask of him there—and that it is well to be so. Every profound spirit needs a mask; nay, more, around every profound spirit there continually grows a mask, owing to the constantly false, that is to say, SUPERFICIAL interpretation of every word he utters, every step he takes, every sign of life he manifests.

41. One must subject oneself to one's own tests that one is destined for independence and command, and do so at the right time. One must not avoid one's tests, although they constitute perhaps the most dangerous game one can play, and are in the end tests made only before ourselves and before no other judge. Not to cleave to any person, be it even the dearest—every person is a prison and also a recess. Not to cleave to a fatherland, be it even the most suffering and necessitous—it is even less difficult to detach one's heart from a victorious fatherland. Not to cleave to a sympathy, be it even for higher men, into whose peculiar torture and helplessness chance has given us an insight. Not to cleave to a science, though it tempt one with the most valuable discoveries, apparently specially reserved for us. Not to cleave to one's own liberation, to the voluptuous distance and remoteness of the bird, which always flies further aloft in order always to see

more under it—the danger of the flier. Not to cleave to our own virtues, nor become as a whole a victim to any of our specialties, to our "hospitality" for instance, which is the danger of dangers for highly developed and wealthy souls, who deal prodigally, almost indifferently with themselves, and push the virtue of liberality so far that it becomes a vice. One must know how TO CONSERVE ONESELF—the best test of independence.

42. A new order of philosophers is appearing; I shall venture to baptize them by a name not without danger. As far as I understand them, as far as they allow themselves to be understood—for it is their nature to WISH to remain something of a puzzle—these philosophers of the future might rightly, perhaps also wrongly, claim to be designated as "tempters." This name itself is after all only an attempt, or, if it be preferred, a temptation.

43. Will they be new friends of "truth," these coming philosophers? Very probably, for all philosophers hitherto have loved their truths. But assuredly they will not be dogmatists. It must be contrary to their pride, and also contrary to their taste, that their truth should still be truth for every one—that which has hitherto been the secret wish and ultimate purpose of all dogmatic efforts. "My opinion is MY opinion: another person has not easily a right to it"—such a philosopher

of the future will say, perhaps. One must renounce the bad taste of wishing to agree with many people. "Good" is no longer good when one's neighbour takes it into his mouth. And how could there be a "common good"! The expression contradicts itself; that which can be common is always of small value. In the end things must be as they are and have always been—the great things remain for the great, the abysses for the profound, the delicacies and thrills for the refined, and, to sum up shortly, everything rare for the rare.

44. Need I say expressly after all this that they will be free, VERY free spirits, these philosophers of the future—as certainly also they will not be merely free spirits, but something more, higher, greater, and fundamentally different, which does not wish to be misunderstood and mistaken? But while I say this, I feel under OBLIGATION almost as much to them as to ourselves (we free spirits who are their heralds and forerunners), to sweep away from ourselves altogether a stupid old prejudice and misunderstanding, which, like a fog, has too long made the conception of "free spirit" obscure. In every country of Europe, and the same in America, there is at present something which makes an abuse of this name a very narrow, prepossessed, enchained class of spirits, who desire almost the opposite of what our intentions and instincts prompt—not to mention that in respect to the NEW philosophers who are appearing, they must still more be

closed windows and bolted doors. Briefly and regrettably, they belong to the LEVELLERS, these wrongly named "free spirits"—as glib-tongued and scribe-fingered slaves of the democratic taste and its "modern ideas" all of them men without solitude, without personal solitude, blunt honest fellows to whom neither courage nor honourable conduct ought to be denied, only, they are not free, and are ludicrously superficial, especially in their innate partiality for seeing the cause of almost ALL human misery and failure in the old forms in which society has hitherto existed—a notion which happily inverts the truth entirely! What they would fain attain with all their strength, is the universal, green-meadow happiness of the herd, together with security, safety, comfort, and alleviation of life for every one, their two most frequently chanted songs and doctrines are called "Equality of Rights" and "Sympathy with All Sufferers"—and suffering itself is looked upon by them as something which must be DONE AWAY WITH. We opposite ones, however, who have opened our eye and conscience to the question how and where the plant "man" has hitherto grown most vigorously, believe that this has always taken place under the opposite conditions, that for this end the dangerousness of his situation had to be increased enormously, his inventive faculty and dissembling power (his "spirit") had to develop into subtlety and daring under long oppression and compulsion, and his Will to Life had to be increased to the unconditioned Will to Power—we believe that severity, violence, slavery, danger in the street and in the heart, secrecy, stoicism, tempter's art and devilry of every kind,—that everything wicked, terrible, tyrannical, predatory, and serpentine in man, serves as well for the elevation of the human species as its opposite—we do not even say enough when we only say THIS MUCH, and in any case we find ourselves here, both with our speech and our silence, at the OTHER extreme of all modern ideology and gregarious desirability, as their antipodes perhaps? What wonder that we "free spirits" are not exactly the most communicative spirits? that we do not wish to betray in every respect WHAT a spirit can free itself from, and WHERE perhaps it will then be driven? And as to the import of the dangerous formula, "Beyond Good and Evil," with which we at least avoid confusion, we ARE something else than "libres-penseurs," "liben pensatori" "free-thinkers," and whatever these honest advocates of "modern ideas" like to call themselves. Having been at home, or at least guests, in many realms of the spirit, having escaped again and again from the gloomy, agreeable nooks in which preferences and prejudices, youth, origin, the accident of men and books, or even the weariness of travel seemed to confine us, full of malice against the seductions of dependency which he concealed in honours, money, positions, or exaltation of the senses, grateful even for distress and the vicissitudes of illness, because they always free us from some rule, and its "prejudice," grateful to the God, devil, sheep, and worm in us, inquisitive to a fault, investigators to the point of cruelty, with unhesitating fingers for the intangible, with teeth and stomachs for the most indigestible, ready for any business that requires sagacity and acute senses, ready for every adventure, owing to an excess of "free will", with anterior and posterior souls, into the ultimate intentions of which it is difficult to pry, with foregrounds and backgrounds to the end of which no foot may run, hidden ones under the mantles of light, appropriators, although we resemble heirs and spendthrifts, arrangers and collectors from morning till night, misers of our wealth and our full-crammed drawers, economical in learning and forgetting, inventive in scheming, sometimes proud of tables of categories, sometimes pedants, sometimes night-owls of work even in full day, yea, if necessary, even scarecrows—and it is necessary nowadays, that is to say, inasmuch as we are the born, sworn, jealous friends of SOLITUDE, of our own profoundest midnight and midday solitude—such kind of men are we, we free spirits! And perhaps ye are also something of the same kind, ye coming ones? ye NEW philosophers?

Chapter III

The religious mood

45. The human soul and its limits, the range of man's inner experiences hitherto attained, the heights, depths, and distances of these experiences, the entire history of the soul UP TO THE PRESENT TIME, and its still unexhausted possibilities: this is the preordained hunting-domain for a born psychologist and lover of a "big hunt". But how often must he say despairingly to himself: "A single individual! alas, only a single individual! and this great forest, this virgin forest!" So he would like to have some hundreds of hunting assistants, and fine trained hounds, that he could send into the history of the human soul, to drive HIS game together. In vain: again and again he experiences, profoundly and bitterly, how difficult it is to find assistants and dogs for all the things that directly excite his curiosity. The evil of sending scholars into new and dangerous hunting-domains, where courage, sagacity, and subtlety in every sense are required, is that they are no longer serviceable just when the "BIG hunt," and also the great danger commences,—it is precisely then that they lose their keen eye and nose. In order, for instance, to divine and determine what sort of history the problem of KNOWLEDGE AND CONSCIENCE

has hitherto had in the souls of homines religiosi, a person would perhaps himself have to possess as profound, as bruised, as immense an experience as the intellectual conscience of Pascal; and then he would still require that wide-spread heaven of clear, wicked spirituality, which, from above, would be able to oversee, arrange, and effectively formulize this mass of dangerous and painful experiences.—But who could do me this service! And who would have time to wait for such servants!—they evidently appear too rarely, they are so improbable at all times! Eventually one must do everything ONESELF in order to know something; which means that one has MUCH to do!—But a curiosity like mine is once for all the most agreeable of vices—pardon me! I mean to say that the love of truth has its reward in heaven, and already upon earth.

46. Faith, such as early Christianity desired, and not infrequently achieved in the midst of a skeptical and southernly free-spirited world, which had centuries of struggle between philosophical schools behind it and in it, counting besides the education in tolerance which the Imperium Romanum gave—this faith is NOT that sincere, austere slave-faith by which perhaps a Luther or a Cromwell, or some other northern barbarian of the spirit remained attached to his God and Christianity, it is much rather the faith of Pascal, which resembles in a terrible manner a continuous suicide of reason—a tough, long-lived, worm-like reason, which is not to be

slain at once and with a single blow. The Christian faith from the beginning, is sacrifice the sacrifice of all freedom, all pride, all self-confidence of spirit, it is at the same time subjection, self-derision, and self-mutilation. There is cruelty and religious Phoenicianism in this faith, which is adapted to a tender, many-sided, and very fastidious conscience, it takes for granted that the subjection of the spirit is indescribably PAINFUL, that all the past and all the habits of such a spirit resist the absurdissimum, in the form of which "faith" comes to it. Modern men, with their obtuseness as regards all Christian nomenclature, have no longer the sense for the terribly superlative conception which was implied to an antique taste by the paradox of the formula, "God on the Cross". Hitherto there had never and nowhere been such boldness in inversion, nor anything at once so dreadful, questioning, and questionable as this formula: it promised a transvaluation of all ancient values—It was the Orient, the PROFOUND Orient, it was the Oriental slave who thus took revenge on Rome and its noble, light-minded toleration, on the Roman "Catholicism" of non-faith, and it was always not the faith, but the freedom from the faith, the half-stoical and smiling indifference to the seriousness of the faith, which made the slaves indignant at their masters and revolt against them. "Enlightenment" causes revolt, for the slave desires the unconditioned, he understands nothing but the tyrannous, even in morals, he loves as he hates, without NUANCE, to the very depths, to the point of pain, to the point of sickness—his many HIDDEN sufferings make him revolt against the noble taste which seems to DENY suffering. The skepticism with regard to suffering, fundamentally only an attitude of aristocratic morality, was not the least of the causes, also, of the last great slave-insurrection which began with the French Revolution.

47. Wherever the religious neurosis has appeared on the earth so far, we find it connected with three dangerous prescriptions as to regimen: solitude, fasting, and sexual abstinence—but without its being possible to determine with certainty which is cause and which is effect, or IF any relation at all of cause and effect exists there. This latter doubt is justified by the fact that one of the most regular symptoms among savage as well as among civilized peoples is the most sudden and excessive sensuality, which then with equal suddenness transforms into penitential paroxysms, world-renunciation, and will-renunciation, both symptoms perhaps explainable as disguised epilepsy? But nowhere is it MORE obligatory to put aside explanations around no other type has there grown such a mass of absurdity and superstition, no other type seems to have been more interesting to men and even to philosophers—perhaps it is time to become just a little indifferent here, to learn caution, or, better still, to look AWAY, TO GO AWAY—Yet in the background of

the most recent philosophy, that of Schopenhauer, we find almost as the problem in itself, this terrible note of interrogation of the religious crisis and awakening. How is the negation of will POSSIBLE? how is the saint possible?—that seems to have been the very question with which Schopenhauer made a start and became a philosopher. And thus it was a genuine Schopenhauerian consequence, that his most convinced adherent (perhaps also his last, as far as Germany is concerned), namely, Richard Wagner, should bring his own life-work to an end just here, and should finally put that terrible and eternal type upon the stage as Kundry, type vecu, and as it loved and lived, at the very time that the mad-doctors in almost all European countries had an opportunity to study the type close at hand, wherever the religious neurosis—or as I call it, "the religious mood"—made its latest epidemical outbreak and display as the "Salvation Army"—If it be a question, however, as to what has been so extremely interesting to men of all sorts in all ages, and even to philosophers, in the whole phenomenon of the saint, it is undoubtedly the appearance of the miraculous therein—namely, the immediate SUCCESSION OF OPPOSITES, of states of the soul regarded as morally antithetical: it was believed here to be self-evident that a "bad man" was all at once turned into a "saint," a good man. The hitherto existing psychology was wrecked at this point, is it not possible it may have happened principally because psychology had placed itself under the dominion of morals, because it BELIEVED in oppositions of moral values, and saw, read, and INTERPRETED these oppositions into the text and facts of the case? What? "Miracle" only an error of interpretation? A lack of philology?

48. It seems that the Latin races are far more deeply attached to their Catholicism than we Northerners are to Christianity generally, and that consequently unbelief in Catholic countries means something quite different from what it does among Protestants—namely, a sort of revolt against the spirit of the race, while with us it is rather a return to the spirit (or non-spirit) of the race.

We Northerners undoubtedly derive our origin from barbarous races, even as regards our talents for religion—we have POOR talents for it. One may make an exception in the case of the Celts, who have theretofore furnished also the best soil for Christian infection in the North: the Christian ideal blossomed forth in France as much as ever the pale sun of the north would allow it. How strangely pious for our taste are still these later French skeptics, whenever there is any Celtic blood in their origin! How Catholic, how un-German does Auguste Comte's Sociology seem to us, with the Roman logic of its instincts! How Jesuitical, that amiable and shrewd cicerone of Port Royal, Sainte-Beuve, in spite of all his hostility to Jesuits! And even Ernest Renan: how inaccessible to us Northerners does the language of such a Renan appear, in whom every instant the merest touch of religious thrill throws his refined voluptuous and comfortably couching soul off its balance! Let us repeat after him these fine sentences—and what wickedness and haughtiness is immediately aroused by way of answer in our probably less beautiful but harder souls, that is to say, in our more German souls!—"DISONS DONC HARDIMENT QUE LA RELIGION EST UN PRODUIT DE L'HOMME NORMAL, QUE L'HOMME EST LE PLUS DANS LE VRAI QUANT IL EST LE PLUS RELIGIEUX ET LE PLUS ASSURE D'UNE DESTINEE INFINIE.... C'EST QUAND IL EST BON QU'IL VEUT QUE LA VIRTU CORRESPONDE A UN ORDER ETERNAL, C'EST QUAND IL CONTEMPLE LES CHOSES D'UNE MANIERE DESINTERESSEE QU'IL TROUVE LA MORT REVOLTANTE ET ABSURDE. COMMENT NE PAS SUPPOSER QUE C'EST DANS CES MOMENTS-LA, QUE L'HOMME VOIT LE MIEUX?"... These sentences are so extremely ANTIPODAL to my ears and habits of thought, that in my first impulse of rage on finding them, I wrote on the margin, "LA NIAISERIE RELIGIEUSE PAR EXCELLENCE!"—until in my later rage I even took a fancy to them, these sentences with their truth absolutely inverted! It is so nice and such a distinction to have one's own antipodes!

49. That which is so astonishing in the religious life of the ancient Greeks is the irrestrainable stream of GRATITUDE which it pours forth—it is a very superior kind of man who takes SUCH an attitude towards nature and life.—Later on, when the populace got the upper hand in Greece, FEAR became rampant also in religion; and Christianity was preparing itself.

50. The passion for God: there are churlish, honest-hearted, and importunate kinds of it, like that of Luther—the whole of Protestantism lacks the southern DELICATEZZA. There is an Oriental exaltation of the mind in it, like that of an undeservedly favoured or elevated slave, as in the case of St. Augustine, for instance, who lacks in an offensive manner, all nobility in bearing and desires. There is a feminine tenderness and sensuality in it, which modestly and unconsciously longs for a UNIO MYSTICA ET PHYSICA, as in the case of Madame de Guyon. In many cases it appears, curiously enough, as the disguise of a girl's or youth's puberty; here and there even as the hysteria of an old maid, also as her last ambition. The Church has frequently canonized the woman in such a case.

51. The mightiest men have hitherto always bowed reverently before the saint, as the enigma of self-subjugation and utter voluntary privation—why did they thus bow? They divined in him—and as it were behind the questionableness of his frail and wretched

appearance—the superior force which wished to test itself by such a subjugation; the strength of will, in which they recognized their own strength and love of power, and knew how to honour it: they honoured something in themselves when they honoured the saint. In addition to this, the contemplation of the saint suggested to them a suspicion: such an enormity of self-negation and anti-naturalness will not have been coveted for nothing—they have said, inquiringly. There is perhaps a reason for it, some very great danger, about which the ascetic might wish to be more accurately informed through his secret interlocutors and visitors? In a word, the mighty ones of the world learned to have a new fear before him, they divined a new power, a strange, still unconquered enemy:—it was the "Will to Power" which obliged them to halt before the saint. They had to question him.

52. In the Jewish "Old Testament," the book of divine justice, there are men, things, and sayings on such an immense scale, that Greek and Indian literature has nothing to compare with it. One stands with fear and reverence before those stupendous remains of what man was formerly, and one has sad thoughts about old Asia and its little out-pushed peninsula Europe, which would like, by all means, to figure before Asia as the "Progress of Mankind." To be sure, he who is himself only a slender, tame house-animal, and knows only the wants of a house-animal (like our cultured people of

today, including the Christians of "cultured" Christianity), need neither be amazed nor even sad amid those ruins—the taste for the Old Testament is a touchstone with respect to "great" and "small": perhaps he will find that the New Testament, the book of grace, still appeals more to his heart (there is much of the odour of the genuine, tender, stupid beadsman and petty soul in it). To have bound up this New Testament (a kind of ROCOCO of taste in every respect) along with the Old Testament into one book, as the "Bible," as "The Book in Itself," is perhaps the greatest audacity and "sin against the Spirit" which literary Europe has upon its conscience.

53. Why Atheism nowadays? "The father" in God is thoroughly refuted; equally so "the judge," "the rewarder." Also his "free will": he does not hear—and even if he did, he would not know how to help. The worst is that he seems incapable of communicating himself clearly; is he uncertain?—This is what I have made out (by questioning and listening at a variety of conversations) to be the cause of the decline of European theism; it appears to me that though the religious instinct is in vigorous growth,—it rejects the theistic satisfaction with profound distrust.

54. What does all modern philosophy mainly do? Since Descartes—and indeed more in defiance of him than on the basis of his procedure—an ATTENTAT has

been made on the part of all philosophers on the old conception of the soul, under the guise of a criticism of the subject and predicate conception—that is to say, an ATTENTAT on the fundamental presupposition of Christian doctrine. Modern philosophy, as epistemological skepticism, is secretly or openly ANTI-CHRISTIAN, although (for keener ears, be it said) by no means anti-religious. Formerly, in effect, one believed in "the soul" as one believed in grammar and the grammatical subject: one said, "I" is the condition, "think" is the predicate and is conditioned—to think is an activity for which one MUST suppose a subject as cause. The attempt was then made, with marvelous tenacity and subtlety, to see if one could not get out of this net,—to see if the opposite was not perhaps true: "think" the condition, and "I" the conditioned; "I," therefore, only a synthesis which has been MADE by thinking itself. KANT really wished to prove that, starting from the subject, the subject could not be proved—nor the object either: the possibility of an APPARENT EXISTENCE of the subject, and therefore of "the soul," may not always have been strange to him,—the thought which once had an immense power on earth as the Vedanta philosophy.

55. There is a great ladder of religious cruelty, with many rounds; but three of these are the most important. Once on a time men sacrificed human beings to their God, and perhaps just those they loved the best—to this

category belong the firstling sacrifices of all primitive religions, and also the sacrifice of the Emperor Tiberius in the Mithra-Grotto on the Island of Capri, that most terrible of all Roman anachronisms. Then, during the moral epoch of mankind, they sacrificed to their God the strongest instincts they possessed, their "nature"; THIS festal joy shines in the cruel glances of ascetics and "anti-natural" fanatics. Finally, what still remained to be sacrificed? Was it not necessary in the end for men to sacrifice everything comforting, holy, healing, all hope, all faith in hidden harmonies, in future blessedness and justice? Was it not necessary to sacrifice God himself, and out of cruelty to themselves to worship stone, stupidity, gravity, fate, nothingness? To sacrifice God for nothingness—this paradoxical mystery of the ultimate cruelty has been reserved for the rising generation; we all know something thereof already.

56. Whoever, like myself, prompted by some enigmatical desire, has long endeavoured to go to the bottom of the question of pessimism and free it from the half-Christian, half-German narrowness and stupidity in which it has finally presented itself to this century, namely, in the form of Schopenhauer's philosophy; whoever, with an Asiatic and super-Asiatic eye, has actually looked inside, and into the most world-renouncing of all possible modes of thought—beyond good and evil, and no longer like Buddha and

Schopenhauer, under the dominion and delusion of morality,—whoever has done this, has perhaps just thereby, without really desiring it, opened his eyes to behold the opposite ideal: the ideal of the most world-approving, exuberant, and vivacious man, who has not only learnt to compromise and arrange with that which was and is, but wishes to have it again AS IT WAS AND IS, for all eternity, insatiably calling out da capo, not only to himself, but to the whole piece and play; and not only the play, but actually to him who requires the play—and makes it necessary; because he always requires himself anew—and makes himself necessary.—What? And this would not be—circulus vitiosus deus?

57. The distance, and as it were the space around man, grows with the strength of his intellectual vision and insight: his world becomes profounder; new stars, new enigmas, and notions are ever coming into view. Perhaps everything on which the intellectual eye has exercised its acuteness and profundity has just been an occasion for its exercise, something of a game, something for children and childish minds. Perhaps the most solemn conceptions that have caused the most fighting and suffering, the conceptions "God" and "sin," will one day seem to us of no more importance than a child's plaything or a child's pain seems to an old man;—and perhaps another plaything and another pain

will then be necessary once more for "the old man"—always childish enough, an eternal child!

58. Has it been observed to what extent outward idleness, or semi-idleness, is necessary to a real religious life (alike for its favourite microscopic labour of self-examination, and for its soft placidity called "prayer," the state of perpetual readiness for the "coming of God"), I mean the idleness with a good conscience, the idleness of olden times and of blood, to which the aristocratic sentiment that work is DISHONOURING—that it vulgarizes body and soul—is not quite unfamiliar? And that consequently the modern, noisy, time-engrossing, conceited, foolishly proud laboriousness educates and prepares for "unbelief" more than anything else? Among these, for instance, who are at present living apart from religion in Germany, I find "free-thinkers" of diversified species and origin, but above all a majority of those in whom laboriousness from generation to generation has dissolved the religious instincts; so that they no longer know what purpose religions serve, and only note their existence in the world with a kind of dull astonishment. They feel themselves already fully occupied, these good people, be it by their business or by their pleasures, not to mention the "Fatherland," and the newspapers, and their "family duties"; it seems that they have no time whatever left for religion; and above all, it is not obvious to them whether it is a question of

a new business or a new pleasure—for it is impossible, they say to themselves, that people should go to church merely to spoil their tempers. They are by no means enemies of religious customs; should certain circumstances, State affairs perhaps, require their participation in such customs, they do what is required, as so many things are done—with a patient and unassuming seriousness, and without much curiosity or discomfort;—they live too much apart and outside to feel even the necessity for a FOR or AGAINST in such matters. Among those indifferent persons may be reckoned nowadays the majority of German Protestants of the middle classes, especially in the great laborious centres of trade and commerce; also the majority of laborious scholars, and the entire University personnel (with the exception of the theologians, whose existence and possibility there always gives psychologists new and more subtle puzzles to solve). On the part of pious, or merely church-going people, there is seldom any idea of HOW MUCH good-will, one might say arbitrary will, is now necessary for a German scholar to take the problem of religion seriously; his whole profession (and as I have said, his whole workmanlike laboriousness, to which he is compelled by his modern conscience) inclines him to a lofty and almost charitable serenity as regards religion, with which is occasionally mingled a slight disdain for the "uncleanliness" of spirit which he takes for granted wherever any one still professes to belong to the

Church. It is only with the help of history (NOT through his own personal experience, therefore) that the scholar succeeds in bringing himself to a respectful seriousness, and to a certain timid deference in presence of religions; but even when his sentiments have reached the stage of gratitude towards them, he has not personally advanced one step nearer to that which still maintains itself as Church or as piety; perhaps even the contrary. The practical indifference to religious matters in the midst of which he has been born and brought up, usually sublimates itself in his case into circumspection and cleanliness, which shuns contact with religious men and things; and it may be just the depth of his tolerance and humanity which prompts him to avoid the delicate trouble which tolerance itself brings with it.—Every age has its own divine type of naivete, for the discovery of which other ages may envy it: and how much naivete—adorable, childlike, and boundlessly foolish naivete is involved in this belief of the scholar in his superiority, in the good conscience of his tolerance, in the unsuspecting, simple certainty with which his instinct treats the religious man as a lower and less valuable type, beyond, before, and ABOVE which he himself has developed—he, the little arrogant dwarf and mob-man, the sedulously alert, head-and-hand drudge of "ideas," of "modern ideas"!

59. Whoever has seen deeply into the world has doubtless divined what wisdom there is in the fact that

men are superficial. It is their preservative instinct which teaches them to be flighty, lightsome, and false. Here and there one finds a passionate and exaggerated adoration of "pure forms" in philosophers as well as in artists: it is not to be doubted that whoever has NEED of the cult of the superficial to that extent, has at one time or another made an unlucky dive BENEATH it. Perhaps there is even an order of rank with respect to those burnt children, the born artists who find the enjoyment of life only in trying to FALSIFY its image (as if taking wearisome revenge on it), one might guess to what degree life has disgusted them, by the extent to which they wish to see its image falsified, attenuated, ultrified, and deified,—one might reckon the homines religiosi among the artists, as their HIGHEST rank. It is the profound, suspicious fear of an incurable pessimism which compels whole centuries to fasten their teeth into a religious interpretation of existence: the fear of the instinct which divines that truth might be attained TOO soon, before man has become strong enough, hard enough, artist enough.... Piety, the "Life in God," regarded in this light, would appear as the most elaborate and ultimate product of the FEAR of truth, as artist-adoration and artist-intoxication in presence of the most logical of all falsifications, as the will to the inversion of truth, to untruth at any price. Perhaps there has hitherto been no more effective means of beautifying man than piety, by means of it man can become so artful, so superficial, so iridescent, and so good, that his appearance no longer offends.

60. To love mankind FOR GOD'S SAKE—this has so far been the noblest and remotest sentiment to which mankind has attained. That love to mankind, without any redeeming intention in the background, is only an ADDITIONAL folly and brutishness, that the inclination to this love has first to get its proportion, its delicacy, its gram of salt and sprinkling of ambergris from a higher inclination—whoever first perceived and "experienced" this, however his tongue may have stammered as it attempted to express such a delicate matter, let him for all time be holy and respected, as the man who has so far flown highest and gone astray in the finest fashion!

61. The philosopher, as WE free spirits understand him—as the man of the greatest responsibility, who has the conscience for the general development of mankind,—will use religion for his disciplining and educating work, just as he will use the contemporary political and economic conditions. The selecting and disciplining influence—destructive, as well as creative and fashioning—which can be exercised by means of religion is manifold and varied, according to the sort of people placed under its spell and protection. For those who are strong and independent, destined and trained to command, in whom the judgment and skill of a ruling

race is incorporated, religion is an additional means for overcoming resistance in the exercise of authority—as a bond which binds rulers and subjects in common, betraying and surrendering to the former the conscience of the latter, their inmost heart, which would fain escape obedience. And in the case of the unique natures of noble origin, if by virtue of superior spirituality they should incline to a more retired and contemplative life, reserving to themselves only the more refined forms of government (over chosen disciples or members of an order), religion itself may be used as a means for obtaining peace from the noise and trouble of managing GROSSER affairs, and for securing immunity from the UNAVOIDABLE filth of all political agitation. The Brahmins, for instance, understood this fact. With the help of a religious organization, they secured to themselves the power of nominating kings for the people, while their sentiments prompted them to keep apart and outside, as men with a higher and super-regal mission. At the same time religion gives inducement and opportunity to some of the subjects to qualify themselves for future ruling and commanding the slowly ascending ranks and classes, in which, through fortunate marriage customs, volitional power and delight in self-control are on the increase. To them religion offers sufficient incentives and temptations to aspire to higher intellectuality, and to experience the sentiments of authoritative self-control, of silence, and of solitude. Asceticism and Puritanism are almost indispensable means of educating and ennobling a race which seeks to rise above its hereditary baseness and work itself upwards to future supremacy. And finally, to ordinary men, to the majority of the people, who exist for service and general utility, and are only so far entitled to exist, religion gives invaluable contentedness with their lot and condition, peace of heart, ennoblement of obedience, additional social happiness and sympathy, with something of transfiguration and embellishment, something of justification of all the commonplaceness, all the meanness, all the semi-animal poverty of their souls. Religion, together with the religious significance of life, sheds sunshine over such perpetually harassed men, and makes even their own aspect endurable to them, it operates upon them as the Epicurean philosophy usually operates upon sufferers of a higher order, in a refreshing and refining manner, almost TURNING suffering TO ACCOUNT, and in the end even hallowing and vindicating it. There is perhaps nothing so admirable in Christianity and Buddhism as their art of teaching even the lowest to elevate themselves by piety to a seemingly higher order of things, and thereby to retain their satisfaction with the actual world in which they find it difficult enough to live—this very difficulty being necessary.

62. To be sure—to make also the bad counter-reckoning against such religions, and to bring to light their secret dangers—the cost is always excessive and

terrible when religions do NOT operate as an educational and disciplinary medium in the hands of the philosopher, but rule voluntarily and PARAMOUNTLY, when they wish to be the final end, and not a means along with other means. Among men, as among all other animals, there is a surplus of defective, diseased, degenerating, infirm, and necessarily suffering individuals; the successful cases, among men also, are always the exception; and in view of the fact that man is THE ANIMAL NOT YET PROPERLY ADAPTED TO HIS ENVIRONMENT, the rare exception. But worse still. The higher the type a man represents, the greater is the improbability that he will SUCCEED; the accidental, the law of irrationality in the general constitution of mankind, manifests itself most terribly in its destructive effect on the higher orders of men, the conditions of whose lives are delicate, diverse, and difficult to determine. What, then, is the attitude of the two greatest religions above-mentioned to the SURPLUS of failures in life? They endeavour to preserve and keep alive whatever can be preserved; in fact, as the religions FOR SUFFERERS, they take the part of these upon principle; they are always in favour of those who suffer from life as from a disease, and they would fain treat every other experience of life as false and impossible. However highly we may esteem this indulgent and preservative care (inasmuch as in applying to others, it has applied, and applies also to the highest and usually the most suffering type of man), the hitherto PARAMOUNT religions—to give a general appreciation of them—are among the principal causes which have kept the type of "man" upon a lower level—they have preserved too much THAT WHICH SHOULD HAVE PERISHED. One has to thank them for invaluable services; and who is sufficiently rich in gratitude not to feel poor at the contemplation of all that the "spiritual men" of Christianity have done for Europe hitherto! But when they had given comfort to the sufferers, courage to the oppressed and despairing, a staff and support to the helpless, and when they had allured from society into convents and spiritual penitentiaries the broken-hearted and distracted: what else had they to do in order to work systematically in that fashion, and with a good conscience, for the preservation of all the sick and suffering, which means, in deed and in truth, to work for the DETERIORATION OF THE EUROPEAN RACE? To REVERSE all estimates of value—THAT is what they had to do! And to shatter the strong, to spoil great hopes, to cast suspicion on the delight in beauty, to break down everything autonomous, manly, conquering, and imperious—all instincts which are natural to the highest and most successful type of "man"—into uncertainty, distress of conscience, and self-destruction; forsooth, to invert all love of the earthly and of supremacy over the earth, into hatred of the earth and earthly things—THAT is the task the Church imposed on itself, and was obliged to impose, until, according to its standard of value, "unworldliness," "unsensuousness," and "higher man" fused into one sentiment. If one could observe the strangely painful, equally coarse and refined comedy of European Christianity with the derisive and impartial eye of an Epicurean god, I should think one would never cease marvelling and laughing; does it not actually seem that some single will has ruled over Europe for eighteen centuries in order to make a SUBLIME ABORTION of man? He, however, who, with opposite requirements (no longer Epicurean) and with some divine hammer in his hand, could approach this almost voluntary degeneration and stunting of mankind, as exemplified in the European Christian (Pascal, for instance), would he not have to cry aloud with rage, pity, and horror: "Oh, you bunglers, presumptuous pitiful bunglers, what have you done! Was that a work for your hands? How you have hacked and botched my finest stone! What have you presumed to do!"—I should say that Christianity has hitherto been the most portentous of presumptions. Men, not great enough, nor hard enough, to be entitled as artists to take part in fashioning MAN; men, not sufficiently strong and far-sighted to ALLOW, with sublime self-constraint, the obvious law of the thousandfold failures and perishings to prevail; men, not sufficiently noble to see the radically different grades of rank and intervals of rank that separate man from man:—SUCH men, with their "equality before God," have hitherto swayed the destiny of Europe; until at last a dwarfed, almost ludicrous species has been produced, a gregarious animal, something obliging, sickly, mediocre, the European of the present day.

Chapter IV
Apophthegms and Interludes

63. He who is a thorough teacher takes things seriously—and even himself—only in relation to his pupils.

64. "Knowledge for its own sake"—that is the last snare laid by morality: we are thereby completely entangled in morals once more.

65. The charm of knowledge would be small, were it not so much shame has to be overcome on the way to it.

65A. We are most dishonourable towards our God: he is not PERMITTED to sin.

66. The tendency of a person to allow himself to be degraded, robbed, deceived, and exploited might be the diffidence of a God among men.

67. Love to one only is a barbarity, for it is exercised at the expense of all others. Love to God also!

68. "I did that," says my memory. "I could not have done that," says my pride, and remains inexorable. Eventually—the memory yields.

69. One has regarded life carelessly, if one has failed to see the hand that—kills with leniency.

70. If a man has character, he has also his typical experience, which always recurs.

71. THE SAGE AS ASTRONOMER.—So long as thou feelest the stars as an "above thee," thou lackest the eye of the discerning one.

72. It is not the strength, but the duration of great sentiments that makes great men.

73. He who attains his ideal, precisely thereby surpasses it.

73A. Many a peacock hides his tail from every eye—and calls it his pride.

74. A man of genius is unbearable, unless he possess at least two things besides: gratitude and purity.

75. The degree and nature of a man's sensuality extends to the highest altitudes of his spirit.

76. Under peaceful conditions the militant man attacks himself.

77. With his principles a man seeks either to dominate, or justify, or honour, or reproach, or conceal his habits: two men with the same principles probably seek fundamentally different ends therewith.

78. He who despises himself, nevertheless esteems himself thereby, as a despiser.

79. A soul which knows that it is loved, but does not itself love, betrays its sediment: its dregs come up.

80. A thing that is explained ceases to concern us—What did the God mean who gave the advice, "Know thyself!" Did it perhaps imply "Cease to be concerned about thyself! become objective!"—And Socrates?—And the "scientific man"?

81. It is terrible to die of thirst at sea. Is it necessary that you should so salt your truth that it will no longer—quench thirst?

82. "Sympathy for all"—would be harshness and tyranny for THEE, my good neighbour.

83. INSTINCT—When the house is on fire one forgets even the dinner—Yes, but one recovers it from among the ashes.

84. Woman learns how to hate in proportion as she—forgets how to charm.

85. The same emotions are in man and woman, but in different TEMPO, on that account man and woman never cease to misunderstand each other.

86. In the background of all their personal vanity, women themselves have still their impersonal scorn—for "woman".

87. FETTERED HEART, FREE SPIRIT—When one firmly fetters one's heart and keeps it prisoner, one can allow one's spirit many liberties: I said this once before But people do not believe it when I say so, unless they know it already.

88. One begins to distrust very clever persons when they become embarrassed.

89. Dreadful experiences raise the question whether he who experiences them is not something dreadful also.

90. Heavy, melancholy men turn lighter, and come temporarily to their surface, precisely by that which makes others heavy—by hatred and love.

91. So cold, so icy, that one burns one's finger at the touch of him! Every hand that lays hold of him shrinks back!—And for that very reason many think him red-hot.

92. Who has not, at one time or another—sacrificed himself for the sake of his good name?

93. In affability there is no hatred of men, but precisely on that account a great deal too much contempt of men.

94. The maturity of man—that means, to have reacquired the seriousness that one had as a child at play.

95. To be ashamed of one's immorality is a step on the ladder at the end of which one is ashamed also of one's morality.

96. One should part from life as Ulysses parted from Nausicaa—blessing it rather than in love with it.

97. What? A great man? I always see merely the play-actor of his own ideal.

98. When one trains one's conscience, it kisses one while it bites.

99. THE DISAPPOINTED ONE SPEAKS—"I listened for the echo and I heard only praise."

100. We all feign to ourselves that we are simpler than we are, we thus relax ourselves away from our fellows.

101. A discerning one might easily regard himself at present as the animalization of God.

102. Discovering reciprocal love should really disenchant the lover with regard to the beloved. "What! She is modest enough to love even you? Or stupid enough? Or—or—-"

103. THE DANGER IN HAPPINESS.—"Everything now turns out best for me, I now love every fate:—who would like to be my fate?"

104. Not their love of humanity, but the impotence of their love, prevents the Christians of today—burning us.

105. The pia fraus is still more repugnant to the taste (the "piety") of the free spirit (the "pious man of knowledge") than the impia fraus. Hence the profound lack of judgment, in comparison with the Church, characteristic of the type "free spirit"—as ITS non-freedom.

106. By means of music the very passions enjoy themselves.

107. A sign of strong character, when once the resolution has been taken, to shut the ear even to the best counter-arguments. Occasionally, therefore, a will to stupidity.

108. There is no such thing as moral phenomena, but only a moral interpretation of phenomena.

109. The criminal is often enough not equal to his deed: he extenuates and maligns it.

110. The advocates of a criminal are seldom artists enough to turn the beautiful terribleness of the deed to the advantage of the doer.

111. Our vanity is most difficult to wound just when our pride has been wounded.

112. To him who feels himself preordained to contemplation and not to belief, all believers are too noisy and obtrusive; he guards against them.

113. "You want to prepossess him in your favour? Then you must be embarrassed before him."

114. The immense expectation with regard to sexual love, and the coyness in this expectation, spoils all the perspectives of women at the outset.

115. Where there is neither love nor hatred in the game, woman's play is mediocre.

116. The great epochs of our life are at the points when we gain courage to rebaptize our badness as the best in us.

117. The will to overcome an emotion, is ultimately only the will of another, or of several other, emotions.

118. There is an innocence of admiration: it is possessed by him to whom it has not yet occurred that he himself may be admired some day.

119. Our loathing of dirt may be so great as to prevent our cleaning ourselves—"justifying" ourselves.

120. Sensuality often forces the growth of love too much, so that its root remains weak, and is easily torn up.

121. It is a curious thing that God learned Greek when he wished to turn author—and that he did not learn it better.

122. To rejoice on account of praise is in many cases merely politeness of heart—and the very opposite of vanity of spirit.

123. Even concubinage has been corrupted—by marriage.

124. He who exults at the stake, does not triumph over pain, but because of the fact that he does not feel pain where he expected it. A parable.

125. When we have to change an opinion about any one, we charge heavily to his account the inconvenience he thereby causes us.

126. A nation is a detour of nature to arrive at six or seven great men.—Yes, and then to get round them.

127. In the eyes of all true women science is hostile to the sense of shame. They feel as if one wished to peep under their skin with it—or worse still! under their dress and finery.

128. The more abstract the truth you wish to teach, the more must you allure the senses to it.

129. The devil has the most extensive perspectives for God; on that account he keeps so far away from him:—the devil, in effect, as the oldest friend of knowledge.

130. What a person IS begins to betray itself when his talent decreases,—when he ceases to show what he CAN do. Talent is also an adornment; an adornment is also a concealment.

131. The sexes deceive themselves about each other: the reason is that in reality they honour and love only themselves (or their own ideal, to express it more agreeably). Thus man wishes woman to be peaceable: but in fact woman is ESSENTIALLY unpeaceable, like the cat, however well she may have assumed the peaceable demeanour.

132. One is punished best for one's virtues.

133. He who cannot find the way to HIS ideal, lives more frivolously and shamelessly than the man without an ideal.

134. From the senses originate all trustworthiness, all good conscience, all evidence of truth.

135. Pharisaism is not a deterioration of the good man; a considerable part of it is rather an essential condition of being good.

136. The one seeks an accoucheur for his thoughts, the other seeks some one whom he can assist: a good conversation thus originates.

137. In intercourse with scholars and artists one readily makes mistakes of opposite kinds: in a remarkable scholar one not infrequently finds a mediocre man; and often, even in a mediocre artist, one finds a very remarkable man.

138. We do the same when awake as when dreaming: we only invent and imagine him with whom we have intercourse—and forget it immediately.

139. In revenge and in love woman is more barbarous than man.

140. ADVICE AS A RIDDLE.—"If the band is not to break, bite it first—secure to make!"

141. The belly is the reason why man does not so readily take himself for a God.

142. The chastest utterance I ever heard: "Dans le veritable amour c'est l'ame qui enveloppe le corps."

143. Our vanity would like what we do best to pass precisely for what is most difficult to us.—

Concerning the origin of many systems of morals.

144. When a woman has scholarly inclinations there is generally something wrong with her sexual nature. Barrenness itself conduces to a certain virility of taste; man, indeed, if I may say so, is "the barren animal."

145. Comparing man and woman generally, one may say that woman would not have the genius for adornment, if she had not the instinct for the SECONDARY role.

146. He who fights with monsters should be careful lest he thereby become a monster. And if thou gaze long into an abyss, the abyss will also gaze into thee.

147. From old Florentine novels—moreover, from life: Buona femmina e mala femmina vuol bastone.—Sacchetti, Nov. 86.

148. To seduce their neighbour to a favourable opinion, and afterwards to believe implicitly in this opinion of their neighbour—who can do this conjuring trick so well as women?

149. That which an age considers evil is usually an unseasonable echo of what was formerly considered good—the atavism of an old ideal.

150. Around the hero everything becomes a tragedy; around the demigod everything becomes a satyr-play; and around God everything becomes—what? perhaps a "world"?

151. It is not enough to possess a talent: one must also have your permission to possess it;—eh, my friends?

152. "Where there is the tree of knowledge, there is always Paradise": so say the most ancient and the most modern serpents.

153. What is done out of love always takes place beyond good and evil.

154. Objection, evasion, joyous distrust, and love of irony are signs of health; everything absolute belongs to pathology.

155. The sense of the tragic increases and declines with sensuousness.

156. Insanity in individuals is something rare—but in groups, parties, nations, and epochs it is the rule.

157. The thought of suicide is a great consolation: by means of it one gets successfully through many a bad night.

158. Not only our reason, but also our conscience, truckles to our strongest impulse—the tyrant in us.

159. One MUST repay good and ill; but why just to the person who did us good or ill?

160. One no longer loves one's knowledge sufficiently after one has communicated it.

161. Poets act shamelessly towards their experiences: they exploit them.

162. "Our fellow-creature is not our neighbour, but our neighbour's neighbour":—so thinks every nation.

163. Love brings to light the noble and hidden qualities of a lover—his rare and exceptional traits: it is thus liable to be deceptive as to his normal character.

164. Jesus said to his Jews: "The law was for servants;—love God as I love him, as his Son! What have we Sons of God to do with morals!"

165. IN SIGHT OF EVERY PARTY.—A shepherd has always need of a bell-wether—or he has himself to be a wether occasionally.

166. One may indeed lie with the mouth; but with the accompanying grimace one nevertheless tells the truth.

167. To vigorous men intimacy is a matter of shame—and something precious.

168. Christianity gave Eros poison to drink; he did not die of it, certainly, but degenerated to Vice.

169. To talk much about oneself may also be a means of concealing oneself.

170. In praise there is more obtrusiveness than in blame.

171. Pity has an almost ludicrous effect on a man of knowledge, like tender hands on a Cyclops.

172. One occasionally embraces some one or other, out of love to mankind (because one cannot embrace all); but this is what one must never confess to the individual.

173. One does not hate as long as one disesteems, but only when one esteems equal or superior.

174. Ye Utilitarians—ye, too, love the UTILE only as a VEHICLE for your inclinations,—ye, too, really find the noise of its wheels insupportable!

175. One loves ultimately one's desires, not the thing desired.

176. The vanity of others is only counter to our taste when it is counter to our vanity.

177. With regard to what "truthfulness" is, perhaps nobody has ever been sufficiently truthful.

178. One does not believe in the follies of clever men: what a forfeiture of the rights of man!

179. The consequences of our actions seize us by the forelock, very indifferent to the fact that we have meanwhile "reformed."

180. There is an innocence in lying which is the sign of good faith in a cause.

181. It is inhuman to bless when one is being cursed.

182. The familiarity of superiors embitters one, because it may not be returned.

183. "I am affected, not because you have deceived me, but because I can no longer believe in you."

184. There is a haughtiness of kindness which has the appearance of wickedness.

185. "I dislike him."—Why?—"I am not a match for him."—Did any one ever answer so?

Chapter V
The natural history of morals

186. The moral sentiment in Europe at present is perhaps as subtle, belated, diverse, sensitive, and refined, as the "Science of Morals" belonging thereto is recent, initial, awkward, and coarse-fingered:—an interesting contrast, which sometimes becomes incarnate and obvious in the very person of a moralist. Indeed, the expression, "Science of Morals" is, in respect to what is designated thereby, far too presumptuous and counter to GOOD taste,—which is always a foretaste of more modest expressions. One ought to avow with the utmost fairness WHAT is still necessary here for a long time, WHAT is alone proper for the present: namely, the collection of material, the comprehensive survey and classification of an immense domain of delicate sentiments of worth, and distinctions of worth, which live, grow, propagate, and perish—and perhaps attempts to give a clear idea of the recurring and more common forms of these living crystallizations—as preparation for a THEORY OF TYPES of morality. To be sure, people have not hitherto been so modest. All the philosophers, with a

pedantic and ridiculous seriousness, demanded of themselves something very much higher, more pretentious, and ceremonious, when they concerned themselves with morality as a science: they wanted to GIVE A BASIC to morality—and every philosopher hitherto has believed that he has given it a basis; morality itself, however, has been regarded as something "given." How far from their awkward pride was the seemingly insignificant problem—left in dust and decay—of a description of forms of morality, notwithstanding that the finest hands and senses could hardly be fine enough for it! It was precisely owing to moral philosophers' knowing the moral facts imperfectly, in an arbitrary epitome, or an accidental abridgement—perhaps as the morality of their environment, their position, their church, their Zeitgeist, their climate and zone—it was precisely because they were badly instructed with regard to nations, eras, and past ages, and were by no means eager to know about these matters, that they did not even come in sight of the real problems of morals—problems which only disclose themselves by a comparison of MANY kinds of morality. In every "Science of Morals" hitherto, strange as it may sound, the problem of morality itself has been OMITTED: there has been no suspicion that there was anything problematic there! That which philosophers called "giving a basis to morality," and endeavoured to realize, has, when seen in a right light, proved merely a learned form of good FAITH in prevailing morality, a new means of its EXPRESSION, consequently just a matter-of-fact within the sphere of a definite morality, yea, in its ultimate motive, a sort of denial that it is LAWFUL for this morality to be called in question—and in any case the reverse of the testing, analyzing, doubting, and vivisecting of this very faith. Hear, for instance, with what innocence—almost worthy of honour—Schopenhauer represents his own task, and draw your conclusions concerning the scientificness of a "Science" whose latest master still talks in the strain of children and old wives: "The principle," he says (page 136 of the Grundprobleme der Ethik), [Footnote: Pages 54-55 of Schopenhauer's Basis of Morality, translated by Arthur B. Bullock, M.A. (1903).] "the axiom about the purport of which all moralists are PRACTICALLY agreed: neminem laede, immo omnes quantum potes juva—is REALLY the proposition which all moral teachers strive to establish, ... the REAL basis of ethics which has been sought, like the philosopher's stone, for centuries."—The difficulty of establishing the proposition referred to may indeed be great—it is well known that Schopenhauer also was unsuccessful in his efforts; and whoever has thoroughly realized how absurdly false and sentimental this proposition is, in a world whose essence is Will to Power, may be reminded that Schopenhauer, although a pessimist, ACTUALLY—played the flute... daily after dinner: one may read about the matter in his biography.

A question by the way: a pessimist, a repudiator of God and of the world, who MAKES A HALT at morality—who assents to morality, and plays the flute to laede-neminem morals, what? Is that really—a pessimist?

187. Apart from the value of such assertions as "there is a categorical imperative in us," one can always ask: What does such an assertion indicate about him who makes it? There are systems of morals which are meant to justify their author in the eyes of other people; other systems of morals are meant to tranquilize him, and make him self-satisfied; with other systems he wants to crucify and humble himself, with others he wishes to take revenge, with others to conceal himself, with others to glorify himself and gave superiority and distinction,—this system of morals helps its author to forget, that system makes him, or something of him, forgotten, many a moralist would like to exercise power and creative arbitrariness over mankind, many another, perhaps, Kant especially, gives us to understand by his morals that "what is estimable in me, is that I know how to obey—and with you it SHALL not be otherwise than with me!" In short, systems of morals are only a SIGN-LANGUAGE OF THE EMOTIONS.

188. In contrast to laisser-aller, every system of morals is a sort of tyranny against "nature" and also against "reason", that is, however, no objection, unless one should again decree by some system of morals, that

all kinds of tyranny and unreasonableness are unlawful What is essential and invaluable in every system of morals, is that it is a long constraint. In order to understand Stoicism, or Port Royal, or Puritanism, one should remember the constraint under which every language has attained to strength and freedom—the metrical constraint, the tyranny of rhyme and rhythm. How much trouble have the poets and orators of every nation given themselves!—not excepting some of the prose writers of today, in whose ear dwells an inexorable conscientiousness—"for the sake of a folly," as utilitarian bunglers say, and thereby deem themselves wise—"from submission to arbitrary laws," as the anarchists say, and thereby fancy themselves "free," even free-spirited. The singular fact remains, however, that everything of the nature of freedom, elegance, boldness, dance, and masterly certainty, which exists or has existed, whether it be in thought itself, or in administration, or in speaking and persuading, in art just as in conduct, has only developed by means of the tyranny of such arbitrary law, and in all seriousness, it is not at all improbable that precisely this is "nature" and "natural"—and not laisser-aller! Every artist knows how different from the state of letting himself go, is his "most natural" condition, the free arranging, locating, disposing, and constructing in the moments of "inspiration"—and how strictly and delicately he then obeys a thousand laws, which, by their very rigidness and precision, defy all formulation by means of ideas (even the most stable idea has, in comparison therewith, something floating, manifold, and ambiguous in it). The essential thing "in heaven and in earth" is, apparently (to repeat it once more), that there should be long OBEDIENCE in the same direction, there thereby results, and has always resulted in the long run, something which has made life worth living; for instance, virtue, art, music, dancing, reason, spirituality—anything whatever that is transfiguring, refined, foolish, or divine. The long bondage of the spirit, the distrustful constraint in the communicability of ideas, the discipline which the thinker imposed on himself to think in accordance with the rules of a church or a court, or conformable to Aristotelian premises, the persistent spiritual will to interpret everything that happened according to a Christian scheme, and in every occurrence to rediscover and justify the Christian God:—all this violence, arbitrariness, severity, dreadfulness, and unreasonableness, has proved itself the disciplinary means whereby the European spirit has attained its strength, its remorseless curiosity and subtle mobility; granted also that much irrecoverable strength and spirit had to be stifled, suffocated, and spoilt in the process (for here, as everywhere, "nature" shows herself as she is, in all her extravagant and INDIFFERENT magnificence, which is shocking, but nevertheless noble). That for centuries European thinkers only thought in order to prove something—nowadays, on the contrary, we are suspicious of every thinker who "wishes to prove something"—that it was always settled beforehand what WAS TO BE the result of their strictest thinking, as it was perhaps in the Asiatic astrology of former times, or as it is still at the present day in the innocent, Christian-moral explanation of immediate personal events "for the glory of God," or "for the good of the soul":—this tyranny, this arbitrariness, this severe and magnificent stupidity, has EDUCATED the spirit; slavery, both in the coarser and the finer sense, is apparently an indispensable means even of spiritual education and discipline. One may look at every system of morals in this light: it is "nature" therein which teaches to hate the laisser-aller, the too great freedom, and implants the need for limited horizons, for immediate duties—it teaches the NARROWING OF PERSPECTIVES, and thus, in a certain sense, that stupidity is a condition of life and development. "Thou must obey some one, and for a long time; OTHERWISE thou wilt come to grief, and lose all respect for thyself"—this seems to me to be the moral imperative of nature, which is certainly neither "categorical," as old Kant wished (consequently the "otherwise"), nor does it address itself to the individual (what does nature care for the individual!), but to nations, races, ages, and ranks; above all, however, to the animal "man" generally, to MANKIND.

189. Industrious races find it a great hardship to be idle: it was a master stroke of ENGLISH instinct to hallow and begloom Sunday to such an extent that the Englishman unconsciously hankers for his week—and work-day again:—as a kind of cleverly devised, cleverly intercalated FAST, such as is also frequently found in the ancient world (although, as is appropriate in southern nations, not precisely with respect to work). Many kinds of fasts are necessary; and wherever powerful influences and habits prevail, legislators have to see that intercalary days are appointed, on which such impulses are fettered, and learn to hunger anew. Viewed from a higher standpoint, whole generations and epochs, when they show themselves infected with any moral fanaticism, seem like those intercalated periods of restraint and fasting, during which an impulse learns to humble and submit itself—at the same time also to PURIFY and SHARPEN itself; certain philosophical sects likewise admit of a similar interpretation (for instance, the Stoa, in the midst of Hellenic culture, with the atmosphere rank and overcharged with Aphrodisiacal odours).—Here also is a hint for the explanation of the paradox, why it was precisely in the most Christian period of European history, and in general only under the pressure of Christian sentiments, that the sexual impulse sublimated into love (amour-passion).

190. There is something in the morality of Plato which does not really belong to Plato, but which only

appears in his philosophy, one might say, in spite of him: namely, Socratism, for which he himself was too noble. "No one desires to injure himself, hence all evil is done unwittingly. The evil man inflicts injury on himself; he would not do so, however, if he knew that evil is evil. The evil man, therefore, is only evil through error; if one free him from error one will necessarily make him—good."—This mode of reasoning savours of the POPULACE, who perceive only the unpleasant consequences of evil-doing, and practically judge that "it is STUPID to do wrong"; while they accept "good" as identical with "useful and pleasant," without further thought. As regards every system of utilitarianism, one may at once assume that it has the same origin, and follow the scent: one will seldom err.—Plato did all he could to interpret something refined and noble into the tenets of his teacher, and above all to interpret himself into them—he, the most daring of all interpreters, who lifted the entire Socrates out of the street, as a popular theme and song, to exhibit him in endless and impossible modifications—namely, in all his own disguises and multiplicities. In jest, and in Homeric language as well, what is the Platonic Socrates, if not prósthe Pláton opithén te Pláton mésse te Chímaira.

191. The old theological problem of "Faith" and "Knowledge," or more plainly, of instinct and reason—

the question whether, in respect to the valuation of things, instinct deserves more authority than rationality, which wants to appreciate and act according to motives, according to a "Why," that is to say, in conformity to purpose and utility—it is always the old moral problem that first appeared in the person of Socrates, and had divided men's minds long before Christianity. Socrates himself, following, of course, the taste of his talent—that of a surpassing dialectician—took first the side of reason; and, in fact, what did he do all his life but laugh at the awkward incapacity of the noble Athenians, who were men of instinct, like all noble men, and could never give satisfactory answers concerning the motives of their actions? In the end, however, though silently and secretly, he laughed also at himself: with his finer conscience and introspection, he found in himself the same difficulty and incapacity. "But why"—he said to himself—"should one on that account separate oneself from the instincts! One must set them right, and the reason ALSO—one must follow the instincts, but at the same time persuade the reason to support them with good arguments." This was the real FALSENESS of that great and mysterious ironist; he brought his conscience up to the point that he was satisfied with a kind of self-outwitting: in fact, he perceived the irrationality in the moral judgment.—Plato, more innocent in such matters, and without the craftiness of the plebeian, wished to prove to himself, at the expenditure of all his strength—the greatest strength a philosopher had ever expended—that reason and instinct lead spontaneously to one goal, to the good, to "God"; and since Plato, all theologians and philosophers have followed the same path—which means that in matters of morality, instinct (or as Christians call it, "Faith," or as I call it, "the herd") has hitherto triumphed. Unless one should make an exception in the case of Descartes, the father of rationalism (and consequently the grandfather of the Revolution), who recognized only the authority of reason: but reason is only a tool, and Descartes was superficial.

192. Whoever has followed the history of a single science, finds in its development a clue to the understanding of the oldest and commonest processes of all "knowledge and cognizance": there, as here, the premature hypotheses, the fictions, the good stupid will to "belief," and the lack of distrust and patience are first developed—our senses learn late, and never learn completely, to be subtle, reliable, and cautious organs of knowledge. Our eyes find it easier on a given occasion to produce a picture already often produced, than to seize upon the divergence and novelty of an impression: the latter requires more force, more "morality." It is difficult and painful for the ear to listen to anything new; we hear strange music badly. When we hear another language spoken, we involuntarily attempt to form the sounds into words with which we

are more familiar and conversant—it was thus, for example, that the Germans modified the spoken word ARCUBALISTA into ARMBRUST (cross-bow). Our senses are also hostile and averse to the new; and generally, even in the "simplest" processes of sensation, the emotions DOMINATE—such as fear, love, hatred, and the passive emotion of indolence.—As little as a reader nowadays reads all the single words (not to speak of syllables) of a page—he rather takes about five out of every twenty words at random, and "guesses" the probably appropriate sense to them—just as little do we see a tree correctly and completely in respect to its leaves, branches, colour, and shape; we find it so much easier to fancy the chance of a tree. Even in the midst of the most remarkable experiences, we still do just the same; we fabricate the greater part of the experience, and can hardly be made to contemplate any event, EXCEPT as "inventors" thereof. All this goes to prove that from our fundamental nature and from remote ages we have been—ACCUSTOMED TO LYING. Or, to express it more politely and hypocritically, in short, more pleasantly—one is much more of an artist than one is aware of.—In an animated conversation, I often see the face of the person with whom I am speaking so clearly and sharply defined before me, according to the thought he expresses, or which I believe to be evoked in his mind, that the degree of distinctness far exceeds the STRENGTH of my visual faculty—the delicacy of the play of the muscles and of the expression of the eyes MUST therefore be imagined by me. Probably the person put on quite a different expression, or none at all.

193. Quidquid luce fuit, tenebris agit: but also contrariwise. What we experience in dreams, provided we experience it often, pertains at last just as much to the general belongings of our soul as anything "actually" experienced; by virtue thereof we are richer or poorer, we have a requirement more or less, and finally, in broad daylight, and even in the brightest moments of our waking life, we are ruled to some extent by the nature of our dreams. Supposing that someone has often flown in his dreams, and that at last, as soon as he dreams, he is conscious of the power and art of flying as his privilege and his peculiarly enviable happiness; such a person, who believes that on the slightest impulse, he can actualize all sorts of curves and angles, who knows the sensation of a certain divine levity, an "upwards" without effort or constraint, a "downwards" without descending or lowering—without TROUBLE!—how could the man with such dream-experiences and dream-habits fail to find "happiness" differently coloured and defined, even in his waking hours! How could he fail—to long DIFFERENTLY for happiness? "Flight," such as is described by poets, must, when compared with his own "flying," be far too

earthly, muscular, violent, far too "troublesome" for him.

194. The difference among men does not manifest itself only in the difference of their lists of desirable things—in their regarding different good things as worth striving for, and being disagreed as to the greater or less value, the order of rank, of the commonly recognized desirable things:—it manifests itself much more in what they regard as actually HAVING and POSSESSING a desirable thing. As regards a woman, for instance, the control over her body and her sexual gratification serves as an amply sufficient sign of ownership and possession to the more modest man; another with a more suspicious and ambitious thirst for possession, sees the "questionableness," the mere apparentness of such ownership, and wishes to have finer tests in order to know especially whether the woman not only gives herself to him, but also gives up for his sake what she has or would like to have—only THEN does he look upon her as "possessed." A third, however, has not even here got to the limit of his distrust and his desire for possession: he asks himself whether the woman, when she gives up everything for him, does not perhaps do so for a phantom of him; he wishes first to be thoroughly, indeed, profoundly well known; in order to be loved at all he ventures to let himself be found out. Only then does he feel the beloved one fully in his possession, when she no longer

deceives herself about him, when she loves him just as much for the sake of his devilry and concealed insatiability, as for his goodness, patience, and spirituality. One man would like to possess a nation, and he finds all the higher arts of Cagliostro and Catalina suitable for his purpose. Another, with a more refined thirst for possession, says to himself: "One may not deceive where one desires to possess"—he is irritated and impatient at the idea that a mask of him should rule in the hearts of the people: "I must, therefore, MAKE myself known, and first of all learn to know myself!" Among helpful and charitable people, one almost always finds the awkward craftiness which first gets up suitably him who has to be helped, as though, for instance, he should "merit" help, seek just THEIR help, and would show himself deeply grateful, attached, and subservient to them for all help. With these conceits, they take control of the needy as a property, just as in general they are charitable and helpful out of a desire for property. One finds them jealous when they are crossed or forestalled in their charity. Parents involuntarily make something like themselves out of their children—they call that "education"; no mother doubts at the bottom of her heart that the child she has borne is thereby her property, no father hesitates about his right to HIS OWN ideas and notions of worth. Indeed, in former times fathers deemed it right to use their discretion concerning the life or death of the newly born (as among the ancient Germans). And like the father, so also do the teacher, the class, the priest, and the prince still see in every new individual an unobjectionable opportunity for a new possession. The consequence is...

195. The Jews—a people "born for slavery," as Tacitus and the whole ancient world say of them; "the chosen people among the nations," as they themselves say and believe—the Jews performed the miracle of the inversion of valuations, by means of which life on earth obtained a new and dangerous charm for a couple of millenniums. Their prophets fused into one the expressions "rich," "godless," "wicked," "violent," "sensual," and for the first time coined the word "world" as a term of reproach. In this inversion of valuations (in which is also included the use of the word "poor" as synonymous with "saint" and "friend") the significance of the Jewish people is to be found; it is with THEM that the SLAVE-INSURRECTION IN MORALS commences.

196. It is to be INFERRED that there are countless dark bodies near the sun—such as we shall never see. Among ourselves, this is an allegory; and the psychologist of morals reads the whole star-writing merely as an allegorical and symbolic language in which much may be unexpressed.

197. The beast of prey and the man of prey (for instance, Caesar Borgia) are fundamentally misunderstood, "nature" is misunderstood, so long as one seeks a "morbidness" in the constitution of these healthiest of all tropical monsters and growths, or even an innate "hell" in them—as almost all moralists have done hitherto. Does it not seem that there is a hatred of the virgin forest and of the tropics among moralists? And that the "tropical man" must be discredited at all costs, whether as disease and deterioration of mankind, or as his own hell and self-torture? And why? In favour of the "temperate zones"? In favour of the temperate men? The "moral"? The mediocre?—This for the chapter: "Morals as Timidity."

198. All the systems of morals which address themselves with a view to their "happiness," as it is called—what else are they but suggestions for behaviour adapted to the degree of DANGER from themselves in which the individuals live; recipes for their passions, their good and bad propensities, insofar as such have the Will to Power and would like to play the master; small and great expediencies and elaborations, permeated with the musty odour of old family medicines and old-wife wisdom; all of them grotesque and absurd in their form—because they address themselves to "all," because they generalize where generalization is not authorized; all of them speaking unconditionally, and taking themselves

unconditionally; all of them flavoured not merely with one grain of salt, but rather endurable only, and sometimes even seductive, when they are over-spiced and begin to smell dangerously, especially of "the other world." That is all of little value when estimated intellectually, and is far from being "science," much less "wisdom"; but, repeated once more, and three times repeated, it is expediency, expediency, expediency, mixed with stupidity, stupidity, stupidity—whether it be the indifference and statuesque coldness towards the heated folly of the emotions, which the Stoics advised and fostered; or the no-more-laughing and no-more-weeping of Spinoza, the destruction of the emotions by their analysis and vivisection, which he recommended so naively; or the lowering of the emotions to an innocent mean at which they may be satisfied, the Aristotelianism of morals; or even morality as the enjoyment of the emotions in a voluntary attenuation and spiritualization by the symbolism of art, perhaps as music, or as love of God, and of mankind for God's sake—for in religion the passions are once more enfranchised, provided that...; or, finally, even the complaisant and wanton surrender to the emotions, as has been taught by Hafis and Goethe, the bold letting-go of the reins, the spiritual and corporeal licentia morum in the exceptional cases of wise old codgers and drunkards, with whom it "no longer has much danger."—This also for the chapter: "Morals as Timidity."

199. Inasmuch as in all ages, as long as mankind has existed, there have also been human herds (family alliances, communities, tribes, peoples, states, churches), and always a great number who obey in proportion to the small number who command—in view, therefore, of the fact that obedience has been most practiced and fostered among mankind hitherto, one may reasonably suppose that, generally speaking, the need thereof is now innate in every one, as a kind of FORMAL CONSCIENCE which gives the command "Thou shalt unconditionally do something, unconditionally refrain from something", in short, "Thou shalt". This need tries to satisfy itself and to fill its form with a content, according to its strength, impatience, and eagerness, it at once seizes as an omnivorous appetite with little selection, and accepts whatever is shouted into its ear by all sorts of commanders—parents, teachers, laws, class prejudices, or public opinion. The extraordinary limitation of human development, the hesitation, protractedness, frequent retrogression, and turning thereof, is attributable to the fact that the herd-instinct of obedience is transmitted best, and at the cost of the art of command. If one imagine this instinct increasing to its greatest extent, commanders and independent individuals will finally be lacking altogether, or they will suffer inwardly from a bad conscience, and will have to impose a deception on themselves in the first

place in order to be able to command just as if they also were only obeying. This condition of things actually exists in Europe at present—I call it the moral hypocrisy of the commanding class. They know no other way of protecting themselves from their bad conscience than by playing the role of executors of older and higher orders (of predecessors, of the constitution, of justice, of the law, or of God himself), or they even justify themselves by maxims from the current opinions of the herd, as "first servants of their people," or "instruments of the public weal". On the other hand, the gregarious European man nowadays assumes an air as if he were the only kind of man that is allowable, he glorifies his qualities, such as public spirit, kindness, deference, industry, temperance, modesty, indulgence, sympathy, by virtue of which he is gentle, endurable, and useful to the herd, as the peculiarly human virtues. In cases, however, where it is believed that the leader and bell-wether cannot be dispensed with, attempt after attempt is made nowadays to replace commanders by the summing together of clever gregarious men all representative constitutions, for example, are of this origin. In spite of all, what a blessing, what a deliverance from a weight becoming unendurable, is the appearance of an absolute ruler for these gregarious Europeans—of this fact the effect of the appearance of Napoleon was the last great proof the history of the influence of Napoleon is almost the history of the higher happiness to which the entire century has attained in its worthiest individuals and periods.

200. The man of an age of dissolution which mixes the races with one another, who has the inheritance of a diversified descent in his body—that is to say, contrary, and often not only contrary, instincts and standards of value, which struggle with one another and are seldom at peace—such a man of late culture and broken lights, will, on an average, be a weak man. His fundamental desire is that the war which is IN HIM should come to an end; happiness appears to him in the character of a soothing medicine and mode of thought (for instance, Epicurean or Christian); it is above all things the happiness of repose, of undisturbedness, of repletion, of final unity—it is the "Sabbath of Sabbaths," to use the expression of the holy rhetorician, St. Augustine, who was himself such a man.—Should, however, the contrariety and conflict in such natures operate as an ADDITIONAL incentive and stimulus to life—and if, on the other hand, in addition to their powerful and irreconcilable instincts, they have also inherited and indoctrinated into them a proper mastery and subtlety for carrying on the conflict with themselves (that is to say, the faculty of self-control and self-deception), there then arise those marvelously incomprehensible and inexplicable beings, those enigmatical men, predestined for conquering and circumventing others, the finest examples of which are Alcibiades and Caesar

(with whom I should like to associate the FIRST of Europeans according to my taste, the Hohenstaufen, Frederick the Second), and among artists, perhaps Leonardo da Vinci. They appear precisely in the same periods when that weaker type, with its longing for repose, comes to the front; the two types are complementary to each other, and spring from the same causes.

201. As long as the utility which determines moral estimates is only gregarious utility, as long as the preservation of the community is only kept in view, and the immoral is sought precisely and exclusively in what seems dangerous to the maintenance of the community, there can be no "morality of love to one's neighbour." Granted even that there is already a little constant exercise of consideration, sympathy, fairness, gentleness, and mutual assistance, granted that even in this condition of society all those instincts are already active which are latterly distinguished by honourable names as "virtues," and eventually almost coincide with the conception "morality": in that period they do not as yet belong to the domain of moral valuations—they are still ULTRA-MORAL. A sympathetic action, for instance, is neither called good nor bad, moral nor immoral, in the best period of the Romans; and should it be praised, a sort of resentful disdain is compatible with this praise, even at the best, directly the sympathetic action is compared with one which

contributes to the welfare of the whole, to the RES PUBLICA. After all, "love to our neighbour" is always a secondary matter, partly conventional and arbitrarily manifested in relation to our FEAR OF OUR NEIGHBOUR. After the fabric of society seems on the whole established and secured against external dangers, it is this fear of our neighbour which again creates new perspectives of moral valuation. Certain strong and dangerous instincts, such as the love of enterprise, foolhardiness, revengefulness, astuteness, rapacity, and love of power, which up till then had not only to be honoured from the point of view of general utility—under other names, of course, than those here given—but had to be fostered and cultivated (because they were perpetually required in the common danger against the common enemies), are now felt in their dangerousness to be doubly strong—when the outlets for them are lacking—and are gradually branded as immoral and given over to calumny. The contrary instincts and inclinations now attain to moral honour, the gregarious instinct gradually draws its conclusions. How much or how little dangerousness to the community or to equality is contained in an opinion, a condition, an emotion, a disposition, or an endowment—that is now the moral perspective, here again fear is the mother of morals. It is by the loftiest and strongest instincts, when they break out passionately and carry the individual far above and beyond the average, and the low level of the gregarious conscience, that the self-reliance of the community is destroyed, its belief in itself, its backbone, as it were, breaks, consequently these very instincts will be most branded and defamed. The lofty independent spirituality, the will to stand alone, and even the cogent reason, are felt to be dangers, everything that elevates the individual above the herd, and is a source of fear to the neighbour, is henceforth called EVIL, the tolerant, unassuming, self-adapting, self-equalizing disposition, the MEDIOCRITY of desires, attains to moral distinction and honour. Finally, under very peaceful circumstances, there is always less opportunity and necessity for training the feelings to severity and rigour, and now every form of severity, even in justice, begins to disturb the conscience, a lofty and rigorous nobleness and self-responsibility almost offends, and awakens distrust, "the lamb," and still more "the sheep," wins respect. There is a point of diseased mellowness and effeminacy in the history of society, at which society itself takes the part of him who injures it, the part of the CRIMINAL, and does so, in fact, seriously and honestly. To punish, appears to it to be somehow unfair—it is certain that the idea of "punishment" and "the obligation to punish" are then painful and alarming to people. "Is it not sufficient if the criminal be rendered HARMLESS? Why should we still punish? Punishment itself is terrible!"—with these questions gregarious morality, the morality of fear, draws its ultimate conclusion. If one could at all do away with danger, the cause of fear, one would have done away with this morality at the same time, it would no longer be necessary, it WOULD NOT CONSIDER ITSELF any longer necessary!—Whoever examines the conscience of the present-day European, will always elicit the same imperative from its thousand moral folds and hidden recesses, the imperative of the timidity of the herd "we wish that some time or other there may be NOTHING MORE TO FEAR!" Some time or other—the will and the way THERETO is nowadays called "progress" all over Europe.

202. Let us at once say again what we have already said a hundred times, for people's ears nowadays are unwilling to hear such truths—OUR truths. We know well enough how offensive it sounds when any one plainly, and without metaphor, counts man among the animals, but it will be accounted to us almost a CRIME, that it is precisely in respect to men of "modern ideas" that we have constantly applied the terms "herd," "herd-instincts," and such like expressions. What avail is it? We cannot do otherwise, for it is precisely here that our new insight is. We have found that in all the principal moral judgments, Europe has become unanimous, including likewise the countries where European influence prevails in Europe people evidently KNOW what Socrates thought he did not know, and what the famous serpent of old once promised to teach—they "know" today what is good

and evil. It must then sound hard and be distasteful to the ear, when we always insist that that which here thinks it knows, that which here glorifies itself with praise and blame, and calls itself good, is the instinct of the herding human animal, the instinct which has come and is ever coming more and more to the front, to preponderance and supremacy over other instincts, according to the increasing physiological approximation and resemblance of which it is the symptom. MORALITY IN EUROPE AT PRESENT IS HERDING-ANIMAL MORALITY, and therefore, as we understand the matter, only one kind of human morality, beside which, before which, and after which many other moralities, and above all HIGHER moralities, are or should be possible. Against such a "possibility," against such a "should be," however, this morality defends itself with all its strength, it says obstinately and inexorably "I am morality itself and nothing else is morality!" Indeed, with the help of a religion which has humoured and flattered the sublimest desires of the herding-animal, things have reached such a point that we always find a more visible expression of this morality even in political and social arrangements: the DEMOCRATIC movement is the inheritance of the Christian movement. That its TEMPO, however, is much too slow and sleepy for the more impatient ones, for those who are sick and distracted by the herding-instinct, is indicated by the increasingly furious howling, and always less disguised teeth-gnashing of the anarchist dogs, who are now roving through the highways of European culture. Apparently in opposition to the peacefully industrious democrats and Revolution-ideologues, and still more so to the awkward philosophasters and fraternity-visionaries who call themselves Socialists and want a "free society," those are really at one with them all in their thorough and instinctive hostility to every form of society other than that of the AUTONOMOUS herd (to the extent even of repudiating the notions "master" and "servant"—ni dieu ni maitre, says a socialist formula); at one in their tenacious opposition to every special claim, every special right and privilege (this means ultimately opposition to EVERY right, for when all are equal, no one needs "rights" any longer); at one in their distrust of punitive justice (as though it were a violation of the weak, unfair to the NECESSARY consequences of all former society); but equally at one in their religion of sympathy, in their compassion for all that feels, lives, and suffers (down to the very animals, up even to "God"—the extravagance of "sympathy for God" belongs to a democratic age); altogether at one in the cry and impatience of their sympathy, in their deadly hatred of suffering generally, in their almost feminine incapacity for witnessing it or ALLOWING it; at one in their involuntary beglooming and heart-softening, under the spell of which Europe seems to be threatened with a new Buddhism; at one in their belief in the morality of MUTUAL sympathy, as though it were morality in itself, the climax, the ATTAINED climax of mankind, the sole hope of the future, the consolation of the present, the great discharge from all the obligations of the past; altogether at one in their belief in the community as the DELIVERER, in the herd, and therefore in "themselves."

203. We, who hold a different belief—we, who regard the democratic movement, not only as a degenerating form of political organization, but as equivalent to a degenerating, a waning type of man, as involving his mediocrising and depreciation: where have WE to fix our hopes? In NEW PHILOSOPHERS—there is no other alternative: in minds strong and original enough to initiate opposite estimates of value, to transvalue and invert "eternal valuations"; in forerunners, in men of the future, who in the present shall fix the constraints and fasten the knots which will compel millenniums to take NEW paths. To teach man the future of humanity as his WILL, as depending on human will, and to make preparation for vast hazardous enterprises and collective attempts in rearing and educating, in order thereby to put an end to the frightful rule of folly and chance which has hitherto gone by the name of "history" (the folly of the "greatest number" is only its last form)—for that purpose a new type of philosopher and commander will some time or other be needed, at the very idea of which everything that has existed in the way of occult, terrible, and benevolent beings might

look pale and dwarfed. The image of such leaders hovers before OUR eyes:—is it lawful for me to say it aloud, ye free spirits? The conditions which one would partly have to create and partly utilize for their genesis; the presumptive methods and tests by virtue of which a soul should grow up to such an elevation and power as to feel a CONSTRAINT to these tasks; a transvaluation of values, under the new pressure and hammer of which a conscience should be steeled and a heart transformed into brass, so as to bear the weight of such responsibility; and on the other hand the necessity for such leaders, the dreadful danger that they might be lacking, or miscarry and degenerate:—these are OUR real anxieties and glooms, ye know it well, ye free spirits! these are the heavy distant thoughts and storms which sweep across the heaven of OUR life. There are few pains so grievous as to have seen, divined, or experienced how an exceptional man has missed his way and deteriorated; but he who has the rare eye for the universal danger of "man" himself DETERIORATING, he who like us has recognized the extraordinary fortuitousness which has hitherto played its game in respect to the future of mankind—a game in which neither the hand, nor even a "finger of God" has participated!—he who divines the fate that is hidden under the idiotic unwariness and blind confidence of "modern ideas," and still more under the whole of Christo-European morality—suffers from an anguish with which no other is to be compared. He sees at a glance all that could still BE MADE OUT OF MAN through a favourable accumulation and augmentation of human powers and arrangements; he knows with all the knowledge of his conviction how unexhausted man still is for the greatest possibilities, and how often in the past the type man has stood in presence of mysterious decisions and new paths:—he knows still better from his painfulest recollections on what wretched obstacles promising developments of the highest rank have hitherto usually gone to pieces, broken down, sunk, and become contemptible. The UNIVERSAL DEGENERACY OF MANKIND to the level of the "man of the future"—as idealized by the socialistic fools and shallow-pates—this degeneracy and dwarfing of man to an absolutely gregarious animal (or as they call it, to a man of "free society"), this brutalizing of man into a pigmy with equal rights and claims, is undoubtedly POSSIBLE! He who has thought out this possibility to its ultimate conclusion knows ANOTHER loathing unknown to the rest of mankind—and perhaps also a new MISSION!

Chapter VI
We Scholars

204. At the risk that moralizing may also reveal itself here as that which it has always been—namely, resolutely MONTRER SES PLAIES, according to Balzac—I would venture to protest against an improper and injurious alteration of rank, which quite unnoticed, and as if with the best conscience, threatens nowadays to establish itself in the relations of science and philosophy. I mean to say that one must have the right out of one's own EXPERIENCE—experience, as it seems to me, always implies unfortunate experience?—to treat of such an important question of rank, so as not to speak of colour like the blind, or AGAINST science like women and artists ("Ah! this dreadful science!" sigh their instinct and their shame, "it always FINDS THINGS OUT!"). The declaration of independence of the scientific man, his emancipation from philosophy, is one of the subtler after-effects of democratic organization and disorganization: the self-glorification and self-conceitedness of the learned man is now everywhere in full bloom, and in its best springtime—which does not mean to imply that in this case self-praise smells sweet. Here also the instinct of the populace cries, "Freedom from all masters!" and after

science has, with the happiest results, resisted theology, whose "hand-maid" it had been too long, it now proposes in its wantonness and indiscretion to lay down laws for philosophy, and in its turn to play the "master"—what am I saying! to play the PHILOSOPHER on its own account. My memory—the memory of a scientific man, if you please!—teems with the naivetes of insolence which I have heard about philosophy and philosophers from young naturalists and old physicians (not to mention the most cultured and most conceited of all learned men, the philologists and schoolmasters, who are both the one and the other by profession). On one occasion it was the specialist and the Jack Horner who instinctively stood on the defensive against all synthetic tasks and capabilities; at another time it was the industrious worker who had got a scent of OTIUM and refined luxuriousness in the internal economy of the philosopher, and felt himself aggrieved and belittled thereby. On another occasion it was the colour-blindness of the utilitarian, who sees nothing in philosophy but a series of REFUTED systems, and an extravagant expenditure which "does nobody any good". At another time the fear of disguised mysticism and of the boundary-adjustment of knowledge became conspicuous, at another time the disregard of individual philosophers, which had involuntarily extended to disregard of philosophy generally. In fine, I found most frequently, behind the proud disdain of philosophy in young scholars, the evil after-effect of some particular philosopher, to whom on the whole obedience had been foresworn, without, however, the spell of his scornful estimates of other philosophers having been got rid of—the result being a general ill-will to all philosophy. (Such seems to me, for instance, the after-effect of Schopenhauer on the most modern Germany: by his unintelligent rage against Hegel, he has succeeded in severing the whole of the last generation of Germans from its connection with German culture, which culture, all things considered, has been an elevation and a divining refinement of the HISTORICAL SENSE, but precisely at this point Schopenhauer himself was poor, irreceptive, and un-German to the extent of ingeniousness.) On the whole, speaking generally, it may just have been the humanness, all-too-humanness of the modern philosophers themselves, in short, their contemptibleness, which has injured most radically the reverence for philosophy and opened the doors to the instinct of the populace. Let it but be acknowledged to what an extent our modern world diverges from the whole style of the world of Heraclitus, Plato, Empedocles, and whatever else all the royal and magnificent anchorites of the spirit were called, and with what justice an honest man of science MAY feel himself of a better family and origin, in view of such representatives of philosophy, who, owing to the fashion of the present day, are just as much aloft as they are down below—in Germany, for instance, the two lions of Berlin, the anarchist Eugen Duhring and the amalgamist Eduard von Hartmann. It is especially the sight of those hotch-potch philosophers, who call themselves "realists," or "positivists," which is calculated to implant a dangerous distrust in the soul of a young and ambitious scholar those philosophers, at the best, are themselves but scholars and specialists, that is very evident! All of them are persons who have been vanquished and BROUGHT BACK AGAIN under the dominion of science, who at one time or another claimed more from themselves, without having a right to the "more" and its responsibility—and who now, creditably, rancorously, and vindictively, represent in word and deed, DISBELIEF in the master-task and supremacy of philosophy After all, how could it be otherwise? Science flourishes nowadays and has the good conscience clearly visible on its countenance, while that to which the entire modern philosophy has gradually sunk, the remnant of philosophy of the present day, excites distrust and displeasure, if not scorn and pity Philosophy reduced to a "theory of knowledge," no more in fact than a diffident science of epochs and doctrine of forbearance a philosophy that never even gets beyond the threshold, and rigorously DENIES itself the right to enter—that is philosophy in its last throes, an end, an agony, something that awakens pity. How could such a philosophy—RULE!

205. The dangers that beset the evolution of the philosopher are, in fact, so manifold nowadays, that one might doubt whether this fruit could still come to maturity. The extent and towering structure of the sciences have increased enormously, and therewith also the probability that the philosopher will grow tired even as a learner, or will attach himself somewhere and "specialize" so that he will no longer attain to his elevation, that is to say, to his superspection, his circumspection, and his DESPECTION. Or he gets aloft too late, when the best of his maturity and strength is past, or when he is impaired, coarsened, and deteriorated, so that his view, his general estimate of things, is no longer of much importance. It is perhaps just the refinement of his intellectual conscience that makes him hesitate and linger on the way, he dreads the temptation to become a dilettante, a millepede, a milleantenna, he knows too well that as a discerner, one who has lost his self-respect no longer commands, no longer LEADS, unless he should aspire to become a great play-actor, a philosophical Cagliostro and spiritual rat-catcher—in short, a misleader. This is in the last instance a question of taste, if it has not really been a question of conscience. To double once more the philosopher's difficulties, there is also the fact that he demands from himself a verdict, a Yea or Nay, not concerning science, but concerning life and the worth of life—he learns unwillingly to believe that it is his right and even his duty to obtain this verdict, and he has

to seek his way to the right and the belief only through the most extensive (perhaps disturbing and destroying) experiences, often hesitating, doubting, and dumbfounded. In fact, the philosopher has long been mistaken and confused by the multitude, either with the scientific man and ideal scholar, or with the religiously elevated, desensualized, desecularized visionary and God-intoxicated man; and even yet when one hears anybody praised, because he lives "wisely," or "as a philosopher," it hardly means anything more than "prudently and apart." Wisdom: that seems to the populace to be a kind of flight, a means and artifice for withdrawing successfully from a bad game; but the GENUINE philosopher—does it not seem so to US, my friends?—lives "unphilosophically" and "unwisely," above all, IMPRUDENTLY, and feels the obligation and burden of a hundred attempts and temptations of life—he risks HIMSELF constantly, he plays THIS bad game.

206. In relation to the genius, that is to say, a being who either ENGENDERS or PRODUCES—both words understood in their fullest sense—the man of learning, the scientific average man, has always something of the old maid about him; for, like her, he is not conversant with the two principal functions of man. To both, of course, to the scholar and to the old maid, one concedes respectability, as if by way of indemnification—in these cases one emphasizes the

respectability—and yet, in the compulsion of this concession, one has the same admixture of vexation. Let us examine more closely: what is the scientific man? Firstly, a commonplace type of man, with commonplace virtues: that is to say, a non-ruling, non-authoritative, and non-self-sufficient type of man; he possesses industry, patient adaptableness to rank and file, equability and moderation in capacity and requirement; he has the instinct for people like himself, and for that which they require—for instance: the portion of independence and green meadow without which there is no rest from labour, the claim to honour and consideration (which first and foremost presupposes recognition and recognisability), the sunshine of a good name, the perpetual ratification of his value and usefulness, with which the inward DISTRUST which lies at the bottom of the heart of all dependent men and gregarious animals, has again and again to be overcome. The learned man, as is appropriate, has also maladies and faults of an ignoble kind: he is full of petty envy, and has a lynx-eye for the weak points in those natures to whose elevations he cannot attain. He is confiding, yet only as one who lets himself go, but does not FLOW; and precisely before the man of the great current he stands all the colder and more reserved—his eye is then like a smooth and irresponsive lake, which is no longer moved by rapture or sympathy. The worst and most dangerous thing of which a scholar is capable results from the instinct of mediocrity of his type, from the Jesuitism of mediocrity, which labours instinctively for the destruction of the exceptional man, and endeavours to break—or still better, to relax—every bent bow To relax, of course, with consideration, and naturally with an indulgent hand—to RELAX with confiding sympathy that is the real art of Jesuitism, which has always understood how to introduce itself as the religion of sympathy.

207. However gratefully one may welcome the OBJECTIVE spirit—and who has not been sick to death of all subjectivity and its confounded IPSISIMOSITY!—in the end, however, one must learn caution even with regard to one's gratitude, and put a stop to the exaggeration with which the unselfing and depersonalizing of the spirit has recently been celebrated, as if it were the goal in itself, as if it were salvation and glorification—as is especially accustomed to happen in the pessimist school, which has also in its turn good reasons for paying the highest honours to "disinterested knowledge" The objective man, who no longer curses and scolds like the pessimist, the IDEAL man of learning in whom the scientific instinct blossoms forth fully after a thousand complete and partial failures, is assuredly one of the most costly instruments that exist, but his place is in the hand of one who is more powerful He is only an instrument, we may say, he is a MIRROR—he is no

"purpose in himself" The objective man is in truth a mirror accustomed to prostration before everything that wants to be known, with such desires only as knowing or "reflecting" implies—he waits until something comes, and then expands himself sensitively, so that even the light footsteps and gliding-past of spiritual beings may not be lost on his surface and film Whatever "personality" he still possesses seems to him accidental, arbitrary, or still oftener, disturbing, so much has he come to regard himself as the passage and reflection of outside forms and events He calls up the recollection of "himself" with an effort, and not infrequently wrongly, he readily confounds himself with other persons, he makes mistakes with regard to his own needs, and here only is he unrefined and negligent Perhaps he is troubled about the health, or the pettiness and confined atmosphere of wife and friend, or the lack of companions and society—indeed, he sets himself to reflect on his suffering, but in vain! His thoughts already rove away to the MORE GENERAL case, and tomorrow he knows as little as he knew yesterday how to help himself He does not now take himself seriously and devote time to himself he is serene, NOT from lack of trouble, but from lack of capacity for grasping and dealing with HIS trouble The habitual complaisance with respect to all objects and experiences, the radiant and impartial hospitality with which he receives everything that comes his way, his habit of inconsiderate good-nature, of dangerous indifference as to Yea and Nay: alas! there are enough of cases in which he has to atone for these virtues of his!—and as man generally, he becomes far too easily the CAPUT MORTUUM of such virtues. Should one wish love or hatred from him—I mean love and hatred as God, woman, and animal understand them—he will do what he can, and furnish what he can. But one must not be surprised if it should not be much—if he should show himself just at this point to be false, fragile, questionable, and deteriorated. His love is constrained, his hatred is artificial, and rather UN TOUR DE FORCE, a slight ostentation and exaggeration. He is only genuine so far as he can be objective; only in his serene totality is he still "nature" and "natural." His mirroring and eternally self-polishing soul no longer knows how to affirm, no longer how to deny; he does not command; neither does he destroy. "JE NE MEPRISE PRESQUE RIEN"—he says, with Leibniz: let us not overlook nor undervalue the PRESQUE! Neither is he a model man; he does not go in advance of any one, nor after, either; he places himself generally too far off to have any reason for espousing the cause of either good or evil. If he has been so long confounded with the PHILOSOPHER, with the Caesarian trainer and dictator of civilization, he has had far too much honour, and what is more essential in him has been overlooked—he is an instrument, something of a slave, though certainly the sublimest sort of slave, but nothing in himself—PRESQUE RIEN! The objective man is an instrument, a costly, easily injured, easily tarnished measuring instrument and mirroring apparatus, which is to be taken care of and respected; but he is no goal, not outgoing nor upgoing, no complementary man in whom the REST of existence justifies itself, no termination—and still less a commencement, an engendering, or primary cause, nothing hardy, powerful, self-centred, that wants to be master; but rather only a soft, inflated, delicate, movable potter's-form, that must wait for some kind of content and frame to "shape" itself thereto—for the most part a man without frame and content, a "selfless" man. Consequently, also, nothing for women, IN PARENTHESI.

208. When a philosopher nowadays makes known that he is not a skeptic—I hope that has been gathered from the foregoing description of the objective spirit?—people all hear it impatiently; they regard him on that account with some apprehension, they would like to ask so many, many questions... indeed among timid hearers, of whom there are now so many, he is henceforth said to be dangerous. With his repudiation of skepticism, it seems to them as if they heard some evil-threatening sound in the distance, as if a new kind of explosive were being tried somewhere, a dynamite of the spirit, perhaps a newly discovered Russian NIHILINE, a pessimism BONAE VOLUNTATIS, that not only denies, means denial, but—dreadful thought!

PRACTISES denial. Against this kind of "good-will"—a will to the veritable, actual negation of life—there is, as is generally acknowledged nowadays, no better soporific and sedative than skepticism, the mild, pleasing, lulling poppy of skepticism; and Hamlet himself is now prescribed by the doctors of the day as an antidote to the "spirit," and its underground noises. "Are not our ears already full of bad sounds?" say the skeptics, as lovers of repose, and almost as a kind of safety police; "this subterranean Nay is terrible! Be still, ye pessimistic moles!" The skeptic, in effect, that delicate creature, is far too easily frightened; his conscience is schooled so as to start at every Nay, and even at that sharp, decided Yea, and feels something like a bite thereby. Yea! and Nay!—they seem to him opposed to morality; he loves, on the contrary, to make a festival to his virtue by a noble aloofness, while perhaps he says with Montaigne: "What do I know?" Or with Socrates: "I know that I know nothing." Or: "Here I do not trust myself, no door is open to me." Or: "Even if the door were open, why should I enter immediately?" Or: "What is the use of any hasty hypotheses? It might quite well be in good taste to make no hypotheses at all. Are you absolutely obliged to straighten at once what is crooked? to stuff every hole with some kind of oakum? Is there not time enough for that? Has not the time leisure? Oh, ye demons, can ye not at all WAIT? The uncertain also has its charms, the Sphinx, too, is a Circe, and Circe, too, was a philosopher."—Thus does a skeptic console himself; and in truth he needs some consolation. For skepticism is the most spiritual expression of a certain many-sided physiological temperament, which in ordinary language is called nervous debility and sickliness; it arises whenever races or classes which have been long separated, decisively and suddenly blend with one another. In the new generation, which has inherited as it were different standards and valuations in its blood, everything is disquiet, derangement, doubt, and tentativeness; the best powers operate restrictively, the very virtues prevent each other growing and becoming strong, equilibrium, ballast, and perpendicular stability are lacking in body and soul. That, however, which is most diseased and degenerated in such nondescripts is the WILL; they are no longer familiar with independence of decision, or the courageous feeling of pleasure in willing—they are doubtful of the "freedom of the will" even in their dreams Our present-day Europe, the scene of a senseless, precipitate attempt at a radical blending of classes, and CONSEQUENTLY of races, is therefore skeptical in all its heights and depths, sometimes exhibiting the mobile skepticism which springs impatiently and wantonly from branch to branch, sometimes with gloomy aspect, like a cloud overcharged with interrogative signs—and often sick unto death of its will! Paralysis of will, where do we not find this cripple sitting nowadays! And yet how bedecked oftentimes' How seductively ornamented! There are the finest gala dresses and disguises for this disease, and that, for instance, most of what places itself nowadays in the show-cases as "objectiveness," "the scientific spirit," "L'ART POUR L'ART," and "pure voluntary knowledge," is only decked-out skepticism and paralysis of will—I am ready to answer for this diagnosis of the European disease—The disease of the will is diffused unequally over Europe, it is worst and most varied where civilization has longest prevailed, it decreases according as "the barbarian" still—or again—asserts his claims under the loose drapery of Western culture It is therefore in the France of today, as can be readily disclosed and comprehended, that the will is most infirm, and France, which has always had a masterly aptitude for converting even the portentous crises of its spirit into something charming and seductive, now manifests emphatically its intellectual ascendancy over Europe, by being the school and exhibition of all the charms of skepticism The power to will and to persist, moreover, in a resolution, is already somewhat stronger in Germany, and again in the North of Germany it is stronger than in Central Germany, it is considerably stronger in England, Spain, and Corsica, associated with phlegm in the former and with hard skulls in the latter—not to mention Italy, which is too young yet to know what it wants, and must first show whether it can exercise will, but it is strongest and most surprising of all in that immense middle empire where

Europe as it were flows back to Asia—namely, in Russia There the power to will has been long stored up and accumulated, there the will—uncertain whether to be negative or affirmative—waits threateningly to be discharged (to borrow their pet phrase from our physicists) Perhaps not only Indian wars and complications in Asia would be necessary to free Europe from its greatest danger, but also internal subversion, the shattering of the empire into small states, and above all the introduction of parliamentary imbecility, together with the obligation of every one to read his newspaper at breakfast I do not say this as one who desires it, in my heart I should rather prefer the contrary—I mean such an increase in the threatening attitude of Russia, that Europe would have to make up its mind to become equally threatening—namely, TO ACQUIRE ONE WILL, by means of a new caste to rule over the Continent, a persistent, dreadful will of its own, that can set its aims thousands of years ahead; so that the long spun-out comedy of its petty-statism, and its dynastic as well as its democratic many-willed-ness, might finally be brought to a close. The time for petty politics is past; the next century will bring the struggle for the dominion of the world—the COMPULSION to great politics.

209. As to how far the new warlike age on which we Europeans have evidently entered may perhaps favour the growth of another and stronger kind of skepticism, I

should like to express myself preliminarily merely by a parable, which the lovers of German history will already understand. That unscrupulous enthusiast for big, handsome grenadiers (who, as King of Prussia, brought into being a military and skeptical genius—and therewith, in reality, the new and now triumphantly emerged type of German), the problematic, crazy father of Frederick the Great, had on one point the very knack and lucky grasp of the genius: he knew what was then lacking in Germany, the want of which was a hundred times more alarming and serious than any lack of culture and social form—his ill-will to the young Frederick resulted from the anxiety of a profound instinct. MEN WERE LACKING; and he suspected, to his bitterest regret, that his own son was not man enough. There, however, he deceived himself; but who would not have deceived himself in his place? He saw his son lapsed to atheism, to the ESPRIT, to the pleasant frivolity of clever Frenchmen—he saw in the background the great bloodsucker, the spider skepticism; he suspected the incurable wretchedness of a heart no longer hard enough either for evil or good, and of a broken will that no longer commands, is no longer ABLE to command. Meanwhile, however, there grew up in his son that new kind of harder and more dangerous skepticism—who knows TO WHAT EXTENT it was encouraged just by his father's hatred and the icy melancholy of a will condemned to solitude?—the skepticism of daring manliness, which is closely related to the genius for war and conquest, and made its first entrance into Germany in the person of the great Frederick. This skepticism despises and nevertheless grasps; it undermines and takes possession; it does not believe, but it does not thereby lose itself; it gives the spirit a dangerous liberty, but it keeps strict guard over the heart. It is the GERMAN form of skepticism, which, as a continued Fredericianism, risen to the highest spirituality, has kept Europe for a considerable time under the dominion of the German spirit and its critical and historical distrust Owing to the insuperably strong and tough masculine character of the great German philologists and historical critics (who, rightly estimated, were also all of them artists of destruction and dissolution), a NEW conception of the German spirit gradually established itself—in spite of all Romanticism in music and philosophy—in which the leaning towards masculine skepticism was decidedly prominent whether, for instance, as fearlessness of gaze, as courage and sternness of the dissecting hand, or as resolute will to dangerous voyages of discovery, to spiritualized North Pole expeditions under barren and dangerous skies. There may be good grounds for it when warm-blooded and superficial humanitarians cross themselves before this spirit, CET ESPRIT FATALISTE, IRONIQUE, MEPHISTOPHELIQUE, as Michelet calls it, not without a shudder. But if one would realize how characteristic is this fear of the "man" in the German spirit which awakened Europe out of its "dogmatic slumber," let us call to mind the former conception which had to be overcome by this new one—and that it is not so very long ago that a masculinized woman could dare, with unbridled presumption, to recommend the Germans to the interest of Europe as gentle, good-hearted, weak-willed, and poetical fools. Finally, let us only understand profoundly enough Napoleon's astonishment when he saw Goethe it reveals what had been regarded for centuries as the "German spirit" "VOILA UN HOMME!"—that was as much as to say "But this is a MAN! And I only expected to see a German!"

210. Supposing, then, that in the picture of the philosophers of the future, some trait suggests the question whether they must not perhaps be skeptics in the last-mentioned sense, something in them would only be designated thereby—and not they themselves. With equal right they might call themselves critics, and assuredly they will be men of experiments. By the name with which I ventured to baptize them, I have already expressly emphasized their attempting and their love of attempting is this because, as critics in body and soul, they will love to make use of experiments in a new, and perhaps wider and more dangerous sense? In their passion for knowledge, will they have to go further in daring and painful attempts than the sensitive and pampered taste of a democratic century can

approve of?—There is no doubt these coming ones will be least able to dispense with the serious and not unscrupulous qualities which distinguish the critic from the skeptic I mean the certainty as to standards of worth, the conscious employment of a unity of method, the wary courage, the standing-alone, and the capacity for self-responsibility, indeed, they will avow among themselves a DELIGHT in denial and dissection, and a certain considerate cruelty, which knows how to handle the knife surely and deftly, even when the heart bleeds They will be STERNER (and perhaps not always towards themselves only) than humane people may desire, they will not deal with the "truth" in order that it may "please" them, or "elevate" and "inspire" them—they will rather have little faith in "TRUTH" bringing with it such revels for the feelings. They will smile, those rigorous spirits, when any one says in their presence "That thought elevates me, why should it not be true?" or "That work enchants me, why should it not be beautiful?" or "That artist enlarges me, why should he not be great?" Perhaps they will not only have a smile, but a genuine disgust for all that is thus rapturous, idealistic, feminine, and hermaphroditic, and if any one could look into their inmost hearts, he would not easily find therein the intention to reconcile "Christian sentiments" with "antique taste," or even with "modern parliamentarism" (the kind of reconciliation necessarily found even among philosophers in our very uncertain and consequently very conciliatory century). Critical discipline, and every habit that conduces to purity and rigour in intellectual matters, will not only be demanded from themselves by these philosophers of the future, they may even make a display thereof as their special adornment—nevertheless they will not want to be called critics on that account. It will seem to them no small indignity to philosophy to have it decreed, as is so welcome nowadays, that "philosophy itself is criticism and critical science—and nothing else whatever!" Though this estimate of philosophy may enjoy the approval of all the Positivists of France and Germany (and possibly it even flattered the heart and taste of KANT: let us call to mind the titles of his principal works), our new philosophers will say, notwithstanding, that critics are instruments of the philosopher, and just on that account, as instruments, they are far from being philosophers themselves! Even the great Chinaman of Konigsberg was only a great critic.

211. I insist upon it that people finally cease confounding philosophical workers, and in general scientific men, with philosophers—that precisely here one should strictly give "each his own," and not give those far too much, these far too little. It may be necessary for the education of the real philosopher that he himself should have once stood upon all those steps upon which his servants, the scientific workers of philosophy, remain standing, and MUST remain

standing he himself must perhaps have been critic, and dogmatist, and historian, and besides, poet, and collector, and traveler, and riddle-reader, and moralist, and seer, and "free spirit," and almost everything, in order to traverse the whole range of human values and estimations, and that he may BE ABLE with a variety of eyes and consciences to look from a height to any distance, from a depth up to any height, from a nook into any expanse. But all these are only preliminary conditions for his task; this task itself demands something else—it requires him TO CREATE VALUES. The philosophical workers, after the excellent pattern of Kant and Hegel, have to fix and formalize some great existing body of valuations—that is to say, former DETERMINATIONS OF VALUE, creations of value, which have become prevalent, and are for a time called "truths"—whether in the domain of the LOGICAL, the POLITICAL (moral), or the ARTISTIC. It is for these investigators to make whatever has happened and been esteemed hitherto, conspicuous, conceivable, intelligible, and manageable, to shorten everything long, even "time" itself, and to SUBJUGATE the entire past: an immense and wonderful task, in the carrying out of which all refined pride, all tenacious will, can surely find satisfaction. THE REAL PHILOSOPHERS, HOWEVER, ARE COMMANDERS AND LAW-GIVERS; they say: "Thus SHALL it be!" They determine first the Whither and the Why of mankind, and thereby set aside the previous labour of all philosophical workers, and all subjugators of the past—they grasp at the future with a creative hand, and whatever is and was, becomes for them thereby a means, an instrument, and a hammer. Their "knowing" is CREATING, their creating is a law-giving, their will to truth is—WILL TO POWER.—Are there at present such philosophers? Have there ever been such philosophers? MUST there not be such philosophers some day? ...

212. It is always more obvious to me that the philosopher, as a man INDISPENSABLE for the morrow and the day after the morrow, has ever found himself, and HAS BEEN OBLIGED to find himself, in contradiction to the day in which he lives; his enemy has always been the ideal of his day. Hitherto all those extraordinary furtherers of humanity whom one calls philosophers—who rarely regarded themselves as lovers of wisdom, but rather as disagreeable fools and dangerous interrogators—have found their mission, their hard, involuntary, imperative mission (in the end, however, the greatness of their mission), in being the bad conscience of their age. In putting the vivisector's knife to the breast of the very VIRTUES OF THEIR AGE, they have betrayed their own secret; it has been for the sake of a NEW greatness of man, a new untrodden path to his aggrandizement. They have always disclosed how much hypocrisy, indolence, self-indulgence, and self-neglect, how much falsehood was

concealed under the most venerated types of contemporary morality, how much virtue was OUTLIVED, they have always said "We must remove hence to where YOU are least at home" In the face of a world of "modern ideas," which would like to confine every one in a corner, in a "specialty," a philosopher, if there could be philosophers nowadays, would be compelled to place the greatness of man, the conception of "greatness," precisely in his comprehensiveness and multifariousness, in his all-roundness, he would even determine worth and rank according to the amount and variety of that which a man could bear and take upon himself, according to the EXTENT to which a man could stretch his responsibility Nowadays the taste and virtue of the age weaken and attenuate the will, nothing is so adapted to the spirit of the age as weakness of will consequently, in the ideal of the philosopher, strength of will, sternness, and capacity for prolonged resolution, must specially be included in the conception of "greatness", with as good a right as the opposite doctrine, with its ideal of a silly, renouncing, humble, selfless humanity, was suited to an opposite age—such as the sixteenth century, which suffered from its accumulated energy of will, and from the wildest torrents and floods of selfishness In the time of Socrates, among men only of worn-out instincts, old conservative Athenians who let themselves go—"for the sake of happiness," as they said, for the sake of pleasure, as their conduct indicated—and who had continually on their lips the old pompous words to which they had long forfeited the right by the life they led, IRONY was perhaps necessary for greatness of soul, the wicked Socratic assurance of the old physician and plebeian, who cut ruthlessly into his own flesh, as into the flesh and heart of the "noble," with a look that said plainly enough "Do not dissemble before me! here—we are equal!" At present, on the contrary, when throughout Europe the herding-animal alone attains to honours, and dispenses honours, when "equality of right" can too readily be transformed into equality in wrong—I mean to say into general war against everything rare, strange, and privileged, against the higher man, the higher soul, the higher duty, the higher responsibility, the creative plenipotence and lordliness—at present it belongs to the conception of "greatness" to be noble, to wish to be apart, to be capable of being different, to stand alone, to have to live by personal initiative, and the philosopher will betray something of his own ideal when he asserts "He shall be the greatest who can be the most solitary, the most concealed, the most divergent, the man beyond good and evil, the master of his virtues, and of super-abundance of will; precisely this shall be called GREATNESS: as diversified as can be entire, as ample as can be full." And to ask once more the question: Is greatness POSSIBLE—nowadays?

213. It is difficult to learn what a philosopher is, because it cannot be taught: one must "know" it by experience—or one should have the pride NOT to know it. The fact that at present people all talk of things of which they CANNOT have any experience, is true more especially and unfortunately as concerns the philosopher and philosophical matters:—the very few know them, are permitted to know them, and all popular ideas about them are false. Thus, for instance, the truly philosophical combination of a bold, exuberant spirituality which runs at presto pace, and a dialectic rigour and necessity which makes no false step, is unknown to most thinkers and scholars from their own experience, and therefore, should any one speak of it in their presence, it is incredible to them. They conceive of every necessity as troublesome, as a painful compulsory obedience and state of constraint; thinking itself is regarded by them as something slow and hesitating, almost as a trouble, and often enough as "worthy of the SWEAT of the noble"—but not at all as something easy and divine, closely related to dancing and exuberance! "To think" and to take a matter "seriously," "arduously"—that is one and the same thing to them; such only has been their "experience."—Artists have here perhaps a finer intuition; they who know only too well that precisely when they no longer do anything "arbitrarily," and everything of necessity, their feeling of freedom, of subtlety, of power, of creatively fixing, disposing, and shaping, reaches its

climax—in short, that necessity and "freedom of will" are then the same thing with them. There is, in fine, a gradation of rank in psychical states, to which the gradation of rank in the problems corresponds; and the highest problems repel ruthlessly every one who ventures too near them, without being predestined for their solution by the loftiness and power of his spirituality. Of what use is it for nimble, everyday intellects, or clumsy, honest mechanics and empiricists to press, in their plebeian ambition, close to such problems, and as it were into this "holy of holies"—as so often happens nowadays! But coarse feet must never tread upon such carpets: this is provided for in the primary law of things; the doors remain closed to those intruders, though they may dash and break their heads thereon. People have always to be born to a high station, or, more definitely, they have to be BRED for it: a person has only a right to philosophy—taking the word in its higher significance—in virtue of his descent; the ancestors, the "blood," decide here also. Many generations must have prepared the way for the coming of the philosopher; each of his virtues must have been separately acquired, nurtured, transmitted, and embodied; not only the bold, easy, delicate course and current of his thoughts, but above all the readiness for great responsibilities, the majesty of ruling glance and contemning look, the feeling of separation from the multitude with their duties and virtues, the kindly patronage and defense of whatever is misunderstood and calumniated, be it God or devil, the delight and practice of supreme justice, the art of commanding, the amplitude of will, the lingering eye which rarely admires, rarely looks up, rarely loves....

Chapter VII
Our Virtues

214. OUR Virtues?—It is probable that we, too, have still our virtues, although naturally they are not those sincere and massive virtues on account of which we hold our grandfathers in esteem and also at a little distance from us. We Europeans of the day after tomorrow, we firstlings of the twentieth century—with all our dangerous curiosity, our multifariousness and art of disguising, our mellow and seemingly sweetened cruelty in sense and spirit—we shall presumably, IF we must have virtues, have those only which have come to agreement with our most secret and heartfelt inclinations, with our most ardent requirements: well, then, let us look for them in our labyrinths!—where, as we know, so many things lose themselves, so many things get quite lost! And is there anything finer than to SEARCH for one's own virtues? Is it not almost to BELIEVE in one's own virtues? But this "believing in one's own virtues"—is it not practically the same as what was formerly called one's "good conscience," that long, respectable pigtail of an idea, which our grandfathers used to hang behind their heads, and often enough also behind their understandings? It seems, therefore, that however little we may imagine ourselves to be old-fashioned and grandfatherly respectable in other respects, in one thing we are nevertheless the

worthy grandchildren of our grandfathers, we last Europeans with good consciences: we also still wear their pigtail.—Ah! if you only knew how soon, so very soon—it will be different!

215. As in the stellar firmament there are sometimes two suns which determine the path of one planet, and in certain cases suns of different colours shine around a single planet, now with red light, now with green, and then simultaneously illumine and flood it with motley colours: so we modern men, owing to the complicated mechanism of our "firmament," are determined by DIFFERENT moralities; our actions shine alternately in different colours, and are seldom unequivocal—and there are often cases, also, in which our actions are MOTLEY-COLOURED.

216. To love one's enemies? I think that has been well learnt: it takes place thousands of times at present on a large and small scale; indeed, at times the higher and sublimer thing takes place:—we learn to DESPISE when we love, and precisely when we love best; all of it, however, unconsciously, without noise, without ostentation, with the shame and secrecy of goodness, which forbids the utterance of the pompous word and the formula of virtue. Morality as attitude—is opposed to our taste nowadays. This is ALSO an advance, as it was an advance in our fathers that religion as an attitude finally became opposed to their taste, including

the enmity and Voltairean bitterness against religion (and all that formerly belonged to freethinker-pantomime). It is the music in our conscience, the dance in our spirit, to which Puritan litanies, moral sermons, and goody-goodness won't chime.

217. Let us be careful in dealing with those who attach great importance to being credited with moral tact and subtlety in moral discernment! They never forgive us if they have once made a mistake BEFORE us (or even with REGARD to us)—they inevitably become our instinctive calumniators and detractors, even when they still remain our "friends."—Blessed are the forgetful: for they "get the better" even of their blunders.

218. The psychologists of France—and where else are there still psychologists nowadays?—have never yet exhausted their bitter and manifold enjoyment of the betise bourgeoise, just as though... in short, they betray something thereby. Flaubert, for instance, the honest citizen of Rouen, neither saw, heard, nor tasted anything else in the end; it was his mode of self-torment and refined cruelty. As this is growing wearisome, I would now recommend for a change something else for a pleasure—namely, the unconscious astuteness with which good, fat, honest mediocrity always behaves towards loftier spirits and the tasks they have to perform, the subtle, barbed,

Jesuitical astuteness, which is a thousand times subtler than the taste and understanding of the middle-class in its best moments—subtler even than the understanding of its victims:—a repeated proof that "instinct" is the most intelligent of all kinds of intelligence which have hitherto been discovered. In short, you psychologists, study the philosophy of the "rule" in its struggle with the "exception": there you have a spectacle fit for Gods and godlike malignity! Or, in plainer words, practise vivisection on "good people," on the "homo bonae voluntatis," ON YOURSELVES!

219. The practice of judging and condemning morally, is the favourite revenge of the intellectually shallow on those who are less so, it is also a kind of indemnity for their being badly endowed by nature, and finally, it is an opportunity for acquiring spirit and BECOMING subtle—malice spiritualises. They are glad in their inmost heart that there is a standard according to which those who are over-endowed with intellectual goods and privileges, are equal to them, they contend for the "equality of all before God," and almost NEED the belief in God for this purpose. It is among them that the most powerful antagonists of atheism are found. If any one were to say to them "A lofty spirituality is beyond all comparison with the honesty and respectability of a merely moral man"—it would make them furious, I shall take care not to say so. I would rather flatter them with my theory that lofty

spirituality itself exists only as the ultimate product of moral qualities, that it is a synthesis of all qualities attributed to the "merely moral" man, after they have been acquired singly through long training and practice, perhaps during a whole series of generations, that lofty spirituality is precisely the spiritualising of justice, and the beneficent severity which knows that it is authorized to maintain GRADATIONS OF RANK in the world, even among things—and not only among men.

220. Now that the praise of the "disinterested person" is so popular one must—probably not without some danger—get an idea of WHAT people actually take an interest in, and what are the things generally which fundamentally and profoundly concern ordinary men— including the cultured, even the learned, and perhaps philosophers also, if appearances do not deceive. The fact thereby becomes obvious that the greater part of what interests and charms higher natures, and more refined and fastidious tastes, seems absolutely "uninteresting" to the average man—if, notwithstanding, he perceive devotion to these interests, he calls it desinteresse, and wonders how it is possible to act "disinterestedly." There have been philosophers who could give this popular astonishment a seductive and mystical, other-worldly expression (perhaps because they did not know the higher nature by experience?), instead of stating the naked and

candidly reasonable truth that "disinterested" action is very interesting and "interested" action, provided that... "And love?"—What! Even an action for love's sake shall be "unegoistic"? But you fools—! "And the praise of the self-sacrificer?"—But whoever has really offered sacrifice knows that he wanted and obtained something for it—perhaps something from himself for something from himself; that he relinquished here in order to have more there, perhaps in general to be more, or even feel himself "more." But this is a realm of questions and answers in which a more fastidious spirit does not like to stay: for here truth has to stifle her yawns so much when she is obliged to answer. And after all, truth is a woman; one must not use force with her.

221. "It sometimes happens," said a moralistic pedant and trifle-retailer, "that I honour and respect an unselfish man: not, however, because he is unselfish, but because I think he has a right to be useful to another man at his own expense. In short, the question is always who HE is, and who THE OTHER is. For instance, in a person created and destined for command, self-denial and modest retirement, instead of being virtues, would be the waste of virtues: so it seems to me. Every system of unegoistic morality which takes itself unconditionally and appeals to every one, not only sins against good taste, but is also an incentive to sins of omission, an ADDITIONAL seduction under the mask of philanthropy—and precisely a seduction

and injury to the higher, rarer, and more privileged types of men. Moral systems must be compelled first of all to bow before the GRADATIONS OF RANK; their presumption must be driven home to their conscience—until they thoroughly understand at last that it is IMMORAL to say that 'what is right for one is proper for another.'"—So said my moralistic pedant and bonhomme. Did he perhaps deserve to be laughed at when he thus exhorted systems of morals to practise morality? But one should not be too much in the right if one wishes to have the laughers on ONE'S OWN side; a grain of wrong pertains even to good taste.

222. Wherever sympathy (fellow-suffering) is preached nowadays—and, if I gather rightly, no other religion is any longer preached—let the psychologist have his ears open through all the vanity, through all the noise which is natural to these preachers (as to all preachers), he will hear a hoarse, groaning, genuine note of SELF-CONTEMPT. It belongs to the overshadowing and uglifying of Europe, which has been on the increase for a century (the first symptoms of which are already specified documentarily in a thoughtful letter of Galiani to Madame d'Epinay)—IF IT IS NOT REALLY THE CAUSE THEREOF! The man of "modern ideas," the conceited ape, is excessively dissatisfied with himself—this is perfectly certain. He suffers, and his vanity wants him only "to suffer with his fellows."

223. The hybrid European—a tolerably ugly plebeian, taken all in all—absolutely requires a costume: he needs history as a storeroom of costumes. To be sure, he notices that none of the costumes fit him properly—he changes and changes. Let us look at the nineteenth century with respect to these hasty preferences and changes in its masquerades of style, and also with respect to its moments of desperation on account of "nothing suiting" us. It is in vain to get ourselves up as romantic, or classical, or Christian, or Florentine, or barocco, or "national," in moribus et artibus: it does not "clothe us"! But the "spirit," especially the "historical spirit," profits even by this desperation: once and again a new sample of the past or of the foreign is tested, put on, taken off, packed up, and above all studied—we are the first studious age in puncto of "costumes," I mean as concerns morals, articles of belief, artistic tastes, and religions; we are prepared as no other age has ever been for a carnival in the grand style, for the most spiritual festival—laughter and arrogance, for the transcendental height of supreme folly and Aristophanic ridicule of the world. Perhaps we are still discovering the domain of our invention just here, the domain where even we can still be original, probably as parodists of the world's history and as God's Merry-Andrews,—perhaps, though nothing else of the present have a future, our laughter itself may have a future!

224. The historical sense (or the capacity for divining quickly the order of rank of the valuations according to which a people, a community, or an individual has lived, the "divining instinct" for the relationships of these valuations, for the relation of the authority of the valuations to the authority of the operating forces),—this historical sense, which we Europeans claim as our specialty, has come to us in the train of the enchanting and mad semi-barbarity into which Europe has been plunged by the democratic mingling of classes and races—it is only the nineteenth century that has recognized this faculty as its sixth sense. Owing to this mingling, the past of every form and mode of life, and of cultures which were formerly closely contiguous and superimposed on one another, flows forth into us "modern souls"; our instincts now run back in all directions, we ourselves are a kind of chaos: in the end, as we have said, the spirit perceives its advantage therein. By means of our semi-barbarity in body and in desire, we have secret access everywhere, such as a noble age never had; we have access above all to the labyrinth of imperfect civilizations, and to every form of semi-barbarity that has at any time existed on earth; and in so far as the most considerable part of human civilization hitherto has just been semi-barbarity, the "historical sense" implies almost the sense and instinct for everything, the taste and tongue for everything: whereby it immediately proves itself to be an IGNOBLE sense. For instance, we enjoy Homer once

more: it is perhaps our happiest acquisition that we know how to appreciate Homer, whom men of distinguished culture (as the French of the seventeenth century, like Saint-Evremond, who reproached him for his ESPRIT VASTE, and even Voltaire, the last echo of the century) cannot and could not so easily appropriate—whom they scarcely permitted themselves to enjoy. The very decided Yea and Nay of their palate, their promptly ready disgust, their hesitating reluctance with regard to everything strange, their horror of the bad taste even of lively curiosity, and in general the averseness of every distinguished and self-sufficing culture to avow a new desire, a dissatisfaction with its own condition, or an admiration of what is strange: all this determines and disposes them unfavourably even towards the best things of the world which are not their property or could not become their prey—and no faculty is more unintelligible to such men than just this historical sense, with its truckling, plebeian curiosity. The case is not different with Shakespeare, that marvelous Spanish-Moorish-Saxon synthesis of taste, over whom an ancient Athenian of the circle of AEschylus would have half-killed himself with laughter or irritation: but we—accept precisely this wild motleyness, this medley of the most delicate, the most coarse, and the most artificial, with a secret confidence and cordiality; we enjoy it as a refinement of art reserved expressly for us, and allow ourselves to be as little disturbed by the repulsive fumes and the proximity of the English populace in which Shakespeare's art and taste lives, as perhaps on the Chiaja of Naples, where, with all our senses awake, we go our way, enchanted and voluntarily, in spite of the drain-odour of the lower quarters of the town. That as men of the "historical sense" we have our virtues, is not to be disputed:—we are unpretentious, unselfish, modest, brave, habituated to self-control and self-renunciation, very grateful, very patient, very complaisant—but with all this we are perhaps not very "tasteful." Let us finally confess it, that what is most difficult for us men of the "historical sense" to grasp, feel, taste, and love, what finds us fundamentally prejudiced and almost hostile, is precisely the perfection and ultimate maturity in every culture and art, the essentially noble in works and men, their moment of smooth sea and halcyon self-sufficiency, the goldenness and coldness which all things show that have perfected themselves. Perhaps our great virtue of the historical sense is in necessary contrast to GOOD taste, at least to the very bad taste; and we can only evoke in ourselves imperfectly, hesitatingly, and with compulsion the small, short, and happy godsends and glorifications of human life as they shine here and there: those moments and marvelous experiences when a great power has voluntarily come to a halt before the boundless and infinite,—when a super-abundance of refined delight has been enjoyed by a sudden checking and petrifying, by standing firmly and planting oneself fixedly on still trembling ground. PROPORTIONATENESS is strange to us, let us confess it to ourselves; our itching is really the itching for the infinite, the immeasurable. Like the rider on his forward panting horse, we let the reins fall before the infinite, we modern men, we semi-barbarians—and are only in OUR highest bliss when we—ARE IN MOST DANGER.

225. Whether it be hedonism, pessimism, utilitarianism, or eudaemonism, all those modes of thinking which measure the worth of things according to PLEASURE and PAIN, that is, according to accompanying circumstances and secondary considerations, are plausible modes of thought and naivetes, which every one conscious of CREATIVE powers and an artist's conscience will look down upon with scorn, though not without sympathy. Sympathy for you!—to be sure, that is not sympathy as you understand it: it is not sympathy for social "distress," for "society" with its sick and misfortuned, for the hereditarily vicious and defective who lie on the ground around us; still less is it sympathy for the grumbling, vexed, revolutionary slave-classes who strive after power—they call it "freedom." OUR sympathy is a loftier and further-sighted sympathy:—we see how MAN dwarfs himself, how YOU dwarf him! and there are moments when we view YOUR sympathy with an indescribable anguish, when we resist it,—when we

regard your seriousness as more dangerous than any kind of levity. You want, if possible—and there is not a more foolish "if possible"—TO DO AWAY WITH SUFFERING; and we?—it really seems that WE would rather have it increased and made worse than it has ever been! Well-being, as you understand it—is certainly not a goal; it seems to us an END; a condition which at once renders man ludicrous and contemptible—and makes his destruction DESIRABLE! The discipline of suffering, of GREAT suffering—know ye not that it is only THIS discipline that has produced all the elevations of humanity hitherto? The tension of soul in misfortune which communicates to it its energy, its shuddering in view of rack and ruin, its inventiveness and bravery in undergoing, enduring, interpreting, and exploiting misfortune, and whatever depth, mystery, disguise, spirit, artifice, or greatness has been bestowed upon the soul—has it not been bestowed through suffering, through the discipline of great suffering? In man CREATURE and CREATOR are united: in man there is not only matter, shred, excess, clay, mire, folly, chaos; but there is also the creator, the sculptor, the hardness of the hammer, the divinity of the spectator, and the seventh day—do ye understand this contrast? And that YOUR sympathy for the "creature in man" applies to that which has to be fashioned, bruised, forged, stretched, roasted, annealed, refined—to that which must necessarily SUFFER, and IS MEANT to suffer? And our sympathy—do ye not understand what our REVERSE sympathy applies to, when it resists your sympathy as the worst of all pampering and enervation?—So it is sympathy AGAINST sympathy!—But to repeat it once more, there are higher problems than the problems of pleasure and pain and sympathy; and all systems of philosophy which deal only with these are naivetes.

226. WE IMMORALISTS.—This world with which WE are concerned, in which we have to fear and love, this almost invisible, inaudible world of delicate command and delicate obedience, a world of "almost" in every respect, captious, insidious, sharp, and tender—yes, it is well protected from clumsy spectators and familiar curiosity! We are woven into a strong net and garment of duties, and CANNOT disengage ourselves—precisely here, we are "men of duty," even we! Occasionally, it is true, we dance in our "chains" and betwixt our "swords"; it is none the less true that more often we gnash our teeth under the circumstances, and are impatient at the secret hardship of our lot. But do what we will, fools and appearances say of us: "These are men WITHOUT duty,"—we have always fools and appearances against us!

227. Honesty, granting that it is the virtue of which we cannot rid ourselves, we free spirits—well, we will labour at it with all our perversity and love, and not tire of "perfecting" ourselves in OUR virtue, which alone

remains: may its glance some day overspread like a gilded, blue, mocking twilight this aging civilization with its dull gloomy seriousness! And if, nevertheless, our honesty should one day grow weary, and sigh, and stretch its limbs, and find us too hard, and would fain have it pleasanter, easier, and gentler, like an agreeable vice, let us remain HARD, we latest Stoics, and let us send to its help whatever devilry we have in us:—our disgust at the clumsy and undefined, our "NITIMUR IN VETITUM," our love of adventure, our sharpened and fastidious curiosity, our most subtle, disguised, intellectual Will to Power and universal conquest, which rambles and roves avidiously around all the realms of the future—let us go with all our "devils" to the help of our "God"! It is probable that people will misunderstand and mistake us on that account: what does it matter! They will say: "Their 'honesty'—that is their devilry, and nothing else!" What does it matter! And even if they were right—have not all Gods hitherto been such sanctified, re-baptized devils? And after all, what do we know of ourselves? And what the spirit that leads us wants TO BE CALLED? (It is a question of names.) And how many spirits we harbour? Our honesty, we free spirits—let us be careful lest it become our vanity, our ornament and ostentation, our limitation, our stupidity! Every virtue inclines to stupidity, every stupidity to virtue; "stupid to the point of sanctity," they say in Russia,—let us be careful lest out of pure honesty we eventually become saints and bores! Is not life a hundred times too short for us—to bore ourselves? One would have to believe in eternal life in order to...

228. I hope to be forgiven for discovering that all moral philosophy hitherto has been tedious and has belonged to the soporific appliances—and that "virtue," in my opinion, has been MORE injured by the TEDIOUSNESS of its advocates than by anything else; at the same time, however, I would not wish to overlook their general usefulness. It is desirable that as few people as possible should reflect upon morals, and consequently it is very desirable that morals should not some day become interesting! But let us not be afraid! Things still remain today as they have always been: I see no one in Europe who has (or DISCLOSES) an idea of the fact that philosophizing concerning morals might be conducted in a dangerous, captious, and ensnaring manner—that CALAMITY might be involved therein. Observe, for example, the indefatigable, inevitable English utilitarians: how ponderously and respectably they stalk on, stalk along (a Homeric metaphor expresses it better) in the footsteps of Bentham, just as he had already stalked in the footsteps of the respectable Helvetius! (no, he was not a dangerous man, Helvetius, CE SENATEUR POCOCURANTE, to use an expression of Galiani). No new thought, nothing of the nature of a finer turning or better expression of an old thought, not even a proper history of what has

been previously thought on the subject: an IMPOSSIBLE literature, taking it all in all, unless one knows how to leaven it with some mischief. In effect, the old English vice called CANT, which is MORAL TARTUFFISM, has insinuated itself also into these moralists (whom one must certainly read with an eye to their motives if one MUST read them), concealed this time under the new form of the scientific spirit; moreover, there is not absent from them a secret struggle with the pangs of conscience, from which a race of former Puritans must naturally suffer, in all their scientific tinkering with morals. (Is not a moralist the opposite of a Puritan? That is to say, as a thinker who regards morality as questionable, as worthy of interrogation, in short, as a problem? Is moralizing not-immoral?) In the end, they all want English morality to be recognized as authoritative, inasmuch as mankind, or the "general utility," or "the happiness of the greatest number,"—no! the happiness of ENGLAND, will be best served thereby. They would like, by all means, to convince themselves that the striving after English happiness, I mean after COMFORT and FASHION (and in the highest instance, a seat in Parliament), is at the same time the true path of virtue; in fact, that in so far as there has been virtue in the world hitherto, it has just consisted in such striving. Not one of those ponderous, conscience-stricken herding-animals (who undertake to advocate the cause of egoism as conducive to the general welfare) wants to have any knowledge or inkling of the facts that the "general welfare" is no ideal, no goal, no notion that can be at all grasped, but is only a nostrum,—that what is fair to one MAY NOT at all be fair to another, that the requirement of one morality for all is really a detriment to higher men, in short, that there is a DISTINCTION OF RANK between man and man, and consequently between morality and morality. They are an unassuming and fundamentally mediocre species of men, these utilitarian Englishmen, and, as already remarked, in so far as they are tedious, one cannot think highly enough of their utility. One ought even to ENCOURAGE them, as has been partially attempted in the following rhymes:

> Hail, ye worthies, barrow wheeling,
> "Longer—better," aye revealing,
>
> Stiffer aye in head and knee;
> Unenraptured, never jesting,
> Mediocre everlasting,
>
> *SANS GENIE ET SANS ESPRIT!*

229. In these later ages, which may be proud of their humanity, there still remains so much fear, so much SUPERSTITION of the fear, of the "cruel wild beast," the mastering of which constitutes the very pride of these humaner ages—that even obvious truths, as if by the agreement of centuries, have long remained unuttered, because they have the appearance of helping the finally slain wild beast back to life again. I perhaps risk something when I allow such a truth to escape; let others capture it again and give it so much "milk of pious sentiment" [FOOTNOTE: An expression from Schiller's William Tell, Act IV, Scene 3.] to drink, that it will lie down quiet and forgotten, in its old corner.—One ought to learn anew about cruelty, and open one's eyes; one ought at last to learn impatience, in order that such immodest gross errors—as, for instance, have been fostered by ancient and modern philosophers with regard to tragedy—may no longer wander about virtuously and boldly. Almost everything that we call "higher culture" is based upon the spiritualising and intensifying of CRUELTY—this is my thesis; the "wild beast" has not been slain at all, it lives, it flourishes, it has only been—transfigured. That which constitutes the painful delight of tragedy is cruelty; that which operates agreeably in so-called tragic sympathy, and at the basis even of everything sublime, up to the highest and most delicate thrills of metaphysics, obtains its sweetness solely from the intermingled ingredient of cruelty. What the Roman enjoys in the arena, the Christian in

the ecstasies of the cross, the Spaniard at the sight of the faggot and stake, or of the bull-fight, the present-day Japanese who presses his way to the tragedy, the workman of the Parisian suburbs who has a homesickness for bloody revolutions, the Wagnerienne who, with unhinged will, "undergoes" the performance of "Tristan and Isolde"—what all these enjoy, and strive with mysterious ardour to drink in, is the philtre of the great Circe "cruelty." Here, to be sure, we must put aside entirely the blundering psychology of former times, which could only teach with regard to cruelty that it originated at the sight of the suffering of OTHERS: there is an abundant, super-abundant enjoyment even in one's own suffering, in causing one's own suffering—and wherever man has allowed himself to be persuaded to self-denial in the RELIGIOUS sense, or to self-mutilation, as among the Phoenicians and ascetics, or in general, to desensualisation, decarnalisation, and contrition, to Puritanical repentance-spasms, to vivisection of conscience and to Pascal-like SACRIFIZIA DELL' INTELLETO, he is secretly allured and impelled forwards by his cruelty, by the dangerous thrill of cruelty TOWARDS HIMSELF.—Finally, let us consider that even the seeker of knowledge operates as an artist and glorifier of cruelty, in that he compels his spirit to perceive AGAINST its own inclination, and often enough against the wishes of his heart:—he forces it to say Nay, where he would like to affirm, love, and adore;

indeed, every instance of taking a thing profoundly and fundamentally, is a violation, an intentional injuring of the fundamental will of the spirit, which instinctively aims at appearance and superficiality,—even in every desire for knowledge there is a drop of cruelty.

230. Perhaps what I have said here about a "fundamental will of the spirit" may not be understood without further details; I may be allowed a word of explanation.—That imperious something which is popularly called "the spirit," wishes to be master internally and externally, and to feel itself master; it has the will of a multiplicity for a simplicity, a binding, taming, imperious, and essentially ruling will. Its requirements and capacities here, are the same as those assigned by physiologists to everything that lives, grows, and multiplies. The power of the spirit to appropriate foreign elements reveals itself in a strong tendency to assimilate the new to the old, to simplify the manifold, to overlook or repudiate the absolutely contradictory; just as it arbitrarily re-underlines, makes prominent, and falsifies for itself certain traits and lines in the foreign elements, in every portion of the "outside world." Its object thereby is the incorporation of new "experiences," the assortment of new things in the old arrangements—in short, growth; or more properly, the FEELING of growth, the feeling of increased power—is its object. This same will has at its service an apparently opposed impulse of the spirit, a suddenly

adopted preference of ignorance, of arbitrary shutting out, a closing of windows, an inner denial of this or that, a prohibition to approach, a sort of defensive attitude against much that is knowable, a contentment with obscurity, with the shutting-in horizon, an acceptance and approval of ignorance: as that which is all necessary according to the degree of its appropriating power, its "digestive power," to speak figuratively (and in fact "the spirit" resembles a stomach more than anything else). Here also belong an occasional propensity of the spirit to let itself be deceived (perhaps with a waggish suspicion that it is NOT so and so, but is only allowed to pass as such), a delight in uncertainty and ambiguity, an exulting enjoyment of arbitrary, out-of-the-way narrowness and mystery, of the too-near, of the foreground, of the magnified, the diminished, the misshapen, the beautified—an enjoyment of the arbitrariness of all these manifestations of power. Finally, in this connection, there is the not unscrupulous readiness of the spirit to deceive other spirits and dissemble before them—the constant pressing and straining of a creating, shaping, changeable power: the spirit enjoys therein its craftiness and its variety of disguises, it enjoys also its feeling of security therein—it is precisely by its Protean arts that it is best protected and concealed!— COUNTER TO this propensity for appearance, for simplification, for a disguise, for a cloak, in short, for an outside—for every outside is a cloak—there operates the sublime tendency of the man of knowledge, which takes, and INSISTS on taking things profoundly, variously, and thoroughly; as a kind of cruelty of the intellectual conscience and taste, which every courageous thinker will acknowledge in himself, provided, as it ought to be, that he has sharpened and hardened his eye sufficiently long for introspection, and is accustomed to severe discipline and even severe words. He will say: "There is something cruel in the tendency of my spirit": let the virtuous and amiable try to convince him that it is not so! In fact, it would sound nicer, if, instead of our cruelty, perhaps our "extravagant honesty" were talked about, whispered about, and glorified—we free, VERY free spirits—and some day perhaps SUCH will actually be our—posthumous glory! Meanwhile—for there is plenty of time until then—we should be least inclined to deck ourselves out in such florid and fringed moral verbiage; our whole former work has just made us sick of this taste and its sprightly exuberance. They are beautiful, glistening, jingling, festive words: honesty, love of truth, love of wisdom, sacrifice for knowledge, heroism of the truthful—there is something in them that makes one's heart swell with pride. But we anchorites and marmots have long ago persuaded ourselves in all the secrecy of an anchorite's conscience, that this worthy parade of verbiage also belongs to the old false adornment, frippery, and gold-dust of unconscious human vanity, and that even under such flattering colour and repainting, the terrible original text HOMO NATURA must again be recognized. In effect, to translate man back again into nature; to master the many vain and visionary interpretations and subordinate meanings which have hitherto been scratched and daubed over the eternal original text, HOMO NATURA; to bring it about that man shall henceforth stand before man as he now, hardened by the discipline of science, stands before the OTHER forms of nature, with fearless Oedipus-eyes, and stopped Ulysses-ears, deaf to the enticements of old metaphysical bird-catchers, who have piped to him far too long: "Thou art more! thou art higher! thou hast a different origin!"—this may be a strange and foolish task, but that it is a TASK, who can deny! Why did we choose it, this foolish task? Or, to put the question differently: "Why knowledge at all?" Every one will ask us about this. And thus pressed, we, who have asked ourselves the question a hundred times, have not found and cannot find any better answer....

231. Learning alters us, it does what all nourishment does that does not merely "conserve"—as the physiologist knows. But at the bottom of our souls, quite "down below," there is certainly something unteachable, a granite of spiritual fate, of predetermined decision and answer to predetermined, chosen questions. In each cardinal problem there speaks an unchangeable "I am this"; a thinker cannot learn

anew about man and woman, for instance, but can only learn fully—he can only follow to the end what is "fixed" about them in himself. Occasionally we find certain solutions of problems which make strong beliefs for us; perhaps they are henceforth called "convictions." Later on—one sees in them only footsteps to self-knowledge, guide-posts to the problem which we ourselves ARE—or more correctly to the great stupidity which we embody, our spiritual fate, the UNTEACHABLE in us, quite "down below."—In view of this liberal compliment which I have just paid myself, permission will perhaps be more readily allowed me to utter some truths about "woman as she is," provided that it is known at the outset how literally they are merely—MY truths.

232. Woman wishes to be independent, and therefore she begins to enlighten men about "woman as she is"—THIS is one of the worst developments of the general UGLIFYING of Europe. For what must these clumsy attempts of feminine scientificality and self-exposure bring to light! Woman has so much cause for shame; in woman there is so much pedantry, superficiality, schoolmasterliness, petty presumption, unbridledness, and indiscretion concealed—study only woman's behaviour towards children!—which has really been best restrained and dominated hitherto by the FEAR of man. Alas, if ever the "eternally tedious in woman"—she has plenty of it!—is allowed to venture forth! if she

begins radically and on principle to unlearn her wisdom and art-of charming, of playing, of frightening away sorrow, of alleviating and taking easily; if she forgets her delicate aptitude for agreeable desires! Female voices are already raised, which, by Saint Aristophanes! make one afraid:—with medical explicitness it is stated in a threatening manner what woman first and last REQUIRES from man. Is it not in the very worst taste that woman thus sets herself up to be scientific? Enlightenment hitherto has fortunately been men's affair, men's gift—we remained therewith "among ourselves"; and in the end, in view of all that women write about "woman," we may well have considerable doubt as to whether woman really DESIRES enlightenment about herself—and CAN desire it. If woman does not thereby seek a new ORNAMENT for herself—I believe ornamentation belongs to the eternally feminine?—why, then, she wishes to make herself feared: perhaps she thereby wishes to get the mastery. But she does not want truth—what does woman care for truth? From the very first, nothing is more foreign, more repugnant, or more hostile to woman than truth—her great art is falsehood, her chief concern is appearance and beauty. Let us confess it, we men: we honour and love this very art and this very instinct in woman: we who have the hard task, and for our recreation gladly seek the company of beings under whose hands, glances, and delicate follies, our seriousness, our gravity, and profundity appear almost like follies to us. Finally, I ask the question: Did a woman herself ever acknowledge profundity in a woman's mind, or justice in a woman's heart? And is it not true that on the whole "woman" has hitherto been most despised by woman herself, and not at all by us?—We men desire that woman should not continue to compromise herself by enlightening us; just as it was man's care and the consideration for woman, when the church decreed: mulier taceat in ecclesia. It was to the benefit of woman when Napoleon gave the too eloquent Madame de Stael to understand: mulier taceat in politicis!—and in my opinion, he is a true friend of woman who calls out to women today: mulier taceat de mulierel.

233. It betrays corruption of the instincts—apart from the fact that it betrays bad taste—when a woman refers to Madame Roland, or Madame de Stael, or Monsieur George Sand, as though something were proved thereby in favour of "woman as she is." Among men, these are the three comical women as they are—nothing more!—and just the best involuntary counter-arguments against feminine emancipation and autonomy.

234. Stupidity in the kitchen; woman as cook; the terrible thoughtlessness with which the feeding of the family and the master of the house is managed! Woman does not understand what food means, and she insists on being cook! If woman had been a thinking creature,

she should certainly, as cook for thousands of years, have discovered the most important physiological facts, and should likewise have got possession of the healing art! Through bad female cooks—through the entire lack of reason in the kitchen—the development of mankind has been longest retarded and most interfered with: even today matters are very little better. A word to High School girls.

235. There are turns and casts of fancy, there are sentences, little handfuls of words, in which a whole culture, a whole society suddenly crystallises itself. Among these is the incidental remark of Madame de Lambert to her son: "MON AMI, NE VOUS PERMETTEZ JAMAIS QUE DES FOLIES, QUI VOUS FERONT GRAND PLAISIR"—the motherliest and wisest remark, by the way, that was ever addressed to a son.

236. I have no doubt that every noble woman will oppose what Dante and Goethe believed about woman—the former when he sang, "ELLA GUARDAVA SUSO, ED IO IN LEI," and the latter when he interpreted it, "the eternally feminine draws us ALOFT"; for THIS is just what she believes of the eternally masculine.

237. SEVEN APOPHTHEGMS FOR WOMEN

How the longest ennui flees, When a man comes to our knees!

Age, alas! and science staid, Furnish even weak virtue aid.

Sombre garb and silence meet: Dress for every dame—discreet.

Whom I thank when in my bliss? God!—and my good tailoress!

Young, a flower-decked cavern home; Old, a dragon thence doth roam.

Noble title, leg that's fine, Man as well: Oh, were HE mine!

Speech in brief and sense in mass—Slippery for the jenny-ass!

237A. Woman has hitherto been treated by men like birds, which, losing their way, have come down among them from an elevation: as something delicate, fragile, wild, strange, sweet, and animating—but as something also which must be cooped up to prevent it flying away.

238. To be mistaken in the fundamental problem of "man and woman," to deny here the profoundest antagonism and the necessity for an eternally hostile tension, to dream here perhaps of equal rights, equal training, equal claims and obligations: that is a TYPICAL sign of shallow-mindedness; and a thinker

who has proved himself shallow at this dangerous spot—shallow in instinct!—may generally be regarded as suspicious, nay more, as betrayed, as discovered; he will probably prove too "short" for all fundamental questions of life, future as well as present, and will be unable to descend into ANY of the depths. On the other hand, a man who has depth of spirit as well as of desires, and has also the depth of benevolence which is capable of severity and harshness, and easily confounded with them, can only think of woman as ORIENTALS do: he must conceive of her as a possession, as confinable property, as a being predestined for service and accomplishing her mission therein—he must take his stand in this matter upon the immense rationality of Asia, upon the superiority of the instinct of Asia, as the Greeks did formerly; those best heirs and scholars of Asia—who, as is well known, with their INCREASING culture and amplitude of power, from Homer to the time of Pericles, became gradually STRICTER towards woman, in short, more Oriental. HOW necessary, HOW logical, even HOW humanely desirable this was, let us consider for ourselves!

239. The weaker sex has in no previous age been treated with so much respect by men as at present—this belongs to the tendency and fundamental taste of democracy, in the same way as disrespectfulness to old age—what wonder is it that abuse should be

immediately made of this respect? They want more, they learn to make claims, the tribute of respect is at last felt to be well-nigh galling; rivalry for rights, indeed actual strife itself, would be preferred: in a word, woman is losing modesty. And let us immediately add that she is also losing taste. She is unlearning to FEAR man: but the woman who "unlearns to fear" sacrifices her most womanly instincts. That woman should venture forward when the fear-inspiring quality in man—or more definitely, the MAN in man—is no longer either desired or fully developed, is reasonable enough and also intelligible enough; what is more difficult to understand is that precisely thereby—woman deteriorates. This is what is happening nowadays: let us not deceive ourselves about it! Wherever the industrial spirit has triumphed over the military and aristocratic spirit, woman strives for the economic and legal independence of a clerk: "woman as clerkess" is inscribed on the portal of the modern society which is in course of formation. While she thus appropriates new rights, aspires to be "master," and inscribes "progress" of woman on her flags and banners, the very opposite realises itself with terrible obviousness: WOMAN RETROGRADES. Since the French Revolution the influence of woman in Europe has DECLINED in proportion as she has increased her rights and claims; and the "emancipation of woman," insofar as it is desired and demanded by women themselves (and not only by masculine shallow-pates), thus proves to be a remarkable symptom of the increased weakening and deadening of the most womanly instincts. There is STUPIDITY in this movement, an almost masculine stupidity, of which a well-reared woman—who is always a sensible woman—might be heartily ashamed. To lose the intuition as to the ground upon which she can most surely achieve victory; to neglect exercise in the use of her proper weapons; to let-herself-go before man, perhaps even "to the book," where formerly she kept herself in control and in refined, artful humility; to neutralize with her virtuous audacity man's faith in a VEILED, fundamentally different ideal in woman, something eternally, necessarily feminine; to emphatically and loquaciously dissuade man from the idea that woman must be preserved, cared for, protected, and indulged, like some delicate, strangely wild, and often pleasant domestic animal; the clumsy and indignant collection of everything of the nature of servitude and bondage which the position of woman in the hitherto existing order of society has entailed and still entails (as though slavery were a counter-argument, and not rather a condition of every higher culture, of every elevation of culture):—what does all this betoken, if not a disintegration of womanly instincts, a defeminising? Certainly, there are enough of idiotic friends and corrupters of woman among the learned asses of the masculine sex, who advise woman to defeminize herself in this manner, and to imitate all the stupidities from which "man" in Europe, European "manliness," suffers,—who would like to lower woman to "general culture," indeed even to newspaper reading and meddling with politics. Here and there they wish even to make women into free spirits and literary workers: as though a woman without piety would not be something perfectly obnoxious or ludicrous to a profound and godless man;—almost everywhere her nerves are being ruined by the most morbid and dangerous kind of music (our latest German music), and she is daily being made more hysterical and more incapable of fulfilling her first and last function, that of bearing robust children. They wish to "cultivate" her in general still more, and intend, as they say, to make the "weaker sex" STRONG by culture: as if history did not teach in the most emphatic manner that the "cultivating" of mankind and his weakening—that is to say, the weakening, dissipating, and languishing of his FORCE OF WILL—have always kept pace with one another, and that the most powerful and influential women in the world (and lastly, the mother of Napoleon) had just to thank their force of will—and not their schoolmasters—for their power and ascendancy over men. That which inspires respect in woman, and often enough fear also, is her NATURE, which is more "natural" than that of man, her genuine, carnivora-like, cunning flexibility, her tiger-claws beneath the glove, her NAIVETE in egoism, her untrainableness and innate wildness, the incomprehensibleness, extent, and deviation of her desires and virtues. That which, in spite of fear, excites one's sympathy for the dangerous and beautiful cat, "woman," is that she seems more afflicted, more vulnerable, more necessitous of love, and more condemned to disillusionment than any other creature. Fear and sympathy it is with these feelings that man has hitherto stood in the presence of woman, always with one foot already in tragedy, which rends while it delights—What? And all that is now to be at an end? And the DISENCHANTMENT of woman is in progress? The tediousness of woman is slowly evolving? Oh Europe! Europe! We know the horned animal which was always most attractive to thee, from which danger is ever again threatening thee! Thy old fable might once more become "history"—an immense stupidity might once again overmaster thee and carry thee away! And no God concealed beneath it—no! only an "idea," a "modern idea"!

Chapter VIII
Peoples and Countries

240. I HEARD, once again for the first time, Richard Wagner's overture to the Mastersinger: it is a piece of magnificent, gorgeous, heavy, latter-day art, which has the pride to presuppose two centuries of music as still living, in order that it may be understood:—it is an honour to Germans that such a pride did not miscalculate! What flavours and forces, what seasons and climes do we not find mingled in it! It impresses us at one time as ancient, at another time as foreign, bitter, and too modern, it is as arbitrary as it is pompously traditional, it is not infrequently roguish, still oftener rough and coarse—it has fire and courage, and at the same time the loose, dun-coloured skin of fruits which ripen too late. It flows broad and full: and suddenly there is a moment of inexplicable hesitation, like a gap that opens between cause and effect, an oppression that makes us dream, almost a nightmare; but already it broadens and widens anew, the old stream of delight— the most manifold delight,—of old and new happiness; including ESPECIALLY the joy of the artist in himself, which he refuses to conceal, his astonished, happy cognizance of his mastery of the expedients here employed, the new, newly acquired, imperfectly tested expedients of art which he apparently betrays to us. All in all, however, no beauty, no South, nothing of the delicate southern clearness of the sky, nothing of grace,

no dance, hardly a will to logic; a certain clumsiness even, which is also emphasized, as though the artist wished to say to us: "It is part of my intention"; a cumbersome drapery, something arbitrarily barbaric and ceremonious, a flirring of learned and venerable conceits and witticisms; something German in the best and worst sense of the word, something in the German style, manifold, formless, and inexhaustible; a certain German potency and super-plenitude of soul, which is not afraid to hide itself under the RAFFINEMENTS of decadence—which, perhaps, feels itself most at ease there; a real, genuine token of the German soul, which is at the same time young and aged, too ripe and yet still too rich in futurity. This kind of music expresses best what I think of the Germans: they belong to the day before yesterday and the day after tomorrow—THEY HAVE AS YET NO TODAY.

241. We "good Europeans," we also have hours when we allow ourselves a warm-hearted patriotism, a plunge and relapse into old loves and narrow views—I have just given an example of it—hours of national excitement, of patriotic anguish, and all other sorts of old-fashioned floods of sentiment. Duller spirits may perhaps only get done with what confines its operations in us to hours and plays itself out in hours—in a considerable time: some in half a year, others in half a lifetime, according to the speed and strength with which they digest and "change their material." Indeed, I

could think of sluggish, hesitating races, which even in our rapidly moving Europe, would require half a century ere they could surmount such atavistic attacks of patriotism and soil-attachment, and return once more to reason, that is to say, to "good Europeanism." And while digressing on this possibility, I happen to become an ear-witness of a conversation between two old patriots—they were evidently both hard of hearing and consequently spoke all the louder. "HE has as much, and knows as much, philosophy as a peasant or a corps-student," said the one—"he is still innocent. But what does that matter nowadays! It is the age of the masses: they lie on their belly before everything that is massive. And so also in politicis. A statesman who rears up for them a new Tower of Babel, some monstrosity of empire and power, they call 'great'—what does it matter that we more prudent and conservative ones do not meanwhile give up the old belief that it is only the great thought that gives greatness to an action or affair. Supposing a statesman were to bring his people into the position of being obliged henceforth to practise 'high politics,' for which they were by nature badly endowed and prepared, so that they would have to sacrifice their old and reliable virtues, out of love to a new and doubtful mediocrity;—supposing a statesman were to condemn his people generally to 'practise politics,' when they have hitherto had something better to do and think about, and when in the depths of their souls they have been unable to free themselves from a prudent loathing of the restlessness, emptiness, and noisy wranglings of the essentially politics-practising nations;—supposing such a statesman were to stimulate the slumbering passions and avidities of his people, were to make a stigma out of their former diffidence and delight in aloofness, an offence out of their exoticism and hidden permanency, were to depreciate their most radical proclivities, subvert their consciences, make their minds narrow, and their tastes 'national'—what! a statesman who should do all this, which his people would have to do penance for throughout their whole future, if they had a future, such a statesman would be GREAT, would he?"—"Undoubtedly!" replied the other old patriot vehemently, "otherwise he COULD NOT have done it! It was mad perhaps to wish such a thing! But perhaps everything great has been just as mad at its commencement!"—"Misuse of words!" cried his interlocutor, contradictorily—"strong! strong! Strong and mad! NOT great!"—The old men had obviously become heated as they thus shouted their "truths" in each other's faces, but I, in my happiness and apartness, considered how soon a stronger one may become master of the strong, and also that there is a compensation for the intellectual superficialising of a nation—namely, in the deepening of another.

242. Whether we call it "civilization," or "humanising," or "progress," which now distinguishes

the European, whether we call it simply, without praise or blame, by the political formula the DEMOCRATIC movement in Europe—behind all the moral and political foregrounds pointed to by such formulas, an immense PHYSIOLOGICAL PROCESS goes on, which is ever extending the process of the assimilation of Europeans, their increasing detachment from the conditions under which, climatically and hereditarily, united races originate, their increasing independence of every definite milieu, that for centuries would fain inscribe itself with equal demands on soul and body,—that is to say, the slow emergence of an essentially SUPER-NATIONAL and nomadic species of man, who possesses, physiologically speaking, a maximum of the art and power of adaptation as his typical distinction. This process of the EVOLVING EUROPEAN, which can be retarded in its TEMPO by great relapses, but will perhaps just gain and grow thereby in vehemence and depth—the still-raging storm and stress of "national sentiment" pertains to it, and also the anarchism which is appearing at present—this process will probably arrive at results on which its naive propagators and panegyrists, the apostles of "modern ideas," would least care to reckon. The same new conditions under which on an average a levelling and mediocrising of man will take place—a useful, industrious, variously serviceable, and clever gregarious man—are in the highest degree suitable to give rise to exceptional men of the most dangerous and attractive qualities. For, while the capacity for adaptation, which is every day trying changing conditions, and begins a new work with every generation, almost with every decade, makes the POWERFULNESS of the type impossible; while the collective impression of such future Europeans will probably be that of numerous, talkative, weak-willed, and very handy workmen who REQUIRE a master, a commander, as they require their daily bread; while, therefore, the democratising of Europe will tend to the production of a type prepared for SLAVERY in the most subtle sense of the term: the STRONG man will necessarily in individual and exceptional cases, become stronger and richer than he has perhaps ever been before—owing to the unprejudicedness of his schooling, owing to the immense variety of practice, art, and disguise. I meant to say that the democratising of Europe is at the same time an involuntary arrangement for the rearing of TYRANTS—taking the word in all its meanings, even in its most spiritual sense.

243. I hear with pleasure that our sun is moving rapidly towards the constellation Hercules: and I hope that the men on this earth will do like the sun. And we foremost, we good Europeans!

244. There was a time when it was customary to call Germans "deep" by way of distinction; but now that the most successful type of new Germanism is covetous of

quite other honours, and perhaps misses "smartness" in all that has depth, it is almost opportune and patriotic to doubt whether we did not formerly deceive ourselves with that commendation: in short, whether German depth is not at bottom something different and worse—and something from which, thank God, we are on the point of successfully ridding ourselves. Let us try, then, to relearn with regard to German depth; the only thing necessary for the purpose is a little vivisection of the German soul.—The German soul is above all manifold, varied in its source, aggregated and super-imposed, rather than actually built: this is owing to its origin. A German who would embolden himself to assert: "Two souls, alas, dwell in my breast," would make a bad guess at the truth, or, more correctly, he would come far short of the truth about the number of souls. As a people made up of the most extraordinary mixing and mingling of races, perhaps even with a preponderance of the pre-Aryan element as the "people of the centre" in every sense of the term, the Germans are more intangible, more ample, more contradictory, more unknown, more incalculable, more surprising, and even more terrifying than other peoples are to themselves:—they escape DEFINITION, and are thereby alone the despair of the French. It IS characteristic of the Germans that the question: "What is German?" never dies out among them. Kotzebue certainly knew his Germans well enough: "We are known," they cried jubilantly to him—but Sand also thought he knew them. Jean Paul knew what he was doing when he declared himself incensed at Fichte's lying but patriotic flatteries and exaggerations,—but it is probable that Goethe thought differently about Germans from Jean Paul, even though he acknowledged him to be right with regard to Fichte. It is a question what Goethe really thought about the Germans?—But about many things around him he never spoke explicitly, and all his life he knew how to keep an astute silence—probably he had good reason for it. It is certain that it was not the "Wars of Independence" that made him look up more joyfully, any more than it was the French Revolution,—the event on account of which he RECONSTRUCTED his "Faust," and indeed the whole problem of "man," was the appearance of Napoleon. There are words of Goethe in which he condemns with impatient severity, as from a foreign land, that which Germans take a pride in, he once defined the famous German turn of mind as "Indulgence towards its own and others' weaknesses." Was he wrong? it is characteristic of Germans that one is seldom entirely wrong about them. The German soul has passages and galleries in it, there are caves, hiding-places, and dungeons therein, its disorder has much of the charm of the mysterious, the German is well acquainted with the bypaths to chaos. And as everything loves its symbol, so the German loves the clouds and all that is obscure, evolving, crepuscular, damp, and shrouded, it seems to him that everything uncertain, undeveloped, self-displacing, and growing is "deep". The German himself does not EXIST, he is BECOMING, he is "developing himself". "Development" is therefore the essentially German discovery and hit in the great domain of philosophical formulas,—a ruling idea, which, together with German beer and German music, is labouring to Germanise all Europe. Foreigners are astonished and attracted by the riddles which the conflicting nature at the basis of the German soul propounds to them (riddles which Hegel systematised and Richard Wagner has in the end set to music). "Good-natured and spiteful"—such a juxtaposition, preposterous in the case of every other people, is unfortunately only too often justified in Germany one has only to live for a while among Swabians to know this! The clumsiness of the German scholar and his social distastefulness agree alarmingly well with his physical rope-dancing and nimble boldness, of which all the Gods have learnt to be afraid. If any one wishes to see the "German soul" demonstrated ad oculos, let him only look at German taste, at German arts and manners what boorish indifference to "taste"! How the noblest and the commonest stand there in juxtaposition! How disorderly and how rich is the whole constitution of this soul! The German DRAGS at his soul, he drags at everything he experiences. He digests his events badly; he never gets "done" with them; and German depth is often only a difficult, hesitating "digestion." And just as all chronic invalids, all dyspeptics like what is convenient, so the German loves "frankness" and "honesty"; it is so CONVENIENT to be frank and honest!—This confidingness, this complaisance, this showing-the-cards of German HONESTY, is probably the most dangerous and most successful disguise which the German is up to nowadays: it is his proper Mephistophelean art; with this he can "still achieve much"! The German lets himself go, and thereby gazes with faithful, blue, empty German eyes—and other countries immediately confound him with his dressing-gown!—I meant to say that, let "German depth" be what it will—among ourselves alone we perhaps take the liberty to laugh at it—we shall do well to continue henceforth to honour its appearance and good name, and not barter away too cheaply our old reputation as a people of depth for Prussian "smartness," and Berlin wit and sand. It is wise for a people to pose, and LET itself be regarded, as profound, clumsy, good-natured, honest, and foolish: it might even be—profound to do so! Finally, we should do honour to our name—we are not called the "TIUSCHE VOLK" (deceptive people) for nothing....

245. The "good old" time is past, it sang itself out in Mozart—how happy are WE that his ROCOCO still speaks to us, that his "good company," his tender enthusiasm, his childish delight in the Chinese and its flourishes, his courtesy of heart, his longing for the elegant, the amorous, the tripping, the tearful, and his

belief in the South, can still appeal to SOMETHING LEFT in us! Ah, some time or other it will be over with it!—but who can doubt that it will be over still sooner with the intelligence and taste for Beethoven! For he was only the last echo of a break and transition in style, and NOT, like Mozart, the last echo of a great European taste which had existed for centuries. Beethoven is the intermediate event between an old mellow soul that is constantly breaking down, and a future over-young soul that is always COMING; there is spread over his music the twilight of eternal loss and eternal extravagant hope,—the same light in which Europe was bathed when it dreamed with Rousseau, when it danced round the Tree of Liberty of the Revolution, and finally almost fell down in adoration before Napoleon. But how rapidly does THIS very sentiment now pale, how difficult nowadays is even the APPREHENSION of this sentiment, how strangely does the language of Rousseau, Schiller, Shelley, and Byron sound to our ear, in whom COLLECTIVELY the same fate of Europe was able to SPEAK, which knew how to SING in Beethoven!—Whatever German music came afterwards, belongs to Romanticism, that is to say, to a movement which, historically considered, was still shorter, more fleeting, and more superficial than that great interlude, the transition of Europe from Rousseau to Napoleon, and to the rise of democracy. Weber—but what do WE care nowadays for "Freischutz" and "Oberon"! Or Marschner's "Hans

Heiling" and "Vampyre"! Or even Wagner's "Tannhauser"! That is extinct, although not yet forgotten music. This whole music of Romanticism, besides, was not noble enough, was not musical enough, to maintain its position anywhere but in the theatre and before the masses; from the beginning it was second-rate music, which was little thought of by genuine musicians. It was different with Felix Mendelssohn, that halcyon master, who, on account of his lighter, purer, happier soul, quickly acquired admiration, and was equally quickly forgotten: as the beautiful EPISODE of German music. But with regard to Robert Schumann, who took things seriously, and has been taken seriously from the first—he was the last that founded a school,—do we not now regard it as a satisfaction, a relief, a deliverance, that this very Romanticism of Schumann's has been surmounted? Schumann, fleeing into the "Saxon Switzerland" of his soul, with a half Werther-like, half Jean-Paul-like nature (assuredly not like Beethoven! assuredly not like Byron!)—his MANFRED music is a mistake and a misunderstanding to the extent of injustice; Schumann, with his taste, which was fundamentally a PETTY taste (that is to say, a dangerous propensity—doubly dangerous among Germans—for quiet lyricism and intoxication of the feelings), going constantly apart, timidly withdrawing and retiring, a noble weakling who revelled in nothing but anonymous joy and sorrow, from the beginning a sort of girl and NOLI ME

TANGERE—this Schumann was already merely a GERMAN event in music, and no longer a European event, as Beethoven had been, as in a still greater degree Mozart had been; with Schumann German music was threatened with its greatest danger, that of LOSING THE VOICE FOR THE SOUL OF EUROPE and sinking into a merely national affair.

246. What a torture are books written in German to a reader who has a THIRD ear! How indignantly he stands beside the slowly turning swamp of sounds without tune and rhythms without dance, which Germans call a "book"! And even the German who READS books! How lazily, how reluctantly, how badly he reads! How many Germans know, and consider it obligatory to know, that there is ART in every good sentence—art which must be divined, if the sentence is to be understood! If there is a misunderstanding about its TEMPO, for instance, the sentence itself is misunderstood! That one must not be doubtful about the rhythm-determining syllables, that one should feel the breaking of the too-rigid symmetry as intentional and as a charm, that one should lend a fine and patient ear to every STACCATO and every RUBATO, that one should divine the sense in the sequence of the vowels and diphthongs, and how delicately and richly they can be tinted and retinted in the order of their arrangement—who among book-reading Germans is complaisant enough to recognize such duties and

requirements, and to listen to so much art and intention in language? After all, one just "has no ear for it"; and so the most marked contrasts of style are not heard, and the most delicate artistry is as it were SQUANDERED on the deaf.—These were my thoughts when I noticed how clumsily and unintuitively two masters in the art of prose-writing have been confounded: one, whose words drop down hesitatingly and coldly, as from the roof of a damp cave—he counts on their dull sound and echo; and another who manipulates his language like a flexible sword, and from his arm down into his toes feels the dangerous bliss of the quivering, over-sharp blade, which wishes to bite, hiss, and cut.

247. How little the German style has to do with harmony and with the ear, is shown by the fact that precisely our good musicians themselves write badly. The German does not read aloud, he does not read for the ear, but only with his eyes; he has put his ears away in the drawer for the time. In antiquity when a man read—which was seldom enough—he read something to himself, and in a loud voice; they were surprised when any one read silently, and sought secretly the reason of it. In a loud voice: that is to say, with all the swellings, inflections, and variations of key and changes of TEMPO, in which the ancient PUBLIC world took delight. The laws of the written style were then the same as those of the spoken style; and these laws depended partly on the surprising development

and refined requirements of the ear and larynx; partly on the strength, endurance, and power of the ancient lungs. In the ancient sense, a period is above all a physiological whole, inasmuch as it is comprised in one breath. Such periods as occur in Demosthenes and Cicero, swelling twice and sinking twice, and all in one breath, were pleasures to the men of ANTIQUITY, who knew by their own schooling how to appreciate the virtue therein, the rareness and the difficulty in the deliverance of such a period;—WE have really no right to the BIG period, we modern men, who are short of breath in every sense! Those ancients, indeed, were all of them dilettanti in speaking, consequently connoisseurs, consequently critics—they thus brought their orators to the highest pitch; in the same manner as in the last century, when all Italian ladies and gentlemen knew how to sing, the virtuosoship of song (and with it also the art of melody) reached its elevation. In Germany, however (until quite recently when a kind of platform eloquence began shyly and awkwardly enough to flutter its young wings), there was properly speaking only one kind of public and APPROXIMATELY artistical discourse—that delivered from the pulpit. The preacher was the only one in Germany who knew the weight of a syllable or a word, in what manner a sentence strikes, springs, rushes, flows, and comes to a close; he alone had a conscience in his ears, often enough a bad conscience: for reasons are not lacking why proficiency in oratory should be especially seldom attained by a German, or almost always too late. The masterpiece of German prose is therefore with good reason the masterpiece of its greatest preacher: the BIBLE has hitherto been the best German book. Compared with Luther's Bible, almost everything else is merely "literature"—something which has not grown in Germany, and therefore has not taken and does not take root in German hearts, as the Bible has done.

248. There are two kinds of geniuses: one which above all engenders and seeks to engender, and another which willingly lets itself be fructified and brings forth. And similarly, among the gifted nations, there are those on whom the woman's problem of pregnancy has devolved, and the secret task of forming, maturing, and perfecting—the Greeks, for instance, were a nation of this kind, and so are the French; and others which have to fructify and become the cause of new modes of life—like the Jews, the Romans, and, in all modesty be it asked: like the Germans?—nations tortured and enraptured by unknown fevers and irresistibly forced out of themselves, amorous and longing for foreign races (for such as "let themselves be fructified"), and withal imperious, like everything conscious of being full of generative force, and consequently empowered "by the grace of God." These two kinds of geniuses seek each other like man and woman; but they also misunderstand each other—like man and woman.

249. Every nation has its own "Tartuffery," and calls that its virtue.—One does not know—cannot know, the best that is in one.

250. What Europe owes to the Jews?—Many things, good and bad, and above all one thing of the nature both of the best and the worst: the grand style in morality, the fearfulness and majesty of infinite demands, of infinite significations, the whole Romanticism and sublimity of moral questionableness—and consequently just the most attractive, ensnaring, and exquisite element in those iridescences and allurements to life, in the aftersheen of which the sky of our European culture, its evening sky, now glows—perhaps glows out. For this, we artists among the spectators and philosophers, are—grateful to the Jews.

251. It must be taken into the bargain, if various clouds and disturbances—in short, slight attacks of stupidity—pass over the spirit of a people that suffers and WANTS to suffer from national nervous fever and political ambition: for instance, among present-day Germans there is alternately the anti-French folly, the anti-Semitic folly, the anti-Polish folly, the Christian-romantic folly, the Wagnerian folly, the Teutonic folly, the Prussian folly (just look at those poor historians, the Sybels and Treitschkes, and their closely bandaged

heads), and whatever else these little obscurations of the German spirit and conscience may be called. May it be forgiven me that I, too, when on a short daring sojourn on very infected ground, did not remain wholly exempt from the disease, but like every one else, began to entertain thoughts about matters which did not concern me—the first symptom of political infection. About the Jews, for instance, listen to the following:—I have never yet met a German who was favourably inclined to the Jews; and however decided the repudiation of actual anti-Semitism may be on the part of all prudent and political men, this prudence and policy is not perhaps directed against the nature of the sentiment itself, but only against its dangerous excess, and especially against the distasteful and infamous expression of this excess of sentiment;—on this point we must not deceive ourselves. That Germany has amply SUFFICIENT Jews, that the German stomach, the German blood, has difficulty (and will long have difficulty) in disposing only of this quantity of "Jew"—as the Italian, the Frenchman, and the Englishman have done by means of a stronger digestion:—that is the unmistakable declaration and language of a general instinct, to which one must listen and according to which one must act. "Let no more Jews come in! And shut the doors, especially towards the East (also towards Austria)!"—thus commands the instinct of a people whose nature is still feeble and uncertain, so that it could be easily wiped out, easily extinguished, by a stronger race. The Jews, however, are beyond all doubt the strongest, toughest, and purest race at present living in Europe, they know how to succeed even under the worst conditions (in fact better than under favourable ones), by means of virtues of some sort, which one would like nowadays to label as vices—owing above all to a resolute faith which does not need to be ashamed before "modern ideas", they alter only, WHEN they do alter, in the same way that the Russian Empire makes its conquest—as an empire that has plenty of time and is not of yesterday—namely, according to the principle, "as slowly as possible"! A thinker who has the future of Europe at heart, will, in all his perspectives concerning the future, calculate upon the Jews, as he will calculate upon the Russians, as above all the surest and likeliest factors in the great play and battle of forces. That which is at present called a "nation" in Europe, and is really rather a RES FACTA than NATA (indeed, sometimes confusingly similar to a RES FICTA ET PICTA), is in every case something evolving, young, easily displaced, and not yet a race, much less such a race AERE PERENNUS, as the Jews are such "nations" should most carefully avoid all hot-headed rivalry and hostility! It is certain that the Jews, if they desired—or if they were driven to it, as the anti-Semites seem to wish—COULD now have the ascendancy, nay, literally the supremacy, over Europe, that they are NOT working and planning for that end is equally certain. Meanwhile, they rather wish and desire, even somewhat importunely, to be insorbed and absorbed by Europe, they long to be finally settled, authorized, and respected somewhere, and wish to put an end to the nomadic life, to the "wandering Jew",—and one should certainly take account of this impulse and tendency, and MAKE ADVANCES to it (it possibly betokens a mitigation of the Jewish instincts) for which purpose it would perhaps be useful and fair to banish the anti-Semitic bawlers out of the country. One should make advances with all prudence, and with selection, pretty much as the English nobility do It stands to reason that the more powerful and strongly marked types of new Germanism could enter into relation with the Jews with the least hesitation, for instance, the nobleman officer from the Prussian border it would be interesting in many ways to see whether the genius for money and patience (and especially some intellect and intellectuality—sadly lacking in the place referred to) could not in addition be annexed and trained to the hereditary art of commanding and obeying—for both of which the country in question has now a classic reputation But here it is expedient to break off my festal discourse and my sprightly Teutonomania for I have already reached my SERIOUS TOPIC, the "European problem," as I understand it, the rearing of a new ruling caste for Europe.

252. They are not a philosophical race—the English: Bacon represents an ATTACK on the philosophical

spirit generally, Hobbes, Hume, and Locke, an abasement, and a depreciation of the idea of a "philosopher" for more than a century. It was AGAINST Hume that Kant uprose and raised himself; it was Locke of whom Schelling RIGHTLY said, "JE MEPRISE LOCKE"; in the struggle against the English mechanical stultification of the world, Hegel and Schopenhauer (along with Goethe) were of one accord; the two hostile brother-geniuses in philosophy, who pushed in different directions towards the opposite poles of German thought, and thereby wronged each other as only brothers will do.—What is lacking in England, and has always been lacking, that half-actor and rhetorician knew well enough, the absurd muddle-head, Carlyle, who sought to conceal under passionate grimaces what he knew about himself: namely, what was LACKING in Carlyle—real POWER of intellect, real DEPTH of intellectual perception, in short, philosophy. It is characteristic of such an unphilosophical race to hold on firmly to Christianity—they NEED its discipline for "moralizing" and humanizing. The Englishman, more gloomy, sensual, headstrong, and brutal than the German—is for that very reason, as the baser of the two, also the most pious: he has all the MORE NEED of Christianity. To finer nostrils, this English Christianity itself has still a characteristic English taint of spleen and alcoholic excess, for which, owing to good reasons, it is used as an antidote—the finer poison to neutralize the coarser:

a finer form of poisoning is in fact a step in advance with coarse-mannered people, a step towards spiritualization. The English coarseness and rustic demureness is still most satisfactorily disguised by Christian pantomime, and by praying and psalm-singing (or, more correctly, it is thereby explained and differently expressed); and for the herd of drunkards and rakes who formerly learned moral grunting under the influence of Methodism (and more recently as the "Salvation Army"), a penitential fit may really be the relatively highest manifestation of "humanity" to which they can be elevated: so much may reasonably be admitted. That, however, which offends even in the humanest Englishman is his lack of music, to speak figuratively (and also literally): he has neither rhythm nor dance in the movements of his soul and body; indeed, not even the desire for rhythm and dance, for "music." Listen to him speaking; look at the most beautiful Englishwoman WALKING—in no country on earth are there more beautiful doves and swans; finally, listen to them singing! But I ask too much...

253. There are truths which are best recognized by mediocre minds, because they are best adapted for them, there are truths which only possess charms and seductive power for mediocre spirits:—one is pushed to this probably unpleasant conclusion, now that the influence of respectable but mediocre Englishmen—I may mention Darwin, John Stuart Mill, and Herbert

Spencer—begins to gain the ascendancy in the middle-class region of European taste. Indeed, who could doubt that it is a useful thing for SUCH minds to have the ascendancy for a time? It would be an error to consider the highly developed and independently soaring minds as specially qualified for determining and collecting many little common facts, and deducing conclusions from them; as exceptions, they are rather from the first in no very favourable position towards those who are "the rules." After all, they have more to do than merely to perceive:—in effect, they have to BE something new, they have to SIGNIFY something new, they have to REPRESENT new values! The gulf between knowledge and capacity is perhaps greater, and also more mysterious, than one thinks: the capable man in the grand style, the creator, will possibly have to be an ignorant person;—while on the other hand, for scientific discoveries like those of Darwin, a certain narrowness, aridity, and industrious carefulness (in short, something English) may not be unfavourable for arriving at them.—Finally, let it not be forgotten that the English, with their profound mediocrity, brought about once before a general depression of European intelligence.

What is called "modern ideas," or "the ideas of the eighteenth century," or "French ideas"—that, consequently, against which the GERMAN mind rose up with profound disgust—is of English origin, there is no doubt about it. The French were only the apes and actors of these ideas, their best soldiers, and likewise, alas! their first and profoundest VICTIMS; for owing to the diabolical Anglomania of "modern ideas," the AME FRANCAIS has in the end become so thin and emaciated, that at present one recalls its sixteenth and seventeenth centuries, its profound, passionate strength, its inventive excellency, almost with disbelief. One must, however, maintain this verdict of historical justice in a determined manner, and defend it against present prejudices and appearances: the European NOBLESSE—of sentiment, taste, and manners, taking the word in every high sense—is the work and invention of FRANCE; the European ignobleness, the plebeianism of modern ideas—is ENGLAND'S work and invention.

254. Even at present France is still the seat of the most intellectual and refined culture of Europe, it is still the high school of taste; but one must know how to find this "France of taste." He who belongs to it keeps himself well concealed:—they may be a small number in whom it lives and is embodied, besides perhaps being men who do not stand upon the strongest legs, in part fatalists, hypochondriacs, invalids, in part persons over-indulged, over-refined, such as have the AMBITION to conceal themselves.

They have all something in common: they keep their ears closed in presence of the delirious folly and noisy spouting of the democratic BOURGEOIS. In fact, a besotted and brutalized France at present sprawls in the foreground—it recently celebrated a veritable orgy of bad taste, and at the same time of self-admiration, at the funeral of Victor Hugo. There is also something else common to them: a predilection to resist intellectual Germanizing—and a still greater inability to do so! In this France of intellect, which is also a France of pessimism, Schopenhauer has perhaps become more at home, and more indigenous than he has ever been in Germany; not to speak of Heinrich Heine, who has long ago been re-incarnated in the more refined and fastidious lyrists of Paris; or of Hegel, who at present, in the form of Taine—the FIRST of living historians—exercises an almost tyrannical influence. As regards Richard Wagner, however, the more French music learns to adapt itself to the actual needs of the AME MODERNE, the more will it "Wagnerite"; one can safely predict that beforehand,—it is already taking place sufficiently! There are, however, three things which the French can still boast of with pride as their heritage and possession, and as indelible tokens of their ancient intellectual superiority in Europe, in spite of all voluntary or involuntary Germanizing and vulgarizing of taste. FIRSTLY, the capacity for artistic emotion, for devotion to "form," for which the expression, L'ART POUR L'ART, along with numerous others, has been invented:—such capacity has not been lacking in France for three centuries; and owing to its reverence for the "small number," it has again and again made a sort of chamber music of literature possible, which is sought for in vain elsewhere in Europe.—The SECOND thing whereby the French can lay claim to a superiority over Europe is their ancient, many-sided, MORALISTIC culture, owing to which one finds on an average, even in the petty ROMANCIERS of the newspapers and chance BOULEVARDIERS DE PARIS, a psychological sensitiveness and curiosity, of which, for example, one has no conception (to say nothing of the thing itself!) in Germany. The Germans lack a couple of centuries of the moralistic work requisite thereto, which, as we have said, France has not grudged: those who call the Germans "naive" on that account give them commendation for a defect. (As the opposite of the German inexperience and innocence IN VOLUPTATE PSYCHOLOGICA, which is not too remotely associated with the tediousness of German intercourse,—and as the most successful expression of genuine French curiosity and inventive talent in this domain of delicate thrills, Henri Beyle may be noted; that remarkable anticipatory and forerunning man, who, with a Napoleonic TEMPO, traversed HIS Europe, in fact, several centuries of the European soul, as a surveyor and discoverer thereof:—it has required two generations to OVERTAKE him one way or other, to divine long afterwards some of the riddles that perplexed and enraptured him—this strange Epicurean and man of interrogation, the last great psychologist of France).—There is yet a THIRD claim to superiority: in the French character there is a successful half-way synthesis of the North and South, which makes them comprehend many things, and enjoins upon them other things, which an Englishman can never comprehend. Their temperament, turned alternately to and from the South, in which from time to time the Provencal and Ligurian blood froths over, preserves them from the dreadful, northern grey-in-grey, from sunless conceptual-spectrism and from poverty of blood—our GERMAN infirmity of taste, for the excessive prevalence of which at the present moment, blood and iron, that is to say "high politics," has with great resolution been prescribed (according to a dangerous healing art, which bids me wait and wait, but not yet hope).—There is also still in France a pre-understanding and ready welcome for those rarer and rarely gratified men, who are too comprehensive to find satisfaction in any kind of fatherlandism, and know how to love the South when in the North and the North when in the South—the born Midlanders, the "good Europeans." For them BIZET has made music, this latest genius, who has seen a new beauty and seduction,—who has discovered a piece of the SOUTH IN MUSIC.

255. I hold that many precautions should be taken against German music. Suppose a person loves the South as I love it—as a great school of recovery for the most spiritual and the most sensuous ills, as a

boundless solar profusion and effulgence which o'erspreads a sovereign existence believing in itself—well, such a person will learn to be somewhat on his guard against German music, because, in injuring his taste anew, it will also injure his health anew. Such a Southerner, a Southerner not by origin but by BELIEF, if he should dream of the future of music, must also dream of it being freed from the influence of the North; and must have in his ears the prelude to a deeper, mightier, and perhaps more perverse and mysterious music, a super-German music, which does not fade, pale, and die away, as all German music does, at the sight of the blue, wanton sea and the Mediterranean clearness of sky—a super-European music, which holds its own even in presence of the brown sunsets of the desert, whose soul is akin to the palm-tree, and can be at home and can roam with big, beautiful, lonely beasts of prey... I could imagine a music of which the rarest charm would be that it knew nothing more of good and evil; only that here and there perhaps some sailor's home-sickness, some golden shadows and tender weaknesses might sweep lightly over it; an art which, from the far distance, would see the colours of a sinking and almost incomprehensible MORAL world fleeing towards it, and would be hospitable enough and profound enough to receive such belated fugitives.

256. Owing to the morbid estrangement which the nationality-craze has induced and still induces among

the nations of Europe, owing also to the short-sighted and hasty-handed politicians, who with the help of this craze, are at present in power, and do not suspect to what extent the disintegrating policy they pursue must necessarily be only an interlude policy—owing to all this and much else that is altogether unmentionable at present, the most unmistakable signs that EUROPE WISHES TO BE ONE, are now overlooked, or arbitrarily and falsely misinterpreted. With all the more profound and large-minded men of this century, the real general tendency of the mysterious labour of their souls was to prepare the way for that new SYNTHESIS, and tentatively to anticipate the European of the future; only in their simulations, or in their weaker moments, in old age perhaps, did they belong to the "fatherlands"—they only rested from themselves when they became "patriots." I think of such men as Napoleon, Goethe, Beethoven, Stendhal, Heinrich Heine, Schopenhauer: it must not be taken amiss if I also count Richard Wagner among them, about whom one must not let oneself be deceived by his own misunderstandings (geniuses like him have seldom the right to understand themselves), still less, of course, by the unseemly noise with which he is now resisted and opposed in France: the fact remains, nevertheless, that Richard Wagner and the LATER FRENCH ROMANTICISM of the forties, are most closely and intimately related to one another. They are akin, fundamentally akin, in all the heights and depths of their requirements; it is Europe, the ONE

Europe, whose soul presses urgently and longingly, outwards and upwards, in their multifarious and boisterous art—whither? into a new light? towards a new sun? But who would attempt to express accurately what all these masters of new modes of speech could not express distinctly? It is certain that the same storm and stress tormented them, that they SOUGHT in the same manner, these last great seekers! All of them steeped in literature to their eyes and ears—the first artists of universal literary culture—for the most part even themselves writers, poets, intermediaries and blenders of the arts and the senses (Wagner, as musician is reckoned among painters, as poet among musicians, as artist generally among actors); all of them fanatics for EXPRESSION "at any cost"—I specially mention Delacroix, the nearest related to Wagner; all of them great discoverers in the realm of the sublime, also of the loathsome and dreadful, still greater discoverers in effect, in display, in the art of the show-shop; all of them talented far beyond their genius, out and out VIRTUOSI, with mysterious accesses to all that seduces, allures, constrains, and upsets; born enemies of logic and of the straight line, hankering after the strange, the exotic, the monstrous, the crooked, and the self-contradictory; as men, Tantaluses of the will, plebeian parvenus, who knew themselves to be incapable of a noble TEMPO or of a LENTO in life and action—think of Balzac, for instance,—unrestrained workers, almost destroying themselves by work;

antinomians and rebels in manners, ambitious and insatiable, without equilibrium and enjoyment; all of them finally shattering and sinking down at the Christian cross (and with right and reason, for who of them would have been sufficiently profound and sufficiently original for an ANTI-CHRISTIAN philosophy?);—on the whole, a boldly daring, splendidly overbearing, high-flying, and aloft-up-dragging class of higher men, who had first to teach their century—and it is the century of the MASSES—the conception "higher man."... Let the German friends of Richard Wagner advise together as to whether there is anything purely German in the Wagnerian art, or whether its distinction does not consist precisely in coming from SUPER-GERMAN sources and impulses: in which connection it may not be underrated how indispensable Paris was to the development of his type, which the strength of his instincts made him long to visit at the most decisive time—and how the whole style of his proceedings, of his self-apostolate, could only perfect itself in sight of the French socialistic original. On a more subtle comparison it will perhaps be found, to the honour of Richard Wagner's German nature, that he has acted in everything with more strength, daring, severity, and elevation than a nineteenth-century Frenchman could have done—owing to the circumstance that we Germans are as yet nearer to barbarism than the French;—perhaps even the most remarkable creation of Richard Wagner is not only at present, but for ever inaccessible, incomprehensible, and inimitable to the whole latter-day Latin race: the figure of Siegfried, that VERY FREE man, who is probably far too free, too hard, too cheerful, too healthy, too ANTI-CATHOLIC for the taste of old and mellow civilized nations. He may even have been a sin against Romanticism, this anti-Latin Siegfried: well, Wagner atoned amply for this sin in his old sad days, when—anticipating a taste which has meanwhile passed into politics—he began, with the religious vehemence peculiar to him, to preach, at least, THE WAY TO ROME, if not to walk therein.—That these last words may not be misunderstood, I will call to my aid a few powerful rhymes, which will even betray to less delicate ears what I mean—what I mean COUNTER TO the "last Wagner" and his Parsifal music:—

—Is this our mode?—From German heart came this vexed ululating? From German body, this self-lacerating? Is ours this priestly hand-dilation, This incense-fuming exaltation? Is ours this faltering, falling, shambling, This quite uncertain ding-dong-dangling? This sly nun-ogling, Ave-hour-bell ringing, This wholly false enraptured heaven-o'erspringing?—Is this our mode?—Think well!—ye still wait for admission—For what ye hear is ROME—ROME'S FAITH BY INTUITION!

Chapter IX

What is noble ?

257. EVERY elevation of the type "man," has hitherto been the work of an aristocratic society and so it will always be—a society believing in a long scale of gradations of rank and differences of worth among human beings, and requiring slavery in some form or other. Without the PATHOS OF DISTANCE, such as grows out of the incarnated difference of classes, out of the constant out-looking and down-looking of the ruling caste on subordinates and instruments, and out of their equally constant practice of obeying and commanding, of keeping down and keeping at a distance—that other more mysterious pathos could never have arisen, the longing for an ever new widening of distance within the soul itself, the formation of ever higher, rarer, further, more extended, more comprehensive states, in short, just the elevation of the type "man," the continued "self-surmounting of man," to use a moral formula in a supermoral sense. To be sure, one must not resign oneself to any humanitarian illusions about the history of the origin of an aristocratic society (that is to say, of the preliminary condition for the elevation of the type "man"): the truth is hard. Let us acknowledge unprejudicedly how every higher civilization hitherto has ORIGINATED! Men

with a still natural nature, barbarians in every terrible sense of the word, men of prey, still in possession of unbroken strength of will and desire for power, threw themselves upon weaker, more moral, more peaceful races (perhaps trading or cattle-rearing communities), or upon old mellow civilizations in which the final vital force was flickering out in brilliant fireworks of wit and depravity. At the commencement, the noble caste was always the barbarian caste: their superiority did not consist first of all in their physical, but in their psychical power—they were more COMPLETE men (which at every point also implies the same as "more complete beasts").

258. Corruption—as the indication that anarchy threatens to break out among the instincts, and that the foundation of the emotions, called "life," is convulsed—is something radically different according to the organization in which it manifests itself. When, for instance, an aristocracy like that of France at the beginning of the Revolution, flung away its privileges with sublime disgust and sacrificed itself to an excess of its moral sentiments, it was corruption:—it was really only the closing act of the corruption which had existed for centuries, by virtue of which that aristocracy had abdicated step by step its lordly prerogatives and lowered itself to a FUNCTION of royalty (in the end even to its decoration and parade-dress). The essential thing, however, in a good and healthy aristocracy is that

it should not regard itself as a function either of the kingship or the commonwealth, but as the SIGNIFICANCE and highest justification thereof—that it should therefore accept with a good conscience the sacrifice of a legion of individuals, who, FOR ITS SAKE, must be suppressed and reduced to imperfect men, to slaves and instruments. Its fundamental belief must be precisely that society is NOT allowed to exist for its own sake, but only as a foundation and scaffolding, by means of which a select class of beings may be able to elevate themselves to their higher duties, and in general to a higher EXISTENCE: like those sun-seeking climbing plants in Java—they are called Sipo Matador,—which encircle an oak so long and so often with their arms, until at last, high above it, but supported by it, they can unfold their tops in the open light, and exhibit their happiness.

259. To refrain mutually from injury, from violence, from exploitation, and put one's will on a par with that of others: this may result in a certain rough sense in good conduct among individuals when the necessary conditions are given (namely, the actual similarity of the individuals in amount of force and degree of worth, and their co-relation within one organization). As soon, however, as one wished to take this principle more generally, and if possible even as the FUNDAMENTAL PRINCIPLE OF SOCIETY, it would immediately disclose what it really is—namely,

a Will to the DENIAL of life, a principle of dissolution and decay. Here one must think profoundly to the very basis and resist all sentimental weakness: life itself is ESSENTIALLY appropriation, injury, conquest of the strange and weak, suppression, severity, obtrusion of peculiar forms, incorporation, and at the least, putting it mildest, exploitation;—but why should one for ever use precisely these words on which for ages a disparaging purpose has been stamped? Even the organization within which, as was previously supposed, the individuals treat each other as equal—it takes place in every healthy aristocracy—must itself, if it be a living and not a dying organization, do all that towards other bodies, which the individuals within it refrain from doing to each other it will have to be the incarnated Will to Power, it will endeavour to grow, to gain ground, attract to itself and acquire ascendancy—not owing to any morality or immorality, but because it LIVES, and because life IS precisely Will to Power. On no point, however, is the ordinary consciousness of Europeans more unwilling to be corrected than on this matter, people now rave everywhere, even under the guise of science, about coming conditions of society in which "the exploiting character" is to be absent—that sounds to my ears as if they promised to invent a mode of life which should refrain from all organic functions. "Exploitation" does not belong to a depraved, or imperfect and primitive society it belongs to the nature of the living being as a primary organic function, it is a consequence of the intrinsic Will to Power, which is precisely the Will to Life—Granting that as a theory this is a novelty—as a reality it is the FUNDAMENTAL FACT of all history let us be so far honest towards ourselves!

260. In a tour through the many finer and coarser moralities which have hitherto prevailed or still prevail on the earth, I found certain traits recurring regularly together, and connected with one another, until finally two primary types revealed themselves to me, and a radical distinction was brought to light. There is MASTER-MORALITY and SLAVE-MORALITY,—I would at once add, however, that in all higher and mixed civilizations, there are also attempts at the reconciliation of the two moralities, but one finds still oftener the confusion and mutual misunderstanding of them, indeed sometimes their close juxtaposition—even in the same man, within one soul. The distinctions of moral values have either originated in a ruling caste, pleasantly conscious of being different from the ruled—or among the ruled class, the slaves and dependents of all sorts. In the first case, when it is the rulers who determine the conception "good," it is the exalted, proud disposition which is regarded as the distinguishing feature, and that which determines the order of rank. The noble type of man separates from himself the beings in whom the opposite of this exalted, proud disposition displays itself he despises them. Let it

at once be noted that in this first kind of morality the antithesis "good" and "bad" means practically the same as "noble" and "despicable",—the antithesis "good" and "EVIL" is of a different origin. The cowardly, the timid, the insignificant, and those thinking merely of narrow utility are despised; moreover, also, the distrustful, with their constrained glances, the self-abasing, the dog-like kind of men who let themselves be abused, the mendicant flatterers, and above all the liars:—it is a fundamental belief of all aristocrats that the common people are untruthful. "We truthful ones"—the nobility in ancient Greece called themselves. It is obvious that everywhere the designations of moral value were at first applied to MEN; and were only derivatively and at a later period applied to ACTIONS; it is a gross mistake, therefore, when historians of morals start with questions like, "Why have sympathetic actions been praised?" The noble type of man regards HIMSELF as a determiner of values; he does not require to be approved of; he passes the judgment: "What is injurious to me is injurious in itself;" he knows that it is he himself only who confers honour on things; he is a CREATOR OF VALUES. He honours whatever he recognizes in himself: such morality equals self-glorification. In the foreground there is the feeling of plenitude, of power, which seeks to overflow, the happiness of high tension, the consciousness of a wealth which would fain give and bestow:—the noble man also helps the unfortunate, but not—or scarcely—out of pity, but rather from an impulse generated by the super-abundance of power. The noble man honours in himself the powerful one, him also who has power over himself, who knows how to speak and how to keep silence, who takes pleasure in subjecting himself to severity and hardness, and has reverence for all that is severe and hard. "Wotan placed a hard heart in my breast," says an old Scandinavian Saga: it is thus rightly expressed from the soul of a proud Viking. Such a type of man is even proud of not being made for sympathy; the hero of the Saga therefore adds warningly: "He who has not a hard heart when young, will never have one." The noble and brave who think thus are the furthest removed from the morality which sees precisely in sympathy, or in acting for the good of others, or in DESINTERESSEMENT, the characteristic of the moral; faith in oneself, pride in oneself, a radical enmity and irony towards "selflessness," belong as definitely to noble morality, as do a careless scorn and precaution in presence of sympathy and the "warm heart."—It is the powerful who KNOW how to honour, it is their art, their domain for invention. The profound reverence for age and for tradition—all law rests on this double reverence,—the belief and prejudice in favour of ancestors and unfavourable to newcomers, is typical in the morality of the powerful; and if, reversely, men of "modern ideas" believe almost instinctively in "progress" and the "future," and are more and more lacking in respect for old age, the ignoble origin of these "ideas" has complacently betrayed itself thereby. A morality of the ruling class, however, is more especially foreign and irritating to present-day taste in the sternness of its principle that one has duties only to one's equals; that one may act towards beings of a lower rank, towards all that is foreign, just as seems good to one, or "as the heart desires," and in any case "beyond good and evil": it is here that sympathy and similar sentiments can have a place. The ability and obligation to exercise prolonged gratitude and prolonged revenge—both only within the circle of equals,—artfulness in retaliation, RAFFINEMENT of the idea in friendship, a certain necessity to have enemies (as outlets for the emotions of envy, quarrelsomeness, arrogance—in fact, in order to be a good FRIEND): all these are typical characteristics of the noble morality, which, as has been pointed out, is not the morality of "modern ideas," and is therefore at present difficult to realize, and also to unearth and disclose.—It is otherwise with the second type of morality, SLAVE-MORALITY. Supposing that the abused, the oppressed, the suffering, the unemancipated, the weary, and those uncertain of themselves should moralize, what will be the common element in their moral estimates? Probably a pessimistic suspicion with regard to the entire situation of man will find expression, perhaps a condemnation of man, together with his situation. The slave has an unfavourable eye for the virtues of the powerful; he has a skepticism and distrust, a REFINEMENT of distrust of everything "good" that is there honoured—he would fain persuade himself that the very happiness there is not genuine. On the other hand, THOSE qualities which serve to alleviate the existence of sufferers are brought into prominence and flooded with light; it is here that sympathy, the kind, helping hand, the warm heart, patience, diligence, humility, and friendliness attain to honour; for here these are the most useful qualities, and almost the only means of supporting the burden of existence. Slave-morality is essentially the morality of utility. Here is the seat of the origin of the famous antithesis "good" and "evil":—power and dangerousness are assumed to reside in the evil, a certain dreadfulness, subtlety, and strength, which do not admit of being despised. According to slave-morality, therefore, the "evil" man arouses fear; according to master-morality, it is precisely the "good" man who arouses fear and seeks to arouse it, while the bad man is regarded as the despicable being. The contrast attains its maximum when, in accordance with the logical consequences of slave-morality, a shade of depreciation—it may be slight and well-intentioned—at last attaches itself to the "good" man of this morality; because, according to the servile mode of thought, the good man must in any case be the SAFE man: he is good-natured, easily deceived, perhaps a little stupid, un bonhomme. Everywhere that slave-morality gains the ascendancy, language shows a tendency to approximate the significations of the words "good" and "stupid."—A last fundamental difference: the desire for FREEDOM, the instinct for happiness and the refinements of the feeling of liberty belong as necessarily to slave-morals and morality, as artifice and enthusiasm in reverence and devotion are the regular symptoms of an aristocratic mode of thinking and estimating.—Hence we can understand without further detail why love AS A PASSION—it is our European specialty—must absolutely be of noble origin; as is well known, its invention is due to the Provencal poet-cavaliers, those brilliant, ingenious men of the "gai saber," to whom Europe owes so much, and almost owes itself.

261. Vanity is one of the things which are perhaps most difficult for a noble man to understand: he will be tempted to deny it, where another kind of man thinks he sees it self-evidently. The problem for him is to represent to his mind beings who seek to arouse a good opinion of themselves which they themselves do not possess—and consequently also do not "deserve,"—and who yet BELIEVE in this good opinion afterwards. This seems to him on the one hand such bad taste and so self-disrespectful, and on the other hand so grotesquely unreasonable, that he would like to consider vanity an exception, and is doubtful about it in most cases when it is spoken of. He will say, for instance: "I may be mistaken about my value, and on

the other hand may nevertheless demand that my value should be acknowledged by others precisely as I rate it:—that, however, is not vanity (but self-conceit, or, in most cases, that which is called 'humility,' and also 'modesty')." Or he will even say: "For many reasons I can delight in the good opinion of others, perhaps because I love and honour them, and rejoice in all their joys, perhaps also because their good opinion endorses and strengthens my belief in my own good opinion, perhaps because the good opinion of others, even in cases where I do not share it, is useful to me, or gives promise of usefulness:—all this, however, is not vanity." The man of noble character must first bring it home forcibly to his mind, especially with the aid of history, that, from time immemorial, in all social strata in any way dependent, the ordinary man WAS only that which he PASSED FOR:—not being at all accustomed to fix values, he did not assign even to himself any other value than that which his master assigned to him (it is the peculiar RIGHT OF MASTERS to create values). It may be looked upon as the result of an extraordinary atavism, that the ordinary man, even at present, is still always WAITING for an opinion about himself, and then instinctively submitting himself to it; yet by no means only to a "good" opinion, but also to a bad and unjust one (think, for instance, of the greater part of the self-appreciations and self-depreciations which believing women learn from their confessors, and which in general the believing Christian learns from his Church). In fact, conformably to the slow rise of the democratic social order (and its cause, the blending of the blood of masters and slaves), the originally noble and rare impulse of the masters to assign a value to themselves and to "think well" of themselves, will now be more and more encouraged and extended; but it has at all times an older, ampler, and more radically ingrained propensity opposed to it—and in the phenomenon of "vanity" this older propensity overmasters the younger. The vain person rejoices over EVERY good opinion which he hears about himself (quite apart from the point of view of its usefulness, and equally regardless of its truth or falsehood), just as he suffers from every bad opinion: for he subjects himself to both, he feels himself subjected to both, by that oldest instinct of subjection which breaks forth in him.—It is "the slave" in the vain man's blood, the remains of the slave's craftiness—and how much of the "slave" is still left in woman, for instance!—which seeks to SEDUCE to good opinions of itself; it is the slave, too, who immediately afterwards falls prostrate himself before these opinions, as though he had not called them forth.—And to repeat it again: vanity is an atavism.

262. A SPECIES originates, and a type becomes established and strong in the long struggle with essentially constant UNFAVOURABLE conditions. On the other hand, it is known by the experience of

breeders that species which receive super-abundant nourishment, and in general a surplus of protection and care, immediately tend in the most marked way to develop variations, and are fertile in prodigies and monstrosities (also in monstrous vices). Now look at an aristocratic commonwealth, say an ancient Greek polis, or Venice, as a voluntary or involuntary contrivance for the purpose of REARING human beings; there are there men beside one another, thrown upon their own resources, who want to make their species prevail, chiefly because they MUST prevail, or else run the terrible danger of being exterminated. The favour, the super-abundance, the protection are there lacking under which variations are fostered; the species needs itself as species, as something which, precisely by virtue of its hardness, its uniformity, and simplicity of structure, can in general prevail and make itself permanent in constant struggle with its neighbours, or with rebellious or rebellion-threatening vassals. The most varied experience teaches it what are the qualities to which it principally owes the fact that it still exists, in spite of all Gods and men, and has hitherto been victorious: these qualities it calls virtues, and these virtues alone it develops to maturity. It does so with severity, indeed it desires severity; every aristocratic morality is intolerant in the education of youth, in the control of women, in the marriage customs, in the relations of old and young, in the penal laws (which have an eye only for the degenerating): it counts intolerance itself among the virtues, under the name of "justice." A type with few, but very marked features, a species of severe, warlike, wisely silent, reserved, and reticent men (and as such, with the most delicate sensibility for the charm and nuances of society) is thus established, unaffected by the vicissitudes of generations; the constant struggle with uniform UNFAVOURABLE conditions is, as already remarked, the cause of a type becoming stable and hard. Finally, however, a happy state of things results, the enormous tension is relaxed; there are perhaps no more enemies among the neighbouring peoples, and the means of life, even of the enjoyment of life, are present in superabundance. With one stroke the bond and constraint of the old discipline severs: it is no longer regarded as necessary, as a condition of existence—if it would continue, it can only do so as a form of LUXURY, as an archaizing TASTE. Variations, whether they be deviations (into the higher, finer, and rarer), or deteriorations and monstrosities, appear suddenly on the scene in the greatest exuberance and splendour; the individual dares to be individual and detach himself. At this turning-point of history there manifest themselves, side by side, and often mixed and entangled together, a magnificent, manifold, virgin-forest-like up-growth and up-striving, a kind of TROPICAL TEMPO in the rivalry of growth, and an extraordinary decay and self-destruction, owing to the savagely opposing and seemingly exploding egoisms, which strive with one another "for sun and light," and can no longer assign any limit, restraint, or forbearance for themselves by means of the hitherto existing morality. It was this morality itself which piled up the strength so enormously, which bent the bow in so threatening a manner:—it is now "out of date," it is getting "out of date." The dangerous and disquieting point has been reached when the greater, more manifold, more comprehensive life IS LIVED BEYOND the old morality; the "individual" stands out, and is obliged to have recourse to his own law-giving, his own arts and artifices for self-preservation, self-elevation, and self-deliverance. Nothing but new "Whys," nothing but new "Hows," no common formulas any longer, misunderstanding and disregard in league with each other, decay, deterioration, and the loftiest desires frightfully entangled, the genius of the race overflowing from all the cornucopias of good and bad, a portentous simultaneousness of Spring and Autumn, full of new charms and mysteries peculiar to the fresh, still inexhausted, still unwearied corruption. Danger is again present, the mother of morality, great danger; this time shifted into the individual, into the neighbour and friend, into the street, into their own child, into their own heart, into all the most personal and secret recesses of their desires and volitions. What will the moral philosophers who appear at this time have to preach? They discover, these sharp onlookers and loafers, that the end is quickly approaching, that everything around them decays and produces decay, that nothing will endure until the day after tomorrow, except one species of man, the incurably MEDIOCRE. The mediocre alone have a prospect of continuing and propagating themselves—they will be the men of the future, the sole survivors; "be like them! become mediocre!" is now the only morality which has still a significance, which still obtains a hearing.—But it is difficult to preach this morality of mediocrity! it can never avow what it is and what it desires! it has to talk of moderation and dignity and duty and brotherly love—it will have difficulty IN CONCEALING ITS IRONY!

263. There is an INSTINCT FOR RANK, which more than anything else is already the sign of a HIGH rank; there is a DELIGHT in the NUANCES of reverence which leads one to infer noble origin and habits. The refinement, goodness, and loftiness of a soul are put to a perilous test when something passes by that is of the highest rank, but is not yet protected by the awe of authority from obtrusive touches and incivilities: something that goes its way like a living touchstone, undistinguished, undiscovered, and tentative, perhaps voluntarily veiled and disguised. He whose task and practice it is to investigate souls, will avail himself of many varieties of this very art to determine the ultimate value of a soul, the unalterable, innate order of rank to which it belongs: he will test it by its INSTINCT FOR REVERENCE. DIFFERENCE

ENGENDRE HAINE: the vulgarity of many a nature spurts up suddenly like dirty water, when any holy vessel, any jewel from closed shrines, any book bearing the marks of great destiny, is brought before it; while on the other hand, there is an involuntary silence, a hesitation of the eye, a cessation of all gestures, by which it is indicated that a soul FEELS the nearness of what is worthiest of respect. The way in which, on the whole, the reverence for the BIBLE has hitherto been maintained in Europe, is perhaps the best example of discipline and refinement of manners which Europe owes to Christianity: books of such profoundness and supreme significance require for their protection an external tyranny of authority, in order to acquire the PERIOD of thousands of years which is necessary to exhaust and unriddle them. Much has been achieved when the sentiment has been at last instilled into the masses (the shallow-pates and the boobies of every kind) that they are not allowed to touch everything, that there are holy experiences before which they must take off their shoes and keep away the unclean hand—it is almost their highest advance towards humanity. On the contrary, in the so-called cultured classes, the believers in "modern ideas," nothing is perhaps so repulsive as their lack of shame, the easy insolence of eye and hand with which they touch, taste, and finger everything; and it is possible that even yet there is more RELATIVE nobility of taste, and more tact for reverence among the people, among the lower classes of the people, especially among peasants, than among the newspaper-reading DEMIMONDE of intellect, the cultured class.

264. It cannot be effaced from a man's soul what his ancestors have preferably and most constantly done: whether they were perhaps diligent economizers attached to a desk and a cash-box, modest and citizen-like in their desires, modest also in their virtues; or whether they were accustomed to commanding from morning till night, fond of rude pleasures and probably of still ruder duties and responsibilities; or whether, finally, at one time or another, they have sacrificed old privileges of birth and possession, in order to live wholly for their faith—for their "God,"—as men of an inexorable and sensitive conscience, which blushes at every compromise. It is quite impossible for a man NOT to have the qualities and predilections of his parents and ancestors in his constitution, whatever appearances may suggest to the contrary. This is the problem of race. Granted that one knows something of the parents, it is admissible to draw a conclusion about the child: any kind of offensive incontinence, any kind of sordid envy, or of clumsy self-vaunting—the three things which together have constituted the genuine plebeian type in all times—such must pass over to the child, as surely as bad blood; and with the help of the best education and culture one will only succeed in DECEIVING with regard to such heredity.—And what else does education and culture try to do nowadays! In

our very democratic, or rather, very plebeian age, "education" and "culture" MUST be essentially the art of deceiving—deceiving with regard to origin, with regard to the inherited plebeianism in body and soul. An educator who nowadays preached truthfulness above everything else, and called out constantly to his pupils: "Be true! Be natural! Show yourselves as you are!"—even such a virtuous and sincere ass would learn in a short time to have recourse to the FURCA of Horace, NATURAM EXPELLERE: with what results? "Plebeianism" USQUE RECURRET. [FOOTNOTE: Horace's "Epistles," I. x. 24.]

265. At the risk of displeasing innocent ears, I submit that egoism belongs to the essence of a noble soul, I mean the unalterable belief that to a being such as "we," other beings must naturally be in subjection, and have to sacrifice themselves. The noble soul accepts the fact of his egoism without question, and also without consciousness of harshness, constraint, or arbitrariness therein, but rather as something that may have its basis in the primary law of things:—if he sought a designation for it he would say: "It is justice itself." He acknowledges under certain circumstances, which made him hesitate at first, that there are other equally privileged ones; as soon as he has settled this question of rank, he moves among those equals and equally privileged ones with the same assurance, as regards modesty and delicate respect, which he enjoys in

intercourse with himself—in accordance with an innate heavenly mechanism which all the stars understand. It is an ADDITIONAL instance of his egoism, this artfulness and self-limitation in intercourse with his equals—every star is a similar egoist; he honours HIMSELF in them, and in the rights which he concedes to them, he has no doubt that the exchange of honours and rights, as the ESSENCE of all intercourse, belongs also to the natural condition of things. The noble soul gives as he takes, prompted by the passionate and sensitive instinct of requital, which is at the root of his nature. The notion of "favour" has, INTER PARES, neither significance nor good repute; there may be a sublime way of letting gifts as it were light upon one from above, and of drinking them thirstily like dew-drops; but for those arts and displays the noble soul has no aptitude. His egoism hinders him here: in general, he looks "aloft" unwillingly—he looks either FORWARD, horizontally and deliberately, or downwards—HE KNOWS THAT HE IS ON A HEIGHT.

266. "One can only truly esteem him who does not LOOK OUT FOR himself."—Goethe to Rath Schlosser.

267. The Chinese have a proverb which mothers even teach their children: "SIAO-SIN" ("MAKE THY HEART SMALL"). This is the essentially fundamental tendency in latter-day civilizations. I have no doubt that

an ancient Greek, also, would first of all remark the self-dwarfing in us Europeans of today—in this respect alone we should immediately be "distasteful" to him.

268. What, after all, is ignobleness?—Words are vocal symbols for ideas; ideas, however, are more or less definite mental symbols for frequently returning and concurring sensations, for groups of sensations. It is not sufficient to use the same words in order to understand one another: we must also employ the same words for the same kind of internal experiences, we must in the end have experiences IN COMMON. On this account the people of one nation understand one another better than those belonging to different nations, even when they use the same language; or rather, when people have lived long together under similar conditions (of climate, soil, danger, requirement, toil) there ORIGINATES therefrom an entity that "understands itself"—namely, a nation. In all souls a like number of frequently recurring experiences have gained the upper hand over those occurring more rarely: about these matters people understand one another rapidly and always more rapidly—the history of language is the history of a process of abbreviation; on the basis of this quick comprehension people always unite closer and closer. The greater the danger, the greater is the need of agreeing quickly and readily about what is necessary; not to misunderstand one another in danger—that is what cannot at all be

dispensed with in intercourse. Also in all loves and friendships one has the experience that nothing of the kind continues when the discovery has been made that in using the same words, one of the two parties has feelings, thoughts, intuitions, wishes, or fears different from those of the other. (The fear of the "eternal misunderstanding": that is the good genius which so often keeps persons of different sexes from too hasty attachments, to which sense and heart prompt them—and NOT some Schopenhauerian "genius of the species"!) Whichever groups of sensations within a soul awaken most readily, begin to speak, and give the word of command—these decide as to the general order of rank of its values, and determine ultimately its list of desirable things. A man's estimates of value betray something of the STRUCTURE of his soul, and wherein it sees its conditions of life, its intrinsic needs. Supposing now that necessity has from all time drawn together only such men as could express similar requirements and similar experiences by similar symbols, it results on the whole that the easy COMMUNICABILITY of need, which implies ultimately the undergoing only of average and COMMON experiences, must have been the most potent of all the forces which have hitherto operated upon mankind. The more similar, the more ordinary people, have always had and are still having the advantage; the more select, more refined, more unique, and difficultly comprehensible, are liable to stand alone; they succumb to accidents in their isolation, and seldom propagate themselves. One must appeal to immense opposing forces, in order to thwart this natural, all-too-natural PROGRESSUS IN SIMILE, the evolution of man to the similar, the ordinary, the average, the gregarious—to the IGNOBLE—!

269. The more a psychologist—a born, an unavoidable psychologist and soul-diviner—turns his attention to the more select cases and individuals, the greater is his danger of being suffocated by sympathy: he NEEDS sternness and cheerfulness more than any other man. For the corruption, the ruination of higher men, of the more unusually constituted souls, is in fact, the rule: it is dreadful to have such a rule always before one's eyes. The manifold torment of the psychologist who has discovered this ruination, who discovers once, and then discovers ALMOST repeatedly throughout all history, this universal inner "desperateness" of higher men, this eternal "too late!" in every sense—may perhaps one day be the cause of his turning with bitterness against his own lot, and of his making an attempt at self-destruction—of his "going to ruin" himself. One may perceive in almost every psychologist a tell-tale inclination for delightful intercourse with commonplace and well-ordered men; the fact is thereby disclosed that he always requires healing, that he needs a sort of flight and forgetfulness, away from what his insight and incisiveness—from

what his "business"—has laid upon his conscience. The fear of his memory is peculiar to him. He is easily silenced by the judgment of others; he hears with unmoved countenance how people honour, admire, love, and glorify, where he has PERCEIVED—or he even conceals his silence by expressly assenting to some plausible opinion. Perhaps the paradox of his situation becomes so dreadful that, precisely where he has learnt GREAT SYMPATHY, together with great CONTEMPT, the multitude, the educated, and the visionaries, have on their part learnt great reverence—reverence for "great men" and marvelous animals, for the sake of whom one blesses and honours the fatherland, the earth, the dignity of mankind, and one's own self, to whom one points the young, and in view of whom one educates them. And who knows but in all great instances hitherto just the same happened: that the multitude worshipped a God, and that the "God" was only a poor sacrificial animal! SUCCESS has always been the greatest liar—and the "work" itself is a success; the great statesman, the conqueror, the discoverer, are disguised in their creations until they are unrecognizable; the "work" of the artist, of the philosopher, only invents him who has created it, is REPUTED to have created it; the "great men," as they are reverenced, are poor little fictions composed afterwards; in the world of historical values spurious coinage PREVAILS. Those great poets, for example, such as Byron, Musset, Poe, Leopardi, Kleist, Gogol (I do not venture to mention much greater names, but I have them in my mind), as they now appear, and were perhaps obliged to be: men of the moment, enthusiastic, sensuous, and childish, light-minded and impulsive in their trust and distrust; with souls in which usually some flaw has to be concealed; often taking revenge with their works for an internal defilement, often seeking forgetfulness in their soaring from a too true memory, often lost in the mud and almost in love with it, until they become like the Will-o'-the-Wisps around the swamps, and PRETEND TO BE stars—the people then call them idealists,—often struggling with protracted disgust, with an ever-reappearing phantom of disbelief, which makes them cold, and obliges them to languish for GLORIA and devour "faith as it is" out of the hands of intoxicated adulators:—what a TORMENT these great artists are and the so-called higher men in general, to him who has once found them out! It is thus conceivable that it is just from woman—who is clairvoyant in the world of suffering, and also unfortunately eager to help and save to an extent far beyond her powers—that THEY have learnt so readily those outbreaks of boundless devoted SYMPATHY, which the multitude, above all the reverent multitude, do not understand, and overwhelm with prying and self-gratifying interpretations. This sympathizing invariably deceives itself as to its power; woman would like to believe that love can do EVERYTHING—it is the SUPERSTITION peculiar to her. Alas, he who knows the heart finds out how poor, helpless, pretentious, and blundering even the best and deepest love is—he finds that it rather DESTROYS than saves!—It is possible that under the holy fable and travesty of the life of Jesus there is hidden one of the most painful cases of the martyrdom of KNOWLEDGE ABOUT LOVE: the martyrdom of the most innocent and most craving heart, that never had enough of any human love, that DEMANDED love, that demanded inexorably and frantically to be loved and nothing else, with terrible outbursts against those who refused him their love; the story of a poor soul insatiated and insatiable in love, that had to invent hell to send thither those who WOULD NOT love him—and that at last, enlightened about human love, had to invent a God who is entire love, entire CAPACITY for love—who takes pity on human love, because it is so paltry, so ignorant! He who has such sentiments, he who has such KNOWLEDGE about love—SEEKS for death!—But why should one deal with such painful matters? Provided, of course, that one is not obliged to do so.

270. The intellectual haughtiness and loathing of every man who has suffered deeply—it almost determines the order of rank HOW deeply men can suffer—the chilling certainty, with which he is thoroughly imbued and coloured, that by virtue of his suffering he KNOWS MORE than the shrewdest and wisest can ever know, that he has been familiar with,

and "at home" in, many distant, dreadful worlds of which "YOU know nothing"!—this silent intellectual haughtiness of the sufferer, this pride of the elect of knowledge, of the "initiated," of the almost sacrificed, finds all forms of disguise necessary to protect itself from contact with officious and sympathizing hands, and in general from all that is not its equal in suffering. Profound suffering makes noble: it separates.—One of the most refined forms of disguise is Epicurism, along with a certain ostentatious boldness of taste, which takes suffering lightly, and puts itself on the defensive against all that is sorrowful and profound. They are "gay men" who make use of gaiety, because they are misunderstood on account of it—they WISH to be misunderstood. There are "scientific minds" who make use of science, because it gives a gay appearance, and because scientificness leads to the conclusion that a person is superficial—they WISH to mislead to a false conclusion. There are free insolent minds which would fain conceal and deny that they are broken, proud, incurable hearts (the cynicism of Hamlet—the case of Galiani); and occasionally folly itself is the mask of an unfortunate OVER-ASSURED knowledge.—From which it follows that it is the part of a more refined humanity to have reverence "for the mask," and not to make use of psychology and curiosity in the wrong place.

271. That which separates two men most profoundly is a different sense and grade of purity. What does it matter about all their honesty and reciprocal usefulness, what does it matter about all their mutual good-will: the fact still remains—they "cannot smell each other!" The highest instinct for purity places him who is affected with it in the most extraordinary and dangerous isolation, as a saint: for it is just holiness—the highest spiritualization of the instinct in question. Any kind of cognizance of an indescribable excess in the joy of the bath, any kind of ardour or thirst which perpetually impels the soul out of night into the morning, and out of gloom, out of "affliction" into clearness, brightness, depth, and refinement:—just as much as such a tendency DISTINGUISHES—it is a noble tendency—it also SEPARATES.—The pity of the saint is pity for the FILTH of the human, all-too-human. And there are grades and heights where pity itself is regarded by him as impurity, as filth.

272. Signs of nobility: never to think of lowering our duties to the rank of duties for everybody; to be unwilling to renounce or to share our responsibilities; to count our prerogatives, and the exercise of them, among our DUTIES.

273. A man who strives after great things, looks upon every one whom he encounters on his way either as a means of advance, or a delay and hindrance—or as a

temporary resting-place. His peculiar lofty BOUNTY to his fellow-men is only possible when he attains his elevation and dominates. Impatience, and the consciousness of being always condemned to comedy up to that time—for even strife is a comedy, and conceals the end, as every means does—spoil all intercourse for him; this kind of man is acquainted with solitude, and what is most poisonous in it.

274. THE PROBLEM OF THOSE WHO WAIT.—Happy chances are necessary, and many incalculable elements, in order that a higher man in whom the solution of a problem is dormant, may yet take action, or "break forth," as one might say—at the right moment. On an average it DOES NOT happen; and in all corners of the earth there are waiting ones sitting who hardly know to what extent they are waiting, and still less that they wait in vain. Occasionally, too, the waking call comes too late—the chance which gives "permission" to take action—when their best youth, and strength for action have been used up in sitting still; and how many a one, just as he "sprang up," has found with horror that his limbs are benumbed and his spirits are now too heavy! "It is too late," he has said to himself—and has become self-distrustful and henceforth for ever useless.—In the domain of genius, may not the "Raphael without hands" (taking the expression in its widest sense) perhaps not be the exception, but the rule?—Perhaps genius is by no

means so rare: but rather the five hundred HANDS which it requires in order to tyrannize over the [GREEK INSERTED HERE], "the right time"—in order to take chance by the forelock!

275. He who does not WISH to see the height of a man, looks all the more sharply at what is low in him, and in the foreground—and thereby betrays himself.

276. In all kinds of injury and loss the lower and coarser soul is better off than the nobler soul: the dangers of the latter must be greater, the probability that it will come to grief and perish is in fact immense, considering the multiplicity of the conditions of its existence.—In a lizard a finger grows again which has been lost; not so in man.—

277. It is too bad! Always the old story! When a man has finished building his house, he finds that he has learnt unawares something which he OUGHT absolutely to have known before he—began to build. The eternal, fatal "Too late!" The melancholia of everything COMPLETED—!

278.—Wanderer, who art thou? I see thee follow thy path without scorn, without love, with unfathomable eyes, wet and sad as a plummet which has returned to the light insatiated out of every depth—what did it seek down there?—with a bosom that never sighs, with lips that conceal their loathing, with a hand which only slowly grasps: who art thou? what hast thou done? Rest thee here: this place has hospitality for every one—refresh thyself! And whoever thou art, what is it that now pleases thee? What will serve to refresh thee? Only name it, whatever I have I offer thee! "To refresh me? To refresh me? Oh, thou prying one, what sayest thou! But give me, I pray thee—-" What? what? Speak out! "Another mask! A second mask!"

279. Men of profound sadness betray themselves when they are happy: they have a mode of seizing upon happiness as though they would choke and strangle it, out of jealousy—ah, they know only too well that it will flee from them!

280. "Bad! Bad! What? Does he not—go back?" Yes! But you misunderstand him when you complain about it. He goes back like every one who is about to make a great spring.

281.—"Will people believe it of me? But I insist that they believe it of me: I have always thought very unsatisfactorily of myself and about myself, only in very rare cases, only compulsorily, always without delight in 'the subject,' ready to digress from 'myself,' and always without faith in the result, owing to an unconquerable distrust of the POSSIBILITY of self-knowledge, which has led me so far as to feel a CONTRADICTIO IN ADJECTO even in the idea of 'direct knowledge' which theorists allow themselves:—this matter of fact is almost the most certain thing I know about myself. There must be a sort of repugnance in me to BELIEVE anything definite about myself.—Is there perhaps some enigma therein? Probably; but fortunately nothing for my own teeth.—Perhaps it betrays the species to which I belong?—but not to myself, as is sufficiently agreeable to me."

282.—"But what has happened to you?"—"I do not know," he said, hesitatingly; "perhaps the Harpies have flown over my table."—It sometimes happens nowadays that a gentle, sober, retiring man becomes suddenly mad, breaks the plates, upsets the table, shrieks, raves, and shocks everybody—and finally withdraws, ashamed, and raging at himself—whither? for what purpose? To famish apart? To suffocate with his memories?—To him who has the desires of a lofty and dainty soul, and only seldom finds his table laid and his food prepared, the danger will always be great—nowadays, however, it is extraordinarily so. Thrown into the midst of a noisy and plebeian age, with which he does not like to eat out of the same dish, he may readily perish of hunger and thirst—or, should he nevertheless finally "fall to," of sudden nausea.—We have probably all sat at tables to which we did not belong; and precisely the most spiritual of us, who are most difficult to nourish, know the dangerous DYSPEPSIA which originates from a sudden insight and disillusionment about our food and our messmates—the AFTER-DINNER NAUSEA.

283. If one wishes to praise at all, it is a delicate and at the same time a noble self-control, to praise only where one DOES NOT agree—otherwise in fact one would praise oneself, which is contrary to good taste:—a self-control, to be sure, which offers excellent opportunity and provocation to constant MISUNDERSTANDING. To be able to allow oneself this veritable luxury of taste and morality, one must not live among intellectual imbeciles, but rather among men whose misunderstandings and mistakes amuse by their refinement—or one will have to pay dearly for it!—"He praises me, THEREFORE he acknowledges me to be right"—this asinine method of inference spoils half of the life of us recluses, for it brings the asses into our neighbourhood and friendship.

284. To live in a vast and proud tranquility; always beyond... To have, or not to have, one's emotions, one's For and Against, according to choice; to lower oneself to them for hours; to SEAT oneself on them as upon horses, and often as upon asses:—for one must know how to make use of their stupidity as well as of their fire. To conserve one's three hundred foregrounds; also

one's black spectacles: for there are circumstances when nobody must look into our eyes, still less into our "motives." And to choose for company that roguish and cheerful vice, politeness. And to remain master of one's four virtues, courage, insight, sympathy, and solitude. For solitude is a virtue with us, as a sublime bent and bias to purity, which divines that in the contact of man and man—"in society"—it must be unavoidably impure. All society makes one somehow, somewhere, or sometime—"commonplace."

285. The greatest events and thoughts—the greatest thoughts, however, are the greatest events—are longest in being comprehended: the generations which are contemporary with them do not EXPERIENCE such events—they live past them. Something happens there as in the realm of stars. The light of the furthest stars is longest in reaching man; and before it has arrived man DENIES—that there are stars there. "How many centuries does a mind require to be understood?"—that is also a standard, one also makes a gradation of rank and an etiquette therewith, such as is necessary for mind and for star.

286. "Here is the prospect free, the mind exalted." [FOOTNOTE: Goethe's "Faust," Part II, Act V. The words of Dr. Marianus.]—But there is a reverse kind of man, who is also upon a height, and has also a free prospect—but looks DOWNWARDS.

287. What is noble? What does the word "noble" still mean for us nowadays? How does the noble man betray himself, how is he recognized under this heavy overcast sky of the commencing plebeianism, by which everything is rendered opaque and leaden?—It is not his actions which establish his claim—actions are always ambiguous, always inscrutable; neither is it his "works." One finds nowadays among artists and scholars plenty of those who betray by their works that a profound longing for nobleness impels them; but this very NEED of nobleness is radically different from the needs of the noble soul itself, and is in fact the eloquent and dangerous sign of the lack thereof. It is not the works, but the BELIEF which is here decisive and determines the order of rank—to employ once more an old religious formula with a new and deeper meaning—it is some fundamental certainty which a noble soul has about itself, something which is not to be sought, is not to be found, and perhaps, also, is not to be lost.—THE NOBLE SOUL HAS REVERENCE FOR ITSELF.—

288. There are men who are unavoidably intellectual, let them turn and twist themselves as they will, and hold their hands before their treacherous eyes—as though the hand were not a betrayer; it always comes out at last that they have something which they hide—namely, intellect. One of the subtlest means of deceiving, at least as long as possible, and of

successfully representing oneself to be stupider than one really is—which in everyday life is often as desirable as an umbrella,—is called ENTHUSIASM, including what belongs to it, for instance, virtue. For as Galiani said, who was obliged to know it: VERTU EST ENTHOUSIASME.

289. In the writings of a recluse one always hears something of the echo of the wilderness, something of the murmuring tones and timid vigilance of solitude; in his strongest words, even in his cry itself, there sounds a new and more dangerous kind of silence, of concealment. He who has sat day and night, from year's end to year's end, alone with his soul in familiar discord and discourse, he who has become a cave-bear, or a treasure-seeker, or a treasure-guardian and dragon in his cave—it may be a labyrinth, but can also be a gold-mine—his ideas themselves eventually acquire a twilight-colour of their own, and an odour, as much of the depth as of the mould, something uncommunicative and repulsive, which blows chilly upon every passer-by. The recluse does not believe that a philosopher—supposing that a philosopher has always in the first place been a recluse—ever expressed his actual and ultimate opinions in books: are not books written precisely to hide what is in us?—indeed, he will doubt whether a philosopher CAN have "ultimate and actual" opinions at all; whether behind every cave in him there is not, and must necessarily be, a still deeper cave: an

ampler, stranger, richer world beyond the surface, an abyss behind every bottom, beneath every "foundation." Every philosophy is a foreground philosophy—this is a recluse's verdict: "There is something arbitrary in the fact that the PHILOSOPHER came to a stand here, took a retrospect, and looked around; that he HERE laid his spade aside and did not dig any deeper—there is also something suspicious in it." Every philosophy also CONCEALS a philosophy; every opinion is also a LURKING-PLACE, every word is also a MASK.

290. Every deep thinker is more afraid of being understood than of being misunderstood. The latter perhaps wounds his vanity; but the former wounds his heart, his sympathy, which always says: "Ah, why would you also have as hard a time of it as I have?"

291. Man, a COMPLEX, mendacious, artful, and inscrutable animal, uncanny to the other animals by his artifice and sagacity, rather than by his strength, has invented the good conscience in order finally to enjoy his soul as something SIMPLE; and the whole of morality is a long, audacious falsification, by virtue of which generally enjoyment at the sight of the soul becomes possible. From this point of view there is perhaps much more in the conception of "art" than is generally believed.

292. A philosopher: that is a man who constantly experiences, sees, hears, suspects, hopes, and dreams extraordinary things; who is struck by his own thoughts as if they came from the outside, from above and below, as a species of events and lightning-flashes PECULIAR TO HIM; who is perhaps himself a storm pregnant with new lightnings; a portentous man, around whom there is always rumbling and mumbling and gaping and something uncanny going on. A philosopher: alas, a being who often runs away from himself, is often afraid of himself—but whose curiosity always makes him "come to himself" again.

293. A man who says: "I like that, I take it for my own, and mean to guard and protect it from every one"; a man who can conduct a case, carry out a resolution, remain true to an opinion, keep hold of a woman, punish and overthrow insolence; a man who has his indignation and his sword, and to whom the weak, the suffering, the oppressed, and even the animals willingly submit and naturally belong; in short, a man who is a MASTER by nature—when such a man has sympathy, well! THAT sympathy has value! But of what account is the sympathy of those who suffer! Or of those even who preach sympathy! There is nowadays, throughout almost the whole of Europe, a sickly irritability and sensitiveness towards pain, and also a repulsive irrestrainableness in complaining, an effeminizing, which, with the aid of religion and philosophical

nonsense, seeks to deck itself out as something superior—there is a regular cult of suffering. The UNMANLINESS of that which is called "sympathy" by such groups of visionaries, is always, I believe, the first thing that strikes the eye.—One must resolutely and radically taboo this latest form of bad taste; and finally I wish people to put the good amulet, "GAI SABER" ("gay science," in ordinary language), on heart and neck, as a protection against it.

294. THE OLYMPIAN VICE.—Despite the philosopher who, as a genuine Englishman, tried to bring laughter into bad repute in all thinking minds—"Laughing is a bad infirmity of human nature, which every thinking mind will strive to overcome" (Hobbes),—I would even allow myself to rank philosophers according to the quality of their laughing—up to those who are capable of GOLDEN laughter. And supposing that Gods also philosophize, which I am strongly inclined to believe, owing to many reasons—I have no doubt that they also know how to laugh thereby in an overman-like and new fashion—and at the expense of all serious things! Gods are fond of ridicule: it seems that they cannot refrain from laughter even in holy matters.

295. The genius of the heart, as that great mysterious one possesses it, the tempter-god and born rat-catcher of consciences, whose voice can descend into the

nether-world of every soul, who neither speaks a word nor casts a glance in which there may not be some motive or touch of allurement, to whose perfection it pertains that he knows how to appear,—not as he is, but in a guise which acts as an ADDITIONAL constraint on his followers to press ever closer to him, to follow him more cordially and thoroughly;—the genius of the heart, which imposes silence and attention on everything loud and self-conceited, which smoothes rough souls and makes them taste a new longing—to lie placid as a mirror, that the deep heavens may be reflected in them;—the genius of the heart, which teaches the clumsy and too hasty hand to hesitate, and to grasp more delicately; which scents the hidden and forgotten treasure, the drop of goodness and sweet spirituality under thick dark ice, and is a divining-rod for every grain of gold, long buried and imprisoned in mud and sand; the genius of the heart, from contact with which every one goes away richer; not favoured or surprised, not as though gratified and oppressed by the good things of others; but richer in himself, newer than before, broken up, blown upon, and sounded by a thawing wind; more uncertain, perhaps, more delicate, more fragile, more bruised, but full of hopes which as yet lack names, full of a new will and current, full of a new ill-will and counter-current... but what am I doing, my friends? Of whom am I talking to you? Have I forgotten myself so far that I have not even told you his name? Unless it be that you have already divined of your own accord who this questionable God and spirit is, that wishes to be PRAISED in such a manner? For, as it happens to every one who from childhood onward has always been on his legs, and in foreign lands, I have also encountered on my path many strange and dangerous spirits; above all, however, and again and again, the one of whom I have just spoken: in fact, no less a personage than the God DIONYSUS, the great equivocator and tempter, to whom, as you know, I once offered in all secrecy and reverence my first-fruits—the last, as it seems to me, who has offered a SACRIFICE to him, for I have found no one who could understand what I was then doing. In the meantime, however, I have learned much, far too much, about the philosophy of this God, and, as I said, from mouth to mouth—I, the last disciple and initiate of the God Dionysus: and perhaps I might at last begin to give you, my friends, as far as I am allowed, a little taste of this philosophy? In a hushed voice, as is but seemly: for it has to do with much that is secret, new, strange, wonderful, and uncanny. The very fact that Dionysus is a philosopher, and that therefore Gods also philosophize, seems to me a novelty which is not unensnaring, and might perhaps arouse suspicion precisely among philosophers;— among you, my friends, there is less to be said against it, except that it comes too late and not at the right time; for, as it has been disclosed to me, you are loth nowadays to believe in God and gods. It may happen, too, that in the frankness of my story I must go further than is agreeable to the strict usages of your ears? Certainly the God in question went further, very much further, in such dialogues, and was always many paces ahead of me... Indeed, if it were allowed, I should have to give him, according to human usage, fine ceremonious tides of lustre and merit, I should have to extol his courage as investigator and discoverer, his fearless honesty, truthfulness, and love of wisdom. But such a God does not know what to do with all that respectable trumpery and pomp. "Keep that," he would say, "for thyself and those like thee, and whoever else require it! I—have no reason to cover my nakedness!" One suspects that this kind of divinity and philosopher perhaps lacks shame?—He once said: "Under certain circumstances I love mankind"—and referred thereby to Ariadne, who was present; "in my opinion man is an agreeable, brave, inventive animal, that has not his equal upon earth, he makes his way even through all labyrinths. I like man, and often think how I can still further advance him, and make him stronger, more evil, and more profound."—"Stronger, more evil, and more profound?" I asked in horror. "Yes," he said again, "stronger, more evil, and more profound; also more beautiful"—and thereby the tempter-god smiled with his halcyon smile, as though he had just paid some charming compliment. One here sees at once that it is not only shame that this divinity lacks;—and in general there are good grounds for supposing that in some things the Gods could all of them come to us men for instruction. We men are—more human.—

296. Alas! what are you, after all, my written and painted thoughts! Not long ago you were so variegated, young and malicious, so full of thorns and secret spices, that you made me sneeze and laugh—and now? You have already doffed your novelty, and some of you, I fear, are ready to become truths, so immortal do they look, so pathetically honest, so tedious! And was it ever otherwise? What then do we write and paint, we mandarins with Chinese brush, we immortalisers of things which LEND themselves to writing, what are we alone capable of painting? Alas, only that which is just about to fade and begins to lose its odour! Alas, only exhausted and departing storms and belated yellow sentiments! Alas, only birds strayed and fatigued by flight, which now let themselves be captured with the hand—with OUR hand! We immortalize what cannot live and fly much longer, things only which are exhausted and mellow! And it is only for your AFTERNOON, you, my written and painted thoughts, for which alone I have colours, many colours, perhaps, many variegated softenings, and fifty yellows and browns and greens and reds;—but nobody will divine thereby how ye looked in your morning, you sudden sparks and marvels of my solitude, you, my old, beloved—EVIL thoughts!

From the heights

1.

MIDDAY of Life! Oh, season of delight!
My summer's park!
Uneaseful joy to look, to lurk, to hark—
I peer for friends, am ready day and night,—
Where linger ye, my friends? The time is right!

2.

Is not the glacier's grey today for you
Rose-garlanded?
The brooklet seeks you, wind, cloud, with
longing thread
And thrust themselves yet higher to the blue,
To spy for you from farthest eagle's view.

3.

My table was spread out for you on high—
Who dwelleth so
Star-near, so near the grisly pit below?—
My realm—what realm hath wider boundary?
My honey—who hath sipped its fragrancy?

4.

Friends, ye are there! Woe me,—yet I am not
He whom ye seek?
Ye stare and stop—better your wrath could speak!
I am not I? Hand, gait, face, changed? And what
I am, to you my friends, now am I not?

5.

Am I an other? Strange am I to Me?
Yet from Me sprung?
A wrestler, by himself too oft self-wrung?
Hindering too oft my own self's potency,
Wounded and hampered by self-victory?

6.

I sought where-so the wind blows keenest. There
I learned to dwell
Where no man dwells, on lonesome ice-lorn fell,
And unlearned Man and God and curse and
prayer?
Became a ghost haunting the glaciers bare?

7.

Ye, my old friends! Look! Ye turn pale, filled o'er
With love and fear!
Go! Yet not in wrath. Ye could ne'er live here.
Here in the farthest realm of ice and scaur,
A huntsman must one be, like chamois soar.

8.

An evil huntsman was I? See how taut
My bow was bent!
Strongest was he by whom such bolt were sent—
  Woe now! That arrow is with peril fraught,
  Perilous as none.—Have yon safe home ye
  sought!

9.

Ye go! Thou didst endure enough, oh, heart;—
Strong was thy hope;
Unto new friends thy portals widely ope,
Let old ones be. Bid memory depart!
Wast thou young then, now—better young thou art!

10.

What linked us once together, one hope's tie—
(Who now doth con
Those lines, now fading, Love once wrote thereon?)—
Is like a parchment, which the hand is shy
To touch—like crackling leaves, all seared, all dry.

11.

Oh! Friends no more! They are—what name for those?—
Friends' phantom-flight
Knocking at my heart's window-pane at night,
Gazing on me, that speaks "We were" and

goes,—
Oh, withered words, once fragrant as the rose!

12.

Pinings of youth that might not understand!
For which I pined,
Which I deemed changed with me, kin of my kind:
But they grew old, and thus were doomed and banned:
None but new kith are native of my land!

13.

Midday of life! My second youth's delight!
My summer's park!
Unrestful joy to long, to lurk, to hark!
I peer for friends!—am ready day and night,
For my new friends. Come! Come! The time is right!

14.

This song is done,—the sweet sad cry of rue
Sang out its end;
A wizard wrought it, he the timely friend,
The midday-friend,—no, do not ask me who;
At midday 'twas, when one became as two.

15.

We keep our Feast of Feasts, sure of our bourne,
Our aims self-same:
The Guest of Guests, friend Zarathustra, came!
  The world now laughs, the grisly veil was torn,
  And Light and Dark were one that wedding-morn.

Deutscher Original Text

(1886)

Jenseits von Gut und Böse

Vorspiel einer Philosophie der Zukunft

Vorrede

Vorausgesetzt, dass die Wahrheit ein Weib ist -, wie? ist der Verdacht nicht gegründet, dass alle Philosophen, sofern sie Dogmatiker waren, sich schlecht auf Weiber verstanden? dass der schauerliche Ernst, die linkische Zudringlichkeit, mit der sie bisher auf die Wahrheit zuzugehen pflegten, ungeschickte und unschickliche Mittel waren, um gerade ein Frauenzimmer für sich einzunehmen? Gewiss ist, dass sie sich nicht hat einnehmen lassen: - und jede Art Dogmatik steht heute mit betrübter und muthloser Haltung da. Wenn sie überhaupt noch steht! Denn es giebt Spötter, welche behaupten, sie sei gefallen, alle Dogmatik liege zu Boden, mehr noch, alle Dogmatik liege in den letzten Zügen. Ernstlich geredet, es giebt gute Gründe zu der Hoffnung, dass alles Dogmatisiren in der Philosophie, so feierlich, so end- und letztgültig es sich auch gebärdet hat, doch nur eine edle Kinderei und Anfängerei gewesen sein möge; und die Zeit ist vielleicht sehr nahe, wo man wieder und wieder begreifen wird, was eigentlich schon ausgereicht hat, um den Grundstein zu solchen erhabenen und unbedingten Philosophen-Bauwerken abzugeben, welche die Dogmatiker bisher aufbauten, - irgend ein Volks-Aberglaube aus unvordenklicher Zeit (wie der Seelen-Aberglaube, der als Subjekt- und Ich-Aberglaube auch heute noch nicht aufgehört hat, Unfug zu stiften), irgend ein Wortspiel vielleicht, eine Verführung von Seiten der Grammatik her oder eine verwegene Verallgemeinerung von sehr engen, sehr persönlichen, sehr menschlich-allzumenschlichen Thatsachen. Die Philosophie der Dogmatiker war hoffentlich nur ein Versprechen über Jahrtausende hinweg: wie es in noch früherer Zeit die Astrologie war, für deren Dienst vielleicht mehr Arbeit, Geld, Scharfsinn, Geduld aufgewendet worden ist, als bisher für irgend eine wirkliche Wissenschaft: - man verdankt ihr und ihren "überirdischen" Ansprüchen in Asien und Ägypten den grossen Stil der Baukunst. Es scheint, dass alle grossen Dinge, um der Menschheit sich mit ewigen Forderungen in das Herz einzuschreiben, erst als ungeheure und furchteinflössende Fratzen über die Erde hinwandeln müssen: eine solche Fratze war die dogmatische Philosophie, zum Beispiel die Vedanta-Lehre in Asien, der Platonismus in Europa. Seien wir nicht undankbar gegen sie, so gewiss es auch zugestanden werden muss, dass der schlimmste, langwierigste und gefährlichste aller Irrthümer bisher ein Dogmatiker-Irrthum gewesen ist, nämlich Plato's Erfindung vom reinen Geiste und vom Guten an sich. Aber nunmehr, wo er überwunden ist, wo Europa von diesem Alpdrucke aufathmet und zum Mindesten eines gesunderen - Schlafs geniessen darf, sind wir, deren Aufgabe das Wachsein selbst ist, die Erben von all der Kraft, welche der Kampf gegen diesen Irrthum grossgezüchtet hat. Es hiess allerdings die Wahrheit auf den Kopf stellen und das Perspektivische, die Grundbedingung alles Lebens, selber verleugnen, so vom Geiste und vom Guten zu reden, wie Plato gethan hat; ja man darf, als Arzt, fragen: "woher eine solche Krankheit am schönsten Gewächse des Alterthums, an Plato? hat ihn doch der böse Sokrates verdorben? wäre Sokrates doch der Verderber der Jugend gewesen? und hätte seinen Schlierling verdient?" - Aber der Kampf gegen Plato, oder, um es verständlicher und für's "Volk" zu sagen, der Kampf gegen den christlich-kirchlichen Druck von Jahrtausenden - denn Christenthum ist Platonismus für's "Volk" - hat in Europa eine prachtvolle Spannung des Geistes geschaffen, wie sie auf Erden noch nicht da war: mit einem so gespannten Bogen kann man nunmehr nach den fernsten Zielen schiessen. Freilich, der europäische Mensch empfindet diese Spannung als Nothstand; und es ist schon zwei Mal im grossen Stile versucht worden, den Bogen abzuspannen, einmal durch den Jesuitismus, zum zweiten Mal durch die demokratische Aufklärung: - als welche mit Hülfe der Pressfreiheit und des Zeitunglesens es in der That erreichen dürfte, dass der Geist sich selbst nicht mehr so leicht als "Noth" empfindet! (Die Deutschen haben das Pulver erfunden - alle Achtung! aber sie haben es wieder quitt gemacht - sie erfanden die Presse.) Aber wir, die wir weder Jesuiten, noch Demokraten, noch selbst Deutsche genug sind, wir guten Europäer und freien, sehr freien Geister - wir haben sie noch, die ganze Noth des Geistes und die ganze Spannung seines Bogens! Und vielleicht auch den Pfeil, die Aufgabe, wer weiss? das Ziel…..

Sils-Maria,

Oberengadin im Juni 1885.

Erstes Hauptstück:

Von den Vorurtheilen der Philosophen.

1. Der Wille zur Wahrheit, der uns noch zu manchem Wagnisse verführen wird, jene berühmte Wahrhaftigkeit, von der alle Philosophen bisher mit Ehrerbietung geredet haben: was für Fragen hat dieser Wille zur Wahrheit uns schon vorgelegt! Welche wunderlichen schlimmen fragwürdigen Fragen! Das ist bereits eine lange Geschichte, - und doch scheint es, dass sie kaum eben angefangen hat? Was Wunder, wenn wir endlich einmal misstrauisch werden, die Geduld verlieren, uns ungeduldig umdrehn? Dass wir von dieser Sphinx auch unserseits das Fragen lernen? Wer ist das eigentlich, der uns hier Fragen stellt? Was in uns will eigentlich "zur Wahrheit"? - In der that, wir

machten langen Halt vor der Frage nach der Ursache dieses Willens, - bis wir, zuletzt, vor einer noch gründlicheren Frage ganz und gar stehen blieben. Wir fragten nach dem Werthe dieses Willens. Gesetzt, wir wollen Wahrheit: warum nicht lieber Unwahrheit? Und Ungewissheit? Selbst Unwissenheit? - Das Problem vom Werthe der Wahrheit trat vor uns hin, - oder waren wir's, die vor das Problem hin traten? Wer von uns ist hier Oedipus? Wer Sphinx? Es ist ein Stelldichein, wie es scheint, von Fragen und Fragezeichen. - Und sollte man's glauben, dass es uns schliesslich bedünken will, als sei das Problem noch nie bisher gestellt, - als sei es von uns zum ersten Male gesehn, in's Auge gefasst, gewagt? Denn es ist ein Wagnis dabei, und vielleicht giebt es kein grösseres.

2. "Wie könnte Etwas aus seinem Gegensatz entstehn? Zum Beispiel die Wahrheit aus dem Irrthume? Oder der Wille zur Wahrheit aus dem Willen zur Täuschung? Oder die selbstlose Handlung aus dem Eigennutze? Oder das reine sonnenhafte Schauen des Weisen aus der Begehrlichkeit? Solcherlei Entstehung ist unmöglich; wer davon träumt, ein Narr, ja Schlimmeres; die Dinge höchsten Werthes müssen einen anderen, eigenen Ursprung haben, - aus dieser vergänglichen verführerischen täuschenden geringen Welt, aus diesem Wirrsal von Wahn und Begierde sind sie unableitbar! Vielmehr im Schoosse des Sein's, im Unvergänglichen, im verborgenen Gotte, im `Ding an

sich` - da muss ihr Grund liegen, und sonst nirgendswo!" - Diese Art zu urtheilen macht das typische Vorurtheil aus, an dem sich die Metaphysiker aller Zeiten wieder erkennen lassen; diese Art von Werthschätzungen steht im Hintergrunde aller ihrer logischen Prozeduren; aus diesem ihrem "Glauben" heraus bemühn sie sich um ihr "Wissen", um Etwas, das feierlich am Ende als "die Wahrheit" getauft wird. Der Grundglaube der Metaphysiker ist der Glaube an die Gegensätze der Werthe. Es ist auch den Vorsichtigsten unter ihnen nicht eingefallen, hier an der Schwelle bereits zu zweifeln, wo es doch am nöthigsten war: selbst wenn sie sich gelobt hatten "de omnibus dubitandum". Man darf nämlich zweifeln, erstens, ob es Gegensätze überhaupt giebt, und zweitens, ob jene volksthümlichen Werthschätzungen und Werth-Gegensätze, auf welche die Metaphysiker ihr Siegel gedrückt haben, nicht vielleicht nur Vordergrunds-Schätzungen sind, nur vorläufige Perspektiven, vielleicht noch dazu aus einem Winkel heraus, vielleicht von Unten hinauf, Frosch-Perspektiven gleichsam, um einen Ausdruck zu borgen, der den Malern geläufig ist? Bei allem Werthe, der dem Wahren, dem Wahrhaftigen, dem Selbstlosen zukommen mag: es wäre möglich, dass dem Scheine, dem Willen zur Täuschung, dem Eigennutz und der Begierde ein für alles Leben höherer und grundsätzlicherer Werth zugeschrieben werden müsste. Es wäre sogar noch möglich, dass was den Werth jener guten und verehrten Dinge ausmacht, gerade darin bestünde, mit jenen schlimmen, scheinbar entgegengesetzten Dingen auf verfängliche Weise verwandt, verknüpft, verhäkelt, vielleicht gar wesensgleich zu sein. Vielleicht! - Aber wer ist Willens, sich um solche gefährliche Vielleichts zu kümmern! Man muss dazu schon die Ankunft einer neuen Gattung von Philosophen abwarten, solcher, die irgend welchen anderen umgekehrten Geschmack und Hang haben als die bisherigen, - Philosophen des gefährlichen Vielleicht in jedem Verstande. - Und allen Ernstes gesprochen: ich sehe solche neue Philosophen heraufkommen.

3. Nachdem ich lange genug den Philosophen zwischen die Zeilen und auf die Finger gesehn habe, sage ich mir: man muss noch den grössten Theil des bewussten Denkens unter die Instinkt-Thätigkeiten rechnen, und sogar im Falle des philosophischen Denkens; man muss hier umlernen, wie man in Betreff der Vererbung und des "Angeborenen" umgelernt hat. So wenig der Akt der Geburt in dem ganzen Vor- und Fortgange der Vererbung in Betracht kommt: ebenso wenig ist "Bewusstsein" in irgend einem entscheidenden Sinne dem Instinktiven entgegengesetzt, - das meiste bewusste Denken eines Philosophen ist durch seine Instinkte heimlich geführt und in bestimmte Bahnen gezwungen. Auch hinter aller Logik und ihrer anscheinenden Selbstherrlichkeit der

Bewegung stehen Werthschätzungen, deutlicher gesprochen, physiologische Forderungen zur Erhaltung einer bestimmten Art von Leben. Zum Beispiel, dass das Bestimmte mehr werth sei als das Unbestimmte, der Schein weniger werth als die "Wahrheit": dergleichen Schätzungen könnten, bei aller ihrer regulativen Wichtigkeit für uns, doch nur Vordergrunds-Schätzungen sein, eine bestimmte Art von niaiserie, wie sie gerade zur Erhaltung von Wesen, wie wir sind, noth thun mag. Gesetzt nämlich, dass nicht gerade der Mensch das "Maass der Dinge" ist…..

4. Die Falschheit eines Urtheils ist uns noch kein Einwand gegen ein Urtheil; darin klingt unsre neue Sprache vielleicht am fremdesten. Die Frage ist, wie weit es lebenfördernd, lebenerhaltend, Arterhaltend, vielleicht gar Art-züchtend ist; und wir sind grundsätzlich geneigt zu behaupten, dass die falschesten Urtheile (zu denen die synthetischen Urtheile a priori gehören) uns die unentbehrlichsten sind, dass ohne ein Geltenlassen der logischen Fiktionen, ohne ein Messen der Wirklichkeit an der rein erfundenen Welt des Unbedingten, Sich-selbst-Gleichen, ohne eine beständige Fälschung der Welt durch die Zahl der Mensch nicht leben könnte, - dass Verzichtleisten auf falsche Urtheile ein Verzichtleisten auf Leben, eine Verneinung des Lebens wäre. Die Unwahrheit als Lebensbedingung zugestehn: das heisst freilich auf eine gefährliche Weise den gewohnten

Werthgefühlen Widerstand leisten; und eine Philosophie, die das wagt, stellt sich damit allein schon jenseits von Gut und Böse.

5. Was dazu reizt, auf alle Philosophen halb misstrauisch, halb spöttisch zu blicken, ist nicht, dass man wieder und wieder dahinter kommt, wie unschuldig sie sind - wie oft und wie leicht sie sich vergreifen und verirren, kurz ihre Kinderei und Kindlichkeit - sondern dass es bei ihnen nicht redlich genug zugeht: während sie allesammt einen grossen und tugendhaften Lärm machen, sobald das Problem der Wahrhaftigkeit auch nur von ferne angerührt wird. Sie stellen sich sämmtlich, als ob sie ihre eigentlichen Meinungen durch die Selbstentwicklung einer kalten, reinen, göttlich unbekümmerten Dialektik entdeckt und erreicht hätten (zum Unterschiede von den Mystikern jeden Rangs, die ehrlicher als sie und tölpelhafter sind - diese reden von "Inspiration" -): während im Grunde ein vorweggenommener Satz, ein Einfall, eine "Eingebung", zumeist ein abstrakt gemachter und durchgesiebter Herzenswunsch von ihnen mit hinterher gesuchten Gründen vertheidigt wird: - sie sind allesammt Advokaten, welche es nicht heissen wollen, und zwar zumeist sogar verschmitzte Fürsprecher ihrer Vorurtheile, die sie "Wahrheiten" taufen - und sehr ferne von der Tapferkeit des Gewissens, das sich dies, eben dies eingesteht, sehr ferne von dem guten Geschmack der Tapferkeit, welche dies auch zu

verstehen giebt, sei es um einen Feind oder Freund zu warnen, sei es aus Übermuth und um ihrer selbst zu spotten. Die ebenso steife als sittsame Tartüfferie des alten Kant, mit der er uns auf die dialektischen Schleichwege lockt, welche zu seinem "kategorischen Imperativ" führen, richtiger verführen - dies Schauspiel macht uns Verwöhnte lächeln, die wir keine kleine Belustigung darin finden, den feinen Tücken alter Moralisten und Moralprediger auf die Finger zu sehn. Oder gar jener Hocuspocus von mathematischer Form, mit der Spinoza seine Philosophie - "die Liebe zu seiner Weisheit" zuletzt, das Wort richtig und billig ausgelegt - wie in Erz panzerte und maskirte, um damit von vornherein den Muth des Angreifenden einzuschüchtern, der auf diese unüberwindliche Jungfrau und Pallas Athene den Blick zu werfen wagen würde: - wie viel eigne Schüchternheit und Angreifbarkeit verräth diese Maskerade eines einsiedlerischen Kranken!

6. Allmählich hat sich mir herausgestellt, was jede grosse Philosophie bisher war: nämlich das Selbstbekenntnis ihres Urhebers und eine Art ungewollter und unvermerkter mémoires; insgleichen, dass die moralischen (oder unmoralischen) Absichten in jeder Philosophie den eigentlichen Lebenskeim ausmachten, aus dem jedesmal die ganze Pflanze gewachsen ist. In der That, man thut gut (und klug), zur Erklärung davon, wie eigentlich die entlegensten

metaphysischen Behauptungen eines Philosophen zu Stande gekommen sind, sich immer erst zu fragen: auf welche Moral will es (will er -) hinaus? Ich glaube demgemäss nicht, dass ein "Trieb zur Erkenntniss" der Vater der Philosophie ist, sondern dass sich ein andrer Trieb, hier wie sonst, der Erkenntniss (und der Verkenntniss!) nur wie eines Werkzeugs bedient hat. Wer aber die Grundtriebe des Menschen darauf hin ansieht, wie weit sie gerade hier als inspirirende Genien (oder Dämonen und Kobolde -) ihr Spiel getrieben haben mögen, wird finden, dass sie Alle schon einmal Philosophie getrieben haben, - und dass jeder Einzelne von ihnen gerade sich gar zu gerne als letzten Zweck des Daseins und als berechtigten Herrn aller übrigen Triebe darstellen möchte. Denn jeder Trieb ist herrschsüchtig: und als solcher versucht er zu philosophiren. - Freilich: bei den Gelehrten, den eigentlich wissenschaftlichen Menschen, mag es anders stehn - "besser", wenn man will -, da mag es wirklich so Etwas wie einen Erkenntnisstrieb geben, irgend ein kleines unabhängiges Uhrwerk, welches, gut aufgezogen, tapfer darauf los arbeitet, ohne dass die gesammten übrigen Triebe des Gelehrten wesentlich dabei betheiligt sind. Die eigentlichen "Interessen" des Gelehrten liegen deshalb gewöhnlich ganz wo anders, etwa in der Familie oder im Gelderwerb oder in der Politik; ja es ist beinahe gleichgültig, ob seine kleine Maschine an diese oder jene Stelle der Wissenschaft gestellt wird, und ob der "hoffnungsvolle" junge

Arbeiter aus sich einen guten Philologen oder Pilzekenner oder Chemiker macht: - es bezeichnet ihn nicht, dass er dies oder jenes wird. Umgekehrt ist an dem Philosophen ganz und gar nichts Unpersönliches; und insbesondere giebt seine Moral ein entschiedenes und entscheidendes Zeugniss dafür ab, wer er ist - das heisst, in welcher Rangordnung die innersten Triebe seiner Natur zu einander gestellt sind.

7. Wie boshaft Philosophen sein können! Ich kenne nichts Giftigeres als den Scherz, den sich Epicur gegen Plato und die Platoniker erlaubte: er nannte sie Dionysiokolakes. Das bedeutet dem Wortlaute nach und im Vordergrunde "Schmeichler des Dionysios", also Tyrannen-Zubehör und Speichellecker; zu alledem will es aber noch sagen "das sind Alles Schauspieler, daran ist nichts Ächtes" (denn Dionysokolax war eine populäre Bezeichnung des Schauspielers). Und das Letztere ist eigentlich die Bosheit, welche Epicur gegen Plato abschoss: ihn verdross die grossartige Manier, das Sich-in-Scene-Setzen, worauf sich Plato sammt seinen Schülern verstand, - worauf sich Epicur nicht verstand! er, der alte Schulmeister von Samos, der in seinem Gärtchen zu Athen versteckt sass und dreihundert Bücher schrieb, wer weiss? vielleicht aus Wuth und Ehrgeiz gegen Plato? - Es brauchte hundert Jahre, bis Griechenland dahinter kam, wer dieser Gartengott Epicur gewesen war. - Kam es dahinter? -

8. In jeder Philosophie giebt es einen Punkt, wo die "Überzeugung" des Philosophen auf die Bühne tritt: oder, um es in der Sprache eines alten Mysteriums zu sagen:

adventavit asinus pulcher et fortissimus.

9. "Gemäss der Natur" wollt ihr leben? Oh ihr edlen Stoiker, welche Betrügerei der Worte! Denkt euch ein Wesen, wie es die Natur ist, verschwenderisch ohne Maass, gleichgültig ohne Maass, ohne Absichten und Rücksichten, ohne Erbarmen und Gerechtigkeit, fruchtbar und öde und ungewiss zugleich, denkt euch die Indifferenz selbst als Macht - wie könntet ihr gemäss dieser Indifferenz leben? Leben - ist das nicht gerade ein Anders-sein-wollen, als diese Natur ist? Ist Leben nicht Abschätzen, Vorziehn, Ungerechtsein, Begrenzt-sein, Different-sein-wollen? Und gesetzt, euer Imperativ "gemäss der Natur leben" bedeute im Grunde soviel als "gemäss dem Leben leben" - wie könntet ihr's denn nicht? Wozu ein Princip aus dem machen, was ihr selbst seid und sein müsst? - In Wahrheit steht es ganz anders: indem ihr entzückt den Kanon eures Gesetzes aus der Natur zu lesen vorgebt, wollt ihr etwas Umgekehrtes, ihr wunderlichen Schauspieler und Selbst-Betrüger! Euer Stolz will der Natur, sogar der Natur, eure Moral, euer Ideal vorschreiben und einverleiben, ihr verlangt, dass sie "der Stoa gemäss" Natur sei und möchtet alles Dasein nur nach eurem

eignen Bilde dasein machen - als eine ungeheure ewige Verherrlichung und Verallgemeinerung des Stoicismus! Mit aller eurer Liebe zur Wahrheit zwingt ihr euch so lange, so beharrlich, so hypnotisch-starr, die Natur falsch, nämlich stoisch zu sehn, bis ihr sie nicht mehr anders zu sehen vermögt, - und irgend ein abgründlicher Hochmuth giebt euch zuletzt noch die Tollhäusler-Hoffnung ein, dass, weil ihr euch selbst zu tyrannisiren versteht - Stoicismus ist Selbst-Tyrannei -, auch die Natur sich tyrannisiren lässt: ist denn der Stoiker nicht ein Stück Natur? Aber dies ist eine alte ewige Geschichte: was sich damals mit den Stoikern begab, begiebt sich heute noch, sobald nur eine Philosophie anfängt, an sich selbst zu glauben. Sie schafft immer die Welt nach ihrem Bilde, sie kann nicht anders; Philosophie ist dieser tyrannische Trieb selbst, der geistigste Wille zur Macht, zur "Schaffung der Welt", zur causa prima.

10. Der Eifer und die Feinheit, ich möchte sogar sagen: Schlauheit, mit denen man heute überall in Europa dem Probleme "von der wirklichen und der scheinbaren Welt" auf den Leib rückt, giebt zu denken und zu horchen; und wer hier im Hintergrunde nur einen "Willen zur Wahrheit" und nichts weiter hört, erfreut sich gewiss nicht der schärfsten Ohren. In einzelnen und seltenen Fällen mag wirklich ein solcher Wille zur Wahrheit, irgend ein ausschweifender und abenteuernder Muth, ein Metaphysiker-Ehrgeiz des

verlornen Postens dabei betheiligt sein, der zuletzt eine Handvoll "Gewissheit" immer noch einem ganzen Wagen voll schöner Möglichkeiten vorzieht; es mag sogar puritanische Fanatiker des Gewissens geben, welche lieber noch sich auf ein sicheres Nichts als auf ein ungewisses Etwas sterben legen. Aber dies ist Nihilismus und Anzeichen einer verzweifelnden sterbensmüden Seele: wie tapfer auch die Gebärden einer solchen Tugend sich ausnehmen mögen. Bei den stärkeren, lebensvolleren, nach Leben noch durstigen Denkern scheint es aber anders zu stehen: indem sie Partei gegen den Schein nehmen und das Wort "perspektivisch" bereits mit Hochmuth aussprechen, indem sie die Glaubwürdigkeit ihres eigenen Leibes ungefähr so gering anschlagen wie die Glaubwürdigkeit des Augenscheins, welcher sagt "die Erde steht still", und dermaassen anscheinend gut gelaunt den sichersten Besitz aus den Händen lassen (denn was glaubt man jetzt sicherer als seinen Leib?) wer weiss, ob sie nicht im Grunde Etwas zurückerobern wollen, das man ehemals noch sicherer besessen hat, irgend Etwas vom alten Grundbesitz des Glaubens von Ehedem, vielleicht "die unsterbliche Seele", vielleicht "den alten Gott", kurz, Ideen, auf welchen sich besser, nämlich kräftiger und heiterer leben liess als auf den "modernen Ideen"? Es ist Misstrauen gegen diese modernen Ideen darin, es ist Unglauben an alles Das, was gestern und heute gebaut worden ist; es ist vielleicht ein leichter Überdruss und Hohn eingemischt, der das bric-à-brac von Begriffen verschiedenster Abkunft nicht mehr aushält, als welches sich heute der sogenannte Positivismus auf den Markt bringt, ein Ekel des verwöhnteren Geschmacks vor der Jahrmarkts-Buntheit und Lappenhaftigkeit aller dieser Wirklichkeits-Philosophaster, an denen nichts neu und ächt ist als diese Buntheit. Man soll darin, wie mich dünkt, diesen skeptischen Anti-Wirklichen und Erkenntniss-Mikroskopikern von heute Recht geben: ihr Instinkt, welcher sie aus der modernen Wirklichkeit hinwegtreibt, ist unwiderlegt, - was gehen uns ihre rückläufigen Schleichwege an! Das Wesentliche an ihnen ist nicht, dass sie "zurück" wollen: sondern, dass sie - weg wollen. Etwas Kraft, Flug, Muth, Künstlerschaft mehr und sie würden hinaus wollen, - und nicht zurück! -

11. Es scheint mir, dass man jetzt überall bemüht ist, von dem eigentlichen Einflusse, den Kant auf die deutsche Philosophie ausgeübt hat, den Blick abzulenken und namentlich über den Werth, den er sich selbst zugestand, klüglich hinwegzuschlüpfen. Kant war vor Allem und zuerst stolz auf seine Kategorientafel, er sagte mit dieser Tafel in den Händen: "das ist das Schwerste, was jemals zum Behufe der Metaphysik unternommen werden konnte". - Man verstehe doch dies "werden konnte"! er war stolz darauf, im Menschen ein neues Vermögen, das Vermögen zu synthetischen Urteilen a priori, entdeckt

zu haben. Gesetzt, dass er sich hierin selbst betrog: aber die Entwicklung und rasche Blüthe der deutschen Philosophie hängt an diesem Stolze und an dem Wetteifer aller Jüngeren, womöglich noch Stolzeres zu entdecken - und jedenfalls "neue Vermögen"! - Aber besinnen wir uns: es ist an der Zeit. Wie sind synthetische Urtheile a priori möglich? fragte sich Kant, - und was antwortete er eigentlich? Vermöge eines Vermögens: leider aber nicht mit drei Worten, sondern so umständlich, ehrwürdig und mit einem solchen Aufwande von deutschem Tief- und Schnörkelsinne, dass man die lustige niaiserie allemande überhörte, welche in einer solchen Antwort steckt. Man war sogar ausser sich über dieses neue Vermögen, und der Jubel kam auf seine Höhe, als Kant auch noch ein moralisches Vermögen im Menschen hinzu entdeckte: - denn damals waren die Deutschen noch moralisch, und ganz und gar noch nicht "real-politisch". - Es kam der Honigmond der deutschen Philosophie; alle jungen Theologen des Tübinger Stifts giengen alsbald in die Büsche, - alle suchten nach "Vermögen". Und was fand man nicht Alles - in jener unschuldigen, reichen, noch jugendlichen Zeit des deutschen Geistes, in welche die Romantik, die boshafte Fee, hineinblies, hineinsang, damals, als man "finden" und "erfinden" noch nicht auseinander zu halten wusste! Vor Allem ein Vermögen für's "übersinnliche": Schelling taufte es die intellektuale Anschauung und kam damit den herzlichsten Gelüsten seiner im Grunde frommgelüsteten Deutschen entgegen. Man kann dieser ganzen übermüthigen und schwärmerischen Bewegung, welche Jugend war, so kühn sie sich auch in graue und greisenhafte Begriffe verkleidete, gar nicht mehr Unrecht thun, als wenn man sie ernst nimmt und gar etwa mit moralischer Entrüstung behandelt; genug, man wurde älter, - der Traum verflog. Es kam eine Zeit, wo man sich die Stirne rieb: man reibt sie sich heute noch. Man hatte geträumt: voran und zuerst - der alte Kant. "Vermöge eines Vermögens" - hatte er gesagt, mindestens gemeint. Aber ist denn das - eine Antwort? Eine Erklärung? Oder nicht vielmehr nur eine Wiederholung der Frage? Wie macht doch das Opium schlafen? "Vermöge eines Vermögens", nämlich der virtus dormitiva - antwortet jener Arzt bei Molière,

quia est in eo virtus dormitiva,

cujus est natura sensus assoupire.

Aber dergleichen Antworten gehören in die Komödie, und es ist endlich an der Zeit, die Kantische Frage "Wie sind synthetische Urtheile a priori möglich?" durch eine andre Frage zu ersetzen "warum ist der Glaube an solche Urtheile nöthig?" - nämlich zu begreifen, dass zum Zweck der Erhaltung von Wesen unsrer Art solche Urtheile als wahr geglaubt werden müssen; weshalb sie natürlich noch falsche Urtheile sein könnten! Oder, deutlicher geredet und grob und gründlich: synthetische

Urtheile a priori sollten gar nicht "möglich sein": wir haben kein Recht auf sie, in unserm Munde sind es lauter falsche Urtheile. Nur ist allerdings der Glaube an ihre Wahrheit nöthig, als ein Vordergrunds-Glaube und Augenschein, der in die Perspektiven-Optik des Lebens gehört. - Um zuletzt noch der ungeheuren Wirkung zu gedenken, welche "die deutsche Philosophie" - man versteht, wie ich hoffe, ihr Anrecht auf Gänsefüsschen? - in ganz Europa ausgeübt hat, so zweifle man nicht, dass eine gewisse virtus dormitiva dabei betheiligt war: man war entzückt, unter edlen Müssiggängern, Tugendhaften, Mystikern, Künstlern, Dreiviertels-Christen und politischen Dunkelmännern aller Nationen, Dank der deutschen Philosophie, ein Gegengift gegen den noch übermächtigen Sensualismus zu haben, der vom vorigen Jahrhundert in dieses hinüberströmte, kurz -"sensus assoupire".......

12. Was die materialistische Atomistik betrifft: so gehört dieselbe zu den bestwiderlegten Dingen, die es giebt; und vielleicht ist heute in Europa Niemand unter den Gelehrten mehr so ungelehrt, ihr ausser zum bequemen Hand- und Hausgebrauch (nämlich als einer Abkürzung der Ausdrucksmittel) noch eine ernstliche Bedeutung zuzumessen - Dank vorerst jenem Polen Boscovich, der, mitsammt dem Polen Kopernicus, bisher der grösste und siegreichste Gegner des Augenscheins war. Während nämlich Kopernicus uns überredet hat zu glauben, wider alle Sinne, dass die

Erde nicht fest steht, lehrte Boscovich dem Glauben an das Letzte, was von der Erde "feststand", abschwören, dem Glauben an den "Stoff", an die "Materie", an das Erdenrest- und Klümpchen-Atom: es war der grösste Triumph über die Sinne, der bisher auf Erden errungen worden ist. - Man muss aber noch weiter gehn und auch dem "atomistischen Bedürfnisse", das immer noch ein gefährliches Nachleben führt, auf Gebieten, wo es Niemand ahnt, gleich jenem berühmteren "metaphysischen Bedürfnisse" - den Krieg erklären, einen schonungslosen Krieg auf's Messer: - man muss zunächst auch jener anderen und verhängnissvolleren Atomistik den Garaus machen, welche das Christenthum am besten und längsten gelehrt hat, der Seelen-Atomistik. Mit diesem Wort sei es erlaubt, jenen Glauben zu bezeichnen, der die Seele als etwas Unvertilgbares, Ewiges, Untheilbares, als eine Monade, als ein Atomon nimmt: diesen Glauben soll man aus der Wissenschaft hinausschaffen! Es ist, unter uns gesagt, ganz und gar nicht nöthig, "die Seele" selbst dabei los zu werden und auf eine der ältesten und ehrwürdigsten Hypothesen Verzicht zu leisten: wie es dem Ungeschick der Naturalisten zu begegnen pflegt, welche, kaum dass sie an "die Seele" rühren, sie auch verlieren. Aber der Weg zu neuen Fassungen und Verfeinerungen der Seelen-Hypothese steht offen: und Begriffe wie "sterbliche Seele" und "Seele als Subjekts-Vielheit" und "Seele als Gesellschaftsbau der Triebe und Affekte" wollen fürderhin in der Wissenschaft

Bürgerrecht haben. Indem der neue Psycholog dem Aberglauben ein Ende bereitet, der bisher um die Seelen-Vorstellung mit einer fast tropischen Üppigkeit wucherte, hat er sich freilich selbst gleichsam in eine neue Öde und ein neues Misstrauen hinaus gestossen - es mag sein, dass die älteren Psychologen es bequemer und lustiger hatten -: zuletzt aber weiss er sich eben damit auch zum Erfinden verurtheilt - und, wer weiss? vielleicht zum Finden. -

13. Die Physiologen sollten sich besinnen, den Selbsterhaltungstrieb als kardinalen Trieb eines organischen Wesens anzusetzen. Vor Allem will etwas Lebendiges seine Kraft auslassen - Leben selbst ist Wille zur Macht -: die Selbsterhaltung ist nur eine der indirekten und häufigsten Folgen davon. - Kurz, hier wie überall, Vorsicht vor überflüssigen teleologischen Principien! - wie ein solches der Selbsterhaltungstrieb ist (man dankt ihn der Inconsequenz Spinoza's -). So nämlich gebietet es die Methode, die wesentlich Principien-Sparsamkeit sein muss.

14. Es dämmert jetzt vielleicht in fünf, sechs Köpfen, dass Physik auch nur eine Welt-Auslegung und -Zurechtlegung (nach uns! mit Verlaub gesagt) und nicht eine Welt-Erklärung ist: aber, insofern sie sich auf den Glauben an die Sinne stellt, gilt sie als mehr und muss auf lange hinaus noch als mehr, nämlich als Erklärung gelten. Sie hat Augen und Finger für sich, sie

hat den Augenschein und die Handgreiflichkeit für sich: das wirkt auf ein Zeitalter mit plebejischem Grundgeschmack bezaubernd, überredend, überzeugend, - es folgt ja instinktiv dem Wahrheits-Kanon des ewig volksthümlichen Sensualismus. Was ist klar, was "erklärt"? Erst Das, was sich sehen und tasten lässt, - bis so weit muss man jedes Problem treiben. Umgekehrt: genau im Widerstreben gegen die Sinnenfälligkeit bestand der Zauber der platonischen Denkweise, welche eine vornehme Denkweise war, - vielleicht unter Menschen, die sich sogar stärkerer und anspruchsvollerer Sinne erfreuten, als unsre Zeitgenossen sie haben, aber welche einen höheren Triumph darin zu finden wussten, über diese Sinne Herr zu bleiben: und dies mittels blasser kalter grauer Begriffs-Netze, die sie über den bunten Sinnen-Wirbel - den Sinnen-Pöbel, wie Plato sagte - warfen. Es war eine andre Art Genuss in dieser Welt-Überwältigung und Welt-Auslegung nach der Manier des Plato, als der es ist, welchen uns die Physiker von Heute anbieten, insgleichen die Darwinisten und Antitheologen unter den physiologischen Arbeitern, mit ihrem Princip der "kleinstmöglichen Kraft" und der grösstmöglichen Dummheit. "Wo der Mensch nichts mehr zu sehen und zu greifen hat, da hat er auch nichts mehr zu suchen" - das ist freilich ein anderer Imperativ als der Platonische, welcher aber doch für ein derbes arbeitsames Geschlecht von Maschinisten und

Brückenbauern der Zukunft, die lauter grobe Arbeit abzuthun haben, gerade der rechte Imperativ sein mag.

15. Um Physiologie mit gutem Gewissen zu treiben, muss man darauf halten, dass die Sinnesorgane nicht Erscheinungen sind im Sinne der idealistischen Philosophie: als solche könnten sie ja keine Ursachen sein! Sensualismus mindestens somit als regulative Hypothese, um nicht zu sagen als heuristisches Princip. - Wie? und Andere sagen gar, die Aussenwelt wäre das Werk unsrer Organe? Aber dann wäre ja unser Leib, als ein Stück dieser Aussenwelt, das Werk unsrer Organe! Aber dann wären ja unsre Organe selbst - das Werk unsrer Organe! Dies ist, wie mir scheint, eine gründliche reductio ad absurdum: gesetzt, dass der Begriff causa sui etwas gründlich Absurdes ist. Folglich ist die Aussenwelt nicht das Werk unsrer Organe -?

16. Es giebt immer noch harmlose Selbst-Beobachter, welche glauben, dass es "unmittelbare Gewissheiten" gebe, zum Beispiel "ich denke", oder, wie es der Aberglaube Schopenhauer's war, "ich will": gleichsam als ob hier das Erkennen rein und nackt seinen Gegenstand zu fassen bekäme, als "Ding an sich", und weder von Seiten des Subjekts, noch von Seiten des Objekts eine Fälschung stattfände. Dass aber "unmittelbare Gewissheit", ebenso wie "absolute Erkenntniss" und "Ding an sich", eine contradictio in

adjecto in sich schliesst, werde ich hundertmal wiederholen: man sollte sich doch endlich von der Verführung der Worte losmachen! Mag das Volk glauben, dass Erkennen ein zu Ende-Kennen sei, der Philosoph muss sich sagen: "wenn ich den Vorgang zerlege, der in dem Satz `ich denke` ausgedrückt ist, so bekomme ich eine Reihe von verwegenen Behauptungen, deren Begründung schwer, vielleicht unmöglich ist, - zum Beispiel, dass ich es bin, der denkt, dass überhaupt ein Etwas es sein muss, das denkt, dass Denken eine Thätigkeit und Wirkung seitens eines Wesens ist, welches als Ursache gedacht wird, dass es ein `Ich` giebt, endlich, dass es bereits fest steht, was mit Denken zu bezeichnen ist, - dass ich weiss, was Denken ist. Denn wenn ich nicht darüber mich schon bei mir entschieden hätte, wonach sollte ich abmessen, dass, was eben geschieht, nicht vielleicht `Wollen` oder `Fühlen` sei? Genug, jenes `ich denke` setzt voraus, dass ich meinen augenblicklichen Zustand mit anderen Zuständen, die ich an mir kenne, vergleiche, um so festzusetzen, was er ist: wegen dieser Rückbeziehung auf anderweitiges `Wissen` hat er für mich jedenfalls keine unmittelbare `Gewissheit`." - An Stelle jener "unmittelbaren Gewissheit", an welche das Volk im gegebenen Falle glauben mag, bekommt dergestalt der Philosoph eine Reihe von Fragen der Metaphysik in die Hand, recht eigentliche Gewissensfragen des Intellekts, welche heissen: "Woher nehme ich den Begriff Denken? Warum glaube ich an Ursache und Wirkung? Was giebt mir das Recht, von einem Ich, und gar von einem Ich als Ursache, und endlich noch von einem Ich als Gedanken-Ursache zu reden?" Wer sich mit der Berufung auf eine Art Intuition der Erkenntniss getraut, jene metaphysischen Fragen sofort zu beantworten, wie es Der thut, welcher sagt: "ich, denke, und weiss, dass dies wenigstens wahr, wirklich, gewiss ist" - der wird bei einem Philosophen heute ein Lächeln und zwei Fragezeichen bereit finden. "Mein Herr, wird der Philosoph vielleicht ihm zu verstehen geben, es ist unwahrscheinlich, dass Sie sich nicht irren: aber warum auch durchaus Wahrheit?" -

17. Was den Aberglauben der Logiker betrifft: so will ich nicht müde werden, eine kleine kurze Thatsache immer wieder zu unterstreichen, welche von diesen Abergläubischen ungern zugestanden wird, - nämlich, dass ein Gedanke kommt, wenn "er" will, und nicht wenn "ich" will; so dass es eine Fälschung des Thatbestandes ist, zu sagen: das Subjekt "ich" ist die Bedingung des Prädikats "denke". Es denkt: aber dass dies "es" gerade jenes alte berühmte "Ich" sei, ist, milde geredet, nur eine Annahme, eine Behauptung, vor Allem keine "unmittelbare Gewissheit". Zuletzt ist schon mit diesem "es denkt" zu viel gethan: schon dies "es" enthält eine Auslegung des Vorgangs und gehört nicht zum Vorgange selbst. Man schliesst hier nach der grammatischen Gewohnheit "Denken ist eine Thätigkeit, zu jeder Thätigkeit gehört Einer, der thätig

ist, folglich -". Ungefähr nach dem gleichen Schema suchte die ältere Atomistik zu der "Kraft", die wirkt, noch jenes Klümpchen Materie, worin sie sitzt, aus der heraus sie wirkt, das Atom; strengere Köpfe lernten endlich ohne diesen "Erdenrest" auskommen, und vielleicht gewöhnt man sich eines Tages noch daran, auch seitens der Logiker ohne jenes kleine "es" (zu dem sich das ehrliche alte Ich verflüchtigt hat) auszukommen.

18. An einer Theorie ist wahrhaftig nicht ihr geringster Reiz, dass sie widerlegbar ist: gerade damit zieht sie feinere Köpfe an. Es scheint, dass die hundertfach widerlegte Theorie vom "freien Willen" ihre Fortdauer nur noch diesem Reize verdankt -: immer wieder kommt jemand und fühlt sich stark genug, sie zu widerlegen.

19. Die Philosophen pflegen vom Willen zu reden, wie als ob er die bekannteste Sache von der Welt sei; ja Schopenhauer gab zu verstehen, der Wille allein sei uns eigentlich bekannt, ganz und gar bekannt, ohne Abzug und Zuthat bekannt. Aber es dünkt mich immer wieder, dass Schopenhauer auch in diesem Falle nur gethan hat, was Philosophen eben zu thun pflegen: dass er ein Volks-Vorurtheil übernommen und übertrieben hat. Wollen scheint mir vor Allem etwas Complicirtes, Etwas, das nur als Wort eine Einheit ist, - und eben im Einen Worte steckt das Volks-Vorurtheil, das über die

allzeit nur geringe Vorsicht der Philosophen Herr geworden ist. Seien wir also einmal vorsichtiger, seien wir "unphilosophisch" -, sagen wir: in jedem Wollen ist erstens eine Mehrheit von Gefühlen, nämlich das Gefühl des Zustandes, von dem weg, das Gefühl des Zustandes, zu dem hin, das Gefühl von diesem "weg" und "hin" selbst, dann noch ein begleitendes Muskelgefühl, welches, auch ohne dass wir "Arme und Beine" in Bewegung setzen, durch eine Art Gewohnheit, sobald wir "wollen", sein Spiel beginnt. Wie also Fühlen und zwar vielerlei Fühlen als Ingredienz des Willens anzuerkennen ist, so zweitens auch noch Denken: in jedem Willensakte giebt es einen commandirenden Gedanken; - und man soll ja nicht glauben, diesen Gedanken von dem "Wollen" abscheiden zu können, wie als ob dann noch Wille übrig bliebe! Drittens ist der Wille nicht nur ein Complex von Fühlen und Denken, sondern vor Allem noch ein Affekt: und zwar jener Affekt des Commando's. Das, was "Freiheit des Willens" genannt wird, ist wesentlich der Überlegenheits-Affekt in Hinsicht auf Den, der gehorchen muss: "ich bin frei, "er" muss gehorchen" - dies Bewusstsein steckt in jedem Willen, und ebenso jene Spannung der Aufmerksamkeit, jener gerade Blick, der ausschliesslich Eins fixirt, jene unbedingte Werthschätzung "jetzt thut dies und nichts Anderes Noth", jene innere Gewissheit darüber, dass gehorcht werden wird, und was Alles noch zum Zustande des

Befehlenden gehört. Ein Mensch, der will -, befiehlt einem Etwas in sich, das gehorcht oder von dem er glaubt, dass es gehorcht. Nun aber beachte man, was das Wunderlichste am Willen ist, - an diesem so vielfachen Dinge, für welches das Volk nur Ein Wort hat: insofern wir im gegebenen Falle zugleich die Befehlenden und Gehorchenden sind, und als Gehorchende die Gefühle des Zwingens, Drängens, Drückens, Widerstehens, Bewegens kennen, welche sofort nach dem Akte des Willens zu beginnen pflegen; insofern wir andererseits die Gewohnheit haben, uns über diese Zweiheit vermöge des synthetischen Begriffs "ich" hinwegzusetzen, hinwegzutäuschen, hat sich an das Wollen noch eine ganze Kette von irrthümlichen Schlüssen und folglich von falschen Werthschätzungen des Willens selbst angehängt, - dergestalt, dass der Wollende mit gutem Glauben glaubt, Wollen genüge zur Aktion. Weil in den allermeisten Fällen nur gewollt worden ist, wo auch die Wirkung des Befehls, also der Gehorsam, also die Aktion erwartet werden durfte, so hat sich der Anschein in das Gefühl übersetzt, als ob es da eine Nothwendigkeit von Wirkung gäbe; genug, der Wollende glaubt, mit einem ziemlichen Grad von Sicherheit, dass Wille und Aktion irgendwie Eins seien -, er rechnet das Gelingen, die Ausführung des Wollens noch dem Willen selbst zu und geniesst dabei einen Zuwachs jenes Machtgefühls, welches alles Gelingen mit sich bringt. "Freiheit des Willens" - das ist das Wort für jenen vielfachen Lust-Zustand des Wollenden, der befiehlt und sich zugleich mit dem Ausführenden als Eins setzt, - der als solcher den Triumph über Widerstände mit geniesst, aber bei sich urtheilt, sein Wille selbst sei es, der eigentlich die Widerstände überwinde. Der Wollende nimmt dergestalt die Lustgefühle der ausführenden, erfolgreichen Werkzeuge, der dienstbaren "Unterwillen" oder Unter-Seelen - unser Leib ist ja nur ein Gesellschaftsbau vieler Seelen - zu seinem Lustgefühle als Befehlender hinzu. L'effet c'est moi: es begiebt sich hier, was sich in jedem gut gebauten und glücklichen Gemeinwesen begiebt, dass die regierende Klasse sich mit den Erfolgen des Gemeinwesens identificirt. Bei allem Wollen handelt es sich schlechterdings um Befehlen und Gehorchen, auf der Grundlage, wie gesagt, eines Gesellschaftsbaus vieler "Seelen": weshalb ein Philosoph sich das Recht nehmen sollte, Wollen an sich schon unter den Gesichtskreis der Moral zu fassen: Moral nämlich als Lehre von den Herrschafts-Verhältnissen verstanden, unter denen das Phänomen "Leben" entsteht. -

20. Dass die einzelnen philosophischen Begriffe nichts Beliebiges, nichts Für-sich-Wachsendes sind, sondern in Beziehung und Verwandtschaft zu einander emporwachsen, dass sie, so plötzlich und willkürlich sie auch in der Geschichte des Denkens anscheinend heraustreten, doch eben so gut einem Systeme angehören als die sämmtlichen Glieder der Fauna eines

Erdtheils: das verräth sich zuletzt noch darin, wie sicher die verschiedensten Philosophen ein gewisses Grundschema von möglichen Philosophien immer wieder ausfüllen. Unter einem unsichtbaren Banne laufen sie immer von Neuem noch einmal die selbe Kreisbahn: sie mögen sich noch so unabhängig von einander mit ihrem kritischen oder systematischen Willen fühlen: irgend Etwas in ihnen führt sie, irgend Etwas treibt sie in bestimmter Ordnung hinter einander her, eben jene eingeborne Systematik und Verwandtschaft der Begriffe. Ihr Denken ist in der That viel weniger ein Entdecken, als ein Wiedererkennen, Wiedererinnern, eine Rück- und Heimkehr in einen fernen uralten Gesammt-Haushalt der Seele, aus dem jene Begriffe einstmals herausgewachsen sind: - Philosophiren ist insofern eine Art von Atavismus höchsten Ranges. Die wunderliche Familien-Ahnlichkeit alles indischen, griechischen, deutschen Philosophirens erklärt sich einfach genug. Gerade, wo Sprach-Verwandtschaft vorliegt, ist es gar nicht zu vermeiden, dass, Dank der gemeinsamen Philosophie der Grammatik - ich meine Dank der unbewussten Herrschaft und Führung durch gleiche grammatische Funktionen - von vornherein Alles für eine gleichartige Entwicklung und Reihenfolge der philosophischen Systeme vorbereitet liegt: ebenso wie zu gewissen andern Möglichkeiten der Welt-Ausdeutung der Weg wie abgesperrt erscheint. Philosophen des ural-altaischen Sprachbereichs (in dem der Subjekt-Begriff am schlechtesten entwickelt ist) werden mit grosser Wahrscheinlichkeit anders "in die Welt" blicken und auf andern Pfaden zu finden sein, als Indogermanen oder Muselmänner: der Bann bestimmter grammatischer Funktionen ist im letzten Grunde der Bann physiologischer Werthurtheile und Rasse-Bedingungen. - So viel zur Zurückweisung von Locke's Oberflächlichkeit in Bezug auf die Herkunft der Ideen.

21. Die causa sui ist der beste Selbst-Widerspruch, der bisher ausgedacht worden ist, eine Art logischer Nothzucht und Unnatur: aber der ausschweifende Stolz des Menschen hat es dahin gebracht, sich tief und schrecklich gerade mit diesem Unsinn zu verstricken. Das Verlangen nach "Freiheit des Willens", in jenem metaphysischen Superlativ-Verstande, wie er leider noch immer in den Köpfen der Halb-Unterrichteten herrscht, das Verlangen, die ganze und letzte Verantwortlichkeit für seine Handlungen selbst zu tragen und Gott, Welt, Vorfahren, Zufall, Gesellschaft davon zu entlasten, ist nämlich nichts Geringeres, als eben jene causa sui zu sein und, mit einer mehr als Münchhausen'schen Verwegenheit, sich selbst aus dem Sumpf des Nichts an den Haaren in's Dasein zu ziehn. Gesetzt, Jemand kommt dergestalt hinter die bäurische Einfalt dieses berühmten Begriffs "freier Wille" und streicht ihn aus seinem Kopfe, so bitte ich ihn nunmehr, seine "Aufklärung" noch um einen Schritt weiter zu treiben und auch die Umkehrung jenes Unbegriffs

"freier Wille" aus seinem Kopfe zu streichen: ich meine den "unfreien Willen", der auf einen Missbrauch von Ursache und Wirkung hinausläuft. Man soll nicht "Ursache" und "Wirkung" fehlerhaft verdinglichen, wie es die Naturforscher thun (und wer gleich ihnen heute im Denken naturalisirt -) gemäss der herrschenden mechanistischen Tölpelei, welche die Ursache drücken und stossen lässt, bis sie "Wirkt"; man soll sich der "Ursache", der "Wirkung" eben nur als reiner Begriffe bedienen, das heisst als conventioneller Fiktionen zum Zweck der Bezeichnung, der Verständigung, nicht der Erklärung. Im "An-sich" giebt es nichts von "Causal-Verbänden", von "Nothwendigkeit", von "psychologischer Unfreiheit", da folgt nicht "die Wirkung auf die Ursache", das regiert kein "Gesetz". Wir sind es, die allein die Ursachen, das Nacheinander, das Für-einander, die Relativität, den Zwang, die Zahl, das Gesetz, die Freiheit, den Grund, den Zweck erdichtet haben; und wenn wir diese Zeichen-Welt als "an sich" in die Dinge hineindichten, hineinmischen, so treiben wir es noch einmal, wie wir es immer getrieben haben, nämlich mythologisch. Der "unfreie Wille" ist Mythologie: im wirklichen Leben handelt es sich nur um starken und schwachen Willen. - Es ist fast immer schon ein Symptom davon, wo es bei ihm selber mangelt, wenn ein Denker bereits in aller "Causal-Verknüpfung" und "psychologischer Nothwendigkeit" etwas von Zwang, Noth, Folgen-Müssen, Druck, Unfreiheit herausfühlt: es ist verrätherisch, gerade so zu fühlen, - die Person verräth sich. Und überhaupt wird, wenn ich recht beobachtet habe, von zwei ganz entgegengesetzten Seiten aus, aber immer auf eine tief persönliche Weise die "Unfreiheit des Willens" als Problem gefasst: die Einen wollen um keinen Preis ihre "Verantwortlichkeit", den Glauben an sich, das persönliche Anrecht auf ihr Verdienst fahren lassen (die eitlen Rassen gehören dahin -); die Anderen wollen umgekehrt nichts verantworten, an nichts schuld sein und verlangen, aus einer innerlichen Selbst-Verachtung heraus, sich selbst irgend wohin abwälzen zu können. Diese Letzteren pflegen sich, wenn sie Bücher schreiben, heute der Verbrecher anzunehmen; eine Art von socialistischem Mitleiden ist ihre gefälligste Verkleidung. Und in der That, der Fatalismus der Willensschwachen verschönert sich erstaunlich, wenn er sich als "la religion de la souffrance humaine" einzuführen versteht: es ist sein "guter Geschmack".

22. Man vergebe es mir als einem alten Philologen, der von der Bosheit nicht lassen kann, auf schlechte Interpretations-Künste den Finger zu legen - aber jene "Gesetzmässigkeit der Natur", von der ihr Physiker so stolz redet, wie als ob - - besteht nur Dank eurer Ausdeutung und schlechten "Philologie", - sie ist kein Thatbestand, kein "Text", vielmehr nur eine naiv-humanitäre Zurechtmachung und Sinnverdrehung, mit der ihr den demokratischen Instinkten der modernen Seele sattsam entgegenkommt! "Überall Gleichheit vor

dem Gesetz, - die Natur hat es darin nicht anders und nicht besser als wir": ein artiger Hintergedanke, in dem noch einmal die pöbelmännische Feindschaft gegen alles Bevorrechtete und Selbstherrliche, insgleichen ein zweiter und feinerer Atheismus verkleidet liegt. "Ni dieu, ni maître" - so wollt auch ihr's.- und darum "hoch das Naturgesetz"! - nicht wahr? Aber, wie gesagt, das ist Interpretation, nicht Text; und es könnte Jemand kommen, der, mit der entgegengesetzten Absicht und Interpretationskunst, aus der gleichen Natur und im Hinblick auf die gleichen Erscheinungen, gerade die tyrannisch-rücksichtenlose und unerbittliche Durchsetzung von Machtansprüchen herauszulesen verstünde, - ein Interpret, der die Ausnahmslosigkeit und Unbedingtheit in allem "Willen zur Macht" dermaassen euch vor Augen stellte, dass fast jedes Wort und selbst das Wort "Tyrannei" schliesslich unbrauchbar oder schon als schwächende und mildernde Metapher - als zu menschlich - erschiene; und der dennoch damit endete, das Gleiche von dieser Welt zu behaupten, was ihr behauptet, nämlich dass sie einen "nothwendigen" und "berechenbaren" Verlauf habe, aber nicht, weil Gesetze in ihr herrschen, sondern weil absolut die Gesetze fehlen, und jede Macht in jedem Augenblicke ihre letzte Consequenz zieht. Gesetzt, dass auch dies nur Interpretation ist - und ihr werdet eifrig genug sein, dies einzuwenden? - nun, um so besser. -

23. Die gesammte Psychologie ist bisher an moralischen Vorurtheilen und Befürchtungen hängen geblieben: sie hat sich nicht in die Tiefe gewagt. Dieselbe als Morphologie und Entwicklungslehre des Willens zur Macht zufassen, wie ich sie fasse - daran hat noch Niemand in seinen Gedanken selbst gestreift: sofern es nämlich erlaubt ist, in dem, was bisher geschrieben wurde, ein Symptom von dem, was bisher verschwiegen wurde, zu erkennen. Die Gewalt der moralischen Vorurtheile ist tief in die geistigste, in die anscheinend kälteste und voraussetzungsloseste Welt gedrungen - und, wie es sich von selbst versteht, schädigend, hemmend, blendend, verdrehend. Eine eigentliche Physio-Psychologie hat mit unbewussten Widerständen im Herzen des Forschers zu kämpfen, sie hat "das Herz" gegen sich: schon eine Lehre von der gegenseitigen Bedingtheit der "guten" und der "schlimmen" Triebe, macht, als feinere Immoralität, einem noch kräftigen und herzhaften Gewissen Noth und Überdruss, - noch mehr eine Lehre von der Ableitbarkeit aller guten Triebe aus den schlimmen. Gesetzt aber, Jemand nimmt gar die Affekte Hass, Neid, Habsucht, Herrschsucht als lebenbedingende Affekte, als Etwas, das im Gesammt-Haushalte des Lebens grundsätzlich und grundwesentlich vorhanden sein muss, folglich noch gesteigert werden muss, falls das Leben noch gesteigert werden soll, - der leidet an einer solchen Richtung seines Urtheils wie an einer Seekrankheit. Und doch ist auch diese Hypothese bei

weitem nicht die peinlichste und fremdeste in diesem ungeheuren fast noch neuen Reiche gefährlicher Erkenntnisse: - und es giebt in der That hundert gute Gründe dafür, dass Jeder von ihm fernbleibt, der es - kann! Andrerseits: ist man einmal mit seinem Schiffe hierhin verschlagen, nun! wohlan! jetzt tüchtig die Zähne zusammengebissen! die Augen aufgemacht! die Hand fest am Steuer! - wir fahren geradewegs über die Moral weg, wir erdrücken, wir zermalmen vielleicht dabei unsren eignen Rest Moralität, indem wir dorthin unsre Fahrt machen und wagen, - aber was liegt an uns! Niemals noch hat sich verwegenen Reisenden und Abenteurern eine tiefere Welt der Einsicht eröffnet: und der Psychologe, welcher dergestalt "Opfer bringt" - es ist nicht das sacrifizio dell'intelletto, im Gegentheil! - wird zum Mindesten dafür verlangen dürfen, dass die Psychologie wieder als Herrin der Wissenschaften anerkannt werde, zu deren Dienste und Vorbereitung die übrigen Wissenschaften da sind. Denn Psychologie ist nunmehr wieder der Weg zu den Grundproblemen.

Zweites Hauptstück:

Der freie Geist.

24. O sancta simplicitas! In welcher seltsamen Vereinfachung und Fälschung lebt der Mensch! Man kann sich nicht zu Ende wundern, wenn man sich erst einmal die Augen für dies Wunder eingesetzt hat! Wie haben wir Alles um uns hell und frei und leicht und einfach gemacht! wie wussten wir unsern Sinnen einen Freipass für alles Oberflächliche, unserm Denken eine göttliche Begierde nach muthwilligen Sprüngen und Fehlschlüssen zu geben! - wie haben wir es von Anfang an verstanden, uns unsre Unwissenheit zu erhalten, um eine kaum begreifliche Freiheit, Unbedenklichkeit, Unvorsichtigkeit, Herzhaftigkeit, Heiterkeit des Lebens, um das Leben zu geniessen! Und erst auf

diesem nunmehr festen und granitnen Grunde von Unwissenheit durfte sich bisher die Wissenschaft erheben, der Wille zum Wissen auf dem Grunde eines viel gewaltigeren Willens, des Willens zum Nichtwissen, zum Ungewissen, zum Unwahren! Nicht als sein Gegensatz, sondern - als seine Verfeinerung! Mag nämlich auch die Sprache, hier wie anderwärts, nicht über ihre Plumpheit hinauskönnen und fortfahren, von Gegensätzen zu reden, wo es nur Grade und mancherlei Feinheit der Stufen giebt; mag ebenfalls die eingefleischte Tartüfferie der Moral, welche jetzt zu unserm unüberwindlichen "Fleisch und Blut" gehört, uns Wissenden selbst die Worte im Munde umdrehen: hier und da begreifen wir es und lachen darüber, wie gerade noch die beste Wissenschaft uns am besten in dieser vereinfachten, durch und durch künstlichen, zurecht gedichteten, zurecht gefälschten Welt festhalten will, wie sie unfreiwillig-willig den Irrthum liebt, weil sie, die Lebendige, - das Leben liebt!

25. Nach einem so fröhlichen Eingang möchte ein ernstes Wort nicht überhört werden: es wendet sich an die Ernstesten. Seht euch vor, ihr Philosophen und Freunde der Erkenntniss, und hütet euch vor dem Martyrium! Vor dem Leiden "um der Wahrheit willen"! Selbst vor der eigenen Vertheidigung! Es verdirbt eurem Gewissen alle Unschuld und feine Neutralität, es macht euch halsstarrig gegen Einwände und rothe Tücher, es verdummt, verthiert und verstiert, wenn ihr

im Kampfe mit Gefahr, Verlästerung, Verdächtigung, Ausstossung und noch gröberen Folgen der Feindschaft, zuletzt euch gar als Vertheidiger der Wahrheit auf Erden ausspielen müsst: - als ob "die Wahrheit" eine so harmlose und täppische Person wäre, dass sie Vertheidiger nöthig hätte! und gerade euch, ihr Ritter von der traurigsten Gestalt, meine Herren Eckensteher und Spinneweber des Geistes! Zuletzt wisst ihr gut genug, dass nichts daran liegen darf, ob gerade ihr Recht behaltet, ebenfalls dass bisher noch kein Philosoph Recht behalten hat, und dass eine preiswürdigere Wahrhaftigkeit in jedem kleinen Fragezeichen liegen dürfte, welches ihr hinter eure Leibworte und Lieblingslehren (und gelegentlich hinter euch selbst) setzt, als in allen feierlichen Gebärden und Trümpfen vor Anklägern und Gerichtshöfen! Geht lieber bei Seite! Flieht in's Verborgene! Und habt eure Maske und Feinheit, dass man euch verwechsele! Oder ein Wenig fürchte! Und vergesst mir den Garten nicht, den Garten mit goldenem Gitterwerk! Und habt Menschen um euch, die wie ein Garten sind, - oder wie Musik über Wassern, zur Zeit des Abends, wo der Tag schon zur Erinnerung wird: - wählt die gute Einsamkeit, die freie muthwillige leichte Einsamkeit, welche euch auch ein Recht giebt, selbst in irgend einem Sinne noch gut zu bleiben! Wie giftig, wie listig, wie schlecht macht jeder lange Krieg, der sich nicht mit offener Gewalt führen lässt! Wie persönlich macht eine lange Furcht, ein langes Augenmerk auf Feinde, auf mögliche Feinde! Diese Ausgestossenen der Gesellschaft, diese Lang-Verfolgten, Schlimm-Gehetzten, - auch die Zwangs-Einsiedler, die Spinoza's oder Giordano Bruno's - werden zuletzt immer, und sei es unter der geistigsten Maskerade, und vielleicht ohne dass sie selbst es wissen, zu raffinirten Rachsüchtigen und Giftmischern (man grabe doch einmal den Grund der Ethik und Theologie Spinoza's auf!) - gar nicht zu reden von der Tölpelei der moralischen Entrüstung, welche an einem Philosophen das unfehlbare Zeichen dafür ist, dass ihm der philosophische Humor davon lief. Das Martyrium des Philosophen, seine "Aufopferung für die Wahrheit" zwingt an's Licht heraus, was vom Agitator und vom Schauspieler in ihm steckte; und gesetzt, dass man ihm nur mit einer artistischen Neugierde bisher zugeschaut hat, so kann in Bezug auf manchen Philosophen der gefährliche Wunsch freilich begreiflich sein, ihn auch einmal in seiner Entartung zu sehn (entartet zum "Märtyrer", zum Bühnen- und Tribünen-Schreihals). Nur dass man sich, mit einem solchen Wunsche, darüber klar sein muss, was man jedenfalls dabei zu sehen bekommen wird: - nur ein Satyrspiel, nur eine Nachspiel-Farce, nur den fortwährenden Beweis dafür, dass die lange eigentliche Tragödie zu Ende ist: vorausgesetzt, dass jede Philosophie im Entstehen eine lange Tragödie war. -

26. Jeder auserlesene Mensch trachtet instinktiv nach seiner Burg und Heimlichkeit, wo er von der Menge,

den Vielen, den Allermeisten erlöst ist, wo er die Regel "Mensch" vergessen darf, als deren Ausnahme: - den Einen Fall ausgenommen, dass er von einem noch stärkeren Instinkte geradewegs auf diese Regel gestossen wird, als Erkennender im grossen und ausnahmsweisen Sinne. Wer nicht im Verkehr mit Menschen gelegentlich in allen Farben der Noth, grün und grau vor Ekel, Überdruss, Mitgefühl, Verdüsterung, Vereinsamung schillert, der ist gewiss kein Mensch höheren Geschmacks; gesetzt aber, er nimmt alle diese Last und Unlust nicht freiwillig auf sich, er weicht ihr immerdar aus und bleibt, wie gesagt, still und stolz auf seiner Burg versteckt, nun, so ist Eins gewiss: er ist zur Erkenntniss nicht gemacht, nicht vorherbestimmt. Denn als solcher würde er eines Tages sich sagen müssen "hole der Teufel meinen guten Geschmack! aber die Regel ist interessanter als die Ausnahme, - als ich, die Ausnahme!" - und würde sich hinab begeben, vor Allem "hinein". Das Studium des durchschnittlichen Menschen, lang, ernsthaft, und zu diesem Zwecke viel Verkleidung, Selbstüberwindung, Vertraulichkeit, schlechter Umgang - jeder Umgang ist schlechter Umgang ausser dem mit Seines-Gleichen -: das macht ein nothwendiges Stück der Lebensgeschichte jedes Philosophen aus, vielleicht das unangenehmste, übelriechendste, an Enttäuschungen reichste Stück. Hat er aber Glück, wie es einem Glückskinde der Erkenntniss geziemt, so begegnet er eigentlichen Abkürzern und Erleichterern seiner

Aufgabe, - ich meine sogenannten Cynikern, also Solchen, welche das Thier, die Gemeinheit, die "Regel" an sich einfach anerkennen und dabei noch jenen Grad von Geistigkeit und Kitzel haben, um über sich und ihres Gleichen vor Zeugen reden zu müssen: - mitunter wälzen sie sich sogar in Büchern wie auf ihrem eignen Miste. Cynismus ist die einzige Form, in welcher gemeine Seelen an Das streifen, was Redlichkeit ist; und der höhere Mensch hat bei jedem gröberen und feineren Cynismus die Ohren aufzumachen und sich jedes Mal Glück zu wünschen, wenn gerade vor ihm der Possenreisser ohne Scham oder der wissenschaftliche Satyr laut werden. Es giebt sogar Fälle, wo zum Ekel sich die Bezauberung mischt: da nämlich, wo an einen solchen indiskreten Bock und Affen, durch eine Laune der Natur, das Genie gebunden ist, wie bei dem Abbé Galiani, dem tiefsten, scharfsichtigsten und vielleicht auch schmutzigsten Menschen seines Jahrhunderts - er war viel tiefer als Voltaire und folglich auch ein gut Theil schweigsamer. Häufiger schon geschieht es, dass, wie angedeutet, der wissenschaftliche Kopf auf einen Affenleib, ein feiner Ausnahme-Verstand auf eine gemeine Seele gesetzt ist, - unter Ärzten und Moral-Physiologen namentlich kein seltenes Vorkommniss. Und wo nur Einer ohne Erbitterung, vielmehr harmlos vom Menschen redet als von einem Bauche mit zweierlei Bedürfnissen und einem Kopfe mit Einem; überall wo Jemand immer nur Hunger, Geschlechts-Begierde und Eitelkeit sieht, sucht und sehn will, als seien es die eigentlichen und einzigen Triebfedern der menschlichen Handlungen; kurz, wo man "schlecht" vom Menschen redet - und nicht einmal schlimm -, da soll der Liebhaber der Erkenntniss fein und fleissig hinhorchen, er soll seine Ohren überhaupt dort haben, wo ohne Entrüstung geredet wird. Denn der entrüstete Mensch, und wer immer mit seinen eignen Zähnen sich selbst (oder, zum Ersatz dafür, die Welt, oder Gott, oder die Gesellschaft) zerreisst und zerfleischt, mag zwar moralisch gerechnet, höher stehn als der lachende und selbstzufriedene Satyr, in jedem anderen Sinne aber ist er der gewöhnlichere, gleichgültigere, unbelehrendere Fall. Und Niemand lügt soviel als der Entrüstete. -

27. Es ist schwer, verstanden zu werden: besonders wenn man gangasrotogati denkt und lebt, unter lauter Menschen, welche anders denken und leben, nämlich kurmagati oder besten Falles "nach der Gangart des Frosches" mandeikagati - ich thue eben Alles, um selbst schwer verstanden zu werden? - und man soll schon für den guten Willen zu einiger Feinheit der Interpretation von Herzen erkenntlich sein. Was aber "die guten Freunde" anbetrifft, welche immer zu bequem sind und gerade als Freunde ein Recht auf Bequemlichkeit zu haben glauben: so thut man gut, ihnen von vornherein einen Spielraum und Tummelplatz des Missverständnisses zuzugestehn: - so hat man noch, zu

lachen; - oder sie ganz abzuschaffen, diese guten Freunde, - und auch zu lachen!

28. Was sich am schlechtesten aus einer Sprache in die andere übersetzen lässt, ist das tempo ihres Stils: als welcher im Charakter der Rasse seinen Grund hat, physiologischer gesprochen, im Durchschnitts-tempo ihres "Stoffwechsels". Es giebt ehrlich gemeinte Übersetzungen, die beinahe Fälschungen sind, als unfreiwillige Vergemeinerungen des Originals, bloss weil sein tapferes und lustiges tempo nicht mit übersetzt werden konnte, welches über alles Gefährliche in Dingen und Worten wegspringt, weghilft. Der Deutsche ist beinahe des Presto in seiner Sprache unfähig: also, wie man billig schliessen darf, auch vieler der ergötzlichsten und verwegensten Nuances des freien, freigeisterischen Gedankens. So gut ihm der Buffo und der Satyr fremd ist, in Leib und Gewissen, so gut ist ihm Aristophanes und Petronius unübersetzbar. Alles Gravitätische, Schwerflüssige, Feierlich-Plumpe, alle langwierigen und langweiligen Gattungen des Stils sind bei den Deutschen in überreicher Mannichfaltigkeit entwickelt, - man vergebe mir die Thatsache, dass selbst Goethe's Prosa, in ihrer Mischung von Steifheit und Zierlichkeit, keine Ausnahme macht, als ein Spiegelbild der "alten guten Zeit", zu der sie gehört, und als Ausdruck des deutschen Geschmacks, zur Zeit, wo es noch einen "deutschen Geschmack" gab: der ein Rokoko-

Geschmack war, in moribus et artibus. Lessing macht eine Ausnahme, Dank seiner Schauspieler-Natur, die Vieles verstand und sich auf Vieles verstand: er, der nicht umsonst der Übersetzer Bayle's war und sich gerne in die Nähe Diderot's und Voltaire's, noch lieber unter die römischen Lustspieldichter flüchtete: - Lessing liebte auch im tempo die Freigeisterei, die Flucht aus Deutschland. Aber wie vermöchte die deutsche Sprache, und sei es selbst in der Prosa eines Lessing, das tempo Macchiavell's nachzuahmen, der, in seinem principe, die trockne feine Luft von Florenz athmen lässt und nicht umhin kann, die ernsteste Angelegenheit in einem unbändigen Allegrissimo vorzutragen: vielleicht nicht ohne ein boshaftes Artisten-Gefühl davon, welchen Gegensatz er wagt, - Gedanken, lang, schwer, hart, gefährlich, und ein tempo des Galopps und der allerbesten muthwilligsten Laune. Wer endlich dürfte gar eine deutsche Übersetzung des Petronius wagen, der, mehr als irgend ein grosser Musiker bisher, der Meister des presto gewesen ist, in Erfindungen, Einfällen, Worten: - was liegt zuletzt an allen Sümpfen der kranken, schlimmen Welt, auch der "alten Welt", wenn man, wie er, die Füsse eines Windes hat, den Zug und Athem, den befreienden Hohn eines Windes, der Alles gesund macht, indem er Alles laufen macht! Und was Aristophanes angeht, jenen verklärenden, complementären Geist, um dessentwillen man dem ganzen Griechenthum verzeiht, dass es da war, gesetzt, dass man in aller Tiefe begriffen hat, was da Alles der Verzeihung, der Verklärung bedarf: - so wüsste ich nichts, was mich über Plato's Verborgenheit und Sphinx-Natur mehr hat träumen lassen als jenes glücklich erhaltene petit falt: dass man unter dem Kopfkissen seines Sterbelagers keine "Bibel" vorfand, nichts Ägyptisches, Pythagoreisches, Platonisches, - sondern den Aristophanes. Wie hätte auch ein Plato das Leben ausgehalten - ein griechisches Leben, zu dem er Nein sagte, - ohne einen Aristophanes! -

29. Es ist die Sache der Wenigsten, unabhängig zu sein: - es ist ein Vorrecht der Starken. Und wer es versucht, auch mit dem besten Rechte dazu, aber ohne es zu müssen, beweist damit, dass er wahrscheinlich nicht nur stark, sondern bis zur Ausgelassenheit verwegen ist. Er begiebt sich in ein Labyrinth, er vertausendfältigt die Gefahren, welche das Leben an sich schon mit sich bringt; von denen es nicht die kleinste ist, dass Keiner mit Augen sieht, wie und wo er sich verirrt, vereinsamt und stückweise von irgend einem Höhlen-Minotaurus des Gewissens zerrissen wird. Gesetzt, ein Solcher geht zu Grunde, so geschieht es so ferne vom Verständniss der Menschen, dass sie es nicht fühlen und mitfühlen: - und er kann nicht mehr zurück! er kann auch zum Mitleiden der Menschen nicht mehr zurück! - -

30. Unsre höchsten Einsichten müssen - und sollen! - wie Thorheiten, unter Umständen wie Verbrechen

klingen, wenn sie unerlaubter Weise Denen zu Ohren kommen, welche nicht dafür geartet und vorbestimmt sind. Das Exoterische und das Esoterische, wie man ehedem unter Philosophen unterschied, bei Indern, wie bei Griechen, Persern und Muselmännern, kurz überall, wo man eine Rangordnung und nicht an Gleichheit und gleiche Rechte glaubte, - das hebt sich nicht sowohl dadurch von einander ab, dass der Exoteriker draussen steht und von aussen her, nicht von innen her, sieht, schätzt, misst, urtheilt: das Wesentlichere ist, dass er von Unten hinauf die Dinge sieht, - der Esoteriker aber von Oben herab! Es giebt Höhen der Seele, von wo aus gesehen selbst die Tragödie aufhört, tragisch zu wirken; und, alles Weh der Welt in Eins genommen, wer dürfte zu entscheiden wagen, ob sein Anblick nothwendig gerade zum Mitleiden und dergestalt zur Verdoppelung des Wehs verführen und zwingen werde?… Was der höheren Art von Menschen zur Nahrung oder zur Labsal dient, muss einer sehr unterschiedlichen und geringeren Art beinahe Gift sein. Die Tugenden des gemeinen Manns würden vielleicht an einem Philosophen Laster und Schwächen bedeuten; es wäre möglich, dass ein hochgearteter Mensch, gesetzt, dass er entartete und zu Grunde gienge, erst dadurch in den Besitz von Eigenschaften käme, derentwegen man nöthig hätte, ihn in der niederen Welt, in welche er hinab sank, nunmehr wie einen Heiligen zu verehren. Es giebt Bücher, welche für Seele und Gesundheit einen umgekehrten Werth haben, je nachdem die niedere Seele, die niedrigere Lebenskraft oder aber die höhere und gewaltigere sich ihrer bedienen: im ersten Falle sind es gefährliche, anbröckelnde, auflösende Bücher, im anderen Heroldsrufe, welche die Tapfersten zu ihrer Tapferkeit herausfordern. Allerwelts-Bücher sind immer übelriechende Bücher: der Kleine-Leute-Geruch klebt daran. Wo das Volk isst und trinkt, selbst wo es verehrt, da pflegt es zu stinken. Man soll nicht in Kirchen gehn, wenn man reine Luft athmen will. - -

31. Man verehrt und verachtet in jungen Jahren noch ohne jene Kunst der Nuance, welche den besten Gewinn des Lebens ausmacht, und muss es billigerweise hart büssen, solchergestalt Menschen und Dinge mit Ja und Nein überfallen zu haben. Es ist Alles darauf eingerichtet, dass der schlechteste aller Geschmäcker, der Geschmack für das Unbedingte grausam genarrt und gemissbraucht werde, bis der Mensch lernt, etwas Kunst in seine Gefühle zu legen und lieber noch mit dem Künstlichen den Versuch zu wagen: wie es die rechten Artisten des Lebens thun. Das Zornige und Ehrfürchtige, das der Jugend eignet, scheint sich keine Ruhe zu geben, bevor es nicht Menschen und Dinge so zurecht gefälscht hat, dass es sich an ihnen auslassen kann: - Jugend ist an sich schon etwas Fälschendes und Betrügerisches. Später, wenn die junge Seele, durch lauter Enttäuschungen gemartert, sich endlich argwöhnisch gegen sich selbst zurück wendet, immer noch heiss und wild, auch in ihrem

Argwohne und Gewissensbisse: wie zürnt sie sich nunmehr, wie zerreisst sie sich ungeduldig, wie nimmt sie Rache für ihre lange Selbst-Verblendung, wie als ob sie eine willkürliche Blindheit gewesen sei! In diesem Übergange bestraft man sich selber, durch Misstrauen gegen sein Gefühl; man foltert seine Begeisterung durch den Zweifel, ja man fühlt schon das gute Gewissen als eine Gefahr, gleichsam als Selbst-Verschleierung und Ermüdung der feineren Redlichkeit; und vor Allem, man nimmt Partei, grundsätzlich Partei gegen "die Jugend". - Ein Jahrzehend später: und man begreift, dass auch dies Alles noch - Jugend war!

32. Die längste Zeit der menschlichen Geschichte hindurch - man nennt sie die prähistorische Zeit - wurde der Werth oder der Unwerth einer Handlung aus ihren Folgen abgeleitet: die Handlung an sich kam dabei ebensowenig als ihre Herkunft in Betracht, sondern ungefähr so, wie heute noch in China eine Auszeichnung oder Schande vom Kinde auf die Eltern zurückgreift, so war es die rückwirkende Kraft des Erfolgs oder Misserfolgs, welche den Menschen anleitete, gut oder schlecht von einer Handlung zu denken. Nennen wir diese Periode die vormoralische Periode der Menschheit: der Imperativ "erkenne dich selbst!" war damals noch unbekannt. In den letzten zehn Jahrtausenden ist man hingegen auf einigen grossen Flächen der Erde Schritt für Schritt so weit

gekommen, nicht mehr die Folgen, sondern die Herkunft der Handlung über ihren Werth entscheiden zu lassen: ein grosses Ereigniss als Ganzes, eine erhebliche Verfeinerung des Blicks und Maassstabs, die unbewusste Nachwirkung von der Herrschaft aristokratischer Werthe und des Glaubens an "Herkunft", das Abzeichen einer Periode, welche man im engeren Sinne als die moralische bezeichnen darf: der erste Versuch zur Selbst-Erkenntniss ist damit gemacht. Statt der Folgen die Herkunft: welche Umkehrung der Perspektive! Und sicherlich eine erst nach langen Kämpfen und Schwankungen erreichte Umkehrung! Freilich: ein verhängnissvoller neuer Aberglaube, eine eigenthümliche Engigkeit der Interpretation kam eben damit zur Herrschaft: man interpretirte die Herkunft einer Handlung im allerbestimmtesten Sinne als Herkunft aus einer Absicht; man wurde Eins im Glauben daran, dass der Werth einer Handlung im Werthe ihrer Absicht belegen sei. Die Absicht als die ganze Herkunft und Vorgeschichte einer Handlung: unter diesem Vorurtheile ist fast bis auf die neueste Zeit auf Erden moralisch gelobt, getadelt, gerichtet, auch philosophirt worden. - Sollten wir aber heute nicht bei der Nothwendigkeit angelangt sein, uns nochmals über eine Umkehrung und Grundverschiebung der Werthe schlüssig zu machen, Dank einer nochmaligen Selbstbesinnung und Vertiefung des Menschen, - sollten wir nicht an der Schwelle einer Periode stehen, welche, negativ, zunächst als die aussermoralische zu, bezeichnen wäre: heute, wo wenigstens unter uns Immoralisten der Verdacht sich regt, dass gerade in dem, was nicht-absichtlich an einer Handlung ist, ihr entscheidender Werth belegen sei, und dass alle ihre Absichtlichkeit, Alles, was von ihr gesehn, gewusst, "bewusst" werden kann, noch zu ihrer Oberfläche und Haut gehöre, - welche, wie jede Haut, Etwas verräth, aber noch mehr verbirgt? Kurz, wir glauben, dass die Absicht nur ein Zeichen und Symptom ist, das erst der Auslegung bedarf, dazu ein Zeichen, das zu Vielerlei und folglich für sich allein fast nichts bedeutet, - dass Moral, im bisherigen Sinne, also Absichten-Moral ein Vorurtheil gewesen ist, eine Voreiligkeit, eine Vorläufigkeit vielleicht, ein Ding etwa vom Range der Astrologie und Alchymie, aber jedenfalls Etwas, das überwunden werden muss. Die Überwindung der Moral, in einem gewissen Verstande sogar die Selbstüberwindung der Moral: mag das der Name für jene lange geheime Arbeit sein, welche den feinsten und redlichsten, auch den boshaftesten Gewissen von heute, als lebendigen Probirsteinen der Seele, vorbehalten blieb. -

33. Es hilft nichts: man muss die Gefühle der Hingebung, der Aufopferung für den Nächsten, die ganze Selbstentäusserungs-Moral erbarmungslos zur Rede stellen und vor Gericht führen: ebenso wie die Ästhetik der "interesselosen Anschauung", unter

welcher sich die Entmännlichung der Kunst verführerisch genug heute ein gutes Gewissen zu schaffen sucht. Es ist viel zu viel Zauber und Zucker in jenen Gefühlen des "für Andere", des "nicht für mich", als dass man nicht nöthig hätte, hier doppelt misstrauisch zu werden und zu fragen: "sind es nicht vielleicht - Verführungen?" - Dass sie gefallen - Dem, der sie hat, und Dem, der ihre Früchte geniesst, auch dem blossen Zuschauer, - dies giebt noch kein Argument für sie ab, sondern fordert gerade zur Vorsicht auf. Seien wir also vorsichtig!

34. Auf welchen Standpunkt der Philosophie man sich heute auch stellen mag: von jeder Stelle aus gesehn ist die Irrthümlichkeit der Welt, in der wir zu leben glauben, das Sicherste und Festeste, dessen unser Auge noch habhaft werden kann: - wir finden Gründe über Gründe dafür, die uns zu Muthmaassungen über ein betrügerisches Princip im "Wesen der Dinge" verlocken möchten. Wer aber unser Denken selbst, also "den Geist" für die Falschheit der Welt verantwortlich macht - ein ehrenhafter Ausweg, den jeder bewusste oder unbewusste advocatus dei geht -: wer diese Welt, sammt Raum, Zeit, Gestalt, Bewegung, als falsch erschlossen nimmt: ein Solcher hätte mindestens guten Anlass, gegen alles Denken selbst endlich Misstrauen zu lernen: hätte es uns nicht bisher den allergrössten Schabernack gespielt? und welche Bürgschaft dafür gäbe es, dass es nicht fortführe, zu thun, was es immer

gethan hat? In allem Ernste: die Unschuld der Denker hat etwas Rührendes und Ehrfurcht Einflössendes, welche ihnen erlaubt, sich auch heute noch vor das Bewusstsein hinzustellen, mit der Bitte, dass es ihnen ehrliche Antworten gebe: zum Beispiel ob es "real" sei, und warum es eigentlich die äussere Welt sich so entschlossen vom Halse halte, und was dergleichen Fragen mehr sind. Der Glaube an "unmittelbare Gewissheiten" ist eine moralische Naivetät, welche uns Philosophen Ehre macht: aber - wir sollen nun einmal nicht "nur moralische" Menschen sein! Von der Moral abgesehn, ist jener Glaube eine Dummheit, die uns wenig Ehre macht! Mag im bürgerlichen Leben das allzeit bereite Misstrauen als Zeichen des "schlechten Charakters" gelten und folglich unter die Unklugheiten gehören: hier unter uns, jenseits der bürgerlichen Welt und ihres Ja's und Nein's, - was sollte uns hindern, unklug zu sein und zu sagen: der Philosoph hat nachgerade ein Recht auf "schlechten Charakter", als das Wesen, welches bisher auf Erden immer am besten genarrt worden ist, - er hat heute die Pflicht zum Misstrauen, zum boshaftesten Schielen aus jedem Abgrunde des Verdachts heraus. - Man vergebe mir den Scherz dieser düsteren Fratze und Wendung: denn ich selbst gerade habe längst über Betrügen und Betrogenwerden anders denken, anders schätzen gelernt und halte mindestens ein paar Rippenstösse für die blinde Wuth bereit, mit der die Philosophen sich dagegen sträuben, betrogen zu werden. Warum nicht?

Es ist nicht mehr als ein moralisches Vorurtheil, dass Wahrheit mehr werth ist als Schein; es ist sogar die schlechtest bewiesene Annahme, die es in der Welt giebt. Man gestehe sich doch so viel ein: es bestünde gar kein Leben, wenn nicht auf dem Grunde perspektivischer Schätzungen und Scheinbarkeiten; und wollte man, mit der tugendhaften Begeisterung und Tölpelei mancher Philosophen, die "scheinbare Welt" ganz abschlaffen, nun, gesetzt, ihr könntet das, - so bliebe mindestens dabei auch von eurer "Wahrheit" nichts mehr übrig! Ja, was zwingt uns überhaupt zur Annahme, dass es einen wesenhaften Gegensatz von "wahr" und "falsch" giebt? Genügt es nicht, Stufen der Scheinbarkeit anzunehmen und gleichsam hellere und dunklere Schatten und Gesammttöne des Scheins, - verschiedene valeurs, um die Sprache der Maler zu reden? Warum dürfte die Welt, die uns etwas angeht -, nicht eine Fiktion sein? Und wer da fragt: "aber zur Fiktion gehört ein Urheber?" - dürfte dem nicht rund geantwortet werden: Warum? Gehört dieses "Gehört" nicht vielleicht mit zur Fiktion? Ist es denn nicht erlaubt, gegen Subjekt, wie gegen Prädikat und Objekt, nachgerade ein Wenig ironisch zu sein? Dürfte sich der Philosoph nicht über die Gläubigkeit an die Grammatik erheben? Alle Achtung vor den Gouvernanten: aber wäre es nicht an der Zeit, dass die Philosophie dem Gouvernanten-Glauben absagte? -

35. Oh Voltaire! Oh Humanität! Oh Blödsinn! Mit der "Wahrheit", mit dem Suchen der Wahrheit hat es etwas auf sich; und wenn der Mensch es dabei gar zu menschlich treibt - "il ne cherche le vrai que pour faire le bien" - ich wette, er findet nichts!

36. Gesetzt, dass nichts Anderes als real "gegeben" ist als unsre Welt der Begierden und Leidenschaften, dass wir zu keiner anderen "Realität" hinab oder hinauf können als gerade zur Realität unsrer Triebe - denn Denken ist nur ein Verhalten dieser Triebe zu einander -: ist es nicht erlaubt, den Versuch zu machen und die Frage zu fragen, ob dies Gegeben nicht ausreicht, um aus Seines-Gleichen auch die sogenannte mechanistische (oder "materielle") Welt zu verstehen? Ich meine nicht als eine Täuschung, einen "Schein", eine "Vorstellung" (im Berkeley'schen und Schopenhauerischen Sinne), sondern als vom gleichen Realitäts-Range, welchen unser Affekt selbst hat, - als eine primitivere Form der Welt der Affekte, in der noch Alles in mächtiger Einheit beschlossen liegt, was sich dann im organischen Prozesse abzweigt und ausgestaltet (auch, wie billig, verzärtelt und abschwächt -), als eine Art von Triebleben, in dem noch sämmtliche organische Funktionen, mit Selbst-Regulirung, Assimilation, Ernährung, Ausscheidung, Stoffwechsel, synthetisch gebunden in einander sind, - als eine Vorform des Lebens? - Zuletzt ist es nicht nur erlaubt, diesen Versuch zu machen: es ist, vom Gewissen der

Methode aus, geboten. Nicht mehrere Arten von Causalität annehmen, so lange nicht der Versuch, mit einer einzigen auszureichen, bis an seine äusserste Grenze getrieben ist (- bis zum Unsinn, mit Verlaub zu sagen): das ist eine Moral der Methode, der man sich heute nicht entziehen darf; - es folgt "aus ihrer Definition", wie ein Mathematiker sagen würde. Die Frage ist zuletzt, ob wir den Willen wirklich als wirkend anerkennen, ob wir an die Causalität des Willens glauben: thun wir das - und im Grunde ist der Glaube daran eben unser Glaube an Causalität selbst -, so müssen wir den Versuch machen, die Willens-Causalität hypothetisch als die einzige zu setzen. "Wille" kann natürlich nur auf "Wille" wirken - und nicht auf "Stoffe" (nicht auf "Nerven" zum Beispiel -): genug, man muss die Hypothese wagen, ob nicht überall, wo "Wirkungen" anerkannt werden, Wille auf Wille wirkt - und ob nicht alles mechanische Geschehen, insofern eine Kraft darin thätig wird, eben Willenskraft, Willens-Wirkung ist. - Gesetzt endlich, dass es gelänge, unser gesammtes Triebleben als die Ausgestaltung und Verzweigung Einer Grundform des Willens zu erklären - nämlich des Willens zur Macht, wie es in ein Satz ist -; gesetzt, dass man alle organischen Funktionen auf diesen Willen zur Macht zurückführen könnte und in ihm auch die Lösung des Problems der Zeugung und Ernährung - es ist Ein Problem - fände, so hätte man damit sich das Recht verschafft, alle wirkende Kraft eindeutig zu bestimmen als: Wille zur Macht. Die Welt von innen gesehen, die Welt auf ihren "intelligiblen Charakter" hin bestimmt und bezeichnet - sie wäre eben "Wille zur Macht" und nichts ausserdem. -

37. "Wie? Heisst das nicht, populär geredet: Gott ist widerlegt, der Teufel aber nicht -?" Im Gegentheil! Im Gegentheil, meine Freunde! Und, zum Teufel auch, wer zwingt euch, populär zu reden! -

38. Wie es zuletzt noch, in aller Helligkeit der neueren Zeiten, mit der französischen Revolution gegangen ist, jener schauerlichen und, aus der Nähe beurtheilt, überflüssigen Posse, in welche aber die edlen und schwärmerischen Zuschauer von ganz Europa aus der Ferne her so lange und so leidenschaftlich ihre eignen Empörungen und Begeisterungen hinein interpretirt haben, bis der Text unter der Interpretation verschwand: so könnte eine edle Nachwelt noch einmal die ganze Vergangenheit missverstehen und dadurch vielleicht erst ihren Anblick erträglich machen. - Oder vielmehr: ist dies nicht bereits geschehen? waren wir nicht selbst - diese "edle Nachwelt"? Und ist es nicht gerade jetzt, insofern wir dies begreifen, - damit vorbei?

39. Niemand wird so leicht eine Lehre, bloss weil sie glücklich macht, oder tugendhaft macht, deshalb für wahr halten: die lieblichen "Idealisten" etwa

ausgenommen, welche für das Gute, Wahre, Schöne schwärmen und in ihrem Teiche alle Arten von bunten plumpen und gutmüthigen Wünschbarkeiten durcheinander schwimmen lassen. Glück und Tugend sind keine Argumente. Man vergisst aber gerne, auch auf Seiten besonnener Geister, dass Unglücklichmachen und Böse-machen ebensowenig Gegenargumente sind. Etwas dürfte wahr sein: ob es gleich im höchsten Grade schädlich und gefährlich wäre; ja es könnte selbst zur Grundbeschaffenheit des Daseins gehören, dass man an seiner völligen Erkenntniss zu Grunde gienge, - so dass sich die Stärke eines Geistes darnach bemässe, wie viel er von der "Wahrheit" gerade noch aushielte, deutlicher, bis zu welchem Grade er sie verdünnt, verhüllt, versüsst, verdumpft, verfälscht nöthig hätte. Aber keinem Zweifel unterliegt es, dass für die Entdeckung gewisser Theile der Wahrheit die Bösen und Unglücklichen begünstigter sind und eine grössere Wahrscheinlichkeit des Gelingens haben; nicht zu reden von den Bösen, die glücklich sind, - eine Species, welche von den Moralisten verschwiegen wird. Vielleicht, dass Härte und List günstigere Bedingungen zur Entstehung des starken, unabhängigen Geistes und Philosophen abgeben, als jene sanfte feine nachgebende Gutartigkeit und Kunst des Leicht-nehmens, welche man an einem Gelehrten schätzt und mit Recht schätzt. Vorausgesetzt, was voran steht, dass man den Begriff "Philosoph" nicht auf den Philosophen einengt, der Bücher schreibt

- oder gar seine Philosophie in Bücher bringt! - Einen letzten Zug zum Bilde des freigeisterischen Philosophen bringt Stendhal bei, den ich um des deutschen Geschmacks willen nicht unterlassen will zu unterstreichen: - denn er geht wider den deutschen Geschmack. "Pour être bon philosophe", sagt dieser letzte grosse Psycholog, "il faut être sec, clair, sans illusion. Un banquier, qui a fait fortune, a une partie du caractère requis pour faire des découvertes en philosophie, c'est-'á-dire pour voir clair dans ce qui est."

40. Alles, was tief ist, liebt die Maske; die allertiefsten Dinge haben sogar einen Hass auf Bild und Gleichniss. Sollte nicht erst der Gegensatz die rechte Verkleidung sein, in der die Scham eines Gottes einhergienge? Eine fragwürdige Frage: es wäre wunderlich, wenn nicht irgend ein Mystiker schon dergleichen bei sich gewagt hätte. Es giebt Vorgänge so zarter Art, dass man gut thut, sie durch eine Grobheit zu verschütten und unkenntlich zu machen; es giebt Handlungen der Liebe und einer ausschweifenden Grossmuth, hinter denen nichts räthlicher ist, als einen Stock zu nehmen und den Augenzeugen durchzuprügeln: damit trübt man dessen Gedächtniss. Mancher versteht sich darauf, das eigne Gedächtniss zu trüben und zu misshandeln, um wenigstens an diesem einzigen Mitwisser seine Rache zu haben: - die Scham ist erfinderisch. Es sind nicht die schlimmsten Dinge,

deren man sich am schlimmsten schämt: es ist nicht nur Arglist hinter einer Maske, - es giebt so viel Güte in der List. Ich könnte mir denken, dass ein Mensch, der etwas Kostbares und Verletzliches zu bergen hätte, grob und rund wie ein grünes altes schwerbeschlagenes Weinfass durch's Leben rollte: die Feinheit seiner Scham will es so. Einem Menschen, der Tiefe in der Scham hat, begegnen auch seine Schicksale und zarten Entscheidungen auf Wegen, zu denen Wenige je gelangen, und um deren Vorhandensein seine Nächsten und Vertrautesten nicht wissen dürfen: seine Lebensgefahr verbirgt sich ihren Augen und ebenso seine wieder eroberte Lebens-Sicherheit. Ein solcher Verborgener, der aus Instinkt das Reden zum Schweigen und Verschweigen braucht und unerschöpflich ist in der Ausflucht vor Mittheilung, will es und fördert es, dass eine Maske von ihm an seiner Statt in den Herzen und Köpfen seiner Freunde herum wandelt; und gesetzt, er will es nicht, so werden ihm eines Tages die Augen darüber aufgehn, dass es trotzdem dort eine Maske von ihm giebt, - und dass es gut so ist. Jeder tiefe Geist braucht eine Maske: mehr noch, um jeden tiefen Geist wächst fortwährend eine Maske, Dank der beständig falschen, nämlich flachen Auslegung jedes Wortes, jedes Schrittes, jedes Lebens-Zeichens, das er giebt. -

41. Man muss sich selbst seine Proben geben, dafür dass man zur Unabhängigkeit und zum Befehlen

bestimmt ist; und dies zur rechten Zeit. Man soll seinen Proben nicht aus dem Wege gehn, obgleich sie vielleicht das gefährlichste Spiel sind, das man spielen kann, und zuletzt nur Proben, die vor uns selber als Zeugen und vor keinem anderen Richter abgelegt werden. Nicht an einer Person hängen bleiben: und sei sie die geliebteste, - jede Person ist ein Gefängniss, auch ein Winkel. Nicht an einem Vaterlande hängen bleiben: und sei es das leidendste und hülfbedürftigste, - es ist schon weniger schwer, sein Herz von einem siegreichen Vaterlande los zu binden. Nicht an einem Mitleiden hängen bleiben: und gälte es höheren Menschen, in deren seltne Marter und Hülflosigkeit uns ein Zufall hat blicken lassen. Nicht an einer Wissenschaft hängen bleiben: und locke sie Einen mit den kostbarsten, anscheinend gerade uns aufgesparten Funden. Nicht an seiner eignen Loslösung hängen bleiben, an jener wollüstigen Ferne und Fremde des Vogels, der immer weiter in die Höhe flieht, um immer mehr unter sich zu sehn: - die Gefahr des Fliegenden. Nicht an unsern eignen Tugenden hängen bleiben und als Ganzes das Opfer irgend einer Einzelheit an uns werden, zum Beispiel unsrer "Gastfreundschaft": wie es die Gefahr der Gefahren bei hochgearteten und reichen Seelen ist, welche verschwenderisch, fast gleichgültig mit sich selbst umgehn und die Tugend der Liberalität bis zum Laster treiben. Man muss wissen, sich zu bewahren: stärkste Probe der Unabhängigkeit.

42. Eine neue Gattung von Philosophen kommt herauf: ich wage es, sie auf einen nicht ungefährlichen Namen zu taufen. So wie ich sie errathe, so wie sie sich errathen lassen - denn es gehört zu ihrer Art, irgend worin Räthsel bleiben zu wollen -, möchten diese Philosophen der Zukunft ein Recht, vielleicht auch ein Unrecht darauf haben, als Versucher bezeichnet zu werden. Dieser Name selbst ist zuletzt nur ein Versuch, und, wenn man will, eine Versuchung.

43. Sind es neue Freunde der "Wahrheit", diese kommenden Philosophen? Wahrscheinlich genug: denn alle Philosophen liebten bisher ihre Wahrheiten. Sicherlich aber werden es keine Dogmatiker sein. Es muss ihnen wider den Stolz gehn, auch wider den Geschmack, wenn ihre Wahrheit gar noch eine Wahrheit für Jedermann sein soll: was bisher der geheime Wunsch und Hintersinn aller dogmatischen Bestrebungen war. "Mein Urtheil ist mein Urtheil: dazu hat nicht leicht auch ein Anderer das Recht" - sagt vielleicht solch ein Philosoph der Zukunft. Man muss den schlechten Geschmack von sich abthun, mit Vielen übereinstimmen zu wollen. "Gut" ist nicht mehr gut, wenn der Nachbar es in den Mund nimmt. Und wie könnte es gar ein "Gemeingut" geben! Das Wort widerspricht sich selbst: was gemein sein kann, hat immer nur wenig Werth. Zuletzt muss es so stehn, wie es steht und immer stand: die grossen Dinge bleiben für die Grossen übrig, die Abgründe für die Tiefen, die

Zartheiten und Schauder für die Feinen, und, im Ganzen und Kurzen, alles Seltene für die Seltenen. -

44. Brauche ich nach alledem noch eigens zu sagen, dass auch sie freie, sehr freie Geister sein werden, diese Philosophen der Zukunft, - so gewiss sie auch nicht bloss freie Geister sein werden, sondern etwas Mehreres, Höheres, Grösseres und Gründlich-Anderes, das nicht verkannt und verwechselt werden will? Aber, indem ich dies sage, fühle ich fast ebenso sehr gegen sie selbst, als gegen uns, die wir ihre Herolde und Vorläufer sind, wir freien Geister! - die Schuldigkeit, ein altes dummes Vorurtheil und Missverständniss von uns gemeinsam fortzublasen, welches allzulange wie ein Nebel den Begriff "freier Geist" undurchsichtig gemacht hat. In allen Ländern Europa's und ebenso in Amerika giebt es jetzt Etwas, das Missbrauch mit diesem Namen treibt, eine sehr enge, eingefangne, an Ketten gelegte Art von Geistern, welche ungefähr das Gegentheil von dem wollen, was in unsern Absichten und Instinkten liegt, - nicht zu reden davon, dass sie in Hinsicht auf jene heraufkommenden neuen Philosophen erst recht zugemachte Fenster und verriegelte Thüren sein müssen. Sie gehören, kurz und schlimm, unter die Nivellirer, diese fälschlich genannten "freien Geister" - als beredte und schreibfingrige Sklaven des demokratischen Geschmacks und seiner "modernen Ideen": allesammt Menschen ohne Einsamkeit, ohne eigne Einsamkeit, plumpe brave Burschen, welchen

weder Muth noch achtbare Sitte abgesprochen werden soll, nur dass sie eben unfrei und zum Lachen oberflächlich sind, vor Allem mit ihrem Grundhange, in den Formen der bisherigen alten Gesellschaft ungefähr die Ursache für alles menschliche Elend und Missrathen zu sehn: wobei die Wahrheit glücklich auf den Kopf zu stehn kommt! Was sie mit allen Kräften erstreben möchten, ist das allgemeine grüne Weide-Glück der Heerde, mit Sicherheit, Ungefährlichkeit, Behagen, Erleichterung des Lebens für Jedermann; ihre beiden am reichlichsten abgesungnen Lieder und Lehren heissen "Gleichheit der Rechte" und "Mitgefühl für alles Leidende", - und das Leiden selbst wird von ihnen als Etwas genommen, das man abschaffen muss. Wir Umgekehrten, die wir uns ein Auge und ein Gewissen für die Frage aufgemacht haben, wo und wie bisher die Pflanze "Mensch" am kräftigsten in die Höhe gewachsen ist, vermeinen, dass dies jedes Mal unter den umgekehrten Bedingungen geschehn ist, dass dazu die Gefährlichkeit seiner Lage erst in's Ungeheure wachsen, seine Erfindungs- und Verstellungskraft (sein "Geist" -) unter langem Druck und Zwang sich in's Feine und Verwegene entwickeln, sein Lebens-Wille bis zum unbedingten Macht-Willen gesteigert werden musste: - wir vermeinen, dass Härte, Gewaltsamkeit, Sklaverei, Gefahr auf der Gasse und im Herzen, Verborgenheit, Stoicismus, Versucherkunst und Teufelei jeder Art, dass alles Böse, Furchtbare, Tyrannische, Raubthier- und Schlangenhafte am

Menschen so gut zur Erhöhung der Species "Mensch" dient, als sein Gegensatz: - wir sagen sogar nicht einmal genug, wenn wir nur so viel sagen, und befinden uns jedenfalls, mit unserm Reden und Schweigen an dieser Stelle, am andern Ende aller modernen Ideologie und Heerden-Wünschbarkeit: als deren Antipoden vielleicht? Was Wunder, dass wir "freien Geister" nicht gerade die mittheilsamsten Geister sind? dass wir nicht in jedem Betrachte zu verrathen wünschen, wovon ein Geist sich frei machen kann und wohin er dann vielleicht getrieben wird? Und was es mit der gefährlichen Formel "jenseits von Gut und Böse" auf sich hat, mit der wir uns zum Mindesten vor Verwechslung behüten: wir sind etwas Anderes als "libres-penseurs", "liberi pensatori", "Freidenker" und wie alle diese braven Fürsprecher der "modernen Ideen" sich zu benennen lieben. In vielen Ländern des Geistes zu Hause, mindestens zu Gaste gewesen; den dumpfen angenehmen Winkeln immer wieder entschlüpft, in die uns Vorliebe und Vorhass, Jugend, Abkunft, der Zufall von Menschen und Büchern, oder selbst die Ermüdungen der Wanderschaft zu bannen schienen; voller Bosheit gegen die Lockmittel der Abhängigkeit, welche in Ehren, oder Geld, oder Ämtern, oder Begeisterungen der Sinne versteckt liegen; dankbar sogar gegen Noth und wechselreiche Krankheit, weil sie uns immer von irgend einer Regel und ihrem "Vorurtheil" losmachte, dankbar gegen Gott, Teufel, Schlaf und Wurm in uns, neugierig bis zum

Laster, Forscher bis zur Grausamkeit, mit unbedenklichen Fingern für Unfassbares, mit Zähnen und Mägen für das Unverdaulichste, bereit zu jedem Handwerk, das Scharfsinn und scharfe Sinne verlangt, bereit zu jedem Wagniss, Dank einem Überschusse von "freiem Willen", mit Vorder- und Hinterseelen, denen Keiner leicht in die letzten Absichten sieht, mit Vorder- und Hintergründen, welche kein Fuss zu Ende laufen dürfte, Verborgene unter den Mänteln des Lichts, Erobernde, ob wir gleich Erben und Verschwendern gleich sehn, Ordner und Sammler von früh bis Abend, Geizhälse unsres Reichthums und unsrer vollgestopften Schubfächer, haushälterisch im Lernen und Vergessen, erfinderisch in Schematen, mitunter stolz auf Kategorien-Tafeln, mitunter Pedanten, mitunter Nachteulen der Arbeit auch am hellen Tage; ja, wenn es noth thut, selbst Vogelscheuchen - und heute thut es noth: nämlich insofern wir die geborenen geschworenen eifersüchtigen Freunde der Einsamkeit sind, unsrer eignen tiefsten mitternächtlichsten mittäglichsten Einsamkeit: - eine solche Art Menschen sind wir, wir freien Geister! und vielleicht seid auch ihr etwas davon, ihr Kommenden? ihr neuen Philosophen? -

Drittes Hauptstück:

Das religiöse Wesen.

45. Die menschliche Seele und ihre Grenzen, der bisher überhaupt erreichte Umfang menschlicher innerer Erfahrungen, die Höhen, Tiefen und Fernen dieser Erfahrungen, die ganze bisherige Geschichte der Seele und ihre noch unausgetrunkenen Möglichkeiten: das ist für einen geborenen Psychologen und Freund der "grossen Jagd" das vorbestimmte Jagdbereich. Aber wie oft muss er sich verzweifelt sagen: "ein Einzelner! ach, nur ein Einzelner! und dieser grosse Wald und Urwald!" Und so wünscht er sich einige hundert Jagdgehülfen und feine gelehrte Spürhunde, welche er in die Geschichte der menschlichen Seele treiben könnte, um dort sein Wild zusammenzutreiben.

Umsonst: er erprobt es immer wieder, gründlich und bitterlich, wie schlecht zu allen Dingen, die gerade seine Neugierde reizen, Gehülfen und Hunde zu finden sind. Der Übelstand, den es hat, Gelehrte auf neue und gefährliche Jagdbereiche auszuschicken, wo Muth, Klugheit, Feinheit in jedem Sinne noth thun, liegt darin, dass sie gerade dort nicht mehr brauchbar sind, wo die "grosse Jagd", aber auch die grosse Gefahr beginnt: - gerade dort verlieren sie ihr Spürauge und ihre Spürnase. Um zum Beispiel zu errathen und festzustellen, was für eine Geschichte bisher das Problem von Wissen und Gewissen in der Seele der homines religiosi gehabt hat, dazu müsste Einer vielleicht selbst so tief, so verwundet, so ungeheuer sein, wie es das intellektuelle Gewissen Pascal's war: und dann bedürfte es immer noch jenes ausgespannten Himmels von heller, boshafter Geistigkeit, welcher von Oben herab dies Gewimmel von gefährlichen und schmerzlichen Erlebnissen zu übersehn, zu ordnen, in Formeln zu zwingen vermöchte. - Aber wer thäte mir diesen Dienst! Aber wer hätte Zeit, auf solche Diener zu warten! - sie wachsen ersichtlich zu selten, sie sind zu allen Zeiten so unwahrscheinlich! Zuletzt muss man Alles selber thun, um selber Einiges zu wissen: das heisst, man hat viel zu thun! - Aber eine Neugierde meiner Art bleibt nun einmal das angenehmste aller Laster, - Verzeihung! ich wollte sagen: die Liebe zur Wahrheit hat ihren Lohn im Himmel und schon auf Erden. -

46. Der Glaube, wie ihn das erste Christenthum verlangt und nicht selten erreicht hat, inmitten einer skeptischen und südlich-freigeisterischen Welt, die einen Jahrhunderte langen Kampf von Philosophenschulen hinter sich und in sich hatte, hinzugerechnet die Erziehung zur Toleranz, welche das imperium Romanum gab, - dieser Glaube ist nicht jener treuherzige und bärbeissige Unterthanen-Glaube, mit dem etwa ein Luther oder ein Cromwell oder sonst ein nordischer Barbar des Geistes an ihrem Gotte und Christenthum gehangen haben; viel eher scholl jener Glaube Pascal's, der auf schreckliche Weise einem dauernden Selbstmorde der Vernunft ähnlich sieht, - einer zähen langlebigen wurmhaften Vernunft, die nicht mit Einem Male und Einem Streiche todtzumachen ist. Der christliche Glaube ist von Anbeginn Opferung: Opferung aller Freiheit, alles Stolzes, aller Selbstgewissheit des Geistes; zugleich Verknechtung und Selbst-Verhöhnung, Selbst-Verstümmelung. Es ist Grausamkeit und religiöser Phönicismus in diesem Glauben, der einem mürben, vielfachen und viel verwöhnten, Gewissen zugemuthet wird: seine Voraussetzung ist, dass die Unterwerfung des Geistes unbeschreiblich wehe thut, dass die ganze Vergangenheit und Gewohnheit eines solchen Geistes sich gegen das Absurdissimum wehrt, als welches ihm der "Glaube" entgegentritt. Die modernen Menschen, mit ihrer Abstumpfung gegen alle christliche Nomenklatur, fühlen das Schauerlich-Superlativische

nicht mehr nach, das für einen antiken Geschmack in der Paradoxie der Formel "Gott am Kreuze" lag. Es hat bisher noch niemals und nirgendswo eine gleiche Kühnheit im Umkehren, etwas gleich Furchtbares, Fragendes und Fragwürdiges gegeben wie diese Formel: sie verhiess eine Umwerthung aller antiken Werthe. - Es ist der Orient, der tiefe Orient, es ist der orientalische Sklave, der auf diese Weise an Rom und seiner vornehmen und frivolen Toleranz, am römischen "Katholicismus" des Glaubens Rache nahm: - und immer war es nicht der Glaube, sondern die Freiheit vom Glauben, jene halb stoische und lächelnde Unbekümmertheit um den Ernst des Glaubens, was die Sklaven an ihren Herrn, gegen ihre Herrn empört hat. Die "Aufklärung" empört: der Sklave nämlich will Unbedingtes, er versteht nur das Tyrannische, auch in der Moral, er liebt wie er hasst, ohne Nuance, bis in die Tiefe, bis zum Schmerz, bis zur Krankheit, - sein vieles verborgenes Leiden empört sich gegen den vornehmen Geschmack, der das Leiden zu leugnen scheint. Die Skepsis gegen das Leiden, im Grunde nur eine Attitude der aristokratischen Moral, ist nicht am wenigsten auch an der Entstehung des letzten grossen Sklaven-Aufstandes betheiligt, welcher mit der französischen Revolution begonnen hat.

47. Wo nur auf Erden bisher die religiöse Neurose aufgetreten ist, finden wir sie verknüpft mit drei gefährlichen Diät-Verordnungen: Einsamkeit, Fasten

und geschlechtlicher Enthaltsamkeit, - doch ohne dass hier mit Sicherheit zu entscheiden wäre, was da Ursache, was Wirkung sei, und ob hier überhaupt ein Verhältniss von Ursache und Wirkung vorliege. Zum letzten Zweifel berechtigt, dass gerade zu ihren regelmässigsten Symptomen, bei wilden wie bei zahmen Völkern, auch die plötzlichste ausschweifendste Wollüstigkeit gehört, welche dann, ebenso plötzlich, in Busskrampf und Welt- und Willens-Verneinung umschlägt: beides vielleicht als maskirte Epilepsie deutbar? Aber nirgendswo sollte man sich der Deutungen mehr entschlagen: um keinen Typus herum ist bisher eine solche Fülle von Unsinn und Aberglauben aufgewachsen, keiner scheint bisher die Menschen, selbst die Philosophen, mehr interessirt zu haben, - es wäre an der Zeit, hier gerade ein Wenig kalt zu werden, Vorsicht zu lernen, besser noch: wegzusehn, wegzugehn. - Noch im Hintergrunde der letztgekommenen Philosophie, der Schopenhauerischen, steht, beinahe als das Problem an sich, dieses schauerliche Fragezeichen der religiösen Krisis und Erweckung. Wie ist Willensverneinung möglich? wie ist der Heilige möglich? - das scheint wirklich die Frage gewesen zu sein, bei der Schopenhauer zum Philosophen wurde und anfieng. Und so war es eine ächt Schopenhauerische Consequenz, dass sein überzeugtester Anhänger (vielleicht auch sein letzter, was Deutschland betrifft -), nämlich Richard Wagner, das eigne Lebenswerk gerade hier zu Ende brachte und zuletzt noch jenen furchtbaren und ewigen Typus als Kundry auf der Bühne vorführte, type vécu, und wie er leibt und lebt; zu gleicher Zeit, wo die Irrenärzte fast aller Länder Europa's einen Anlass hatten, ihn aus der Nähe zu studiren, überall, wo die religiöse Neurose - oder, wie ich es nenne, "das religiöse Wesen" - als "Heilsarmee" ihren letzten epidemischen Ausbruch und Aufzug gemacht hat. - Fragt man sich aber, was eigentlich am ganzen Phänomen des Heiligen den Menschen aller Art und Zeit, auch den Philosophen, so unbändig interessant gewesen ist: so ist es ohne allen Zweifel der ihm, anhaftende Anschein des Wunders, nämlich der unmittelbaren Aufeinanderfolge von Gegensätzen, von moralisch entgegengesetzt gewertheten Zuständen der Seele: man glaubte hier mit Händen zu greifen, dass aus einem "schlechten Menschen" mit Einem Male ein "Heiliger", ein guter Mensch werde. Die bisherige Psychologie litt an dieser Stelle Schiffbruch: sollte es nicht vornehmlich darum geschehen sein, weil sie sich unter die Herrschaft der Moral gestellt hatte, weil sie an die moralischen Werth-Gegensätze selbst glaubte, und diese Gegensätze in den Text und Thatbestand hineinsah, hineinlas, hinein deutete? - Wie? Das "Wunder" nur ein Fehler der Interpretation? Ein Mangel an Philologie? -

48. Es scheint, dass den lateinischen Rassen ihr Katholicismus viel innerlicher zugehört, als uns

Nordländern das ganze Christentum überhaupt: und dass folglich der Unglaube in katholischen Ländern etwas ganz Anderes zu bedeuten hat, als in protestantischen - nämlich eine Art Empörung gegen den Geist der Rasse, während er bei uns eher eine Rückkehr zum Geist (oder Ungeist -) der Rasse ist. Wir Nordländer stammen unzweifelhaft aus Barbaren-Rassen, auch in Hinsicht auf unsere Begabung zur Religion: wir sind schlecht für sie begabt. Man darf die Kelten ausnehmen, welche deshalb auch den besten Boden für die Aufnahme der christlichen Infektion im Norden abgegeben haben: - in Frankreich kam das christliche Ideal, soweit es nur die blasse Sonne des Nordens erlaubt hat, zum Ausblühen. Wie fremdartig fromm sind unserm Geschmack selbst diese letzten französischen Skeptiker noch, sofern etwas keltisches Blut in ihrer Abkunft ist! Wie katholisch, wie undeutsch riecht uns Auguste Comte's Sociologie mit ihrer römischen Logik der Instinkte! Wie jesuitisch jener liebenswürdige und kluge Cicerone von Port-Royal, Sainte-Beuve, trotz all seiner Jesuiten-Feindschaft! Und gar Ernest Renan: wie unzugänglich klingt uns Nordländern die Sprache solch eines Renan, in dem alle Augenblicke irgend ein Nichts von religiöser Spannung seine in feinerem Sinne wollüstige und bequem sich bettende Seele um ihr Gleichgewicht bringt! Man spreche ihm einmal diese schönen Sätze nach, - und was für Bosheit und Übermuth regt sich sofort in unserer wahrscheinlich weniger schönen und härteren, nämlich deutscheren Seele als Antwort! - "disons donc hardiment que la religion est un produit de l'homme normal, que l'homme est le plus dans le vrai quand il est le plus religieux et le plus assuré d'une destinée infinie.... C'est quand il est bon qu'il veut que la vertu corresponde à un ordre éternel, c'est quand il contemple les choses d'une manière désintéressée qu'il trouve la mort révoltante et absurde. Comment ne pas supposer que c'est dans ces moments-là, que l'homme voit le mieux?...." Diese Sätze sind meinen Ohren und Gewohnheiten so sehr antipodisch, dass, als ich sie fand, mein erster Ingrimm daneben schrieb "la niaiserie religieuse par excellence!" - bis mein letzter Ingrimm sie gar noch lieb gewann, diese Sätze mit ihrer auf den Kopf gestellten Wahrheit! Es ist so artig, so auszeichnend, seine eignen Antipoden zu haben!

49. Das, was an der Religiosität der alten Griechen staunen macht, ist die unbändige Fülle von Dankbarkeit, welche sie ausströmt: - es ist eine sehr vornehme Art Mensch, welche so vor der Natur und vor dem Leben steht! - Später, als der Pöbel in Griechenland zum Übergewicht kommt, überwuchert die Furcht auch in der Religion; und das Christenthum bereitete sich vor.-

50. Die Leidenschaft für Gott: es giebt bäurische, treuherzige und zudringliche Arten, wie die Luther's, - der ganze Protestantismus entbehrt der südlichen

delicatezza. Es giebt ein orientalisches Aussersichsein darin, wie bei einem unverdient begnadeten oder erhobenen Sklaven, zum Beispiel bei Augustin, der auf eine beleidigende Weise aller Vornehmheit der Gebärden und Begierden ermangelt. Es giebt frauenhafte Zärtlichkeit und Begehrlichkeit darin, welche schamhaft und unwissend nach einer unio mystica et physica drängt: wie bei Madame de Guyon. In vielen Fällen erscheint sie wunderlich genug als Verkleidung der Pubertät eines Mädchens oder Jünglings; hier und da selbst als Hysterie einer alten Jungfer, auch als deren letzter Ehrgeiz: - die Kirche hat das Weib schon mehrfach in einem solchen Falle heilig gesprochen.

51. Bisher haben sich die mächtigsten Menschen immer noch verehrend vor dem Heiligen gebeugt, als dem Räthsel der Selbstbezwingung und absichtlichen letzten Entbehrung: warum beugten sie sich? Sie ahnten in ihm - und gleichsam hinter dem Fragezeichen seines gebrechlichen und kläglichen Anscheins - die überlegene Kraft, welche sich an einer solchen Bezwingung erproben wollte, die Stärke des Willens, in der sie die eigne Stärke und herrschaftliche Lust wieder erkannten und zu ehren wussten: sie ehrten Etwas an sich, wenn sie den Heiligen ehrten. Es kam hinzu, dass der Anblick des Heiligen ihnen einen Argwohn eingab: ein solches Ungeheures von Verneinung, von Wider-Natur wird nicht umsonst begehrt worden sein, so

sagten und fragten sie sich. Es giebt vielleicht einen Grund dazu, eine ganz grosse Gefahr, über welche der Asket, Dank seinen geheimen Zusprechern und Besuchern, näher unterrichtet sein möchte? Genug, die Mächtigen der Welt lernten vor ihm eine neue Furcht, sie ahnten eine neue Macht, einen fremden, noch unbezwungenen Feind: - der "Wille zur Macht" war es, der sie nöthigte, vor dem Heiligen stehen zu bleiben. Sie mussten ihn fragen - -

52. Im jüdischen "alten Testament", dem Buche von der göttlichen Gerechtigkeit, giebt es Menschen, Dinge und Reden in einem so grossen Stile, dass das griechische und indische Schriftenthum ihm nichts zur Seite zu stellen hat. Man steht mit Schrecken und Ehrfurcht vor diesen ungeheuren Überbleibseln dessen, was der Mensch einstmals war, und wird dabei über das alte Asien und sein vorgeschobenes Halbinselchen Europa, das durchaus gegen Asien den "Fortschritt des Menschen" bedeuten möchte, seine traurigen Gedanken haben. Freilich: wer selbst nur ein dünnes zahmes Hausthier ist und nur Hausthier-Bedürfnisse kennt (gleich unsren Gebildeten von heute, die Christen des "gebildeten" Christenthums hinzugenommen -), der hat unter jenen Ruinen weder sich zu verwundern, noch gar sich zu betrüben - der Geschmack am alten Testament ist ein Prüfstein in Hinsicht auf "Gross" und "Klein" -: vielleicht, dass er das neue Testament, das Buch von der Gnade, immer noch eher nach seinem Herzen findet

(in ihm ist viel von dem rechten zärtlichen dumpfen Betbrüder- und Kleinen-Seelen-Geruch). Dieses neue Testament, eine Art Rokoko des Geschmacks in jedem Betrachte, mit dem alten Testament zu Einem Buche zusammengeleimt zu haben, als "Bibel", als "das Buch an sich": das ist vielleicht die grösste Verwegenheit und "Sünde wider den Geist", welche das litterarische Europa auf dem Gewissen hat.

53. Warum heute Atheismus? - "Der Vater" in Gott ist gründlich widerlegt; ebenso "der Richter", "der Belohner". Insgleichen sein "freier Wille": er hört nicht, - und wenn er hörte, wüsste er trotzdem nicht zu helfen. Das Schlimmste ist: er scheint unfähig, sich deutlich mitzutheilen: ist er unklar? - Dies ist es, was ich, als Ursachen für den Niedergang des europäischen Theismus, aus vielerlei Gesprächen, fragend, hinhorchend, ausfindig gemacht habe; es scheint mir, dass zwar der religiöse Instinkt mächtig im Wachsen ist, - dass er aber gerade die theistische Befriedigung mit tiefem Misstrauen ablehnt.

54. Was thut denn im Grunde die ganze neuere Philosophie? Seit Descartes - und zwar mehr aus Trotz gegen ihn, als auf Grund seines Vorgangs - macht man seitens aller Philosophen ein Attentat auf den alten Seelen-Begriff, unter dem Anschein einer Kritik des Subjekt- und Prädikat-Begriffs - das heisst: ein Attentat auf die Grundvoraussetzung der christlichen Lehre. Die

neuere Philosophie, als eine erkenntnisstheoretische Skepsis, ist, versteckt oder offen, antichristlich: obschon, für feinere Ohren gesagt, keineswegs antireligiös. Ehemals nämlich glaubte man an "die Seele", wie man an die Grammatik und das grammatische Subjekt glaubte: man sagte, "Ich" ist Bedingung, "denke" ist Prädikat und bedingt - Denken ist eine Thätigkeit, zu der ein Subjekt als Ursache gedacht werden muss. Nun versuchte man, mit einer bewunderungswürdigen Zähigkeit und List, ob man nicht aus diesem Netze heraus könne, - ob nicht vielleicht das Umgekehrte wahr sei: "denke" Bedingung, "Ich" bedingt; "Ich" also erst eine Synthese, welche durch das Denken selbst gemacht wird. Kant wollte im Grunde beweisen, dass vom Subjekt aus das Subjekt nicht bewiesen werden könne, - das Objekt auch nicht: die Möglichkeit einer Scheinexistenz des Subjekts, also "der Seele", mag ihm nicht immer fremd gewesen sein, jener Gedanke, welcher als Vedanta-Philosophie schon einmal und in ungeheurer Macht auf Erden dagewesen ist.

55. Es giebt eine grosse Leiter der religiösen Grausamkeit, mit vielen Sprossen; aber drei davon sind die wichtigsten. Einst opferte man seinem Gotte Menschen, vielleicht gerade solche, welche man am besten liebte, - dahin gehören die Erstlings-Opfer aller Vorzeit-Religionen, dahin auch das Opfer des Kaisers Tiberius in der Mithrasgrotte der Insel Capri, jener

schauerlichste aller römischen Anachronismen. Dann, in der moralischen Epoche der Menschheit, opferte man seinem Gotte die stärksten Instinkte, die man besass, seine "Natur"; diese Festfreude glänzt im grausamen Blicke des Asketen, des begeisterten "Wider-Natürlichen". Endlich: was blieb noch übrig zu opfern? Musste man nicht endlich einmal alles Tröstliche, Heilige, Heilende, alle Hoffnung, allen Glauben an verborgene Harmonie, an zukünftige Seligkeiten und Gerechtigkeiten opfern? musste man nicht Gott selber opfern und, aus Grausamkeit gegen sich, den Stein, die Dummheit, die Schwere, das Schicksal, das Nichts anbeten? Für das Nichts Gott opfern - dieses paradoxe Mysterium der letzten Grausamkeit blieb dem Geschlechte, welches jetzt eben herauf kommt, aufgespart: wir Alle kennen schon etwas davon. -

56. Wer, gleich mir, mit irgend einer räthselhaften Begierde sich lange darum bemüht hat, den Pessimismus in die Tiefe zu denken und aus der halb christlichen, halb deutschen Enge und Einfalt zu erlösen, mit der er sich diesem Jahrhundert zuletzt dargestellt hat, nämlich in Gestalt der Schopenhauerischen Philosophie; wer wirklich einmal mit einem asiatischen und überasiatischen Auge in die weltverneinendste aller möglichen Denkweisen hinein und hinunter geblickt hat - jenseits von Gut und Böse, und nicht mehr, wie Buddha und Schopenhauer, im Bann und Wahne der Moral -, der hat vielleicht

ebendamit, ohne dass er es eigentlich wollte, sich die Augen für das umgekehrte Ideal aufgemacht: für das Ideal des übermüthigsten lebendigsten und weltbejahendsten Menschen, der sich nicht nur mit dem, was war und ist, abgefunden und vertragen gelernt hat, sondern es, so wie es war und ist, wieder haben will, in alle Ewigkeit hinaus, unersättlich da capo rufend, nicht nur zu sich, sondern zum ganzen Stücke und Schauspiele, und nicht nur zu einem Schauspiele, sondern im Grunde zu Dem, der gerade dies Schauspiel nöthig hat - und nöthig macht: weil er immer wieder sich nöthig hat - und nöthig macht - - Wie? Und dies wäre nicht - circulus vitiosus deus?

57. Mit der Kraft seines geistigen Blicks und Einblicks wächst die Ferne und gleichsam der Raum um den Menschen: seine Welt wird tiefer, immer neue Sterne, immer neue Räthsel und Bilder kommen ihm in Sicht. Vielleicht war Alles, woran das Auge des Geistes seinen Scharfsinn und Tiefsinn geübt hat, eben nur ein Anlass zu seiner Übung, eine Sache des Spiels, Etwas für Kinder und Kindsköpfe. Vielleicht erscheinen uns einst die feierlichsten Begriffe, um die am meisten gekämpft und gelitten worden ist, die Begriffe "Gott" und "Sünde", nicht wichtiger, als dem alten Manne ein Kinder-Spielzeug und Kinder-Schmerz erscheint, - und vielleicht hat dann "der alte Mensch" wieder ein andres Spielzeug und einen andren Schmerz nöthig, - immer noch Kinds genug, ein ewiges Kind!

58. Hat man wohl beachtet, in wiefern zu einem eigentlich religiösen Leben (und sowohl zu seiner mikroskopischen Lieblings-Arbeit der Selbstprüfung, als zu jener zarten Gelassenheit, welche sich "Gebet" nennt und eine beständige Bereitschaft für das "Kommen Gottes" ist) der äussere Müssiggang oder Halb-Müssiggang noth thut, ich meine der Müssiggang mit gutem Gewissen, von Alters her, von Geblüt, dem das Aristokraten-Gefühl nicht ganz fremd ist, dass Arbeit schändet, - nämlich Seele und Leib gemein macht? Und dass folglich die moderne, lärmende, Zeit-auskaufende, auf sich stolze, dumm-stolze Arbeitsamkeit, mehr als alles Übrige, gerade zum "Unglauben" erzieht und vorbereitet? Unter Denen, welche zum Beispiel jetzt in Deutschland abseits von der Religion leben, finde ich Menschen von vielerlei Art und Abkunft der "Freidenkerei", vor Allem aber eine Mehrzahl solcher, denen Arbeitsamkeit, von Geschlecht zu Geschlecht, die religiösen Instinkte aufgelöst hat: so dass sie gar nicht mehr wissen, wozu Religionen nütze sind, und nur mit einer Art stumpfen Erstaunens ihr Vorhandensein in der Welt gleichsam registriren. Sie fühlen sich schon reichlich in Anspruch genommen, diese braven Leute, sei es von ihren Geschäften, sei es von ihren Vergnügungen, gar nicht zu reden vom "Vaterlande" und den Zeitungen und den "Pflichten der Familie": es scheint, dass sie gar keine Zeit für die Religion übrig haben, zumal es ihnen unklar bleibt, ob es sich dabei um ein neues Geschäft

oder ein neues Vergnügen handelt, - denn unmöglich, sagen sie sich, geht man in die Kirche, rein um sich die gute Laune zu verderben. Sie sind keine Feinde der religiösen Gebräuche; verlangt man in gewissen Fällen, etwa von Seiten des Staates, die Betheiligung an solchen Gebräuchen, so thun sie, was man verlangt, wie man so Vieles thut -, mit einem geduldigen und bescheidenen Ernste und ohne viel Neugierde und Unbehagen: - sie leben eben zu sehr abseits und ausserhalb, um selbst nur ein Für und Wider in solchen Dingen bei sich nöthig zu finden. Zu diesen Gleichgültigen gehört heute die Überzahl der deutschen Protestanten in den mittleren Ständen, sonderlich in den arbeitsamen grossen Handels- und Verkehrscentren; ebenfalls die Überzahl der arbeitsamen Gelehrten und der ganze Universitäts-Zubehör (die Theologen ausgenommen, deren Dasein und Möglichkeit daselbst dem Psychologen immer mehr und immer feinere Räthsel zu rathen giebt). Man macht sich selten von Seiten frommer oder auch nur kirchlicher Menschen eine Vorstellung davon, wieviel guter Wille, man könnte sagen, willkürlicher Wille jetzt dazu gehört, dass ein deutscher Gelehrter das Problem der Religion ernst nimmt; von seinem ganzen Handwerk her (und, wie gesagt, von der handwerkerhaften Arbeitsamkeit her, zu welcher ihn sein modernes Gewissen verpflichtet) neigt er zu einer überlegenen, beinahe gütigen Heiterkeit gegen die Religion, zu der sich bisweilen eine leichte Geringschätzung mischt, gerichtet gegen die "Unsauberkeit" des Geistes, welche er überall dort voraussetzt, wo man sich, noch zur Kirche bekennt. Es gelingt dem Gelehrten erst mit Hülfe der Geschichte (also nicht von seiner persönlichen Erfahrung aus), es gegenüber den Religionen zu einem ehrfurchtsvollen Ernste und zu einer gewissen scheuen Rücksicht zu bringen; aber wenn er sein Gefühl sogar bis zur Dankbarkeit gegen sie gehoben hat, so ist er mit seiner Person auch noch keinen Schritt weit dem, was noch als Kirche oder Frömmigkeit besteht, näher gekommen: vielleicht umgekehrt. Die praktische Gleichgültigkeit gegen religiöse Dinge, in welche hinein er geboren und erzogen ist, pflegt sich bei ihm zur Behutsamkeit und Reinlichkeit zu sublimiren, welche die Berührung mit religiösen Menschen und Dingen scheut; und es kann gerade die Tiefe seiner Toleranz und Menschlichkeit sein, die ihn vor dem feinen Nothstande ausweichen heisst, welchen das Toleriren selbst mit sich bringt. - Jede Zeit hat ihre eigene göttliche Art von Naivetät, um deren Erfindung sie andre Zeitalter beneiden dürfen: - und wie viel Naivetät, verehrungswürdige, kindliche und unbegrenzt tölpelhafte Naivetät liegt in diesem Überlegenheits-Glauben des Gelehrten, im guten Gewissen seiner Toleranz, in der ahnungslosen schlichten Sicherheit, mit der sein Instinkt den religiösen Menschen als einen minderwerthigen und niedrigeren Typus behandelt, über den er selbst hinaus, hinweg, hinauf gewachsen ist, - er, der kleine anmaassliche Zwerg und Pöbelmann, der fleissig-flinke Kopf- und Handarbeiter der "Ideen", der "modernen Ideen"!

59. Wer tief in die Welt gesehen hat, erräth wohl, welche Weisheit darin liegt, dass die Menschen oberflächlich sind. Es ist ihr erhaltender Instinkt, der sie lehrt, flüchtig, leicht und falsch zu sein. Man findet hier und da eine leidenschaftliche und übertreibende Anbetung der "reinen Formen", bei Philosophen wie bei Künstlern: möge Niemand zweifeln, dass wer dergestalt den Cultus der Oberfläche nöthig hat, irgend wann einmal einen unglückseligen Griff unter sie gethan hat. Vielleicht giebt es sogar hinsichtlich dieser verbrannten Kinder, der geborenen Künstler, welche den Genuss des Lebens nur noch in der Absicht finden, sein Bild zu fälschen (gleichsam in einer langwierigen Rache am Leben -), auch noch eine Ordnung des Ranges: man könnte den Grad, in dem ihnen das Leben verleidet ist, daraus abnehmen, bis wie weit sie sein Bild verfälscht, verdünnt, verjenseitigt, vergöttlicht zu sehn wünschen, - man könnte die homines religiosi mit unter die Künstler rechnen, als ihren höchsten Rang. Es ist die tiefe argwöhnische Furcht vor einem unheilbaren Pessimismus, der ganze Jahrtausende zwingt, sich mit den Zähnen in eine religiöse Interpretation des Daseins zu verbeissen: die Furcht jenes Instinktes, welcher ahnt, dass man der Wahrheit zu früh habhaft werden könnte, ehe der Mensch stark genug, hart genug, Künstler

genug geworden ist.... Die Frömmigkeit, das "Leben in Gott", mit diesem Blicke betrachtet, erschiene dabei als die feinste und letzte Ausgeburt der Furcht vor der Wahrheit, als Künstler-Anbetung und -Trunkenheit vor der consequentesten aller Fälschungen, als der Wille zur Umkehrung der Wahrheit, zur Unwahrheit um jeden Preis. Vielleicht, dass es bis jetzt kein stärkeres Mittel gab, den Menschen selbst zu verschönern, als eben Frömmigkeit: durch sie kann der Mensch so sehr Kunst, Oberfläche, Farbenspiel, Güte werden, dass man an seinem Anblicke nicht mehr leidet. -

60. Den Menschen zu lieben um Gottes Willen - das war bis jetzt das vornehmste und entlegenste Gefühl, das unter Menschen erreicht worden ist. Dass die Liebe zum Menschen ohne irgendeine heiligende Hinterabsicht eine Dummheit und Thierheit mehr ist, dass der Hang zu dieser Menschenliebe erst von einem höheren Hange sein Maass, seine Feinheit, sein Körnchen Salz und Stäubchen Ambra zu bekommen hat: - welcher Mensch es auch war, der dies zuerst empfunden und "erlebt" hat, wie sehr auch seine Zunge gestolpert haben mag, als sie versuchte, solch eine Zartheit auszudrücken, er bleibe uns in alle Zeiten heilig und verehrenswerth, als der Mensch, der am höchsten bisher geflogen und am schönsten sich verirrt hat!

61. Der Philosoph, wie wir ihn verstehen, wir freien Geister als der Mensch der umfänglichsten Verantwortlichkeit, der das Gewissen für die Gesammt-Entwicklung des Menschen hat: dieser Philosoph wird sich der Religionen zu seinem Züchtungs- und Erziehungswerke bedienen, wie er sich der jeweiligen politischen und wirthschaftlichen Zustände bedienen wird. Der auslesende, züchtende, das heisst immer ebensowohl der zerstörende als der schöpferische und gestaltende Einfluss, welcher mit Hülfe der Religionen ausgeübt werden kann, ist je nach der Art Menschen, die unter ihren Bann und Schutz gestellt werden, ein vielfacher und verschiedener. Für die Starken, Unabhängigen, zum Befehlen, Vorbereiteten und Vorbestimmten, in denen die Vernunft und Kunst einer regierenden Rasse leibhaft wird, ist, Religion ein Mittelmehr, um Widerstände zu überwinden, um herrschen zu können: als ein Band, das Herrscher und Unterthanen gemeinsam bindet und die Gewissen der Letzteren, ihr Verborgenes und Innerlichstes, das sich gerne dem Gehorsam entziehen möchte, den Ersteren verräth und überantwortet; und falls einzelne Naturen einer solchen vornehmen Herkunft, durch hohe Geistigkeit, einem abgezogeneren und beschaulicheren Leben sich zuneigen und nur die feinste Artung des Herrschens (über ausgesuchte Jünger oder Ordensbrüder) sich vorbehalten, so kann Religion selbst als Mittel benutzt werden, sich Ruhe vor dem Lärm und der Mühsal des gröberen Regierens und

Reinheit vor dem nothwendigen Schmutz alles Politik-Machens zu schaffen. So verstanden es zum Beispiel die Brahmanen: mit Hülfe einer religiösen Organisation gaben sie sich die Macht, dem Volke seine Könige zu ernennen, während sie sich selber abseits und ausserhalb hielten und fühlten, als die Menschen höherer und überköniglicher Aufgaben. Inzwischen giebt die Religion auch einem Theile der Beherrschten Anleitung und Gelegenheit, sich auf einstmaliges Herrschen und Befehlen vorzubereiten, jenen langsam heraufkommenden Klassen und Ständen nämlich, in denen, durch glückliche Ehesitten, die Kraft und Lust des Willens, der Wille zur Selbstbeherrschung, immer im Steigen ist: - ihnen bietet die Religion Anstösse und Versuchungen genug, die Wege zur höheren Geistigkeit zu gehen, die Gefühle der grossen Selbstüberwindung, des Schweigens und der Einsamkeit zu erproben: - Asketismus und Puritanismus sind fast unentbehrliche Erziehungs- und Veredelungsmittel, wenn eine Rasse über ihre Herkunft aus dem Pöbel Herr werden will und sich zur einstmaligen Herrschaft emporarbeitet. Den gewöhnlichen Menschen endlich, den Allermeisten, welche zum Dienen und zum allgemeinen Nutzen da sind und nur insofern dasein dürfen, giebt die Religion eine unschätzbare Genügsamkeit mit ihrer Lage und Art, vielfachen Frieden des Herzens, eine Veredelung des Gehorsams, ein Glück und Leid mehr mit Ihres-Gleichen und Etwas von Verklärung und Verschönerung, Etwas von Rechtfertigung des ganzen

Alltags, der ganzen Niedrigkeit, der ganzen Halbthier-Armuth ihrer Seele. Religion und religiöse Bedeutsamkeit des Lebens legt Sonnenglanz auf solche immer geplagte Menschen und macht ihnen selbst den eigenen Anblick erträglich, sie wirkt, wie eine epikurische Philosophie auf Leidende höheren Ranges zu wirken pflegt, erquickend, verfeinernd, das Leiden gleichsam ausnützend, zuletzt gar heiligend und rechtfertigend. Vielleicht ist am Christenthum und Buddhismus nichts so ehrwürdig als ihre Kunst, noch den Niedrigsten anzulehren, sich durch Frömmigkeit in eine höhere Schein-Ordnung der Dinge zu stellen und damit das Genügen an der wirklichen Ordnung, innerhalb deren sie hart genug leben, - und gerade diese Härte thut Noth! - bei sich festzuhalten.

62. Zuletzt freilich, um solchen Religionen auch die schlimme Gegenrechnung zu machen und ihre unheimliche Gefährlichkeit an's Licht zu stellen: - es bezahlt sich immer theuer und fürchterlich, wenn Religionen nicht als Züchtungs- und Erziehungsmittel in der Hand des Philosophen, sondern von sich aus und souverän walten, wenn sie selber letzte Zwecke und nicht Mittel neben anderen Mitteln sein wollen. Es giebt bei dem Menschen wie bei jeder anderen Thierart einen Überschuss von Missrathenen, Kranken, Entartenden, Gebrechlichen, nothwendig Leidenden; die gelungenen Fälle sind auch beim Menschen immer die Ausnahme und sogar in Hinsicht darauf, dass der

Mensch das noch nicht festgestellte Thier ist, die spärliche Ausnahme. Aber noch schlimmer: je höher geartet der Typus eines Menschen ist, der durch ihn dargestellt wird, um so mehr steigt noch die Unwahrscheinlichkeit, dass er geräth: das Zufällige, das Gesetz des Unsinns im gesammten Haushalte der Menschheit zeigt sich am erschrecklichsten in seiner zerstörerischen Wirkung auf die höheren Menschen, deren Lebensbedingungen fein, vielfach und schwer auszurechnen sind. Wie verhalten sich nun die genannten beiden grössten Religionen zu diesem Überschuss der misslungenen Fälle? Sie suchen zu erhalten, im Leben festzuhalten, was sich nur irgend halten lässt, ja sie nehmen grundsätzlich für sie Partei, als Religionen für Leidende, sie geben allen Denen Recht, welche am Leben wie an einer Krankheit leiden, und möchten es durchsetzen, dass jede andre Empfindung des Lebens als falsch gelte und unmöglich werde. Möchte man diese schonende und erhaltende Fürsorge, insofern sie neben allen anderen auch dem höchsten, bisher fast immer auch leidendsten Typus des Menschen gilt und galt, noch so hoch anschlagen: in der Gesammt-Abrechnung gehören die bisherigen, nämlich souveränen Religionen zu den Hauptursachen, welche den Typus "Mensch" auf einer niedrigeren Stufe festhielten, - sie erhielten zu viel von dem, was zu Grunde gehn sollte. Man hat ihnen Unschätzbares zu danken; und wer ist reich genug an Dankbarkeit, um nicht vor alle dem arm zu werden, was zum Beispiel die "geistlichen Menschen" des Christenthums bisher für Europa gethan haben! Und doch, wenn sie den Leidenden Trost, den Unterdrückten und Verzweifelnden Muth, den Unselbständigen einen Stab und Halt gaben und die Innerlich-Zerstörten und Wild-Gewordenen von der Gesellschaft weg in Klöster und seelische Zuchthäuser lockten: was mussten sie ausserdem thun, um mit gutem Gewissen dergestalt grundsätzlich an der Erhaltung alles Kranken und Leidenden, das heisst in That und Wahrheit an der Verschlechterung der europäischen Rasse zu arbeiten? Alle Werthschätzungen auf den Kopf stellen - das mussten sie! Und die Starken zerbrechen, die grossen Hoffnungen ankränkeln, das Glück in der Schönheit verdächtigen, alles Selbstherrliche, Männliche, Erobernde, Herrschsüchtige, alle Instinkte, welche dem höchsten und wohlgerathensten Typus "Mensch" zu eigen sind, in Unsicherheit, Gewissens-Noth, Selbstzerstörung umknicken, ja die ganze Liebe zum Irdischen und zur Herrschaft über die Erde in Hass gegen die Erde und das Irdische verkehren - das stellte sich die Kirche zur Aufgabe und musste es sich stellen, bis für ihre Schätzung endlich "Entweltlichung", "Entsinnlichung" und "höherer Mensch" in Ein Gefühl zusammenschmolzen. Gesetzt, dass man mit dem spöttischen und unbetheiligten Auge eines epikurischen Gottes die wunderlich schmerzliche und ebenso grobe wie feine Komödie des europäischen Christenthums zu überschauen vermöchte, ich glaube, man fände kein

Ende mehr zu staunen und zu lachen: scheint es denn nicht, dass Ein Wille über Europa durch achtzehn Jahrhunderte geherrscht hat, aus dem Menschen eine sublime Missgeburt zu machen? Wer aber mit umgekehrten Bedürfnissen, nicht epikurisch mehr, sondern mit irgend einem göttlichen Hammer in der Hand auf diese fast willkürliche Entartung und Verkümmerung des Menschen zuträte, wie sie der christliche Europäer ist (Pascal zum Beispiel), müsste er da nicht mit Grimm, mit Mitleid, mit Entsetzen schreien: "Oh ihr Tölpel, ihr anmaassenden mitleidigen Tölpel, was habt ihr da gemacht! War das eine Arbeit für eure Hände! Wie habt ihr mir meinen schönsten Stein verhauen und verhunzt! Was nahmt ihr euch heraus!" - Ich wollte sagen: das Christenthum war bisher die verhängnissvollste Art von Selbst-Überhebung. Menschen, nicht hoch und hart genug, um am Menschen als Künstler gestalten zu dürfen; Menschen, nicht stark und fernsichtig genug, um, mit einer erhabenen Selbst-Bezwingung, das Vordergrund-Gesetz des tausendfältigen Missrathens und Zugrundegehns walten zu lassen; Menschen, nicht vornehm genug, um die abgründlich verschiedene Rangordnung und Rangkluft zwischen Mensch und Mensch zu sehen: - solche Menschen haben, mit ihrem "Gleich vor Gott", bisher über dem Schicksale Europa's gewaltet, bis endlich eine verkleinerte, fast lächerliche Art, ein Heerdenthier, etwas Gutwilliges, Kränkliches und Mittelmässiges, herangezüchtet ist, der heutige Europäer....

Viertes Hauptstück:

Sprüche und Zwischenspiele.

63. Wer von Grund aus Lehrer ist, nimmt alle Dinge nur in Bezug auf seine Schüler ernst, - sogar sich selbst.

64. "Die Erkenntniss um ihrer selbst willen" - das ist der letzte Fallstrick, den die Moral legt: damit verwickelt man sich noch einmal völlig in sie.

65. Der Reiz der Erkenntniss wäre gering, wenn nicht auf dem Wege zu ihr so viel Scham zu überwinden wäre.

65 A. Man ist am unehrlichsten gegen seinen Gott: er darf nicht sündigen!

66. Die Neigung, sich herabzusetzen, sich bestehlen, belügen und ausbeuten zu lassen, könnte die Scham eines Gottes unter Menschen sein.

67. Die Liebe zu Einem ist eine Barbarei: denn sie wird auf Unkosten aller Übrigen ausgeübt. Auch die Liebe zu Gott.

68. "Das habe ich gethan" sagt mein Gedächtniss. Das kann ich nicht gethan haben - sagt mein Stolz und bleibt unerbittlich. Endlich - giebt das Gedächtniss nach.

69. Man hat schlecht dem Leben zugeschaut, wenn man nicht auch die Hand gesehn hat, die auf eine schonende Weise - tödtet.

70. Hat man Charakter, so hat man auch sein typisches Erlebniss, das immer wiederkommt.

71. Der Weise als Astronom. - So lange du noch die Sterne fühlst als ein "Über-dir", fehlt dir noch der Blick des Erkennenden.

72. Nicht die Stärke, sondern die Dauer der hohen Empfindung macht die hohen Menschen.

73. Wer sein Ideal erreicht, kommt eben damit über dasselbe hinaus.

73 A. Mancher Pfau verdeckt vor Aller Augen seinen Pfauenschweif - und heisst es seinen Stolz.

74. Ein Mensch mit Genie ist unausstehlich, wenn er nicht mindestens noch zweierlei dazu besitzt: Dankbarkeit und Reinlichkeit.

75. Grad und Art der Geschlechtlichkeit eines Menschen reicht bis in den letzten Gipfel seines Geistes hinauf.

76. Unter friedlichen Umständen fällt der kriegerische Mensch über sich selber her.

77. Mit seinen Grundsätzen will man seine Gewohnheiten tyrannisiren oder rechtfertgen oder ehren oder beschimpfen oder verbergen: - zwei Menschen mit gleichen Grundsätzen wollen damit wahrscheinlich noch etwas Grund-Verschiedenes.

78. Wer sich selbst verachtet, achtet sich doch immer noch dabei als Verächter.

79. Eine Seele, die sich geliebt weiss, aber selbst nicht liebt, verräth ihren Bodensatz: - ihr Unterstes kommt herauf.

80. Eine Sache, die sich aufklärt, hört auf, uns etwas anzugehn. - Was meinte jener Gott, welcher anrieth: "erkenne dich selbst"! Hiess es vielleicht: "höre auf, dich etwas anzugehn! werde objektiv!" - Und Sokrates? - Und der "wissenschaftliche Mensch"? -

81. Es ist furchtbar, im Meere vor Durst zu sterben. Müsst ihr denn gleich eure Wahrheit so salzen, dass sie nicht einmal mehr - den Durst löscht?

82. "Mitleiden mit Allen" - wäre Härte und Tyrannei mit dir, mein Herr Nachbar! -

83. Der Instinkt. - Wenn das Haus brennt, vergisst man sogar das Mittagsessen. - Ja: aber man holt es auf der Asche nach.

84. Das Weib lernt hassen, in dem Maasse, in dem es zu bezaubern - verlernt.

85. Die gleichen Affekte sind bei Mann und Weib doch im Tempo verschieden: deshalb hören Mann und Weib nicht auf, sich misszuverstehn.

86. Die Weiber selber haben im Hintergrunde aller persönlichen Eitelkeit immer noch ihre unpersönliche Verachtung - für das "Weib".

87. Gebunden Herz, freier Geist. - Wenn man sein Herz hart bindet und gefangen legt, kann man seinem Geist viele Freiheiten geben: ich sagte das schon Ein Mal. Aber man glaubt mir's nicht, gesetzt, dass man's nicht schon weiss…..

88. Sehr klugen Personen fängt man an zu misstrauen, wenn sie verlegen werden.

89. Fürchterliche Erlebnisse geben zu rathen, ob Der, welcher sie erlebt, nicht etwas Fürchterliches ist.

90. Schwere, Schwermüthige Menschen werden gerade durch das, was Andre schwer macht, durch Hass und Liebe, leichter und kommen zeitweilig an ihre Oberfläche.

91. So kalt, so eisig, dass man sich an ihm die Finger verbrennt! Jede Hand erschrickt, die ihn anfasst! - Und gerade darum halten Manche ihn für glühend.

92. Wer hat nicht für seinen guten Ruf schon einmal - sich selbst geopfert? -

93. In der Leutseligkeit ist Nichts von Menschenhass, aber eben darum allzuviel von Menschenverachtung.

94. Reife des Mannes: das heisst den Ernst wiedergefunden haben, den man als Kind hatte, beim Spiel.

95. Sich seiner Unmoralität schämen: das ist eine Stufe auf der Treppe, an deren Ende man sich auch seiner Moralität schämt.

96. Man soll vom Leben scheiden wie Odysseus von Nausikaa schied, - mehr segnend als verliebt.

97. Wie? Ein grosser Mann? Ich sehe immer nur den Schauspieler seines eignen Ideals.

98. Wenn man sein Gewissen dressirt, so küsst es uns zugleich, indem es beisst.

99. Der Enttäuschte spricht. - "Ich horchte auf Widerhall, und ich hörte nur Lob -"

100. Vor uns selbst stellen wir uns Alle einfältiger als wir sind: wir ruhen uns so von unsern Mitmenschen aus.

101. Heute möchte sich ein Erkennender leicht als Thierwerdung Gottes fühlen.

102. Gegenliebe entdecken sollte eigentlich den Liebenden über das geliebte Wesen ernüchtern. "Wie? es ist bescheiden genug, sogar dich zu lieben? Oder dumm genug? Oder - oder -"

103. Die Gefahr im Glücke. - "Nun gereicht mir Alles zum Besten, nunmehr liebe ich jedes Schicksal: - wer hat Lust, mein Schicksal zu sein?"

104. Nicht ihre Menschenliebe, sondern die Ohnmacht ihrer Menschenliebe hindert die Christen von heute, uns - zu verbrennen.

105. Dem freien Geiste, dem "Frommen der Erkenntniss" - geht die pia fraus noch mehr wider den Geschmack (wider seine "Frömmigkeit") als die impia fraus. Daher sein tiefer Unverstand gegen die Kirche, wie er zum Typus "freier Geist" gehört, - als seine Unfreiheit.

106. Vermöge der Musik geniessen sich die Leidenschaften selbst.

107. Wenn der Entschluss einmal gefasst ist, das Ohr auch für den besten Gegengrund zu schliessen: Zeichen des starken Charakters. Also ein gelegentlicher Wille zur Dummheit.

108. Es giebt gar keine moralischen Phänomene, sondern nur eine moralische Ausdeutung von Phänomenen…..

109. Der Verbrecher ist häufig genug seiner That nicht gewachsen: er verkleinert und verleumdet sie.

110. Die Advokaten eines Verbrechers sind selten Artisten genug, um das schöne Schreckliche der That zu Gunsten ihres Thäters zu wenden.

111. Unsre Eitelkeit ist gerade dann am schwersten zu verletzen, wenn eben unser Stolz verletzt wurde.

112. Wer sich zum Schauen und nicht zum Glauben vorherbestimmt fühlt, dem sind alle Gläubigen zu lärmend und zudringlich: er erwehrt sich ihrer.

113. "Du willst ihn für dich einnehmen? So stelle dich vor ihm verlegen -"

114. Die ungeheure Erwartung in Betreff der Geschlechtsliebe, und die Scham in dieser Erwartung, verdirbt den Frauen von vornherein alle Perspektiven.

115. Wo nicht Liebe oder Hass mitspielt, spielt das Weib mittelmässig.

116. Die grossen Epochen unsres Lebens liegen dort, wo wir den Muth gewinnen, unser Böses als unser Bestes umzutaufen.

117. Der Wille, einen Affekt zu überwinden, ist zuletzt doch nur der Wille eines anderen oder mehrer anderer Affekte.

118. Es giebt eine Unschuld der Bewunderung: Der hat sie, dem es noch nicht in den Sinn gekommen ist, auch er könne einmal bewundert werden.

119. Der Ekel vor dem Schmutze kann so gross sein, dass er uns hindert, uns zu reinigen, - uns zu "rechtfertigen".

120. Die Sinnlichkeit übereilt oft das Wachsthum der Liebe, so dass die Wurzel schwach bleibt und leicht auszureissen ist.

121. Es ist eine Feinheit, dass Gott griechisch lernte, als er Schriftsteller werden wollte - und dass er es nicht besser lernte.

122. Sich über ein Lob freuen ist bei Manchem nur eine Höflichkeit des Herzens - und gerade das Gegenstück einer Eitelkeit des Geistes.

123. Auch das Concubinat ist corrumpirt worden: - durch die Ehe.

124. Wer auf dem Scheiterhaufen noch frohlockt, triumphirt nicht über den Schmerz, sondern darüber, keinen Schmerz zu fühlen, wo er ihn erwartete. Ein Gleichniss.

125. Wenn wir über Jemanden umlernen müssen, so rechnen wir ihm die Unbequemlichkeit hart an, die er uns damit macht.

126. Ein Volk ist der Umschweif der Natur, um zu sechs, sieben grossen Männern zu kommen. - Ja: und um dann um sie herum zu kommen.

127. Allen rechten Frauen geht Wissenschaft wider die Scham. Es ist ihnen dabei zu Muthe, als ob man damit ihnen unter die Haut, - schlimmer noch! unter Kleid und Putz gucken wolle.

128. Je abstrakter die Wahrheit ist, die du lehren willst, um so mehr musst du noch die Sinne zu ihr verführen.

129. Der Teufel hat die weitesten Perspektiven für Gott, deshalb hält er sich von ihm so fern: - der Teufel nämlich als der älteste Freund der Erkenntniss.

130. Was jemand ist, fängt an, sich zu verrathen, wenn sein Talent nachlässt, - wenn er aufhört, zu zeigen, was er kann. Das Talent ist auch ein Putz; ein Putz ist auch ein Versteck.

131. Die Geschlechter täuschen sich über einander: das macht, sie ehren und lieben im Grunde nur sich selbst (oder ihr eigenes ideal, um es gefälliger auszudrücken -). So will der Mann das Weib friedlich, - aber gerade das Weib ist wesentlich unfriedlich, gleich der Katze, so gut es sich auch auf den Anschein des Friedens eingeübt hat.

132. Man wird am besten für seine Tugenden bestraft.

133. Wer den Weg zu seinem Ideale nicht zu finden weiss, lebt leichtsinniger und frecher, als der Mensch ohne Ideal.

134. Von den Sinnen her kommt erst alle Glaubwürdigkeit, alles gute Gewissen, aller Augenschein der Wahrheit.

135. Der Pharisäismus ist nicht eine Entartung am guten Menschen: ein gutes Stück davon ist vielmehr die Bedingung von allem Gutsein.

136. Der Eine sucht einen Geburtshelfer für seine Gedanken, der Andre Einen, dem er helfen kann: so entsteht ein gutes Gespräch.

137. Im Verkehre mit Gelehrten und Künstlern verrechnet man sich leicht in umgekehrter Richtung: man findet hinter einem merkwürdigen Gelehrten nicht selten einen mittelmässigen Menschen, und hinter einem mittelmässigen Künstler sogar oft - einen sehr merkwürdigen Menschen.

138. Wir machen es auch im Wachen wie im Traume: wir erfinden und erdichten erst den Menschen, mit dem wir verkehren - und vergessen es sofort.

139. In der Rache und in der Liebe ist das Weib barbarischer, als der Mann.

140. Rath als Räthsel. - "Soll das Band nicht reissen, - musst du erst drauf beissen."

141. Der Unterleib ist der Grund dafür, dass der Mensch sich nicht so leicht für einen Gott hält.

142. Das züchtigste Wort, das ich gehört habe: "Dans le véritable amour c'est l'âme, qui enveloppe le corps."

143. Was wir am besten thun, von dem möchte unsre Eitelkeit, dass es grade als Das gelte, was uns am schwersten werde. Zum Ursprung mancher Moral.

144. Wenn ein Weib gelehrte Neigungen hat, so ist gewöhnlich Etwas an ihrer Geschlechtlichkeit nicht in Ordnung. Schon Unfruchtbarkeit disponirt zu einer gewissen Männlichkeit des Geschmacks; der Mann ist nämlich, mit Verlaub, "das unfruchtbare Thier".

145. Mann und Weib im Ganzen verglichen, darf man sagen: das Weib hätte nicht das Genie des Putzes, wenn es nicht den Instinkt der zweiten Rolle hätte.

146. Wer mit Ungeheuern kämpft, mag zusehn, dass er nicht dabei zum Ungeheuer wird. Und wenn du lange

in einen Abgrund blickst, blickt der Abgrund auch in dich hinein.

147. Aus alten florentinischen Novellen, überdies - aus dem Leben: buona femmina e mala femmina vuol bastone. Sacchetti Nov. 86.

148. Den Nächsten zu einer guten Meinung verführen und hinterdrein an diese Meinung des Nächsten gläubig glauben: wer thut es in diesem Kunststück den Weibern gleich? -

149. Was eine Zeit als böse empfindet, ist gewöhnlich ein unzeitgemässer Nachschlag dessen, was ehemals als gut empfunden wurde, - der Atavismus eines älteren Ideals.

150. Um den Helden herum wird Alles zur Tragödie, um den Halbgott herum Alles zum Satyrspiel; und um Gott herum wird Alles - wie? vielleicht zur "Welt"? -

151. Ein Talent haben ist nicht genug: man muss auch eure Erlaubniss dazu haben, - wie? meine Freunde?

152. "Wo der Baum der Erkenntniss steht, ist immer das Paradies": so reden die ältesten und die jüngsten Schlangen.

153. Was aus Liebe gethan wird, geschieht immer jenseits von Gut und Böse.

154. Der Einwand, der Seitensprung, das fröhliche Misstrauen, die Spottlust sind Anzeichen der Gesundheit: alles Unbedingte gehört in die Pathologie.

155. Der Sinn für das Tragische nimmt mit der Sinnlichkeit ab und zu.

156. Der Irrsinn ist bei Einzelnen etwas Seltenes, - aber bei Gruppen, Parteien, Völkern, Zeiten die Regel.

157. Der Gedanke an den Selbstmord ist ein starkes Trostmittel: mit ihm kommt man gut über manche böse Nacht hinweg.

158. Unserm stärksten Triebe, dem Tyrannen in uns, unterwirft sich nicht nur unsre Vernunft, sondern auch unser Gewissen.

159. Man muss vergelten, Gutes und Schlimmes: aber warum gerade an der Person, die uns Gutes oder Schlimmes that?

160. Man liebt seine Erkenntniss nicht genug mehr, sobald man sie mittheilt.

161. Die Dichter sind gegen ihre Erlebnisse schamlos: sie beuten sie aus.

162. "Unser Nächster ist nicht unser Nachbar, sondern dessen Nachbar" - so denkt jedes Volk.

163. Die Liebe bringt die hohen und verborgenen Eigenschaften eines Liebenden an's Licht, - sein Seltenes, Ausnahmsweises: insofern täuscht sie leicht über Das, was Regel an ihm ist.

164. Jesus sagte zu seinen Juden: "das Gesetz war für Knechte, - liebt Gott, wie ich ihn liebe, als sein Sohn! Was geht uns Söhne Gottes die Moral an!" -

165. Angesichts jeder Partei. - Ein Hirt hat immer auch noch einen Leithammel nöthig, - oder er muss selbst gelegentlich Hammel sein.

166. Man lügt wohl mit dem Munde; aber mit dem Maule, das man dabei macht, sagt man doch noch die Wahrheit.

167. Bei harten Menschen ist die Innigkeit eine Sache der Scham - und etwas Kostbares.

168. Das Christenthum gab dem Eros Gift zu trinken: - er starb zwar nicht daran, aber entartete, zum Laster.

169. Viel von sich reden kann auch ein Mittel sein, sich zu verbergen.

170. Im Lobe ist mehr Zudringlichkeit, als im Tadel.

171. Mitleiden wirkt an einem Menschen der Erkenntniss beinahe zum Lachen, wie zarte Hände an einem Cyklopen.

172. Man umarmt aus Menschenliebe bisweilen einen Beliebigen (weil man nicht Alle umarmen kann): aber gerade Das darf man dem Beliebigen nicht verrathen…..

173. Man hasst nicht, so lange man noch gering schätzt, sondern erst, wenn man gleich oder höher schätzt.

174. Ihr Utilitarier, auch ihr liebt alles utile nur als ein Fuhrwerk eurer Neigungen, - auch ihr findet eigentlich den Lärm seiner Räder unausstehlich?

175. Man liebt zuletzt seine Begierde, und nicht das Begehrte.

176. Die Eitelkeit Andrer geht uns nur dann wider den Geschmack, wenn sie wider unsre Eitelkeit geht.

177. Ober Das, was "Wahrhaftigkeit" ist, war vielleicht noch Niemand wahrhaftig genug.

178. Klugen Menschen glaubt man ihre Thorheiten nicht: welche Einbusse an Menschenrechten!

179. Die Folgen unsrer Handlungen fassen uns am Schopfe, sehr gleichgültig dagegen, dass wir uns inzwischen "gebessert" haben.

180. Es giebt eine Unschuld in der Lüge, welche das Zeichen des guten Glaubens an eine Sache ist.

181. Es ist unmenschlich, da zu segnen, wo Einem geflucht wird.

182. Die Vertraulichkeit des überlegenen erbittert, weil sie nicht zurückgegeben werden darf. -

183. "Nicht dass du mich belogst, sondern dass ich dir nicht mehr glaube, hat mich erschüttert." -

184. Es giebt einen Übermuth der Güte, welcher sich wie Bosheit ausnimmt.

185. "Er missfällt mir." - Warum? - "Ich bin ihm nicht gewachsen." - Hat je ein Mensch so geantwortet?

Fünftes Hauptstück:

Zur Naturgeschichte der Moral.

186. Die moralische Empfindung ist jetzt in Europa ebenso fein, spät, vielfach, reizbar, raffinirt, als die dazu gehörige "Wissenschaft der Moral" noch jung, anfängerhaft, plump und grobfingrig ist: - ein anziehender Gegensatz, der bisweilen in der Person eines Moralisten selbst sichtbar und leibhaft wird. Schon das Wort "Wissenschaft der Moral" ist in Hinsicht auf Das, was damit bezeichnet wird, viel zu hochmüthig und wider den guten Geschmack: welcher immer ein Vorgeschmack für die bescheideneren Worte zu sein pflegt. Man sollte, in aller Strenge, sich eingestehn, was hier auf lange hinaus noch noth thut, was vorläufig allein Recht hat: nämlich Sammlung des Materials, begriffliche Fassung und Zusammenordnung eines ungeheuren Reichs zarter Werthgefühle und Werthunterschiede, welche leben, wachsen, zeugen und

zu Grunde gehn, - und, vielleicht, Versuche, die wiederkehrenden und häufigeren Gestaltungen dieser lebenden Krystallisation anschaulich zu machen, - als Vorbereitung zu einer Typenlehre der Moral. Freilich: man war bisher nicht so bescheiden. Die Philosophen allesammt forderten, mit einem steifen Ernste, der lachen macht, von sich etwas sehr viel Höheres, Anspruchsvolleres, Feierlicheres, sobald sie sich mit der Moral als Wissenschaft befassten: sie wollten die Begründung der Moral, - und jeder Philosoph hat bisher geglaubt, die Moral begründet zu haben; die Moral selbst aber galt als "gegeben". Wie ferne lag ihrem plumpen Stolze jene unscheinbar dünkende und in Staub und Moder belassene Aufgabe einer Beschreibung, obwohl für sie kaum die feinsten Hände und Sinne fein genug sein könnten! Gerade dadurch, dass die Moral-Philosophen die moralischen facta nur gröblich, in einem willkürlichen Auszuge oder als zufällige Abkürzung kannten, etwa als Moralität ihrer Umgebung, ihres Standes, ihrer Kirche, ihres Zeitgeistes, ihres Klima's und Erdstriches, - gerade dadurch, dass sie in Hinsicht auf Völker, Zeiten, Vergangenheiten schlecht unterrichtet und selbst wenig wissbegierig waren, bekamen sie die eigentlichen Probleme der Moral gar nicht zu Gesichte: - als welche alle erst bei einer Vergleichung vieler Moralen auftauchen. In aller bisherigen "Wissenschaft der Moral" fehlte, so wunderlich es klingen mag, noch das Problem der Moral selbst: es fehlte der Argwohn dafür, dass es hier etwas Problematisches gebe. Was die Philosophen "Begründung der Moral" nannten und von sich forderten, war, im rechten Lichte gesehn, nur eine gelehrte Form des guten Glaubens an die herrschende Moral, ein neues Mittel ihres Ausdrucks, also ein Thatbestand selbst innerhalb einer bestimmten Moralität, ja sogar, im letzten Grunde, eine Art Leugnung, dass diese Moral als Problem gefasst werden dürfe: - und jedenfalls das Gegenstück einer Prüfung, Zerlegung, Anzweiflung, Vivisektion eben dieses Glaubens. Man höre zum Beispiel, mit welcher beinahe verehrenswürdigen Unschuld noch Schopenhauer seine eigene Aufgabe hinstellt, und man mache seine Schlüsse über die Wissenschaftlichkeit einer "Wissenschaft", deren letzte Meister noch wie die Kinder und die alten Weibchen reden: - "das Princip, sagt er (p. 136 der Grundprobleme der Moral), der Grundsatz, über dessen Inhalt alle Ethiker eigentlich einig sind; neminem laede, immo omnes, quantum potes, juva - das ist eigentlich der Satz, welchen zu begründen alle Sittenlehrer sich abmühen…. das eigentliche Fundament der Ethik, welches man wie den Stein der Weisen seit Jahrtausenden sucht." - Die Schwierigkeit, den angeführten Satz zu begründen, mag freilich gross sein - bekanntlich ist es auch Schopenhauern damit nicht geglückt -; und wer einmal gründlich nachgefühlt hat, wie abgeschmackt-falsch und sentimental dieser Satz ist, in einer Welt, deren Essenz Wille zur Macht ist -, der mag sich daran erinnern lassen, dass Schopenhauer, obschon Pessimist, eigentlich - die Flöte blies…. Täglich, nach Tisch: man lese hierüber seinen Biographen. Und beiläufig gefragt: ein Pessimist, ein Gott- und Welt-Verneiner, der vor der Moral Haltmacht, - der zur Moral Ja sagt und Flöte bläst, zur laede-neminem-Moral: wie? ist das eigentlich - ein Pessimist?

187. Abgesehn noch vom Werthe solcher Behauptungen wie "es giebt in uns einen kategorischen Imperativ", kann man immer noch fragen: was sagt eine solche Behauptung von dem sie Behauptenden aus? Es giebt Moralen, welche ihren Urheber vor Anderen rechtfertigen sollen; andre Moralen sollen ihn beruhigen und mit sich zufrieden stimmen; mit anderen will er sich selbst an's Kreuz schlagen und demüthigen; mit andern will er Rache üben, mit andern sich verstecken, mit andern sich verklären und hinaus, in die Höhe und Ferne setzen; diese Moral dient ihrem Urheber, um zu vergessen, jene, um sich oder Etwas von sich vergessen zu machen; mancher Moralist möchte an der Menschheit Macht und schöpferische Laune ausüben; manch Anderer, vielleicht gerade auch Kant, giebt mit seiner Moral zu verstehn: "was an mir achtbar ist, das ist, dass ich gehorchen kann, - und bei euch soll es nicht anders stehn, als bei mir!" - kurz, die Moralen sind auch nur eine Zeichensprache der Affekte.

188. Jede Moral ist, im Gegensatz zum laisser aller, ein Stück Tyrannei gegen die "Natur", auch gegen die "Vernunft": das ist aber noch kein Einwand gegen sie, man müsste denn selbst schon wieder von irgend einer Moral aus dekretiren, dass alle Art Tyrannei und Unvernunft unerlaubt sei. Das Wesentliche und Unschätzbare an jeder Moral ist, dass sie ein langer Zwang ist: um den Stoicismus oder Port-Royal oder das Puritanerthum zu verstehen, mag man sich des Zwangs erinnern, unter dem bisher jede Sprache es zur Stärke und Freiheit gebracht, - des metrischen Zwangs, der Tyrannei von Reim und Rhythmus. Wie viel Noth haben sich in jedem Volke die Dichter und die Redner gemacht! - einige Prosaschreiber von heute nicht ausgenommen, in deren Ohr ein unerbittliches Gewissen wohnt - "um einer Thorheit willen", wie utilitarische Tölpel sagen, welche sich damit klug dünken, - "aus Unterwürfigkeit gegen Willkür-Gesetze", wie die Anarchisten sagen, die sich damit "frei", selbst freigeistisch wähnen. Der wunderliche Thatbestand ist aber, dass Alles, was es von Freiheit, Feinheit, Kühnheit, Tanz und meisterlicher Sicherheit auf Erden giebt oder gegeben hat, sei es nun in dem Denken selbst, oder im Regieren, oder im Reden und überreden, in den Künsten ebenso wie in den Sittlichkeiten, sich erst vermöge der "Tyrannei solcher Willkür-Gesetze" entwickelt hat; und allen Ernstes, die Wahrscheinlichkeit dafür ist nicht gering, dass gerade dies "Natur" und "natürlich" sei - und nicht jenes laisser

aller! jeder Künstler weiss, wie fern vom Gefühl des Sichgehen-lassens sein "natürlichster" Zustand ist, das freie Ordnen, Setzen, Verfügen, Gestalten in den Augenblicken der "Inspiration", - und wie streng und fein er gerade da tausendfältigen Gesetzen gehorcht, die aller Formulirung durch Begriffe gerade auf Grund ihrer Härte und Bestimmtheit spotten (auch der festeste Begriff hat, dagegen gehalten, etwas Schwimmendes, Vielfaches, Vieldeutiges -). Das Wesentliche, "im Himmel und auf Erden", wie es scheint, ist, nochmals gesagt, dass lange und in Einer Richtung gehorcht werde: dabei kommt und kam auf die Dauer immer Etwas heraus, dessentwillen es sich lohnt, auf Erden zu leben, zum Beispiel Tugend, Kunst, Musik, Tanz, Vernunft, Geistigkeit, - irgend etwas Verklärendes, Raffinirtes, Tolles und Göttliches. Die lange Unfreiheit des Geistes, der misstrauische Zwang in der Mittheilbarkeit der Gedanken, die Zucht, welche sich der Denker auferlegte, innerhalb einer kirchlichen und höfischen Richtschnur oder unter aristotelischen Voraussetzungen zu denken, der lange geistige Wille, Alles, was geschieht, nach einem christlichen Schema auszulegen und den christlichen Gott noch in jedem Zufalle wieder zu entdecken und zu rechtfertigen, - all dies Gewaltsame, Willkürliche, Harte, Schauerliche, Widervernünftige hat sich als das Mittel herausgestellt, durch welches dem europäischen Geiste seine Stärke, seine rücksichtslose Neugierde und feine Beweglichkeit angezüchtet wurde: zugegeben, dass dabei ebenfalls unersetzbar viel an Kraft und Geist erdrückt, erstickt und verdorben werden musste (denn hier wie überall zeigt sich "die Natur", wie sie ist, in ihrer ganzen verschwenderischen und gleichgültigen Grossartigkeit, welche empört, aber vornehm ist). Dass Jahrtausende lang die europäischen Denker nur dachten, um Etwas zu beweisen -heute ist uns umgekehrt jeder Denker verdächtig, der "Etwas beweisen will" -, dass ihnen bereits immer feststand, was als Resultat ihres strengsten Nachdenkens herauskommen sollte, etwa wie ehemals bei der asiatischen Astrologie oder wie heute noch bei der harmlosen christlich-moralischen Auslegung der nächsten persönlichen Ereignisse "zu Ehren Gottes" und "zum Heil der Seele": - diese Tyrannei, diese Willkür, diese strenge und grandiose Dummheit hat den Geist erzogen; die Sklaverei ist, wie es scheint, im gröberen und feineren Verstande das unentbehrliche Mittel auch der geistigen Zucht und Züchtung. Man mag jede Moral darauf hin ansehn: die "Natur" in ihr ist es, welche das laisser aller, die allzugrosse Freiheit hassen lehrt und das Bedürfniss nach beschränkten Horizonten, nach nächsten Aufgaben pflanzt, - welche die Verengerung der Perspektive, und also in gewissem Sinne die Dummheit, als eine Lebens- und Wachsthums-Bedingung lehrt. "Du sollst gehorchen, irgend wem, und auf lange: sonst gehst du zu Grunde und verlierst die letzte Achtung vor dir selbst" - dies scheint mir der moralische Imperativ der Natur zu sein, welcher freilich weder "kategorisch" ist, wie es der alte Kant von ihm verlangte (daher das "sonst" -), noch an den Einzelnen sich wendet (was liegt ihr am Einzelnen!), wohl aber an Völker, Rassen, Zeitalter, Stände, vor Allem aber an das ganze Thier "Mensch", an den Menschen.

189. Die arbeitsamen Rassen finden eine grosse Beschwerde darin, den Müssiggang zu ertragen: es war ein Meisterstück des englischen Instinktes, den Sonntag in dem Maasse zu heiligen und zu langweiligen, dass der Engländer dabei wieder unvermerkt nach seinem Wochen- und Werktage lüstern wird: - als eine Art klug erfundenen, klug eingeschalteten Fastens, wie dergleichen auch in der antiken Welt reichlich wahrzunehmen ist (wenn auch, wie billig bei südländischen Völkern, nicht gerade in Hinsicht auf Arbeit -). Es muss Fasten von vielerlei Art geben; und überall, wo mächtige Triebe und Gewohnheiten herrschen, haben die Gesetzgeber dafür zu sorgen, Schalttage einzuschieben, an denen solch ein Trieb in Ketten gelegt wird und wieder einmal hungern lernt. Von einem höheren Orte aus gesehn, erscheinen ganze Geschlechter und Zeitalter, wenn sie mit irgend einem moralischen Fanatismus behaftet auftreten, als solche eingelegte Zwangs- und Fastenzeiten, während welchen ein Trieb sich ducken und niederwerfen, aber auch sich reinigen und schärfen lernt; auch einzelne philosophische Sekten (zum Beispiel die Stoa inmitten der hellenistischen Cultur und ihrer mit aphrodisischen

Düften überladenen und geil gewordenen Luft) erlauben eine derartige Auslegung. - Hiermit ist auch ein Wink zur Erklärung jenes Paradoxons gegeben, warum gerade in der christlichsten Periode Europa's und überhaupt erst unter dem Druck christlicher Werthurtheile der Geschlechtstrieb sich bis zur Liebe (amour-passion) sublimirt hat.

190. Es giebt Etwas in der Moral Plato's, das nicht eigentlich zu Plato gehört, sondern sich nur an seiner Philosophie vorfindet, man könnte sagen, trotz Plato: nämlich der Sokratismus, für den er eigentlich zu vornehm war. "Keiner will sich selbst Schaden thun, daher geschieht alles Schlechte unfreiwillig. Denn der Schlechte fügt sich selbst Schaden zu: das würde er nicht thun, falls er wüsste, dass das Schlechte schlecht ist. Demgemäss ist der Schlechte nur aus einem Irrthum schlecht; nimmt man ihm seinen Irrthum, so macht man ihn notwendig - gut." - Diese Art zu schliessen riecht nach dem Pöbel, der am Schlechthandeln nur die leidigen Folgen in's Auge fasst und eigentlich urtheilt "es ist dumm, schlecht zu handeln"; während er "gut" mit "nützlich und angenehm" ohne Weiteres als identisch nimmt. Man darf bei jedem Utilitarismus der Moral von vornherein auf diesen gleichen Ursprung rathen und seiner Nase folgen: man wird selten irre gehn. - Plato hat Alles gethan, um etwas Feines und Vornehmes in den Satz seines Lehrers hinein zu interpretiren, vor Allem sich selbst -, er, der

verwegenste aller Interpreten, der den ganzen Sokrates nur wie ein populäres Thema und Volkslied von der Gasse nahm, um es in's Unendliche und Unmögliche zu variiren: nämlich in alle seine eignen Masken und Vielfältigkeiten. Im Scherz gesprochen, und noch dazu homerisch: was ist denn der platonische Sokrates, wenn nicht prósthe Pláton opithén te Pláton mésse te Chímaira.

191. Das alte theologische Problem von "Glauben" und "Wissen" - oder, deutlicher, von Instinkt und Vernunft - also die Frage, ob in Hinsicht auf Werthschätzung der Dinge der Instinkt mehr Autorität verdiene, als die Vernünftigkeit, welche nach Gründen, nach einem "Warum?", als nach Zweckmässigkeit und Nützlichkeit geschätzt und gehandelt wissen will, - es ist immer noch jenes alte moralische Problem, wie es zuerst in der Person des Sokrates auftrat und lange vor dem Christenthum schon die Geister gespaltet hat. Sokrates selbst hatte sich zwar mit dem Geschmack seines Talentes - dem eines überlegenen Dialektikers - zunächst auf Seiten der Vernunft gestellt; und in Wahrheit, was hat er sein Leben lang gethan, als über die linkische Unfähigkeit seiner vornehmen Athener zu lachen, welche Menschen des Instinktes waren gleich allen vornehmen Menschen und niemals genügend über die Gründe ihres Handelns Auskunft geben konnten? Zuletzt aber, im Stillen und Geheimen, lachte er auch über sich selbst: er fand bei sich, vor seinem feineren

Gewissen und Selbstverhör, die gleiche Schwierigkeit und Unfähigkeit. Wozu aber, redete er sich zu, sich deshalb von den Instinkten lösen! Man muss ihnen und auch der Vernunft zum Recht verhelfen, - man muss den Instinkten folgen, aber die Vernunft überreden, ihnen dabei mit guten Gründen nachzuhelfen. Dies war die eigentliche Falschheit jenes grossen geheimnissreichen Ironikers; er brachte sein Gewissen dahin, sich mit einer Art Selbstüberlistung zufrieden zu geben: im Grunde hatte er das Irrationale im moralischen Urtheile durchschaut. - Plato, in solchen Dingen unschuldiger und ohne die Verschmitztheit des Plebejers, wollte mit Aufwand aller Kraft - der grössten Kraft, die bisher ein Philosoph aufzuwenden hatte! - sich beweisen, dass Vernunft und Instinkt von selbst auf Ein Ziel zugehen, auf das Gute, auf "Gott"; und seit Plato sind alle Theologen und Philosophen auf der gleichen Bahn, - das heisst, in Dingen der Moral hat bisher der Instinkt, oder wie die Christen es nennen, "der Glaube", oder wie ich es nenne, "die Heerde" gesiegt. Man müsse denn Descartes ausnehmen, den Vater des Rationalismus (und folglich Grossvater der Revolution), welcher der Vernunft allein Autorität zuerkannte: aber die Vernunft ist nur ein Werkzeug, und Descartes war oberflächlich.

192. Wer der Geschichte einer einzelnen Wissenschaft nachgegangen ist, der findet in ihrer Entwicklung einen Leitfaden zum Verständniss der

ältesten und gemeinsten Vorgänge alles "Wissens und Erkennens": dort wie hier sind die voreiligen Hypothesen, die Erdichtungen, der gute dumme Wille zum "Glauben", der Mangel an Misstrauen und Geduld zuerst entwickelt, - unsre Sinne lernen es spät, und lernen es nie ganz, feine treue vorsichtige Organe der Erkenntniss zu sein. Unserm Auge fällt es bequemer, auf einen gegebenen Anlass hin ein schon öfter erzeugtes Bild wieder zu erzeugen, als das Abweichende und Neue eines Eindrucks bei sich festzuhalten: letzteres braucht mehr Kraft, mehr "Moralität". Etwas Neues hören ist dem Ohre peinlich und schwierig; fremde Musik hören wir schlecht. Unwillkürlich versuchen wir, beim Hören einer andren Sprache, die gehörten Laute in Worte einzuformen, welche uns vertrauter und heimischer klingen: so machte sich zum Beispiel der Deutsche ehemals aus dem gehörten arcubalista das Wort Armbrust zurecht. Das Neue findet auch unsre Sinne feindlich und widerwillig; und überhaupt herrschen schon bei den "einfachsten" Vorgängen der Sinnlichkeit die Affekte, wie Furcht, Liebe, Hass, eingeschlossen die passiven Affekte der Faulheit. - So wenig ein Leser heute die einzelnen Worte (oder gar Silben) einer Seite sämmtlich abliest - er nimmt vielmehr aus zwanzig Worten ungefähr fünf nach Zufall heraus und "erräth" den zu diesen fünf Worten muthmaasslich zugehörigen Sinn -, eben so wenig sehen wir einen Baum genau und vollständig, in Hinsicht auf Blätter, Zweige, Farbe,

Gestalt; es fällt uns so sehr viel leichter, ein Ungefähr von Baum hin zu phantasiren. Selbst inmitten der seltsamsten Erlebnisse machen wir es noch ebenso: wir erdichten uns den grössten Theil des Erlebnisses und sind kaum dazu zu zwingen, nicht als "Erfinder" irgend einem Vorgange zuzuschauen. Dies Alles will sagen: wir sind von Grund aus, von Alters her - an's Lügen gewöhnt. Oder, um es tugendhafter und heuchlerischer, kurz angenehmer auszudrücken: man ist viel mehr Künstler als man weiss. - In einem lebhaften Gespräch sehe ich oftmals das Gesicht der Person, mit der ich rede, je nach dem Gedanken, den sie äussert, oder den ich bei ihr hervorgerufen glaube, so deutlich und feinbestimmt vor mir, dass dieser Grad von Deutlichkeit weit über die Kraft meines Sehvermögens hinausgeht: - die Feinheit des Muskelspiels und des Augen-Ausdrucks muss also von mir hinzugedichtet sein. Wahrscheinlich machte die Person ein ganz anderes Gesicht oder gar keins.

193. Quidquid luce fuit, tenebris agit: aber auch umgekehrt. Was wir im Traume erleben, vorausgesetzt, dass wir es oftmals erleben, gehört zuletzt so gut zum Gesammt-Haushalt unsrer Seele, wie irgend etwas "wirklich" Erlebtes: wir sind vermöge desselben reicher oder ärmer, haben ein Bedürfniss mehr oder weniger und werden schliesslich am hellen lichten Tage, und selbst in den heitersten Augenblicken unsres wachen Geistes, ein Wenig von den Gewöhnungen unsrer

Träume gegängelt. Gesetzt, dass Einer in seinen Träumen oftmals geflogen ist und endlich, sobald er träumt, sich einer Kraft und Kunst des Fliegens wie seines Vorrechtes bewusst wird, auch wie seines eigensten beneidenswerthen Glücks: ein Solcher, der jede Art von Bogen und Winkeln mit dem leisesten Impulse verwirklichen zu können glaubt, der das Gefühl einer gewissen göttlichen Leichtfertigkeit kennt, ein "nach, Oben" ohne Spannung und Zwang, ein "nach Unten" ohne Herablassung und Erniedrigung - ohne Schwere! - wie sollte der Mensch solcher Traum-Erfahrungen und Traum-Gewohnheiten nicht endlich auch für seinen wachen Tag das Wort "Glück" anders gefärbt und bestimmt finden! wie sollte er nicht anders nach Glück - verlangen "Aufschwung", so wie dies von Dichtern beschrieben wird, muss ihm, gegen jenes "Fliegen" gehalten, schon zu erdenhaft, muskelhaft, gewaltsam, schon zu "schwer" sein.

194. Die Verschiedenheit der Menschen zeigt sich nicht nur in der Verschiedenheit ihrer Gütertafeln, also darin, dass sie verschiedene Güter für erstrebenswerth halten und auch über das Mehr und Weniger des Werthes, über die Rangordnung der gemeinsam anerkannten Güter mit einander uneins sind: - sie zeigt sich noch mehr in dem, was ihnen als wirkliches Haben und Besitzen eines Gutes gilt. In Betreff eines Weibes zum Beispiel gilt dem Bescheideneren schon die Verfügung über den Leib und der Geschlechtsgenuss

als ausreichendes und genugthuendes Anzeichen des Habens, des Besitzens; ein Anderer, mit seinem argwöhnischeren und anspruchsvolleren Durste nach Besitz, sieht das "Fragezeichen", das nur Scheinbare eines solchen Habens, und will feinere Proben, vor Allem, um zu wissen, ob das Weib nicht nur ihm sich giebt, sondern auch für ihn lässt, was sie hat oder gerne hätte -: so erst gilt es ihm als "besessen". Ein Dritter aber ist auch hier noch nicht am Ende seines Misstrauens und Habenwollens, er fragt sich, ob das Weib, wenn es Alles für ihn lässt, dies nicht etwa für ein Phantom von ihm thut: er will erst gründlich, ja abgründlich gut gekannt sein, um überhaupt geliebt werden zu können, er wagt es, sich errathen zu lassen -. Erst dann fühlt er die Geliebte völlig in seinem Besitze, wenn sie sich nicht mehr über ihn betrügt, wenn sie ihn um seiner Teufelei und versteckten Unersättlichkeit willen eben so sehr liebt, als um seiner Güte, Geduld und Geistigkeit willen. Jener möchte ein Volk besitzen: und alle höheren Cagliostro- und Catilina-Künste sind ihm zu diesem Zwecke recht. Ein Anderer, mit einem feineren Besitzdurste, sagt sich "man darf nicht betrügen, wo man besitzen will" -, er ist gereizt und ungeduldig bei der Vorstellung, dass eine Maske von ihm über das Herz des Volks gebietet: "also muss ich mich kennen lassen und, vorerst, mich selbst kennen!" Unter hülfreichen und wohlthätigen Menschen findet man jene plumpe Arglist fast regelmässig vor, welche sich Den, dem geholfen werden soll, erst zurecht macht: als ob er zum Beispiel Hülfe "verdiene", gerade nach ihrer Hülfe verlange, und für alle Hülfe sich ihnen tief dankbar, anhänglich, unterwürfig beweisen werde, - mit diesen Einbildungen verfügen sie über den Bedürftigen wie über ein Eigenthum, wie sie aus einem Verlangen nach Eigenthum überhaupt wohlthätige und hülfreiche Menschen sind. Man findet sie eifersüchtig, wenn man sie beim Helfen kreuzt oder ihnen zuvorkommt. Die Eltern machen unwillkürlich aus dem Kinde etwas ihnen Ähnliches - sie nennen das "Erziehung" -, keine Mutter zweifelt im Grunde ihres Herzens daran, am Kinde sich ein Eigenthum geboren zu haben, kein Vater bestreitet sich das Recht, es seinen Begriffen und Werthschätzungen unterwerfen zu dürfen. Ja, ehemals schien es den Vätern billig, über Leben und Tod des Neugebornen (wie unter den alten Deutschen) nach Gutdünken zu verfügen. Und wie der Vater, so sehen auch jetzt noch der Lehrer, der Stand, der Priester, der Fürst in jedem neuen Menschen eine unbedenkliche Gelegenheit zu neuem Besitze. Woraus folgt…..

195. Die Juden - ein Volk "geboren zur Sklaverei", wie Tacitus und die ganze antike Welt sagt, "das auserwählte Volk unter den Völkern", wie sie selbst sagen und glauben - die Juden haben jenes Wunderstück von Umkehrung der Werthe zu Stande gebracht, Dank welchem das Leben auf der Erde für ein Paar Jahrtausende einen neuen und gefährlichen Reiz

erhalten hat: - ihre Propheten haben "reich" "gottlos" "böse" "gewaltthätig" "sinnlich" in Eins geschmolzen und zum ersten Male das Wort "Welt", zum Schandwort gemünzt. In dieser Umkehrung der Werthe (zu der es gehört, das Wort für "Arm" als synonym mit "Heilig" und "Freund" zu brauchen) liegt die Bedeutung des jüdischen Volks: mit ihm beginnt der Sklaven-Aufstand in der Moral.

196. Es giebt unzählige dunkle Körper neben der Sonne zu erschliessen, - solche die wir nie sehen werden. Das ist, unter uns gesagt, ein Gleichniss; und ein Moral-Psycholog liest die gesammte Sternenschrift nur als eine Gleichniss- und Zeichensprache, mit der sich Vieles verschweigen lässt.

197. Man missversteht das Raubthier und den Raubmenschen (zum Beispiele Cesare Borgia) gründlich, man missversteht die "Natur", so lange man noch nach einer "Krankhaftigkeit" im Grunde dieser gesündesten aller tropischen Unthiere und Gewächse sucht, oder gar nach einer ihnen eingeborenen "Hölle" -: wie es bisher fast alle Moralisten gethan haben. Es scheint, dass es bei den Moralisten einen Hass gegen den Urwald und gegen die Tropen giebt? Und dass der "tropische Mensch" um jeden Preis diskreditirt werden muss, sei es als Krankheit und Entartung des Menschen, sei es als eigne Hölle und Selbst-Marterung? Warum doch? Zu Gunsten der

"gemässigten Zonen"? Zu Gunsten der gemässigten Menschen? Der "Moralischen"? Der Mittelmässigen? - Dies zum Kapitel "Moral als Furchtsamkeit". -

198. Alle diese Moralen, die sich an die einzelne Person wenden, zum Zwecke ihres "Glückes", wie es heisst, - was sind sie Anderes, als Verhaltungs-Vorschläge im Verhältniss zum Grade der Gefährlichkeit, in welcher die einzelne Person mit sich selbst lebt; Recepte gegen ihre Leidenschaften, ihre guten und schlimmen Hänge, so fern sie den Willen zur Macht haben und den Herrn spielen möchten; kleine und grosse Klugheiten und Künsteleien, behaftet mit dem Winkelgeruch alter Hausmittel und Altweiber-Weisheit; allesammt in der Form barock und unvernünftig - weil sie sich an "Alle" wenden, weil sie generalisiren, wo nicht generalisirt werden darf -, allesammt unbedingt redend, sich unbedingt nehmend, allesammt nicht nur mit Einem Korne Salz gewürzt, vielmehr erst erträglich, und bisweilen sogar verführerisch, wenn sie überwürzt und gefährlich zu riechen lernen, vor Allem "nach der anderen Welt": Das ist Alles, intellektuell gemessen, wenig werth und noch lange nicht "Wissenschaft", geschweige denn "Weisheit", sondern, nochmals gesagt und dreimal gesagt, Klugheit, Klugheit, Klugheit, gemischt mit Dummheit, Dummheit, Dummheit, - sei es nun jene Gleichgültigkeit und Bildsäulenkälte gegen die hitzige Narrheit der Affekte, welche die Stoiker anriethen und

ankurirten; oder auch jenes Nicht-mehr-Lachen und Nicht-mehr-Weinen des Spinoza, seine so naiv befürwortete Zerstörung der Affekte durch Analysis und Vivisektion derselben; oder jene Herabstimmung der Affekte auf ein unschädliches Mittelmaass, bei welchem sie befriedigt werden dürfen, der Aristotelismus der Moral; selbst Moral als Genuss der Affekte in einer absichtlichen Verdünnung und Vergeistigung durch die Symbolik der Kunst, etwa als Musik, oder als Liebe zu Gott und zum Menschen um Gotteswillen - denn in der Religion haben die Leidenschaften wieder Bürgerrecht, vorausgesetzt dass; zuletzt selbst jene entgegenkommende und muthwillige Hingebung an die Affekte, wie sie Hafis und Goethe gelehrt haben, jenes kühne Fallen-lassen der Zügel, jene geistig- leibliche licentia morum in dem Ausnahmefalle alter weiser Käuze und Trunkenbolde, bei denen es "wenig Gefahr mehr hat". Auch Dies zum Kapitel "Moral als Furchtsamkeit".

199. Insofern es zu allen Zeiten, so lange es Menschen giebt, auch Menschenheerden gegeben hat (Geschlechts-Verbände, Gemeinden, Stämme, Völker, Staaten, Kirchen) und immer sehr viel Gehorchende im Verhältniss zu der kleinen Zahl Befehlender, - in Anbetracht also, dass Gehorsam bisher am besten und längsten unter Menschen geübt und gezüchtet worden ist, darf man billig voraussetzen, dass durchschnittlich jetzt einem jeden das Bedürfniss darnach angeboren ist,

als eine Art formalen Gewissens, welches gebietet: "du sollst irgend Etwas unbedingt thun, irgend Etwas unbedingt lassen", kurz "du sollst". Dies Bedürfniss sucht sich zu sättigen und seine Form mit einem Inhalte zu füllen; es greift dabei, gemäss seiner Stärke, Ungeduld und Spannung, wenig wählerisch, als ein grober Appetit, zu und nimmt an, was ihm nur von irgend welchen Befehlenden - Eltern, Lehrern, Gesetzen, Standesvorurtheilen, öffentlichen Meinungen - in's Ohr gerufen wird. Die seltsame Beschränktheit der menschlichen Entwicklung, das Zögernde, Langwierige, oft Zurücklaufende und Sich-Drehende derselben beruht darauf, dass der Heerden-Instinkt des Gehorsams am besten und auf Kosten der Kunst des Befehlens vererbt wird. Denkt man sich diesen Instinkt einmal bis zu seinen letzten Ausschweifungen schreitend, so fehlen endlich geradezu die Befehlshaber und Unabhängigen; oder sie leiden innerlich am schlechten Gewissen und haben nöthig, sich selbst erst eine Täuschung vorzumachen, um befehlen zu können: nämlich als ob auch sie nur gehorchten. Dieser Zustand besteht heute thatsächlich in Europa: ich nenne ihn die moralische Heuchelei der Befehlenden. Sie wissen sich nicht anders vor ihrem schlechten Gewissen zu schützen als dadurch, dass sie sich als Ausführer älterer oder höherer Befehle gebärden (der Vorfahren, der Verfassung, des Rechts, der Gesetze oder gar Gottes) oder selbst von der Heerden-Denkweise her sich Heerden-Maximen borgen, zum Beispiel als "erste

Diener ihres Volks" oder als "Werkzeuge des gemeinen Wohls". Auf der anderen Seite giebt sich heute der Heerdenmensch in Europa das Ansehn, als sei er die einzig erlaubte Art Mensch, und verherrlicht seine Eigenschaften, vermöge deren er zahm, verträglich und der Heerde nützlich ist, als die eigentlich menschlichen Tugenden: also Gemeinsinn, Wohlwollen, Rücksicht, Fleiss, Mässigkeit, Bescheidenheit, Nachsicht, Mitleiden. Für die Fälle aber, wo man der Führer und Leithammel nicht entrathen zu können glaubt, macht man heute Versuche über Versuche, durch Zusammen-Addiren kluger Heerdenmenschen die Befehlshaber zu ersetzen: dieses Ursprungs sind zum Beispiel alle repräsentativen Verfassungen. Welche Wohlthat, welche Erlösung von einem unerträglich werdenden Druck trotz Alledem das Erscheinen eines unbedingt Befehlenden für diese Heerdenthier-Europäer ist, dafür gab die Wirkung, welche das Erscheinen Napoleon's machte, das letzte grosse Zeugniss: - die Geschichte der Wirkung Napoleon's ist beinahe die Geschichte des höheren Glücks, zu dem es dieses ganze Jahrhundert in seinen werthvollsten Menschen und Augenblicken gebracht hat.

200. Der Mensch aus einem Auflösungs-Zeitalter, welches die Rassen durch einander wirft, der als Solcher die Erbschaft einer vielfältigen Herkunft im Leibe hat, das heisst gegensätzliche und oft nicht einmal nur gegensätzliche Triebe und Werthmaasse,

welche mit einander kämpfen und sich selten Ruhe geben, - ein solcher Mensch der späten Culturen und der gebrochenen Lichter wird durchschnittlich ein schwächerer Mensch sein: sein gründlichstes Verlangen geht darnach, dass der Krieg, der er ist, einmal ein Ende habe; das Glück erscheint ihm, in Übereinstimmung mit einer beruhigenden (zum Beispiel epikurischen oder christlichen) Medizin und Denkweise, vornehmlich als das Glück des Ausruhens, der Ungestörtheit, der Sattheit, der endlichen Einheit, als "Sabbat der Sabbate", um mit dem heiligen Rhetor Augustin zu reden, der selbst ein solcher Mensch war. - Wirkt aber der Gegensatz und Krieg in einer solchen Natur wie ein Lebensreiz und -Kitzel mehr -, und ist andererseits zu ihren mächtigen und unversöhnlichen Trieben auch die eigentliche Meisterschaft und Feinheit im Kriegführen mit sich, also Selbst-Beherrschung, Selbst-Überlistung hinzuvererbt und angezüchtet: so entstehen jene zauberhaften Unfassbaren und Unausdenklichen, jene zum Siege und zur Verführung vorherbestimmten Räthselmenschen, deren schönster Ausdruck Alciblades und Caesar (- denen ich gerne jenen ersten Europäer nach meinem Geschmack, den Hohenstaufen Friedrich den Zweiten zugesellen möchte), unter Künstlern vielleicht Lionardo da Vinci ist. Sie erscheinen genau in den selben Zeiten, wo jener schwächere Typus, mit seinem Verlangen nach Ruhe, in den Vordergrund tritt.- beide Typen gehören zu einander und entspringen den gleichen Ursachen.

201. So lange die Nützlichkeit, die in den moralischen Werthurtheilen herrscht, allein die Heerden-Nützlichkeit ist, so lange der Blick einzig der Erhaltung der Gemeinde zugewendet ist, und das Unmoralische genau und ausschliesslich in dem gesucht wird, was dem Gemeinde-Bestand gefährlich scheint: so lange kann es noch keine "Moral der Nächstenliebe" geben. Gesetzt, es findet sich auch da bereits eine beständige kleine Übung von Rücksicht, Mitleiden, Billigkeit, Milde, Gegenseitigkeit der Hülfeleistung, gesetzt, es sind auch auf diesem Zustande der Gesellschaft schon alle jene Triebe thätig, welche später mit Ehrennamen, als "Tugenden" bezeichnet werden und schliesslich fast mit dem Begriff "Moralität" in Eins zusammenfallen: in jener Zeit gehören sie noch gar nicht in das Reich der moralischen Werthschätzungen - sie sind noch aussermoralisch. Eine mitleidige Handlung zum Beispiel heisst in der besten Römerzeit weder gut noch böse, weder moralisch noch unmoralisch; und wird sie selbst gelobt, so verträgt sich mit diesem Lobe noch auf das Beste eine Art unwilliger Geringschätzung, sobald sie nämlich mit irgend einer Handlung zusammengehalten wird, welche der Förderung des Ganzen, der res publica, dient. Zuletzt ist die "Liebe zum Nächsten" immer etwas Nebensächliches, zum Theil Conventionelles und Willkürlich-Scheinbares im Verhältniss zur Furcht vor dem Nächsten. Nachdem das Gefüge der Gesellschaft im Ganzen festgestellt und gegen äussere Gefahren gesichert erscheint, ist es diese

Furcht vor dem Nächsten, welche wieder neue Perspektiven der moralischen Werthschätzung schafft. Gewisse starke und gefährliche Triebe, wie Unternehmungslust, Tollkühnheit, Rachsucht, Verschlagenheit, Raubgier, Herrschsucht, die bisher in einem gemeinnützigen Sinne nicht nur geehrt unter anderen Namen, wie billig, als den eben gewählten sondern gross-gezogen und -gezüchtet werden mussten (weil man ihrer in der Gefahr des Ganzen gegen die Feinde des Ganzen beständig bedurfte), werden nunmehr in ihrer Gefährlichkeit doppelt stark empfunden - jetzt, wo die Abzugskanäle für sie fehlen - und schrittweise, als unmoralisch, gebrandmarkt und der Verleumdung preisgegeben. Jetzt kommen die gegensätzlichen Triebe und Neigungen zu moralischen Ehren; der Heerden-Instinkt zieht, Schritt für Schritt, seine Folgerung. Wie viel oder wie wenig Gemein-Gefährliches, der Gleichheit Gefährliches in einer Meinung, in einem Zustand und Affekte, in einem Willen, in einer Begabung liegt, das ist jetzt die moralische Perspektive: die Furcht ist auch hier wieder die Mutter der Moral. An den höchsten und stärksten Trieben, wenn sie, leidenschaftlich ausbrechend, den Einzelnen weit über den Durchschnitt und die Niederung des Heerdengewissens hinaus und hinauf treiben, geht das Selbstgefühl der Gemeinde zu Grunde, ihr Glaube an sich, ihr Rückgrat gleichsam, zerbricht: folglich wird man gerade diese Triebe am besten brandmarken und verleumden. Die hohe unabhängige

Geistigkeit, der Wille zum Alleinstehn, die grosse Vernunft schon werden als Gefahr empfunden; Alles, was den Einzelnen über die Heerde hinaushebt und dem Nächsten Furcht macht, heisst von nun an böse; die billige, bescheidene, sich einordnende, gleichsetzende Gesinnung, das Mittelmaass der Begierden kommt zu moralischen Namen und Ehren. Endlich, unter sehr friedfertigen Zuständen, fehlt die Gelegenheit und Nöthigung immer mehr, sein Gefühl zur Strenge und Härte zu erziehn; und jetzt beginnt jede Strenge, selbst in der Gerechtigkeit, die Gewissen zu stören; eine hohe und harte Vornehmheit und Selbst-Verantwortlichkeit beleidigt beinahe und erweckt Misstrauen, "das Lamm", noch mehr "das Schlaf" gewinnt an Achtung. Es giebt einen Punkt von krankhafter Vermürbung und Verzärtlichung in der Geschichte der Gesellschaft, wo sie selbst für ihren Schädiger, den Verbrecher Partei nimmt, und zwar ernsthaft und ehrlich. Strafen: das scheint ihr irgendworin unbillig, - gewiss ist, dass die Vorstellung "Strafe" und "Strafen-Sollen" ihr wehe thut, ihr Furcht macht. "Genügt es nicht, ihn ungefährlich machen? Wozu noch strafen? Strafen selbst ist fürchterlich!" - mit dieser Frage zieht die Heerden-Moral, die Moral der Furchtsamkeit ihre letzte Consequenz. Gesetzt, man könnte überhaupt die Gefahr, den Grund zum Fürchten abschaffen, so hätte man diese Moral mit abgeschafft: sie wäre nicht mehr nöthig, sie hielte sich selbst nicht mehr für nöthig! - Wer das Gewissen des heutigen Europäers prüft, wird aus tausend moralischen Falten und Verstecken immer den gleichen Imperativ herauszuziehen haben, den Imperativ der Heerden-Furchtsamkeit: "wir wollen, dass es irgendwann einmal Nichts mehr zu fürchten giebt!" Irgendwann einmal - der Wille und Weg dorthin heisst heute in Europa überall der "Fortschritt".

202. Sagen wir es sofort noch einmal, was wir schon hundert Mal gesagt haben: denn die Ohren sind für solche Wahrheiten - für unsere Wahrheiten - heute nicht gutwillig. Wir wissen es schon genug, wie beleidigend es klingt, wenn Einer überhaupt den Menschen ungeschminkt und ohne Gleichniss zu den Thieren rechnet; aber es wird beinahe als Schuld uns angerechnet werden, dass wir gerade in Bezug auf die Menschen der "modernen Ideen" beständig die Ausdrücke "Heerde", "Heerden-Instinkte" und dergleichen gebrauchen. Was hilft es! Wir können nicht anders: denn gerade hier liegt unsre neue Einsicht. Wir fanden, dass in allen moralischen Haupturtheilen Europa einmüthig geworden ist, die Länder noch hinzugerechnet, wo Europa's Einfluss herrscht: man weiss ersichtlich in Europa, was Sokrates nicht zu wissen meinte, und was jene alte berühmte Schlange einst zu lehren verhiess, - man "weiss" heute, was Gut und Böse ist. Nun muss es hart klingen und schlecht zu Ohren gehn, wenn wir immer von Neuem darauf bestehn: was hier zu wissen glaubt, was hier mit seinem Loben und Tadeln sich selbst verherrlicht, sich selbst

gut heisst, ist der Instinkt des Heerdenthiers Mensch: als welcher zum Durchbruch, zum Übergewicht, zur Vorherrschaft über andere Instinkte gekommen ist und immer mehr kommt, gemäss der wachsenden physiologischen Annäherung und Anähnlichung, deren Symptom er ist. Moral ist heute in Europa Heerdenthier-Moral: - also nur, wie wir die Dinge verstehn, Eine Art von menschlicher Moral, neben der, vor der, nach der viele andere, vor Allem höhere Moralen möglich sind oder sein sollten. Gegen eine solche "Möglichkeit", gegen ein solches "Sollte" wehrt sich aber diese Moral mit allen Kräften: sie sagt hartnäckig und unerbittlich "ich bin die Moral selbst, und Nichts ausserdem ist Moral!" - ja mit Hülfe einer Religion, welche den sublimsten Heerdenthier-Begierden zu Willen war und schmeichelte, ist es dahin gekommen, dass wir selbst in den politischen und gesellschaftlichen Einrichtungen einen immer sichtbareren Ausdruck dieser Moral finden: die demokratische Bewegung macht die Erbschaft der christlichen. Dass aber deren Tempo für die Ungeduldigeren, für die Kranken und Süchtigen des genannten Instinktes noch viel zu langsam und schläfrig ist, dafür spricht das immer rasender werdende Geheul, das immer unverhülltere Zähnefletschen der Anarchisten-Hunde, welche jetzt durch die Gassen der europäischen Cultur schweifen: anscheinend im Gegensatz zu den friedlich-arbeitsamen Demokraten und Revolutions-Ideologen, noch mehr zu den tölpelhaften Philosophastern und Bruderschafts-Schwärmern, welche sich Socialisten nennen und die "freie Gesellschaft" wollen, in Wahrheit aber Eins mit ihnen Allen in der gründlichen und instinktiven Feindseligkeit gegen jede andre Gesellschafts-Form als die der autonomen Heerde (bis hinaus zur Ablehnung selbst der Begriffe "Herr" und "Knecht" - ni dieu ni maître heisst eine socialistische Formel -); Eins im zähen Widerstande gegen jeden Sonder-Anspruch, jedes Sonder-Recht und Vorrecht (das heisst im letzten Grunde gegen jedes Recht: denn dann, wenn Alle gleich sind, braucht Niemand mehr "Rechte" -); Eins im Misstrauen gegen die strafende Gerechtigkeit (wie als ob sie eine Vergewaltigung am Schwächeren, ein Unrecht an der nothwendigen Folge aller früheren Gesellschaft wäre -); aber ebenso Eins in der Religion des Mitleidens, im Mitgefühl, soweit nur gefühlt, gelebt, gelitten wird (bis hinab zum Thier, bis hinauf zu "Gott": - die Ausschweifung eines Mitleidens mit "Gott" gehört in ein demokratisches Zeitalter -); Eins allesammt im Schrei und der Ungeduld des Mitleidens, im Todhass gegen das Leiden überhaupt, in der fast weiblichen Unfähigkeit, Zuschauer dabei bleiben zu können, leiden lassen zu können; Eins in der unfreiwilligen Verdüsterung und Verzärtlichung, unter deren Bann Europa von einem neuen Buddhismus bedroht scheint; Eins im Glauben an die Moral des gemeinsamen Mitleidens, wie als ob sie die Moral an sich sei, als die Höhe, die erreichte Höhe des

Menschen, die alleinige Hoffnung der Zukunft, das Trostmittel der Gegenwärtigen, die grosse Ablösung aller Schuld von Ehedem: - Eins allesammt im Glauben an die Gemeinschaft als die Erlöserin, an die Heerde also, an sich……

203. Wir, die wir eines andren Glaubens sind -, wir, denen die demokratische Bewegung nicht bloss als eine Verfalls-Form der politischen Organisation, sondern als Verfalls-, nämlich Verkleinerungs-Form des Menschen gilt, als seine Vermittelmässigung und Werth-Erniedrigung: wohin müssen wir mit unsren Hoffnungen greifen? - Nach neuen Philosophen, es bleibt keine Wahl; nach Geistern, stark und ursprünglich genug, um die Anstösse zu entgegengesetzten Werthschätzungen zu geben und "ewige Werthe" umzuwerthen, umzukehren; nach Vorausgesandten, nach Menschen der Zukunft, welche in der Gegenwart den Zwang und Knoten anknüpfen, der den Willen von Jahrtausenden auf neue Bahnen zwingt. Dem Menschen die Zukunft des Menschen als seinen Willen, als abhängig von einem Menschen-Willen zu lehren und grosse Wagnisse und Gesammt-Versuche von Zucht und Züchtung vorzubereiten, um damit jener schauerlichen Herrschaft des Unsinns und Zufalls, die bisher "Geschichte" hiess, ein Ende zu machen - der Unsinn der "grössten Zahl" ist nur seine letzte Form -: dazu wird irgendwann einmal eine neue Art von Philosophen und Befehlshabern nöthig sein, an

deren Bilde sich Alles, was auf Erden an verborgenen, furchtbaren und wohlwollenden Geistern dagewesen ist, blass und verzwergt ausnehmen möchte. Das Bild solcher Führer ist es, das vor unsern Augen schwebt: - darf ich es laut sagen, ihr freien Geister? Die Umstände, welche man zu ihrer Entstehung theils schaffen, theils ausnützen müsste; die muthmaasslichen Wege und Proben, vermöge deren eine Seele zu einer solchen Höhe und Gewalt aufwüchse, um den Zwang zu diesen Aufgaben zu empfinden; eine Umwerthung der Werthe, unter deren neuem Druck und Hammer ein Gewissen gestählt, ein Herz in Erz verwandelt würde, dass es das Gewicht einer solchen Verantwortlichkeit ertrüge; andererseits die Nothwendigkeit solcher Führer, die erschreckliche Gefahr, dass sie ausbleiben oder missrathen und entarten könnten - das sind unsre eigentlichen Sorgen und Verdüsterungen, ihr wisst es, ihr freien Geister? das sind die schweren fernen Gedanken und Gewitter, welche über den Himmel unseres Lebens hingehn. Es giebt wenig so empfindliche Schmerzen, als einmal gesehn, errathen, mitgefühlt zu haben, wie ein ausserordentlicher Mensch aus seiner Bahn gerieth und entartete: wer aber das seltene Auge für die Gesammt-Gefahr hat, dass "der Mensch" selbst entartet, wer, gleich uns, die ungeheuerliche Zufälligkeit erkannt hat, welche bisher in Hinsicht auf die Zukunft des Menschen ihr Spiel spielte - ein Spiel, an dem keine Hand und nicht einmal ein "Finger Gottes" mitspielte! - wer das Verhängniss, erräth, das in der blödsinnigen Arglosigkeit und Vertrauensseligkeit der "modernen Ideen", noch mehr in der ganzen christlich-europäischen Moral verborgen liegt: der leidet an einer Beängstigung, mit der sich keine andere vergleichen lässt, - er fasst es ja mit Einem Blicke, was Alles noch, bei einer günstigen Ansammlung und Steigerung von Kräften und Aufgaben, aus dem Menschen zu züchten wäre, er weiss es mit allem Wissen seines Gewissens, wie der Mensch noch unausgeschöpft für die grössten Möglichkeiten ist, und wie oft schon der Typus Mensch an geheimnissvollen Entscheidungen und neuen Wegen gestanden hat: - er weiss es noch besser, aus seiner schmerzlichsten Erinnerung, an was für erbärmlichen Dingen ein Werdendes höchsten Ranges bisher gewöhnlich zerbrach, abbrach, absank, erbärmlich ward. Die Gesammt-Entartung des Menschen, hinab bis zu dem, was heute den socialistischen Tölpeln und Flachköpfen als ihr "Mensch der Zukunft" erscheint, - als ihr Ideal! - diese Entartung und Verkleinerung des Menschen zum vollkommenen Heerdenthiere (oder, wie sie sagen, zum Menschen der "freien Gesellschaft"), diese Verthierung des Menschen zum Zwergthiere der gleichen Rechte und Ansprüche ist möglich, es ist kein Zweifel! Wer diese Möglichkeit einmal bis zu Ende gedacht hat, kennt einen Ekel mehr, als die übrigen Menschen, - und vielleicht auch eine neue Aufgabe!....

Sechstes Hauptstück:

Wir Gelehrten.

204. Auf die Gefahr hin, dass Moralisiren sich auch hier als Das herausstellt, was es immer war - nämlich als ein unverzagtes montrer ses plaies, nach Balzac -, möchte ich wagen, einer ungebührlichen und schädlichen Rangverschiebung entgegenzutreten, welche sich heute, ganz unvermerkt und wie mit dem besten Gewissen, zwischen Wissenschaft und Philosophie herzustellen droht. Ich meine, man muss von seiner Erfahrung aus - Erfahrung bedeutet, wie mich dünkt, immer schlimme Erfahrung? - ein Recht haben, über eine solche höhere Frage des Rangs mitzureden: um nicht wie die Blinden von der Farbe oder wie Frauen und Künstler gegen die Wissenschaft zu reden ("ach, diese schlimme Wissenschaft! seufzt deren Instinkt und Scham, sie kommt immer dahinter!" -). Die Unabhängigkeits-Erklärung des wissenschaftlichen Menschen, seine Emancipation von der Philosophie, ist eine der feineren Nachwirkungen

des demokratischen Wesens und Unwesens: die Selbstverherrlichung und Selbstüberhebung des Gelehrten steht heute überall in voller Blüthe und in ihrem besten Frühlinge, - womit noch nicht gesagt sein soll, dass in diesem Falle Eigenlob lieblich röche. "Los von allen Herren!" - so will es auch hier der pöbelmännische Instinkt; und nachdem sich die Wissenschaft mit glücklichstem Erfolge der Theologie erwehrt hat, deren "Magd" sie zu lange war, ist sie nun in vollem Übermuthe und Unverstande darauf hin aus, der Philosophie Gesetze zu machen und ihrerseits einmal den "Herrn" - was sage ich! den Philosophen zu spielen. Mein Gedächtniss - das Gedächtniss eines wissenschaftlichen Menschen, mit Verlaub! - strotzt von Naivetäten des Hochmuths, die ich seitens junger Naturforscher und alter Ärzte über Philosophie und Philosophen gehört habe (nicht zu reden von den gebildetsten und eingebildetsten aller Gelehrten, den Philologen und Schulmännern, welche Beides von Berufs wegen sind -). Bald war es der Spezialist und Eckensteher, der sich instinktiv überhaupt gegen alle synthetischen Aufgaben und Fähigkeiten zur Wehre setzte; bald der fleissige Arbeiter, der einen Geruch von otium und der vornehmen Üppigkeit im Seelen-Haushalte des Philosophen bekommen hatte und sich dabei beeinträchtigt und verkleinert fühlte. Bald war es jene Farben-Blindheit des Nützlichkeits-Menschen, der in der Philosophie Nichts sieht, als eine Reihe widerlegter Systeme und einen verschwenderischen

Aufwand, der Niemandem "zu Gute kommt". Bald sprang die Furcht vor verkappter Mystik und Grenzberichtigung des Erkennens hervor; bald die Missachtung einzelner Philosophen, welche sich unwillkürlich zur Missachtung der Philosophie verallgemeinert hatte. Am häufigsten endlich fand ich bei jungen Gelehrten hinter der hochmüthigen Geringschätzung der Philosophie die schlimme Nachwirkung eines Philosophen selbst, dem man zwar im Ganzen den Gehorsam gekündigt hatte, ohne doch aus dem Banne seiner wegwerfenden Werthschätzungen anderer Philosophen herausgetreten zu sein: - mit dem Ergebniss einer Gesammt-Verstimmung gegen alle Philosophie. (Dergestalt scheint mir zum Beispiel die Nachwirkung Schopenhauer's auf das neueste Deutschland zu sein: - er hat es mit seiner unintelligenten Wuth auf Hegel dahin gebracht, die ganze letzte Generation von Deutschen aus dem Zusammenhang mit der deutschen Cultur herauszubrechen, welche Cultur, Alles wohl erwogen, eine Höhe und divinatorische Feinheit des historischen Sinns gewesen ist: aber Schopenhauer selbst war gerade an dieser Stelle bis zur Genialität arm, unempfänglich, undeutsch.) Überhaupt in's Grosse gerechnet, mag es vor Allem das Menschliche, Allzumenschliche, kurz die Armseligkeit der neueren Philosophen selbst gewesen sein, was am gründlichsten der Ehrfurcht vor der Philosophie Abbruch gethan und dem pöbelmännischen Instinkte die Thore aufgemacht hat. Man gestehe es sich doch ein, bis zu welchem Grade unsrer modernen Welt die ganze Art der Heraklite, Plato's, Empedokles', und wie alle diese königlichen und prachtvollen Einsiedler des Geistes geheissen haben, abgeht; und mit wie gutem Rechte Angesichts solcher Vertreter der Philosophie, die heute Dank der Mode ebenso oben-auf als unten-durch sind - in Deutschland zum Beispiel die beiden Löwen von Berlin, der Anarchist Eugen Dühring und der Amalgamist Eduard von Hartmann - ein braver Mensch der Wissenschaft sich besserer Art und Abkunft fühlen darf. Es ist in Sonderheit der Anblick jener Mischmasch-Philosophen, die sich "Wirklichkeits-Philosophen" oder "Positivisten" nennen, welcher ein gefährliches Misstrauen in die Seele eines jungen, ehrgeizigen Gelehrten zu werfen im Stande ist: das sind ja besten Falls selbst Gelehrte und Spezialisten, man greift es mit Händen! - das sind ja allesammt überwundene und unter die Botmässigkeit der Wissenschaft Zurückgebrachte, welche irgendwann einmal mehr von sich gewollt haben, ohne ein Recht zu diesem "mehr" und seiner Verantwortlichkeit zu haben - und die jetzt, ehrsam, ingrimmig, rachsüchtig, den Unglauben an die Herren-Aufgabe und Herrschaftlichkeit der Philosophie mit Wort und That repräsentiren. Zuletzt: wie könnte es auch anders sein! Die Wissenschaft blüht heute und hat das gute Gewissen reichlich im Gesichte, während Das, wozu die ganze neuere Philosophie allmählich gesunken ist, dieser Rest Philosophie von heute, Misstrauen und Missmuth, wenn nicht Spott und Mitleiden gegen sich rege macht. Philosophie auf "Erkenntnisstheorie" reduzirt, thatsächlich nicht mehr als eine schüchterne Epochistik und Enthaltsamkeitslehre: eine Philosophie, die gar nicht über die Schwelle hinweg kommt und sich peinlich das Recht zum Eintritt verweigert - das ist Philosophie in den letzten Zügen, ein Ende, eine Agonie, Etwas das Mitleiden macht. Wie könnte eine solche Philosophie - herrschen!

205. Die Gefahren für die Entwicklung des Philosophen sind heute in Wahrheit so vielfach, dass man zweifeln möchte, ob diese Frucht überhaupt noch reif werden kann. Der Umfang und der Thurmbau der Wissenschaften ist in's Ungeheure gewachsen, und damit auch die Wahrscheinlichkeit, dass der Philosoph schon als Lernender müde wird oder sich irgendwo festhalten und "spezialisiren" lässt: so dass er gar nicht mehr auf seine Höhe, nämlich zum Überblick, Umblick, Niederblick kommt. Oder er gelangt zu spät hinauf, dann, wenn seine beste Zeit und Kraft schon vorüber ist; oder beschädigt, vergröbert, entartet, so dass sein Blick, sein Gesammt-Werthurtheil wenig mehr bedeutet. Gerade die Feinheit seines intellektuellen Gewissens lässt ihn vielleicht unterwegs zögern und sich verzögern; er fürchtet die Verführung zum Dilettanten, zum Tausendfuss und Tausend-Fühlhorn, er weiss es zu gut, dass Einer, der vor sich

selbst die Ehrfurcht verloren hat, auch als Erkennender nicht mehr befiehlt, nicht mehr führt: er müsste denn schon zum grossen Schauspieler werden wollen, zum philosophischen Cagliostro und Rattenfänger der Geister, kurz zum Verführer. Dies ist zuletzt eine Frage des Geschmacks: wenn es selbst nicht eine Frage des Gewissens wäre. Es kommt hinzu, um die Schwierigkeit des Philosophen noch einmal zu verdoppeln, dass er von sich ein Urtheil, ein ja oder Nein, nicht über die Wissenschaften, sondern über das Leben und den Werth des Lebens verlangt, - dass er ungern daran glauben lernt, ein Recht oder gar eine Pflicht zu diesem Urtheile zu haben, und sich nur aus den umfänglichsten - vielleicht störendsten, zerstörendsten - Erlebnissen heraus und oft zögernd, zweifelnd, verstummend seinen Weg zu jenem Rechte und jenem Glauben suchen muss. In der That, die Menge hat den Philosophen lange Zeit verwechselt und verkannt, sei es mit dem wissenschaftlichen Menschen und idealen Gelehrten, sei es mit dem religiös-gehobenen entsinnlichten "entweltlichten" Schwärmer und Trunkenbold Gottes; und hört man gar heute jemanden loben, dafür, dass er "weise" lebe oder "als ein Philosoph", so bedeutet es beinahe nicht mehr, als "klug und abseits". Weisheit: das scheint dem Pöbel eine Art Flucht zu sein, ein Mittel und Kunststück, sich gut aus einem schlimmen Spiele herauszuziehn; aber der rechte Philosoph - so scheint es uns, meine Freunde? - lebt "unphilosophisch" und "unweise", vor

Allem unklug, und fühlt die Last und Pflicht zu hundert Versuchen und Versuchungen des Lebens: - er risquirt sich beständig, er spielt das schlimme Spiel.....

206. Im Verhältnisse zu einem Genie, das heisst zu einem Wesen, welches entweder zeugt oder gebiert, beide Worte in ihrem höchsten Umfange genommen -, hat der Gelehrte, der wissenschaftliche Durchschnittsmensch immer etwas von der alten Jungfer: denn er versteht sich gleich dieser nicht auf die zwei werthvollsten Verrichtungen des Menschen. In der That, man gesteht ihnen Beiden, den Gelehrten und den alten Jungfern, gleichsam zur Entschädigung die Achtbarkeit zu - man unterstreicht in diesen Fällen die Achtbarkeit - und hat noch an dem Zwange dieses Zugeständnisses den gleichen Beisatz von Verdruss. Sehen wir genauer zu: was ist der wissenschaftliche Mensch? Zunächst eine unvornehme Art Mensch, mit den Tugenden einer unvornehmen, das heisst nicht herrschenden, nicht autoritativen und auch nicht selbstgenugsamen Art Mensch: er hat Arbeitsamkeit, geduldige Einordnung in Reih und Glied, Gleichmässigkeit und Maass im Können und Bedürfen, er hat den Instinkt für Seines gleichen und für Das, was Seinesgleichen nöthig hat, zum Beispiel jenes Stück Unabhängigkeit und grüner Weide, ohne welches es keine Ruhe der Arbeit giebt, jenen Anspruch auf Ehre und Anerkennung (die zuerst und zuoberst Erkennung, Erkennbarkeit voraussetzt -), jenen Sonnenschein des

guten Namens, jene beständige Besiegelung seines Werthes und seiner Nützlichkeit, mit der das innerliche Misstrauen, der Grund im Herzen aller abhängigen Menschen und Heerdenthiere, immer wieder überwunden werden muss. Der Gelehrte hat, wie billig, auch die Krankheiten und Unarten einer unvornehmen Art: er ist reich am kleinen Neide und hat ein Luchsauge für das Niedrige solcher Naturen, zu deren Höhen er nicht hinauf kann. Er ist zutraulich, doch nur wie Einer, der sich gehen, aber nicht strömen lässt; und gerade vor dem Menschen des grossen Stroms steht er um so kälter und verschlossener da, - sein Auge ist dann wie ein glatter widerwilliger See, in dem sich kein Entzücken, kein Mitgefühl mehr kräuselt. Das Schlimmste und Gefährlichste, dessen ein Gelehrter fähig ist, kommt ihm vom Instinkte der Mittelmässigkeit seiner Art: von jenem Jesuitismus der Mittelmässigkeit, welcher an der Vernichtung des ungewöhnlichen Menschen instinktiv arbeitet und jeden gespannten Bogen zu brechen oder - noch lieber! - abzuspannen sucht. Abspannen nämlich, mit Rücksicht, mit schonender Hand natürlich -, mit zutraulichem Mitleiden abspannen: das ist die eigentliche Kunst des Jesuitismus, der es immer verstanden hat, sich als Religion des Mitleidens einzuführen. -

207. Wie dankbar man auch immer dem objektiven Geiste entgegenkommen mag - und wer wäre nicht schon einmal alles Subjektiven und seiner verfluchten

Ipsissimosität bis zum Sterben satt gewesen! - zuletzt muss man aber auch gegen seine Dankbarkeit Vorsicht lernen und der Übertreibung Einhalt thun, mit der die Entselbstung und Entpersönlichung des Geistes gleichsam als Ziel an sich, als Erlösung und Verklärung neuerdings gefeiert wird: wie es namentlich innerhalb der Pessimisten-Schule zu geschehn pflegt, die auch gute Gründe hat, dem "interesselosen Erkennen" ihrerseits die höchsten Ehren zu geben. Der objektive Mensch, der nicht mehr flucht und schimpft, gleich dem Pessimisten, der ideale Gelehrte, in dem der wissenschaftliche Instinkt nach tausendfachem Ganz- und Halb-Missrathen einmal zum Auf- und Ausblühen kommt, ist sicherlich eins der kostbarsten Werkzeuge, die es giebt: aber er gehört in die Hand eines Mächtigeren. Er ist nur ein Werkzeug, sagen wir: er ist ein Spiegel, - er ist kein "Selbstzweck". Der objektive Mensch ist in der That ein Spiegel: vor Allem, was erkannt werden will, zur Unterwerfung gewohnt, ohne eine andre Lust, als wie sie das Erkennen, das "Abspiegeln" giebt, - er wartet, bis Etwas kommt, und breitet sich dann zart hin, dass auch leichte Fusstapfen und das Vorüberschlüpfen geisterhafter Wesen nicht auf seiner Fläche und Haut verloren gehen. Was von "Person" an ihm noch übrig ist, dünkt ihm zufällig, oft willkürlich, noch öfter störend: so sehr ist er sich selbst zum Durchgang und Wiederschein fremder Gestalten und Ereignisse geworden. Er besinnt sich auf "Sich" zurück, mit Anstrengung, nicht selten falsch; er verwechselt sich leicht, er vergreift sich in Bezug auf die eignen Nothdürfte und ist hier allein unfein und nachlässig. Vielleicht quält ihn die Gesundheit oder die Kleinlichkeit und Stubenluft von Weib und Freund, oder der Mangel an Gesellen und Gesellschaft, - ja, er zwingt sich, über seine Qual nachzudenken: umsonst! Schon schweift sein Gedanke weg, zum allgemeineren Falle, und morgen weiss er so wenig als er es gestern wusste, wie ihm zu helfen ist. Er hat den Ernst für sich verloren, auch die Zeit: er ist heiter, nicht aus Mangel an Noth, sondern aus Mangel an Fingern und Handhaben für seine Noth. Das gewohnte Entgegenkommen gegen jedes Ding und Erlebniss, die sonnige und unbefangene Gastfreundschaft, mit der er Alles annimmt, was auf ihn stösst, seine Art von rücksichtslosem Wohlwollen, von gefährlicher Unbekümmertheit um Ja und Nein: ach, es giebt genug Fälle, wo er diese seine Tugenden büssen muss! - und als Mensch überhaupt wird er gar zu leicht das caput mortuum dieser Tugenden. Will man Liebe und Hass von ihm, ich meine Liebe und Hass, wie Gott, Weib und Thier sie verstehn -: er wird thun, was er kann, und geben, was er kann. Aber man soll sich nicht wundern, wenn es nicht viel ist, - wenn er da gerade sich unächt, zerbrechlich, fragwürdig und morsch zeigt. Seine Liebe ist gewollt, sein Hass künstlich und mehr un tour de force, eine kleine Eitelkeit und Übertreibung. Er ist eben nur ächt, so weit er objektiv sein darf: allein in seinem heitern Totalismus ist er noch "Natur" und "natürlich". Seine spiegelnde und ewig sich glättende Seele weiss nicht mehr zu bejahen, nicht mehr zu verneinen; er befiehlt nicht; er zerstört auch nicht. "Je ne méprise presque rien" - sagt er mit Leibnitz: man überhöre und unterschätze das presque nicht! Er ist auch kein Mustermensch; er geht Niemandem voran, noch nach; er stellt sich überhaupt zu ferne, als dass er Grund hätte, zwischen Gut und Böse Partei zu ergreifen. Wenn man ihn so lange mit dem Philosophen verwechselt hat, mit dem cäsarischen Züchter und Gewaltmenschen der Cultur: so hat man ihm viel zu hohe Ehren gegeben und das Wesentlichste an ihm übersehen, - er ist ein Werkzeug, ein Stück Sklave, wenn gewiss auch die sublimste Art des Sklaven, an sich aber Nichts, - presque rien! Der objektive Mensch ist ein Werkzeug, ein kostbares, leicht verletzliches und getrübtes Mess-Werkzeug und Spiegel-Kunstwerk, das man schonen und ehren soll; aber er ist kein Ziel, kein Ausgang und Aufgang, kein complementärer Mensch, in dem das übrige Dasein sich rechtfertigt, kein Schluss - und noch weniger ein Anfang, eine Zeugung und erste Ursache, nichts Derbes, Mächtiges, Auf-sich-Gestelltes, das Herr sein will: vielmehr nur ein zarter ausgeblasener feiner beweglicher Formen-Topf, der auf irgend einen Inhalt und Gehalt erst warten muss, um sich nach ihm "zu gestalten", - für gewöhnlich ein Mensch ohne Gehalt und Inhalt, ein "selbstloser" Mensch. Folglich auch Nichts für Weiber, in parenthesi. -

208. Wenn heute ein Philosoph zu verstehen giebt, er sei kein Skeptiker, - ich hoffe, man hat Das aus der eben gegebenen Abschilderung des objektiven Geistes herausgehört? - so hört alle Welt das ungern; man sieht ihn darauf an, mit einiger Scheu, man möchte so Vieles fragen, fragen… ja, unter furchtsamen Horchern, wie es deren jetzt in Menge giebt, heisst er von da an gefährlich. Es ist ihnen, als ob sie, bei seiner Ablehnung der Skepsis, von Ferne her irgend ein böses bedrohliches Geräusch hörten, als ob irgendwo ein neuer Sprengstoff versucht werde, ein Dynamit des Geistes, vielleicht ein neuentdecktes Russisches Nihilin, ein Pessimismus bonae voluntatis, der nicht bloss Nein sagt, Nein will, sondern - schrecklich zu denken! Nein thut. Gegen diese Art von "gutem Willen" - einem Willen zur wirklichen thätlichen Verneinung des Lebens - giebt es anerkanntermaassen heute kein besseres Schlaf- und Beruhigungsmittel, als Skepsis, den sanften holden einlullenden Mohn Skepsis; und Hamlet selbst wird heute von den Ärzten der Zeit gegen den "Geist" und sein Rumoren unter dem Boden verordnet. "Hat man denn nicht alle Ohren schon voll von schlimmen Geräuschen? sagt der Skeptiker, als ein Freund der Ruhe und beinahe als eine Art von Sicherheits-Polizei: dies unterirdische Nein ist fürchterlich! Stille endlich, ihr pessimistischen Maulwürfe!" Der Skeptiker nämlich, dieses zärtliche Geschöpf, erschrickt allzuleicht; sein Gewissen ist darauf eingeschult, bei jedem Nein, ja schon bei einem

entschlossenen harten Ja zu zucken und etwas wie einen Biss zu spüren. Ja! und Nein! - das geht ihm wider die Moral; umgekehrt liebt er es, seiner Tugend mit der edlen Enthaltung ein Fest zu machen, etwa indem er mit Montaigne spricht: "was weiss ich?" Oder mit Sokrates: "ich weiss, dass ich Nichts weiss". Oder: "hier traue ich mir nicht, hier steht mir keine Thür offen." Oder: "gesetzt, sie stünde offen, wozu gleich eintreten!" Oder: "wozu nützen alle vorschnellen Hypothesen? Gar keine Hypothesen machen könnte leicht zum guten Geschmack gehören. Müsst ihr denn durchaus etwas Krummes gleich gerade biegen? Durchaus jedes Loch mit irgend welchem Werge ausstopfen? Hat das nicht Zeit? Hat die Zeit nicht Zeit? Oh ihr Teufelskerle, könnt ihr denn gar nicht warten? Auch das Ungewisse hat seine Reize, auch die Sphinx ist eine Circe, auch die Circe war eine Philosophin." - Also tröstet sich ein Skeptiker; und es ist wahr, dass er einigen Trost nöthig hat. Skepsis nämlich ist der geistigste Ausdruck einer gewissen vielfachen physiologischen Beschaffenheit, welche man in gemeiner Sprache Nervenschwäche und Kränklichkeit nennt; sie entsteht jedes Mal, wenn sich in entscheidender und plötzlicher Weise lang von einander abgetrennte Rassen oder Stände kreuzen. In dem neuen Geschlechte, das gleichsam verschiedene Maasse und Werthe in's Blut vererbt bekommt, ist Alles Unruhe, Störung, Zweifel, Versuch; die besten Kräfte wirken hemmend, die Tugenden selbst lassen einander nicht wachsen und stark werden, in Leib und Seele fehlt Gleichgewicht, Schwergewicht, perpendikuläre Sicherheit. Was aber in solchen Mischlingen am tiefsten krank wird und entartet, das ist der Wille: sie kennen das Unabhängige im Entschlusse, das tapfere Lustgefühl im Wollen gar nicht mehr, - sie zweifeln an der "Freiheit des Willens" auch noch in ihren Träumen. Unser Europa von heute, der Schauplatz eines unsinnig plötzlichen Versuchs von radikaler Stände- und folglich Rassenmischung, ist deshalb skeptisch in allen Höhen und Tiefen, bald mit jener beweglichen Skepsis, welche ungeduldig und lüstern von einem Ast zum andern springt, bald trübe wie eine mit Fragezeichen überladene Wolke, - und seines Willens oft bis zum Sterben satt! Willenslähmung: wo findet man nicht heute diesen Krüppel sitzen! Und oft noch wie geputzt! Wie verführerisch herausgeputzt! Es giebt die schönsten Prunk- und Lügenkleider für diese Krankheit; und dass zum Beispiel das Meiste von dem, was sich heute als "Objektivität", "Wissenschaftlichkeit", "l'art pour l'art", "reines willensfreies Erkennen" in die Schauläden stellt, nur aufgeputzte Skepsis und Willenslähmung ist, - für diese Diagnose der europäischen Krankheit will ich einstehn. - Die Krankheit des Willens ist ungleichmässig über Europa verbreitet: sie zeigt sich dort am grössten und vielfältigsten, wo die Cultur schon am längsten heimisch ist, sie verschwindet im dem Maasse, als "der Barbar" noch - oder wieder - unter dem schlotterichten

Gewande von westländischer Bildung sein Recht geltend macht. Im jetzigen Frankreich ist demnach, wie man es ebenso leicht erschliessen als mit Händen greifen kann, der Wille am schlimmsten erkrankt; und Frankreich, welches immer eine meisterhafte Geschicklichkeit gehabt hat, auch die verhängnisvollen Wendungen seines Geistes in's Reizende und Verführerische umzukehren, zeigt heute recht eigentlich als Schule und Schaustellung aller Zauber der Skepsis sein Cultur-Übergewicht über Europa. Die Kraft zu wollen, und zwar einen Willen lang zu wollen, ist etwas stärker schon in Deutschland, und im deutschen Norden wiederum stärker als in der deutschen Mitte; erheblich stärker in England, Spanien und Corsika, dort an das Phlegma, hier an harte Schädel gebunden, - um nicht von Italien zu reden, welches zu jung ist, als dass es schon wüsste, was es wollte, und das erst beweisen muss, ob es wollen kann -, aber am allerstärksten und erstaunlichsten in jenem ungeheuren Zwischenreiche, wo Europa gleichsam nach Asien zurückfliesst, in Russland. Da ist die Kraft zu wollen seit langem zurückgelegt und aufgespeichert, da wartet der Wille - ungewiss, ob als Wille der Verneinung oder der Bejahung - in bedrohlicher Weise darauf, ausgelöst zu werden, um den Physikern von heute ihr Leibwort abzuborgen. Es dürften nicht nur indische Kriege und Verwicklungen in Asien dazu nöthig sein, damit Europa von seiner grössten Gefahr entlastet werde, sondern innere Umstürze, die Zersprengung des Reichs in kleine Körper und vor Allem die Einführung des parlamentarischen Blödsinns, hinzugerechnet die Verpflichtung für Jedermann, zum Frühstück seine Zeitung zu lesen. Ich sage dies nicht als Wünschender: mir würde das Entgegengesetzte eher nach dem Herzen sein, - ich meine eine solche Zunahme der Bedrohlichkeit Russlands, dass Europa sich entschliessen müsste, gleichermaassen bedrohlich zu werden, nämlich Einen Willen zu bekommen, durch das Mittel einer neuen über Europa herrschenden Kaste, einen langen furchtbaren eigenen Willen, der sich über Jahrtausende hin Ziele setzen könnte: - damit endlich die langgesponnene Komödie seiner Kleinstaaterei und ebenso seine dynastische wie demokratische Vielwollerei zu einem Abschluss käme. Die Zeit für kleine Politik ist vorbei: schon das nächste Jahrhundert bringt den Kampf um die Erd-Herrschaft, - den Zwang zur grossen Politik.

209. Inwiefern das neue kriegerische Zeitalter, in welches wir Europäer ersichtlich eingetreten sind, vielleicht auch der Entwicklung einer anderen und stärkeren Art von Skepsis günstig sein mag, darüber möchte ich mich vorläufig nur durch ein Gleichniss ausdrücken, welches die Freunde der deutschen Geschichte schon verstehen werden. Jener unbedenkliche Enthusiast für schöne grossgewachsene Grenadiere, welcher, als König von Preussen, einem militärischen und skeptischen Genie - und damit im

Grunde jenem neuen, jetzt eben siegreich heraufgekommenen Typus des Deutschen - das Dasein gab, der fragwürdige tolle Vater Friedrichs des Grossen, hatte in Einem Punkte selbst den Griff und die Glücks-Kralle des Genies: er wusste, woran es damals in Deutschland fehlte, und welcher Mangel hundert Mal ängstlicher und dringender war, als etwa der Mangel an Bildung und gesellschaftlicher Form, - sein Widerwille gegen den jungen Friedrich kam aus der Angst eines tiefen Instinktes. Männer fehlten; und er argwöhnte zu seinem bittersten Verdrusse, dass sein eigner Sohn nicht Manns genug sei. Darin betrog er sich: aber wer hätte an seiner Stelle sich nicht betrogen? Er sah seinen Sohn dem Atheismus, dem esprit, der genüsslichen Leichtlebigkeit geistreicher Franzosen verfallen: - er sah im Hintergrunde die grosse Blutaussaugerin, die Spinne Skepsis, er argwöhnte das unheilbare Elend eines Herzens, das zum Bösen wie zum Guten nicht mehr hart genug ist, eines zerbrochnen Willens, der nicht mehr befiehlt, nicht mehr befehlen kann. Aber inzwischen wuchs in seinem Sohne jene gefährlichere und härtere neue Art der Skepsis empor - wer weiss, wie sehr gerade durch den Hass des Vaters und durch die eisige Melancholie eines einsam gemachten Willens begünstigt? - die Skepsis der verwegenen Männlichkeit, welche dem Genie zum Kriege und zur Eroberung nächst verwandt ist und in der Gestalt des grossen Friedrich ihren ersten Einzug in Deutschland hielt. Diese Skepsis verachtet und reisst trotzdem an sich; sie untergräbt und nimmt in Besitz; sie glaubt nicht, aber sie verliert sich nicht dabei; sie giebt dem Geiste gefährliche Freiheit, aber sie hält das Herz streng; es ist die deutsche Form der Skepsis, welche, als ein fortgesetzter und in's Geistigste gesteigerter Fridericianismus, Europa eine gute Zeit unter die Botmässigkeit des deutschen Geistes und seines kritischen und historischen Misstrauens gebracht hat. Dank dem unbezwinglich starken und zähen Manns-Charakter der grossen deutschen Philologen und Geschichts-Kritiker (welche, richtig angesehn, allesammt auch Artisten der Zerstörung und Zersetzung waren) stellte sich allmählich und trotz aller Romantik in Musik und Philosophie ein neuer Begriff vom deutschen Geiste fest, in dem der Zug zur männlichen Skepsis entscheidend hervortrat: sei es zum Beispiel als Unerschrockenheit des Blicks, als Tapferkeit und Härte der zerlegenden Hand, als zäher Wille zu gefährlichen Entdeckungsreisen, zu vergeistigten Nordpol-Expeditionen unter öden und gefährlichen Himmeln. Es mag seine guten Gründe haben, wenn sich warmblütige und oberflächliche Menschlichkeits-Menschen gerade vor diesem Geiste bekreuzigen: cet esprit fataliste, ironique, méphistophélique nennt ihn, nicht ohne Schauder, Michelet. Aber will man nachfühlen, wie auszeichnend diese Furcht vor dem "Mann" im deutschen Geiste ist, durch den Europa aus seinem "dogmatischen Schlummer" geweckt wurde, so möge man sich des ehemaligen Begriffs erinnern, der mit ihm überwunden werden musste, - und wie es noch nicht zu lange her ist, dass ein vermännlichtes Weib es in zügelloser Anmaassung wagen durfte, die Deutschen als sanfte herzensgute willensschwache und dichterische Tölpel der Theilnahme Europa's zu empfehlen. Man verstehe doch endlich das Erstaunen Napoleon's tief genug, als er Goethen zu sehen bekam: es verräth, was man sich Jahrhunderte lang unter dem "deutschen Geiste" gedacht hatte. "Voilà un homme!" - das wollte sagen: Das ist ja ein Mann! Und ich hatte nur einen Deutschen erwartet! - -

210. Gesetzt also, dass im Bilde der Philosophen der Zukunft irgend ein Zug zu rathen giebt, ob sie nicht vielleicht, in dem zuletzt angedeuteten Sinne, Skeptiker sein müssen, so wäre damit doch nur ein Etwas an ihnen bezeichnet - und nicht sie selbst. Mit dem gleichen Rechte dürften sie sich Kritiker nennen lassen; und sicherlich werden es Menschen der Experimente sein. Durch den Namen, auf welchen ich sie zu taufen wagte, habe ich das Versuchen und die Lust am Versuchen schon ausdrücklich unterstrichen: geschah dies deshalb, weil sie, als Kritiker an Leib und Seele, sich des Experiments in einem neuen, vielleicht weiteren, vielleicht gefährlicheren Sinne zu bedienen lieben? Müssen sie, in ihrer Leidenschaft der Erkenntniss, mit verwegenen und schmerzhaften Versuchen weiter gehn, als es der weichmüthige und verzärtelte Geschmack eines demokratischen

Jahrhunderts gut heissen kann? - Es ist kein Zweifel: diese Kommenden werden am wenigsten jener ernsten und nicht unbedenklichen Eigenschaften entrathen dürfen, welche den Kritiker vom Skeptiker abheben, ich meine die Sicherheit der Werthmaasse, die bewusste Handhabung einer Einheit von Methode, den gewitzten Muth, das Alleinstehn und Sich-verantworten-können; ja, sie gestehen bei sich eine Lust am Neinsagen und Zergliedern und eine gewisse besonnene Grausamkeit zu, welche das Messer sicher und fein zu führen weiss, auch noch, wenn das Herz blutet. Sie werden härter sein (und vielleicht nicht immer nur gegen sich), als humane Menschen wünschen mögen, sie werden sich nicht mit der "Wahrheit" einlassen, damit sie ihnen "gefalle" oder sie "erhebe" und "begeistere": - ihr Glaube wird vielmehr gering sein, dass gerade die Wahrheit solche Lustbarkeiten für das Gefühl mit sich bringe. Sie werden lächeln, diese strengen Geister, wenn Einer vor ihnen sagte "jener Gedanke erhebt mich: wie sollte er nicht wahr sein?" Oder: "jenes Werk entzückt mich: wie sollte es nicht schön sein?" Oder: "jener Künstler vergrössert mich: wie sollte er nicht gross sein?" - sie haben vielleicht nicht nur ein Lächeln, sondern einen ächten Ekel vor allem derartig Schwärmerischen, Idealistischen, Femininischen, Hermaphroditischen bereit, und wer ihnen bis in ihre geheimen Herzenskammern zu folgen wüsste, würde schwerlich dort die Absicht vorfinden, "christliche Gefühle" mit dem "antiken Geschmacke" und etwa gar noch mit dem "modernen Parlamentarismus" zu versöhnen (wie dergleichen Versöhnlichkeit in unserm sehr unsicheren, folglich sehr versöhnlichen Jahrhundert sogar bei Philosophen vorkommen soll). Kritische Zucht und jede Gewöhnung, welche zur Reinlichkeit und Strenge in Dingen des Geistes führt, werden diese Philosophen der Zukunft nicht nur von sich verlangen: sie dürften sie wie ihre Art Schmuck selbst zur Schau tragen, - trotzdem wollen sie deshalb noch nicht Kritiker heissen. Es scheint ihnen keine kleine Schmach, die der Philosophie angethan wird, wenn man dekretirt, wie es heute so gern geschieht: "Philosophie selbst ist Kritik und kritische Wissenschaft - und gar nichts ausserdem!" Mag diese Werthschätzung der Philosophie sich des Beifalls aller Positivisten Frankreichs und Deutschlands erfreuen (- und es wäre möglich, dass sie sogar dem Herzen und Geschmacke Kant's geschmeichelt hätte: man erinnere sich der Titel seiner Hauptwerke -): unsre neuen Philosophen werden trotzdem sagen: Kritiker sind Werkzeuge des Philosophen und eben darum, als Werkzeuge, noch lange nicht selbst Philosophen! Auch der grosse Chinese von Königsberg war nur ein grosser Kritiker. -

211. Ich bestehe darauf, dass man endlich aufhöre, die philosophischen Arbeiter und überhaupt die wissenschaftlichen Menschen mit den Philosophen zu verwechseln, - dass man gerade hier mit Strenge

"Jedem das Seine" und Jenen nicht zu Viel, Diesen nicht viel zu Wenig gebe. Es mag zur Erziehung des wirklichen Philosophen nöthig sein, dass er selbst auch auf allen diesen Stufen einmal gestanden hat, auf welchen seine Diener, die wissenschaftlichen Arbeiter der Philosophie, stehen bleiben, - stehen bleiben müssen; er muss selbst vielleicht Kritiker und Skeptiker und Dogmatiker und Historiker und überdies Dichter und Sammler und Reisender und Räthselrather und Moralist und Seher und "freier Geist" und beinahe Alles gewesen sein, um den Umkreis menschlicher Werthe und Werth-Gefühle zu durchlaufen und mit vielerlei Augen und Gewissen, von der Höhe in jede Ferne, von der Tiefe in jede Höhe, von der Ecke in jede Weite, blicken zu können. Aber dies Alles sind nur Vorbedingungen seiner Aufgabe: diese Aufgabe selbst will etwas Anderes, - sie verlangt, dass er Werthe schaffe. Jene philosophischen Arbeiter nach dem edlen Muster Kant's und Hegel's haben irgend einen grossen Thatbestand von Werthschätzungen - das heisst ehemaliger Werthsetzungen, Werthschöpfungen, welche herrschend geworden sind und eine Zeit lang "Wahrheiten" genannt werden - festzustellen und in Formeln zu drängen, sei es im Reiche des Logischen oder des Politischen (Moralischen) oder des Künstlerischen. Diesen Forschern liegt es ob, alles bisher Geschehene und Geschätzte übersichtlich, überdenkbar, fasslich, handlich zu machen, alles Lange, ja "die Zeit" selbst, abzukürzen und die ganze

Vergangenheit zu überwältigen: eine ungeheure und wundervolle Aufgabe, in deren Dienst sich sicherlich jeder feine Stolz, jeder zähe Wille befriedigen kann. Die eigentlichen Philosophen aber sind Befehlende und Gesetzgeber: sie sagen "so soll es sein!", sie bestimmen erst das Wohin? und Wozu? des Menschen und verfügen dabei über die Vorarbeit aller philosophischen Arbeiter, aller Überwältiger der Vergangenheit, - sie greifen mit schöpferischer Hand nach der Zukunft, und Alles, was ist und war, wird ihnen dabei zum Mittel, zum Werkzeug, zum Hammer. Ihr "Erkennen" ist Schaffen, ihr Schaffen ist eine Gesetzgebung, ihr Wille zur Wahrheit ist - Wille zur Macht. - Giebt es heute solche Philosophen? Gab es schon solche Philosophen? Muss es nicht solche Philosophen geben?....

212. Es will mir immer mehr so scheinen, dass der Philosoph als ein nothwendiger Mensch des Morgens und Übermorgens sich jederzeit mit seinem Heute in Widerspruch befunden hat und befinden musste: sein Feind war jedes Mal das Ideal von Heute. Bisher haben alle diese ausserordentlichen Förderer des Menschen, welche man Philosophen nennt, und die sich selbst selten als Freunde der Weisheit, sondern eher als unangenehme Narren und gefährliche Fragezeichen fühlten -, ihre Aufgabe, ihre harte, ungewollte, unabweisliche Aufgabe, endlich aber die Grösse ihrer Aufgabe darin gefunden, das böse Gewissen ihrer Zeit zu sein. Indem sie gerade den Tugenden der Zeit das

Messer vivisektorisch auf die Brust setzten, verriethen sie, was ihr eignes Geheimniss war: um eine neue Grösse des Menschen zu wissen, um einen neuen ungegangenen Weg zu seiner Vergrösserung. Jedes Mal deckten sie auf, wie viel Heuchelei, Bequemlichkeit, Sich-gehen-lassen und Sich-fallen lassen, wie viel Lüge unter dem bestgeehrten Typus ihrer zeitgenössischen Moralität versteckt, wie viel Tugend überlebt sei; jedes Mal sagten sie: "wir müssen dorthin, dorthinaus, wo ihr heute am wenigsten zu Hause seid." Angesichts einer Welt der "modernen Ideen", welche Jedermann in eine Ecke und "Spezialität" bannen möchte, würde ein Philosoph, falls es heute Philosophen geben könnte, gezwungen sein, die Grösse des Menschen, den Begriff "Grösse" gerade in seine Umfänglichkeit und Vielfältigkeit, in seine Ganzheit im Vielen zu setzen: er würde sogar den Werth und Rang darnach bestimmen, wie viel und vielerlei Einer tragen und auf sich nehmen, wie weit Einer seine Verantwortlichkeit spannen könnte. Heute schwächt und verdünnt der Zeitgeschmack und die Zeittugend den Willen, Nichts ist so sehr zeitgemäss als Willensschwäche: also muss, im Ideale des Philosophen, gerade Stärke des Willens, Härte und Fähigkeit zu langen Entschliessungen in den Begriff "Grösse" hineingehören; mit so gutem Rechte als die umgekehrte Lehre und das Ideal einer blöden entsagenden demüthigen selbstlosen Menschlichkeit einem umgekehrten Zeitalter angemessen war, einem solchen, das gleich dem sechszehnten Jahrhundert an seiner aufgestauten Energie des Willens und den wildesten Wässern und Sturmfluthen der Selbstsucht litt. Zur Zeit des Sokrates, unter lauter Menschen des ermüdeten Instinktes, unter conservativen Altathenern, welche sich gehen liessen - "zum Glück", wie sie sagten, zum Vergnügen, wie sie thaten - und die dabei immer noch die alten prunkvollen Worte in den Mund nahmen, auf die ihnen ihr Leben längst kein Recht mehr gab, war vielleicht Ironie zur Grösse der Seele nöthig, jene sokratische boshafte Sicherheit des alten Arztes und Pöbelmanns, welcher schonungslos in's eigne Fleisch schnitt, wie in's Fleisch und Herz des "Vornehmen", mit einem Blick, welcher verständlich genug sprach: "verstellt euch vor mir nicht! Hier - sind wir gleich!" Heute umgekehrt, wo in Europa das Heerdenthier allein zu Ehren kommt und Ehren vertheilt, wo die "Gleichheit der Rechte" allzuleicht sich in die Gleichheit im Unrecht umwandeln könnte: ich will sagen in gemeinsame Bekriegung alles Seltenen, Fremden, Bevorrechtigten, des höheren Menschen, der höheren Seele, der höheren Pflicht, der höheren Verantwortlichkeit, der schöpferischen Machtfülle und Herrschaftlichkeit - heute gehört das Vornehm-sein, das Für-sich-sein-wollen, das Anders-sein-können, das Allein-stehn und auf-eigne-Faust-leben-müssen zum Begriff "Grösse"; und der Philosoph wird Etwas von seinem eignen Ideal verrathen, wenn er aufstellt: "der soll der Grösste sein, der der Einsamste sein kann, der Verborgenste, der Abweichendste, der

Mensch jenseits von Gut und Böse, er Herr seiner Tugenden, der überreiche des Willens; dies eben soll Grösse heissen: ebenso vielfach als ganz, ebenso weit als voll sein können." Und nochmals gefragt: ist heute - Grösse möglich?

213. Was ein Philosoph ist, das ist deshalb schlecht zu lernen, weil es nicht zu lehren ist: man muss es "wissen", aus Erfahrung, - oder man soll den Stolz haben, es nicht zu wissen. Dass aber heutzutage alle Welt von Dingen redet, in Bezug auf welche sie keine Erfahrung haben kann, gilt am meisten und schlimmsten vom Philosophen und den philosophischen Zuständen: - die Wenigsten kennen sie, dürfen sie kennen, und alle populären Meinungen über sie sind falsch. So ist zum Beispiel jenes ächt philosophische Beieinander einer kühnen ausgelassenen Geistigkeit, welche presto läuft, und einer dialektischen Strenge und Nothwendigkeit, die keinen Fehltritt thut, den meisten Denkern und Gelehrten von ihrer Erfahrung her unbekannt und darum, falls jemand davon vor ihnen reden wollte, un glaubwürdig. Sie stellen sich jede Nothwendigkeit als Noth, als peinliches Folgen-müssen und Gezwungen-werden vor; und das Denken selbst gilt ihnen als etwas Langsames, Zögerndes, beinahe als eine Mühsal und oft genug als "des Schweisses der Edlen werth" - aber ganz und gar nicht als etwas Leichtes, Göttliches und dem Tanze, dem Übermuthe, Nächst-Verwandtes! "Denken" und

eine Sache "ernst nehmen", "schwer nehmen" - das gehört bei ihnen zu einander: so allein haben sie es "erlebt" -. Die Künstler mögen hier schon eine feinere Witterung haben.- sie, die nur zu gut wissen, dass gerade dann, wo sie Nichts mehr "willkürlich" und Alles nothwendig machen, ihr Gefühl von Freiheit, Feinheit, Vollmacht, von schöpferischem Setzen, Verfügen, Gestalten auf seine Höhe kommt, - kurz, dass Nothwendigkeit und "Freiheit des Willens" dann bei ihnen Eins sind. Es giebt zuletzt eine Rangordnung seelischer Zustände, welcher die Rangordnung der Probleme gemäss ist; und die höchsten Probleme stossen ohne Gnade Jeden zurück, der ihnen zu nahen wagt, ohne durch Höhe und Macht seiner Geistigkeit zu ihrer Lösung vorherbestimmt zu sein. Was hilft es, wenn gelenkige Allerwelts-Köpfe oder ungelenke brave Mechaniker und Empiriker sich, wie es heute so vielfach geschieht, mit ihrem Plebejer-Ehrgeize in ihre Nähe und gleichsam an diesen "Hof der Höfe" drängen! Aber auf solche Teppiche dürfen grobe Füsse nimmermehr treten: dafür ist im Urgesetz der Dinge schon gesorgt; die Thüren bleiben diesen Zudringlichen geschlossen, mögen sie sich auch die Köpfe daran stossen und zerstossen! Für jede hohe Welt muss man geboren sein; deutlicher gesagt, man muss für sie gezüchtet sein: ein Recht auf Philosophie - das Wort im grossen Sinne genommen - hat man nur Dank seiner Abkunft, die Vorfahren, das "Geblüt" entscheidet auch hier. Viele Geschlechter müssen der Entstehung des

Philosophen vorgearbeitet haben; jede seiner Tugenden muss einzeln erworben, gepflegt, fortgeerbt, einverleibt worden sein, und nicht nur der kühne leichte zarte Gang und Lauf seiner Gedanken, sondern vor Allem die Bereitwilligkeit zu grossen Verantwortungen, die Hoheit herrschender Blicke und Niederblicke, das Sich-Abgetrennt-Fühlen von der Menge und ihren Pflichten und Tugenden, das leutselige Beschützen und Vertheidigen dessen, was missverstanden und verleumdet wird, sei es Gott, sei es Teufel, die Lust und Übung in der grossen Gerechtigkeit, die Kunst des Befehlens, die Weite des Willens, das langsame Auge, welches selten bewundert, selten hinauf blickt, selten liebt....

Siebentes Hauptstück:

Unsere Tugenden.

214. Unsere Tugenden? - Es ist wahrscheinlich, dass auch wir noch unsere Tugenden haben, ob es schon billigerweise nicht jene treuherzigen und vierschrötigen Tugenden sein werden, um derentwillen wir unsere Grossväter in Ehren, aber auch ein wenig uns vom Leibe halten. Wir Europäer von übermorgen, wir Erstlinge des zwanzigsten Jahrhunderts, - mit aller unsrer gefährlichen Neugierde, unsrer Vielfältigkeit und Kunst der Verkleidung, unsrer mürben und gleichsam versüssten Grausamkeit in Geist und Sinnen, - wir werden vermuthlich, wenn wir Tugenden haben sollten, nur solche haben, die sich mit unsren

heimlichsten und herzlichsten Hängen, mit unsern heissesten Bedürfnissen am besten vertragen lernten: wohlan, suchen wir einmal nach ihnen in unsren Labyrinthen! - woselbst sich, wie man weiss, so mancherlei verliert, so mancherlei ganz verloren geht. Und giebt es etwas Schöneres, als nach seinen eigenen Tugenden suchen? Heisst dies nicht beinahe schon: an seine eigne Tugend glauben? Dies aber "an seine Tugend glauben" - ist dies nicht im Grunde dasselbe, was man ehedem sein "gutes Gewissen" nannte, jener ehrwürdige langschwänzige Begriffs-Zopf, den sich unsre Grossväter hinter ihren Kopf, oft genug auch hinter ihren Verstand hängten? Es scheint demnach, wie wenig wir uns auch sonst altmodisch und grossväterhaft-ehrbar dünken mögen, in Einem sind wir dennoch die würdigen Enkel dieser Grossväter, wir letzten Europäer mit gutem Gewissen: auch wir noch tragen ihren Zopf. - Ach! Wenn ihr wüsstet, wie es bald, so bald schon - anders kommt!.....

215. Wie es im Reich der Sterne mitunter zwei Sonnen sind, welche die Bahn Eines Planeten bestimmen, wie in gewissen Fällen Sonnen verschiedener Farbe um einen einzigen Planeten leuchten, bald mit rothem Lichte, bald mit grünen Lichte, und dann wieder gleichzeitig ihn treffend und bunt überfluthend: so sind wir modernen Menschen, Dank der complicirten Mechanik unsres "Sternenhimmels" - durch verschiedene Moralen

bestimmt; unsre Handlungen leuchten abwechselnd in verschiedenen Farben, sie sind selten eindeutig, - und es giebt genug Fälle, wo wir bunte Handlungen thun.

216. Seine Feinde lieben? Ich glaube, das ist gut gelernt worden: es geschieht heute tausendfältig, im Kleinen und im Grossen; ja es geschieht bisweilen schon das Höhere und Sublimere - wir lernen verachten, wenn wir lieben, und gerade wenn wir am besten lieben: - aber alles dies unbewusst, ohne Lärm, ohne Prunk, mit jener Scham und Verborgenheit der Güte, welche dem Munde das feierliche, Wort und die Tugend-Formel verbietet. Moral als Attitüde - geht uns heute wider den Geschmack. Dies ist auch ein Fortschritt: wie es der Fortschritt unsrer Väter war, dass ihnen endlich Religion als Attitüde wider den Geschmack gieng, eingerechnet die Feindschaft und Voltairische Bitterkeit gegen die Religion (und was Alles ehemals zur Freigeist-Gebärdensprache gehörte). Es ist die Musik in unserm Gewissen, der Tanz in unserm Geiste, zu dem alle Puritaner-Litanei, alle Moral-Predigt und Biedermännerei nicht klingen will.

217. Sich vor Denen in Acht nehmen, welche einen hohen Werth darauf legen, dass man ihnen moralischen Takt und Feinheit in der moralischen Unterscheidung zutraue! Sie vergeben es uns nie, wenn sie sich einmal vor uns (oder gar an uns) vergriffen haben, - sie werden unvermeidlich zu unsern instinktiven Verleumdern und

Beeinträchtigern, selbst wenn sie noch unsre "Freunde" bleiben. - Selig sind die Vergesslichen: denn sie werden auch mit ihren Dummheiten "fertig".

218. Die Psychologen Frankreichs - und wo giebt es heute sonst noch Psychologen? - haben immer noch ihr bitteres und vielfältiges Vergnügen an der bêtise bourgeoise nicht ausgekostet, gleichsam als wenn genug, sie verrathen etwas damit. Flaubert zum Beispiel, der brave Bürger von Rouen, sah, hörte und schmeckte zuletzt nichts Anderes mehr: es war seine Art von Selbstquälerei und feinerer Grausamkeit. Nun empfehle ich, zur Abwechslung - denn es wird langweilig -, ein anderes Ding zum Entzücken: das ist die unbewusste Verschlagenheit, mit der sich alle guten dicken braven Geister des Mittelmaasses zu höheren Geistern und deren Aufgaben verhalten, jene feine verhäkelte jesuitische Verschlagenheit, welche tausend Mal feiner ist, als der Verstand und Geschmack dieses Mittelstandes in seinen besten Augenblicken - sogar auch als der Verstand seiner Opfer -: zum abermaligen Beweise dafür, dass der "Instinkt" unter allen Arten von Intelligenz, welche bisher entdeckt wurden, die intelligenteste ist. Kurz, studirt, ihr Psychologen, die Philosophie der "Regel" im Kampfe mit der "Ausnahme": da habt ihr ein Schauspiel, gut genug für Götter und göttliche Boshaftigkeit! Oder, noch heutlicher: treibt Vivisektion am "guten Menschen", am "homo bonae voluntatis" an euch!

219. Das moralische Urtheilen und Verurtheilen ist die Lieblings-Rache der Geistig-Beschränkten an Denen, die es weniger sind, auch eine Art Schadenersatz dafür, dass sie von der Natur schlecht bedacht wurden, endlich eine Gelegenheit, Geist zu bekommen und fein zu werden: - Bosheit vergeistigt. Es thut ihnen im Grunde ihres Herzens wohl, dass es einen Maassstab giebt, vor dem auch die mit Gütern und Vorrechten des Geistes überhäuften ihnen gleich stehn: - sie kämpfen für die "Gleichheit Aller vor Gott" und brauchen beinahe dazu schon den Glauben an Gott. Unter ihnen sind die kräftigsten Gegner des Atheismus. Wer ihnen sagte "eine hohe Geistigkeit ist ausser Vergleich mit irgend welcher Bravheit und Achtbarkeit eines eben nur moralischen Menschen", würde sie rasend machen: - ich werde mich hüten, es zu thun. Vielmehr möchte ich ihnen mit meinem Satze schmeicheln, dass eine hohe Geistigkeit selber nur als letzte Ausgeburt moralischer Qualitäten besteht; dass sie eine Synthesis aller jener Zustände ist, welche den "nur moralischen" Menschen nachgesagt werden, nachdem sie, einzeln, durch lange Zucht und Übung, vielleicht in ganzen Ketten von Geschlechtern erworben sind; dass die hohe Geistigkeit eben die Vergeistigung der Gerechtigkeit und jener gütigen Strenge ist, welche sich beauftragt weiss, die Ordnung des Ranges in der Welt aufrecht zu erhalten, unter den Dingen selbst - und nicht nur unter Menschen.

220. Bei dem jetzt so volksthümlichen Lobe des "Uninteressirten" muss man sich, vielleicht nicht ohne einige Gefahr, zum Bewusstsein bringen, woran eigentlich das Volk Interesse nimmt, und was überhaupt die Dinge sind, um die sich der gemeine Mann gründlich und tief kümmert: die Gebildeten eingerechnet, sogar die Gelehrten, und wenn nicht Alles trügt, beinahe auch die Philosophen. Die Thatsache kommt dabei heraus, dass das Allermeiste von dem, was feinere und verwöhntere Geschmäcker, was jede höhere Natur interessirt und reizt, dem durchschnittlichen Menschen gänzlich "uninteressant" scheint: - bemerkt er trotzdem eine Hingebung daran, so nennt er sie "désintéressé" und wundert sich, wie es möglich ist, "uninteressirt" zu handeln. Es hat Philosophen gegeben, welche dieser Volks-Verwunderung noch einen verführerischen und mystisch-jenseitigen Ausdruck zu verleihen wussten (- vielleicht weil sie die höhere Natur nicht aus Erfahrung kannten?) - statt die nackte und herzlich billige Wahrheit hinzustellen, dass die "uninteressirte" Handlung eine sehr interessante und interessirte Handlung ist, vorausgesetzt….. "Und die Liebe?" - Wie! Sogar eine Handlung aus Liebe soll "unegoistisch" sein? Aber ihr Tölpel -! "Und das Lob des Aufopfernden?" - Aber wer wirklich Opfer gebracht hat, weiss, dass er etwas dafür wollte und bekam, - vielleicht etwas von sich für etwas von sich - dass er hier hingab, um dort mehr zu haben, vielleicht

um überhaupt mehr zu sein oder sich doch als "mehr" zu fühlen. Aber dies ist ein Reich von Fragen und Antworten, in dem ein verwöhnterer Geist sich ungern aufhält: so sehr hat hier bereits die Wahrheit nöthig, das Gähnen zu unterdrücken, wenn sie antworten muss. Zuletzt ist sie ein Weib: man soll ihr nicht Gewalt anthun.

221. Es kommt vor, sagte ein moralistischer Pedant und Kleinigkeitskrämer, dass ich einen uneigennützigen Menschen ehre und auszeichne: nicht aber, weil er uneigennützig ist, sondern weil er mir ein Recht darauf zu haben scheint, einem anderen Menschen auf seine eignen Unkosten zu nützen. Genug, es fragt sich immer, wer er ist und wer Jener ist. An Einem zum Beispiele, der zum Befehlen bestimmt und gemacht wäre, würde Selbst-Verleugnung und bescheidenes Zurücktreten nicht eine Tugend, sondern die Vergeudung einer Tugend sein: so scheint es mir. Jede unegoistische Moral, welche sich unbedingt nimmt und an Jedermann wendet, sündigt nicht nur gegen den Geschmack: sie ist eine Aufreizung zu Unterlassungs-Sünden, eine Verführung mehr unter der Maske der Menschenfreundlichkeit - und gerade eine Verführung und Schädigung der Höheren, Seltneren, Bevorrechteten. Man muss die Moralen zwingen, sich zu allererst vor der Rangordnung zu beugen, man muss ihnen ihre Anmaassung in's Gewissen schieben, - bis sie endlich mit einander darüber in's Klare kommen,

das es unmoralisch ist zu sagen: "was dem Einen recht ist, ist dem Andern billig". - Also mein moralistischer Pedant und bonhomme: verdiente er es wohl, dass man ihn auslachte, als er die Moralen dergestalt zur Moralität ermahnte? Aber man soll nicht zu viel Recht haben, wenn man die Lacher auf seiner Seite haben will; ein Körnchen Unrecht gehört sogar zum guten Geschmack.

222. Wo heute Mitleiden gepredigt wird - und, recht gehört, wird jetzt keine andre Religion mehr gepredigt - möge der Psycholog seine Ohren aufmachen: durch alle Eitelkeit, durch allen Lärm hindurch, der diesen Predigern (wie allen Predigern) zu eigen ist, wird er einen heiseren, stöhnenden, ächten Laut von Selbst-Verachtung hören. Sie gehört zu jener Verdüsterung und Verhässlichung Europa's, welche jetzt ein Jahrhundert lang im Wachsen ist (und deren erste Symptome schon in einem nachdenklichen Briefe Galiani's an Madame d'Epinay urkundlich verzeichnet sind): wenn sie nicht deren Ursache ist! Der Mensch der "modernen Ideen", dieser stolze Affe, ist unbändig mit sich selbst unzufrieden: dies steht fest. Er leidet: und seine Eitelkeit will, dass er nur "mit leidet"……

223. Der europäische Mischmensch - ein leidlich hässlicher Plebejer, Alles in Allem - braucht schlechterdings ein Kostüm: er hat die Historie nöthig als die Vorrathskammer der Kostüme. Freilich bemerkt

er dabei, dass ihm keines recht auf den Leib passt, - er wechselt und wechselt. Man sehe sich das neunzehnte Jahrhundert auf diese schnellen Vorlieben und Wechsel der Stil-Maskeraden an; auch auf die Augenblicke der Verzweiflung darüber, dass uns "nichts steht" -. Unnütz, sich romantisch oder klassisch oder christlich oder florentinisch oder barokko oder "national" vorzuführen, in moribus et artibus: "es kleidet nicht"! Aber der "Geist", insbesondere der "historische Geist", ersieht sich auch noch an dieser Verzweiflung seinen Vortheil: immer wieder wird ein neues Stück Vorzeit und Ausland versucht, umgelegt, abgelegt, eingepackt, vor allem studirt: - wir sind das erste studirte Zeitalter in puncto der "Kostüme", ich meine der Moralen, Glaubensartikel, Kunstgeschmäcker und Religionen, vorbereitet wie noch keine Zeit es war, zum Karneval grossen Stils, zum geistigsten Fasching-Gelächter und Übermuth, zur transscendentalen Höhe des höchsten Blödsinns und der aristophanischen Welt-Verspottung. Vielleicht, dass wir hier gerade das Reich unsrer Erfindung noch entdecken, jenes Reich, wo auch wir noch original sein können, etwa als Pazodisten der Weltgeschichte und Hanswürste Gottes, - vielleicht dass, wenn auch Nichts von heute sonst Zukunft hat, doch gerade unser Lachen noch Zukunft hat!

224. Der historische Sinn (oder die Fähigkeit, die Rangordnung von Werthschätzungen schnell zu errathen, nach welchen ein Volk, eine Gesellschaft, ein

Mensch gelebt hat, der "divinatorische Instinkt" für die Beziehungen dieser Werthschätzungen, für das Verhältniss der Autorität der Werthe zur Autorität der wirkenden Kräfte): dieser historische Sinn, auf welchen wir Europäer als auf unsre Besonderheit Anspruch machen, ist uns im Gefolge der bezaubernden und tollen Halbbarbarei gekommen, in welche Europa durch die demokratische Vermengung der Stände und Rassen gestürzt worden ist, - erst das neunzehnte Jahrhundert kennt diesen Sinn, als seinen sechsten Sinn. Die Vergangenheit von jeder Form und Lebensweise, von Culturen, die früher hart neben einander, über einander lagen, strömt Dank jener Mischung in uns "moderne Seelen" aus, unsre Instinkte laufen nunmehr überallhin zurück, wir selbst sind eine Art Chaos -: schliesslich ersieht sich "der Geist", wie gesagt, seinen Vortheil dabei. Durch unsre Halbbarbarei in Leib und Begierde haben wir geheime Zugänge überallhin, wie sie ein vornehmes Zeitalter nie besessen hat, vor Allem die Zugänge zum Labyrinthe der unvollendeten Culturen und zu jeder Halbbarbarei, die nur jemals auf Erden dagewesen ist; und insofern der beträchtlichste Theil der menschlichen Cultur bisher eben Halbbarbarei war, bedeutet "historischer Sinn" beinahe den Sinn und Instinkt für Alles, den Geschmack und die Zunge für Alles: womit er sich sofort als ein unvornehmer Sinn ausweist. Wir geniessen zum Beispiel Homer wieder: vielleicht ist es unser glücklichster Vorsprung, dass wir Homer zu schmecken verstehen, welchen die Menschen einer vornehmen Cultur (etwa die Franzosen des siebzehnten Jahrhunderts, wie Saint-Evremond, der ihm den esprit vaste vorwirft, selbst noch ihr Ausklang Voltaire) nicht so leicht sich anzueignen wissen und wussten, - welchen zu geniessen sie sich kaum erlaubten. Das sehr bestimmte Ja und Nein ihres Gaumens, ihr leicht bereiter Ekel, ihre zögernde Zurückhaltung in Bezug auf alles Fremdartige, ihre Scheu vor dem Ungeschmack selbst der lebhaften Neugierde, und überhaupt jener schlechte Wille jeder vornehmen und selbstgenügsamen Cultur, sich eine neue Begehrlichkeit, eine Unbefriedigung am Eignen, eine Bewunderung des Fremden einzugestehen: alles dies stellt und stimmt sie ungünstig selbst gegen die besten Dinge der Welt, welche nicht ihr Eigenthum sind oder ihre Beute werden könnten, - und kein Sinn ist solchen Menschen unverständlicher, als gerade der historische Sinn und seine unterwürfige Plebejer-Neugierde. Nicht anders steht es mit Shakespeare, dieser erstaunlichen spanisch-maurisch-sächsischen Geschmacks-Synthesis, über welchen sich ein Altathener aus der Freundschaft des Aeschylus halbtodt gelacht oder geärgert haben würde: aber wir - nehmen gerade diese wilde Buntheit, dies Durcheinander des Zartesten, Gröbsten und Künstlichsten, mit einer geheimen Vertraulichkeit und Herzlichkeit an, wir geniessen ihn als das gerade uns aufgesparte Raffinement der Kunst und lassen uns dabei von den widrigen Dämpfen und der Nähe des englischen Pöbels, in welcher Shakespeare's Kunst und Geschmack lebt, so wenig stören, als etwa auf der Chiaja Neapels: wo wir mit allen unsren Sinnen, bezaubert und willig, unsres Wegs gehn, wie sehr auch die Cloaken der Pöbel-Quartiere in der Luft sind. Wir Menschen des "historischen Sinns": wir haben als solche unsre Tugenden, es ist nicht zu bestreiten, - wir sind anspruchslos, selbstlos, bescheiden, tapfer, voller Selbstüberwindung, voller Hingebung, sehr dankbar, sehr geduldig, sehr entgegenkommend: - wir sind mit Alledem vielleicht nicht sehr "geschmackvoll". Gestehen wir es uns schliesslich zu: was uns Menschen des "historischen Sinns" am schwersten zu fassen, zu fühlen, nachzuschmecken, nachzulieben ist, was uns im Grunde voreingenommen und fast feindlich findet, das ist gerade das Vollkommene und Letzthin - Reife in jeder Cultur und Kunst, das eigentlich Vornehme an Werken und Menschen, ihr Augenblick glatten Meers und halkyonischer Selbstgenugsamkeit, das Goldene und Kalte, welches alle Dinge zeigen, die sich vollendet haben. Vielleicht steht unsre grosse Tugend des historischen Sinns in einem nothwendigen Gegensatz zum guten Geschmacke, mindestens zum allerbesten Geschmacke, und wir vermögen gerade die kleinen kurzen und höchsten Glücksfälle und Verklärungen des menschlichen Lebens, wie sie hier und da einmal aufglänzen, nur schlecht, nur zögernd, nur mit Zwang in uns nachzubilden: jene Augenblicke und Wunder, wo eine grosse Kraft freiwillig vor dem Maasslosen und Unbegrenzten stehen blieb -, wo ein Überfluss von feiner Lust in der plötzlichen Bändigung und Versteinerung, im Feststehen und Sich-Fest-Stellen auf einem noch zitternden Boden genossen wurde. Das Maass ist uns fremd, gestehen wir es uns; unser Kitzel ist gerade der Kitzel des Unendlichen, Ungemessenen. Gleich dem Reiter auf vorwärts schnaubendem Rosse lassen wir vor dem Unendlichen die Zügel fallen, wir modernen Menschen, wir Halbbarbaren - und sind erst dort in unsrer Seligkeit, wo wir auch am meisten - in Gefahr sind.

225. Ob Hedonismus, ob Pessimismus, ob Utilitarismus, ob Eudämonismus: alle diese Denkweisen, welche nach Lust und Leid, das heisst nach Begleitzuständen und Nebensachen den Werth der Dinge messen, sind Vordergrunds-Denkweisen und Naivetäten, auf welche ein Jeder, der sich gestaltender Kräfte und eines Künstler-Gewissens bewusst ist, nicht ohne Spott, auch nicht ohne Mitleid herabblicken wird. Mitleiden mit euch! das ist freilich nicht das Mitleiden, wie ihr es meint: das ist nicht Mitleiden mit der socialen "Noth", mit der "Gesellschaft" und ihren Kranken und Verunglückten, mit Lasterhaften und Zerbrochnen von Anbeginn, wie sie rings um uns zu Boden liegen; das ist noch weniger Mitleiden mit murrenden gedrückten aufrührerischen Sklaven-Schichten, welche nach Herrschaft - sie nennen's "Freiheit" - trachten. Unser Mitleiden ist ein höheres

fernsichtigeres Mitleiden: - wir sehen, wie der Mensch sich verkleinert, wie ihr ihn verkleinert! - und es giebt Augenblicke, wo wir gerade eurem Mitleiden mit einer unbeschreiblichen Beängstigung zusehn, wo wir uns gegen dies Mitleiden wehren -, wo wir euren Ernst gefährlicher als irgend welche Leichtfertigkeit finden. Ihr wollt womöglich - und es giebt kein tolleres "womöglich" - das Leiden abschaffen; und wir? - es scheint gerade, wir wollen es lieber noch höher und schlimmer haben, als je es war! Wohlbefinden, wie ihr es versteht - das ist ja kein Ziel, das scheint uns ein Ende! Ein Zustand, welcher den Menschen alsbald lächerlich und verächtlich macht, - der seinen Untergang wünschen macht! Die Zucht des Leidens, des grossen Leidens - wisst ihr nicht, dass nur diese Zucht alle Erhöhungen des Menschen bisher geschaffen hat? Jene Spannung der Seele im Unglück, welche ihr die Stärke anzüchtet, ihre Schauer im Anblick des grossen Zugrundegehens, ihre Erfindsamkeit und Tapferkeit im Tragen, Ausharren, Ausdeuten, Ausnützen des Unglücks, und was ihr nur je von Tiefe, Geheimniss, Maske, Geist, List, Grösse geschenkt worden ist: - ist es nicht ihr unter Leiden, unter der Zucht des grossen Leidens geschenkt worden? Im Menschen ist Geschöpf und Schöpfer vereint: im Menschen ist Stoff, Bruchstück, Überfluss, Lehm, Koth, Unsinn, Chaos; aber im Menschen ist auch Schöpfer, Bildner, Hammer-Härte, Zuschauer-Göttlichkeit und siebenter Tag: - versteht ihr diesen

Gegensatz? Und dass euer Mitleid dem "Geschöpf im Menschen" gilt, dem, was geformt, gebrochen, geschmiedet, gerissen, gebrannt, geglüht, geläutert werden muss, - dem, was nothwendig leiden muss und leiden soll? Und unser Mitleid - begreift ihr's nicht, wem unser umgekehrtes Mitleid gilt, wenn es sich gegen euer Mitleid wehrt, als gegen die schlimmste aller Verzärtelungen und Schwächen? - Mitleid also gegen Mitleid! - Aber, nochmals gesagt, es giebt höhere Probleme als alle Lust- und Leid- und Mitleid-Probleme; und jede Philosophie, die nur auf diese hinausläuft, ist eine Naivetät. -

226. Wir Immoralisten! - Diese Welt, die uns angeht, in der wir zu fürchten und zu lieben haben, diese beinahe unsichtbare unhörbare Welt feinen Befehlens, feinen Gehorchens, eine Welt des "Beinahe" in jedem Betrachte, häklich, verfänglich, spitzig, zärtlich: ja, sie ist gut vertheidigt gegen plumpe Zuschauer und vertrauliche Neugierde! Wir sind in ein strenges Garn und Hemd von Pflichten eingesponnen und können da nicht heraus -, darin eben sind wir "Menschen der Pflicht", auch wir! Bisweilen, es ist wahr, tanzen wir wohl in unsern "Ketten" und zwischen unsern "Schwertern"; öfter, es ist nicht minder wahr, knirschen wir darunter und sind ungeduldig über all die heimliche Härte unsres Geschicks. Aber wir mögen thun, was wir wollen: die Tölpel und der Augenschein sagen gegen

uns "das sind Menschen ohne Pflicht" - wir haben immer die Tölpel und den Augenschein gegen uns!

227. Redlichkeit, gesetzt, dass dies unsre Tugend ist, von der wir nicht loskönnen, wir freien Geister - nun, wir wollen mit aller Bosheit und Liebe an ihr arbeiten und nicht müde werden, uns in unsrer Tugend, die allein uns übrig blieb, zu "vervollkommnen": mag ihr Glanz einmal wie ein vergoldetes blaues spöttisches Abendlicht über dieser alternden Cultur und ihrem dumpfen düsteren Ernste liegen bleiben! Und wenn dennoch unsre Redlichkeit eines Tages müde wird und seufzt und die Glieder streckt und uns zu hart findet und es besser, leichter, zärtlicher haben möchte, gleich einem angenehmen Laster: bleiben wir hart, wir letzten Stoiker! und schicken wir ihr zu Hülfe, was wir nur an Teufelei in uns haben - unsern Ekel am Plumpen und Ungefähren, unser "nitimur in vetitum", unsern Abenteuerer-Muth, unsre gewitzte und verwöhnte Neugierde, unsern feinsten verkapptesten geistigsten Willen zur Macht und Welt-Überwindung, der begehrlich um alle Reiche der Zukunft schweift und schwärmt, - kommen wir unserm "Gotte" mit allen unsern "Teufeln" zu Hülfe! Es ist wahrscheinlich, dass man uns darob verkennt und verwechselt: was liegt daran! Man wird sagen: "ihre "Redlichkeit" - das ist ihre Teufelei, und gar nichts mehr!" was liegt daran! Und selbst wenn man Recht hätte! Waren nicht alle Götter bisher dergleichen heilig gewordne umgetaufte

Teufel? Und was wissen wir zuletzt von uns? Und wie der Geist heissen will, der uns führt? (es ist eine Sache der Namen.) Und wie viele Geister wir bergen? Unsre Redlichkeit, wir freien Geister, - sorgen wir dafür, dass sie nicht unsre Eitelkeit, unser Putz und Prunk, unsre Grenze, unsre Dummheit werde! Jede Tugend neigt zur Dummheit, jede Dummheit zur Tugend; "dumm bis zur Heiligkeit" sagt man in Russland, - sorgen wir dafür, dass wir nicht aus Redlichkeit zuletzt noch zu Heiligen und Langweiligen werden! Ist das Leben nicht hundert Mal zu kurz, sich in ihm - zu langweilen? Man müsste schon an's ewige Leben glauben, um....

228. Man vergebe mir die Entdeckung, dass alle Moral-Philosophie bisher langweilig war und zu den Schlafmitteln gehörte - und dass "die Tugend" durch nichts mehr in meinen Augen beeinträchtigt worden ist, als durch diese Langweiligkeit ihrer Fürsprecher; womit ich noch nicht deren allgemeine Nützlichkeit verkannt haben möchte. Es liegt viel daran, dass so wenig Menschen als möglich über Moral nachdenken, - es liegt folglich sehr viel daran, dass die Moral nicht etwa eines Tages interessant werde! Aber man sei unbesorgt! Es steht auch heute noch so, wie es immer stand: ich sehe Niemanden in Europa, der einen Begriff davon hätte (oder gäbe), dass das Nachdenken über Moral gefährlich, verfänglich, verführerisch getrieben werden könnte, - dass Verhängniss darin liegen könnte! Man sehe sich zum Beispiel die unermüdlichen

unvermeidlichen englischen Utilitarier an, wie sie plump und ehrenwerth in den Fusstapfen Bentham's, daher wandeln, dahin wandeln (ein homerisches Gleichniss sagt es deutlicher), so wie er selbst schon in den Fusstapfen des ehrenwerthen Helvétius wandelte (nein, das war kein gefährlicher Mensch, dieser Helvétius!). Kein neuer Gedanke, Nichts von feinerer Wendung und Faltung eines alten Gedankens, nicht einmal eine wirkliche Historie des früher Gedachten: eine unmögliche Litteratur im Ganzen, gesetzt, dass man sie nicht mit einiger Bosheit sich einzusäuern versteht. Es hat sich nämlich auch in diese Moralisten (welche man durchaus mit Nebengedanken lesen muss, falls man sie lesen muss-), jenes alte englische Laster eingeschlichen, das cant heisst und moralische Tartüfferie ist, dies Mal unter die neue Form der Wissenschaftlichkeit versteckt; es fehlt auch nicht an geheimer Abwehr von Gewissensbissen, an denen billigerweise eine Rasse von ehemaligen Puritanern bei aller wissenschaftlichen Befassung mit Moral leiden wird. (Ist ein Moralist nicht das Gegenstück eines Puritaners? Nämlich als ein Denker, der die Moral als fragwürdig, fragezeichenwürdig, kurz als Problem nimmt? Sollte Moralisiren nicht - unmoralisch sein?) Zuletzt wollen sie Alle, dass die englische Moralität Recht bekomme: insofern gerade damit der Menschheit, oder dem "allgemeinen Nutzen" oder "dem Glück der Meisten", nein! dem Glücke Englands am besten gedient wird; sie möchten mit allen Kräften sich beweisen, dass das Streben nach englischem Glück, ich meine nach comfort und fashion (und, an höchster Stelle, einem Sitz im Parlament) zugleich auch der rechte Pfad der Tugend sei, ja dass, so viel Tugend es bisher in der Welt gegeben hat, es eben in einem solchen Streben bestanden habe. Keins von allen diesen schwerfälligen, im Gewissen beunruhigten Heerdenthieren (die die Sache des Egoismus als Sache der allgemeinen Wohlfahrt zu führen unternehmen -) will etwas davon wissen und riechen, dass die "allgemeine Wohlfahrt" kein Ideal, kein Ziel, kein irgendwie fassbarer Begriff, sondern nur ein Brechmittel ist, - dass, was dem Einen billig ist, durchaus noch nicht dem Andern billig sein kann, dass die Forderung Einer Moral für Alle die Beeinträchtigung gerade der höheren Menschen ist, kurz, dass es eine Rangordnung zwischen Mensch und Mensch, folglich auch zwischen Moral und Moral giebt. Es ist eine bescheidene und gründlich mittelmässige Art Mensch, diese utilitarischen Engländer, und, wie gesagt: insofern sie langweilig sind, kann man nicht hoch genug von ihrer Utilität denken. Man sollte sie noch ermuthigen: wie es, zum Theil, mit nachfolgenden Reimen versucht worden ist.

  Heil euch, brave Karrenschieber,
  Stets "je länger, desto lieber",
  Steifer stets an Kopf und Knie,
  Unbegeistert, ungespässig,

Unverwüstlich-mittelmässig,
Sans genie et sans esprit!

229. Es bleibt in jenen späten Zeitaltern, die auf Menschlichkeit stolz sein dürfen, so viel Furcht, so viel Aberglaube der Furcht vor dem "wilden grausamen Thiere" zurück, über welches Herr geworden zu sein eben den Stolz jener menschlicheren Zeitalter ausmacht, dass selbst handgreifliche Wahrheiten wie auf Verabredung Jahrhunderte lang unausgesprochen bleiben, weil sie den Anschein haben, jenem wilden, endlich abgetödteten Thiere wieder zum Leben zu verhelfen. Ich wage vielleicht etwas, wenn ich eine solche Wahrheit mir entschlüpfen lasse: mögen Andre sie wieder einfangen und ihr so viel "Milch der frommen Denkungsart" zu trinken geben, bis sie still und vergessen in ihrer alten Ecke liegt. - Man soll über die Grausamkeit umlernen und die Augen aufmachen; man soll endlich Ungeduld lernen, damit nicht länger solche unbescheidne dicke Irrthümer tugendhaft und dreist herumwandeln, wie sie zum Beispiel in Betreff der Tragödie von alten und neuen Philosophen aufgefüttert worden sind. Fast Alles, was wir "höhere Cultur" nennen, beruht auf der Vergeistigung und Vertiefung der Grausamkeit - dies ist mein Satz; jenes "wilde Thier" ist gar nicht abgetödtet worden, es lebt, es blüht, es hat sich nur - vergöttlicht. Was die schmerzliche Wollust der Tragödie ausmacht, ist Grausamkeit; was im sogenannten tragischen

Mitleiden, im Grunde sogar in allem Erhabenen bis hinauf zu den höchsten und zartesten Schaudern der Metaphysik, angenehm wirkt, bekommt seine Süssigkeit allein von der eingemischten Ingredienz der Grausamkeit. Was der Römer in der Arena, der Christ in den Entzückungen des Kreuzes, der Spanier Angesichts von Scheiterhaufen oder Stierkämpfen, der Japanese von heute, der sich zur Tragödie drängt, der Pariser Vorstadt-Arbeiter, der ein Heimweh nach blutigen Revolutionen hat, die Wagnerianerin, welche mit ausgehängtem Willen Tristan und Isolde über sich "ergehen lässt", - was diese Alle geniessen und mit geheimnissvoller Brunst in sich hineinzutrinken trachten, das sind die Würztränke der grossen Circe "Grausamkeit". Dabei muss man freilich die tölpelhafte Psychologie von Ehedem davon jagen, welche von der Grausamkeit nur zu lehren wusste, dass sie beim Anblicke fremden Leides entstünde: es giebt einen reichlichen, überreichlichen Genuss auch am eignen Leiden, am eignen Sich-leiden-machen, - und wo nur der Mensch zur Selbst-Verleugnung im religiösen Sinne oder zur Selbstverstümmelung, wie bei Phöniziern und Asketen, oder überhaupt zur Entsinnlichung, Entfleischung, Zerknirschung, zum puritanischen Busskrampfe, zur Gewissens-Vivisektion und zum Pascalischen sacrifizio dell'intelletto sich überreden lässt, da wird er heimlich durch seine Grausamkeit gelockt und vorwärts gedrängt, durch jene gefährlichen Schauder der gegen sich selbst gewendeten Grausamkeit. Zuletzt erwäge man, dass selbst der Erkennende, indem er seinen Geist zwingt, wider den Hang des Geistes und oft genug auch wider die Wünsche seines Herzens zu erkennen - nämlich Nein zu sagen, wo er bejahen, lieben, anbeten möchte -, als Künstler und Verklärer der Grausamkeit waltet; schon jedes Tief- und Gründlich-Nehmen ist eine Vergewaltigung, ein Wehe-thun-wollen am Grundwillen des Geistes, welcher unablässig zum Scheine und zu den Oberflächen hin will, - schon in jedem Erkennen-Wollen ist ein Tropfen Grausamkeit.

230. Vielleicht versteht man nicht ohne Weiteres, was ich hier von einem "Grundwillen des Geistes" gesagt habe: man gestatte mir eine Erläuterung. - Das befehlerische Etwas, das vom Volke "der Geist" genannt wird, will in sich und um sich herum Herr sein und sich als Herrn fühlen: es hat den Willen aus der Vielheit zur Einfachheit, einen zusammenschnürenden, bändigenden, herrschsüchtigen und wirklich herrschaftlichen Willen. Seine Bedürfnisse und Vermögen sind hierin die selben, wie sie die Physiologen für Alles, was lebt, wächst und sich vermehrt, aufstellen. Die Kraft des Geistes, Fremdes sich anzueignen, offenbart sich in einem starken Hange, das Neue dem Alten anzuähnlichen, das Mannichfaltige zu vereinfachen, das gänzlich Widersprechende zu übersehen oder wegzustossen: ebenso wie er bestimmte Züge und Linien am Fremden, an jedem Stück

"Aussenwelt" willkürlich stärker unterstreicht, heraushebt, sich zurecht fälscht. Seine Absicht geht dabei auf Einverleibung neuer "Erfahrungen" auf Einreihung neuer Dinge unter alte Reihen, - auf Wachsthum also; bestimmter noch, auf das Gefühl des Wachsthums, auf das Gefühl der vermehrten Kraft. Diesem selben Willen dient ein scheinbar entgegengesetzter Trieb des Geistes, ein plötzlich herausbrechender Entschluss zur Unwissenheit, zur willkürlichen Abschliessung, ein Zumachen seiner Fenster, ein inneres Neinsagen zu diesem oder jenem Dinge, ein Nicht-heran-kommen-lassen, eine Art Vertheidigungs-Zustand gegen vieles Wissbare, eine Zufriedenheit mit dem Dunkel, mit dem abschliessenden Horizonte, ein Ja-sagen und Gutheissen der Unwissenheit: wie dies Alles nöthig ist je nach dem Grade seiner aneignenden Kraft, seiner "Verdauungskraft", im Bilde geredet - und wirklich gleicht "der Geist" am meisten noch einem Magen. Insgleichen gehört hierher der gelegentliche Wille des Geistes, sich täuschen zu lassen, vielleicht mit einer muthwilligen Ahnung davon, dass es so und so nicht steht, dass man es so und so eben nur gelten lässt, eine Lust an aller Unsicherheit und Mehrdeutigkeit, ein frohlockender Selbstgenuss an der willkürlichen Enge und Heimlichkeit eines Winkels, am Allzunahen, am Vordergrunde, am Vergrösserten, Verkleinerten, Verschobenen, Verschönerten, ein Selbstgenuss an der Willkürlichkeit aller dieser Machtäusserungen. Endlich gehört hierher jene nicht unbedenkliche Bereitwilligkeit des Geistes, andere Geister zu täuschen und sich vor ihnen zu verstellen, jener beständige Druck und Drang einer schaffenden, bildenden, wandelfähigen Kraft: der Geist geniesst darin seine Masken-Vielfältigkeit und Verschlagenheit, er geniesst auch das Gefühl seiner Sicherheit darin, - gerade durch seine Proteuskünste ist er ja am besten vertheidigt und versteckt! - Diesem Willen zum Schein, zur Vereinfachung, zur Maske, zum Mantel, kurz zur Oberfläche - denn jede Oberfläche ist ein Mantel - wirkt jener sublime Hang des Erkennenden entgegen, der die Dinge tief, vielfach, gründlich nimmt und nehmen will: als eine Art Grausamkeit des intellektuellen Gewissens und Geschmacks, welche jeder tapfere Denker bei sich anerkennen wird, gesetzt dass er, wie sich gebührt, sein Auge für sich selbst lange genug gehärtet und gespitzt hat und an strenge Zucht, auch an strenge Worte gewöhnt ist. Er wird sagen "es ist etwas Grausames im Hange meines Geistes": - mögen die Tugendhaften und Liebenswürdigen es ihm auszureden suchen! In der That, es klänge artiger, wenn man uns, statt der Grausamkeit, etwa eine "ausschweifende Redlichkeit" nachsagte, nachraunte, nachrühmte, - uns freien, sehr freien Geistern: - und so klingt vielleicht wirklich einmal unser - Nachruhm? Einstweilen - denn es hat Zeit bis dahin - möchten wir selbst wohl am wenigsten geneigt sein, uns mit dergleichen moralischen Wort-Flittern und -Franzen aufzuputzen: unsre ganze bisherige Arbeit verleidet uns gerade diesen Geschmack und seine muntere Üppigkeit. Es sind schöne glitzernde klirrende festliche Worte: Redlichkeit, Liebe zur Wahrheit, Liebe zur Weisheit, Aufopferung für die Erkenntniss, Heroismus des Wahrhaftigen, - es ist Etwas daran, das Einem den Stolz schwellen macht. Aber wir Einsiedler und Murmelthiere, wir haben uns längst in aller Heimlichkeit eines Einsiedler-Gewissens überredet, dass auch dieser würdige Wort-Prunk zu dem alten Lügen-Putz, -Plunder und -Goldstaub der unbewussten menschlichen Eitelkeit gehört, und dass auch unter solcher schmeichlerischen Farbe und Übermalung der schreckliche Grundtext homo natura wieder heraus erkannt werden muss. Den Menschen nämlich zurückübersetzen in die Natur; über die vielen eitlen und schwärmerischen Deutungen und Nebensinne Herr werden, welche bisher über jenen ewigen Grundtext homo natura gekritzelt und gemalt wurden; machen, dass der Mensch fürderhin vor dem Menschen steht, wie er heute schon, hart geworden in der Zucht der Wissenschaft, vor der anderen Natur steht, mit unerschrocknen Oedipus-Augen und verklebten Odysseus-Ohren, taub gegen die Lockweisen alter metaphysischer Vogelfänger, welche ihm allzulange zugeflötet haben: "du bist mehr! du bist höher! du bist anderer Herkunft!" - das mag eine seltsame und tolle Aufgabe sein, aber es ist eine Aufgabe - wer wollte das leugnen! Warum wir sie wählten, diese tolle Aufgabe?

Oder anders gefragt: "warum überhaupt Erkenntniss?" - Jedermann wird uns darnach fragen. Und wir, solchermaassen gedrängt, wir, die wir uns hunderte Male selbst schon ebenso gefragt haben, wir fanden und finden keine bessere Antwort….

231. Das Lernen verwandelt uns, es thut Das, was alle Ernährung thut, die auch nicht bloss "erhält" -: wie der Physiologe weiss. Aber im Grunde von uns, ganz "da unten", giebt es freilich etwas Unbelehrbares, einen Granit von geistigem Fatum, von vorherbestimmter Entscheidung und Antwort auf vorherbestimmte ausgelesene Fragen. Bei jedem kardinalen Probleme redet ein unwandelbares "das bin ich"; über Mann und Weib zum Beispiel kann ein Denker nicht umlernen, sondern nur auslernen, - nur zu Ende entdecken, was darüber bei ihm "feststeht". Man findet bei Zeiten gewisse Lösungen von Problemen, die gerade uns starken Glauben machen; vielleicht nennt man sie fürderhin seine "Überzeugungen". Später - sieht man in ihnen nur Fusstapfen zur Selbsterkenntniss, Wegweiser zum Probleme, das wir sind, - richtiger, zur grossen Dummheit, die wir sind, zu unserem geistigen Fatum, zum Unbelehrbaren ganz "da unten". - Auf diese reichliche Artigkeit hin, wie ich sie eben gegen mich selbst begangen habe, wird es mir vielleicht eher schon gestattet sein, über das "Weib an sich" einige Wahrheiten herauszusagen: gesetzt, dass man es von

vornherein nunmehr weiss, wie sehr es eben nur - meine Wahrheiten sind. -

232. Das Weib will selbständig werden: und dazu fängt es an, die Männer über das "Weib an sich" aufzuklären - das gehört zu den schlimmsten Fortschritten der allgemeinen Verhässlichung Europa's. Denn was müssen diese plumpen Versuche der weiblichen Wissenschaftlichkeit und Selbst-Entblössung Alles an's Licht bringen! Das Weib hat so viel Grund zur Scham; im Weibe ist so viel Pedantisches, Oberflächliches, Schulmeisterliches, Kleinlich-Anmaassliches, Kleinlich-Zügelloses und - Unbescheidenes versteckt - man studire nur seinen Verkehr mit Kindern! -, das im Grunde bisher durch die Furcht vor dem Manne am besten zurückgedrängt und gebändigt wurde. Wehe, wenn erst das "Ewig-Langweilige am Weibe" - es ist reich daran! - sich hervorwagen darf! wenn es seine Klugheit und Kunst, die der Anmuth, des Spielens, Sorgen-Wegscheuchens, Erleichterns und Leicht-Nehmens, wenn es seine feine Anstelligkeit zu angenehmen Begierden gründlich und grundsätzlich zu verlernen beginnt! Es werden schon jetzt weibliche Stimmen laut, welche, beim heiligen Aristophanes! Schrecken machen, es wird mit medizinischer Deutlichkeit gedroht, was zuerst und zuletzt das Weib vom Manne will. Ist es nicht vom schlechtesten Geschmacke, wenn das Weib sich dergestalt anschickt, wissenschaftlich zu werden?

Bisher war glücklicher Weise das Aufklären Männer-Sache, Männer-Gabe - man blieb damit "unter sich"; und man darf sich zuletzt, bei Allem, was Weiber über "das Weib" schreiben, ein gutes Misstrauen vorbehalten, ob das Weib über sich selbst eigentlich Aufklärung will - und wollen kann Wenn ein Weib damit nicht einen neuen Putz für sich sucht - ich denke doch, das Sich-Putzen gehört zum Ewig-Weiblichen? - nun, so will es vor sich Furcht erregen: - es will damit vielleicht Herrschaft. Aber es will nicht Wahrheit: was liegt dem Weibe an Wahrheit! Nichts ist von Anbeginn an dem Weibe fremder, widriger, feindlicher als Wahrheit, - seine grosse Kunst ist die Lüge, seine höchste Angelegenheit ist der Schein und die Schönheit. Gestehen wir es, wir Männer: wir ehren und lieben gerade diese Kunst und diesen Instinkt am Weibe: wir, die wir es schwer haben und uns gerne zu unsrer Erleichterung zu Wesen gesellen, unter deren Händen, Blicken und zarten Thorheiten uns unser Ernst, unsre Schwere und Tiefe beinahe wie eine Thorheit erscheint. Zuletzt stelle ich die Frage: hat jemals ein Weib selber schon einem Weibskopfe Tiefe, einem Weibsherzen Gerechtigkeit zugestanden? Und ist es nicht wahr, dass, im Grossen gerechnet, "das Weib" bisher vom Weibe selbst am meisten missachtet wurde - und ganz und gar nicht von uns? - Wir Männer wünschen, dass das Weib nicht fortfahre, sich durch Aufklärung zu compromittiren: wie es Manns-Fürsorge und Schonung des Weibes war, als die Kirche dekretirte: mulier taceat in ecclesia! Es geschah zum Nutzen des Weibes, als Napoleon der allzuberedten Madame de Staël zu verstehen gab: mulier taceat in politicis! - und ich denke, dass es ein rechter Weiberfreund ist, der den Frauen heute zuruft: mulier taceat de muliere!

233. Es verräth Corruption der Instinkte - noch abgesehn davon, dass es schlechten Geschmack verräth -. wenn ein Weib sich gerade auf Madame Roland oder Madame de Staël oder Monsieur George Sand beruft, wie als ob damit etwas zu Gunsten des "Weibes an sich" bewiesen wäre. Unter Männern sind die Genannten die drei komischen Weiber an sich - nichts mehr! - und gerade die besten unfreiwilligen Gegen-Argumente gegen Emancipation und weibliche Selbstherrlichkeit.

234. Die Dummheit in der Küche; das Weib als Köchin; die schauerliche Gedankenlosigkeit, mit der die Ernährung der Familie und des Hausherrn besorgt wird! Das Weib versteht nicht, was die Speise bedeutet: und will Köchin sein! Wenn das Weib ein denkendes Geschöpf wäre, so hätte es ja, als Köchin seit Jahrtausenden, die grössten physiologischen Thatsachen finden, insgleichen die Heilkunst in seinen Besitz bringen müssen! Durch schlechte Köchinnen - durch den vollkommenen Mangel an Vernunft in der Küche ist die Entwicklung des Menschen am längsten

aufgehalten, am schlimmsten beeinträchtigt worden: es steht heute selbst noch wenig besser. Eine Rede an höhere Töchter.

235. Es giebt Wendungen und Würfe des Geistes, es giebt Sentenzen, eine kleine Handvoll Worte, in denen eine ganze Cultur, eine ganze Gesellschaft sich plötzlich krystallisirt. Dahin gehört jenes gelegentliche Wort der Madame de Lambert an ihren Sohn: "mon ami, ne vous permettez jamais que de folies, qui vous feront grand plaisir": - beiläufig das mütterlichste und klügste Wort, das je an einen Sohn gerichtet worden ist.

236. Das, was Dante und Goethe vom Weibe geglaubt haben - jener, indem er sang "ella guardava suso, ed io in lei", dieser, indem er es übersetzte "das Ewig-Weibliche zieht uns hinan" -: ich zweifle nicht, dass jedes edlere Weib sich gegen diesen Glauben wehren wird, denn es glaubt eben das vom Ewig-Männlichen…

237. Sieben Weibs-Sprüchlein.

Wie die längste Weile fleucht,
kommt ein Mann zu uns gekreucht!

Alter, ach! und Wissenschaft
giebt auch schwacher Tugend Kraft.

Schwarz Gewand und Schweigsamkeit
kleidet jeglich Weib - gescheidt.

Wem im Glück ich dankbar bin?
Gott! - und meiner Schneiderin.

Jung: beblümtes Höhlenhaus.
Alt: ein Drache fährt heraus.

Edler Name, hübsches Bein,
Mann dazu: oh wär' *er* mein!

Kurze Rede, langer Sinn
- Glatteis für die Eselin!

237. Die Frauen sind von den Männern bisher wie Vögel behandelt worden, die von irgend welcher Höhe sich hinab zu ihnen verirrt haben: als etwas Feineres, Verletzlicheres, Wilderes, Wunderlicheres, Süsseres, Seelenvolleres, - aber als Etwas, das man einsperren muss, damit es nicht davonfliegt.

238. Sich im Grundprobleme "Mann und Weib" zu vergreifen, hier den abgründlichsten Antagonismus und die Nothwendigkeit einer ewig-feindseligen Spannung zu leugnen, hier vielleicht von gleichen Rechten, gleicher Erziehung, gleichen Ansprüchen und Verpflichtungen zu träumen: das ist ein typisches Zeichen von Flachköpfigkeit, und ein Denker, der an dieser gefährlichen Stelle sich flach erwiesen hat - flach im Instinkte! -, darf überhaupt als verdächtig, mehr noch, als verrathen, als aufgedeckt gelten: wahrscheinlich wird er für alle Grundfragen des

Lebens, auch des zukünftigen Lebens, zu "kurz" sein und in keine Tiefe hinunter können. Ein Mann hingegen, der Tiefe hat, in seinem Geiste, wie in seinen Begierden, auch jene Tiefe des Wohlwollens, welche der Strenge und Härte fähig ist, und leicht mit ihnen verwechselt wird, kann über das Weib immer nur orientalisch denken: er muss das Weib als Besitz, als verschliessbares Eigenthum, als etwas zur Dienstbarkeit Vorbestimmtes und in ihr sich Vollendendes fassen, - er muss sich hierin auf die ungeheure Vernunft Asiens, auf Asiens Instinkt-Überlegenheit stellen: wie dies ehemals die Griechen gethan haben, diese besten Erben und Schüler Asiens, welche, wie bekannt, von Homer bis zu den Zeiten des Perikles, mit zunehmen - der Cultur und Umfänglichkeit an Kraft, Schritt für Schritt auch strenger gegen das Weib, kurz orientalischer geworden sind. Wie nothwendig, wie logisch, wie selbst menschlich-wünschbar dies war: möge man darüber bei sich nachdenken!

239. Das schwache Geschlecht ist in keinem Zeitalter mit solcher Achtung von Seiten der Männer behandelt worden als in unserm Zeitalter - das gehört zum demokratischen Hang und Grundgeschmack, ebenso wie die Unehrerbietigkeit vor dem Alter -: was Wunder, dass sofort wieder mit dieser Achtung Missbrauch getrieben wird? Man will mehr, man lernt fordern, man findet zuletzt jenen Achtungszoll beinahe schon kränkend, man würde den Wettbewerb um

Rechte, ja ganz eigentlich den Kampf vorziehn: genug, das Weib verliert an Scham. Setzen wir sofort hinzu, dass es auch an Geschmack verliert. Es verlernt den Mann zu fürchten: aber das Weib, das "das Fürchten verlernt", giebt seine weiblichsten Instinkte preis. Dass das Weib sich hervor wagt, wenn das Furcht-Einflössende am Manne, sagen wir bestimmter, wenn der Mann im Manne nicht mehr gewollt und grossgezüchtet wird, ist billig genug, auch begreiflich genug; was sich schwerer begreift, ist, dass ebendamit - das Weib entartet. Dies geschieht heute: täuschen wir uns nicht darüber! Wo nur der industrielle Geist über den militärischen und aristokratischen Geist gesiegt hat, strebt jetzt das Weib nach der wirthschaftlichen und rechtlichen Selbständigkeit eines Commis: "das Weib als Commis" steht an der Pforte der sich bildenden modernen Gesellschaft. Indem es sich dergestalt neuer Rechte bemächtigt, "Herr" zu werden trachtet und den "Fortschritt" des Weibes auf seine Fahnen und Fähnchen schreibt, vollzieht sich mit schrecklicher Deutlichkeit das Umgekehrte: das Weib geht zurück. Seit der französischen Revolution ist in Europa der Einfluss des Weibes in dem Maasse geringer geworden, als es an Rechten und Ansprüchen zugenommen hat; und die "Emancipation des Weibes", insofern sie von den Frauen selbst (und nicht nur von männlichen Flachköpfen) verlangt und gefördert wird, ergiebt sich dergestalt als ein merkwürdiges Symptom von der zunehmenden Schwächung und Abstumpfung der allerweiblichsten Instinkte. Es ist Dummheit in dieser Bewegung, eine beinahe maskulinische Dummheit, deren sich ein wohlgerathenes Weib - das immer ein kluges Weib ist - von Grund aus zu schämen hätte. Die Witterung dafür verlieren, auf welchem Boden man am sichersten zum Siege kommt; die Übung in seiner eigentlichen Waffenkunst vernachlässigen; sich vor dem Manne gehen lassen, vielleicht sogar "bis zum Buche", wo man sich früher in Zucht und feine listige Demuth nahm; dem Glauben des Mannes an ein im Weibe verhülltes grundverschiedenes Ideal, an irgend ein Ewig- und Nothwendig-Weibliches mit tugendhafter Dreistigkeit entgegenarbeiten; dem Manne es nachdrücklich und geschwätzig ausreden, dass das Weib gleich einem zarteren, wunderlich wilden und oft angenehmen Hausthiere erhalten, versorgt, geschützt, geschont werden müsse; das täppische und entrüstete Zusammensuchen all des Sklavenhaften und Leibeigenen, das die Stellung des Weibes in der bisherigen Ordnung der Gesellschaft an sich gehabt hat und noch hat (als ob Sklaverei ein Gegenargument und nicht vielmehr eine Bedingung jeder höheren Cultur, jeder Erhöhung der Cultur sei): - was bedeutet dies Alles, wenn nicht eine Anbröckelung der weiblichen Instinkte, eine Entweiblichung? Freilich, es giebt genug blödsinnige Frauen-Freunde und Weibs-Verderber unter den gelehrten Eseln männlichen Geschlechts, die dem Weibe anrathen, sich dergestalt zu entweiblichen und alle die Dummheiten nachzumachen, an denen der

"Mann" in Europa, die europäische "Mannhaftigkeit" krankt, - welche das Weib bis zur "allgemeinen Bildung", wohl gar zum Zeitungslesen und Politisiren herunterbringen möchten. Man will hier und da selbst Freigeister und Litteraten aus den Frauen machen: als ob ein Weib ohne Frömmigkeit für einen tiefen und gottlosen Mann nicht etwas vollkommen Widriges oder Lächerliches wäre -; man verdirbt fast überall ihre Nerven mit der krankhaftesten und gefährlichsten aller Arten Musik (unsrer deutschen neuesten Musik) und macht sie täglich hysterischer und zu ihrem ersten und letzten Berufe, kräftige Kinder zu gebären, unbefähigter. Man will sie überhaupt noch mehr "cultiviren" und, wie man sagt, das "schwache Geschlecht" durch Cultur stark machen: als ob nicht die Geschichte so eindringlich wie möglich lehrte, dass "Cultivirung" des Menschen und Schwächung - nämlich Schwächung, Zersplitterung, Ankränkelung der Willenskraft, immer mit einander Schritt gegangen sind, und dass die mächtigsten und einflussreichsten Frauen der Welt (zuletzt noch die Mutter Napoleon's) gerade ihrer Willenskraft - und nicht den Schulmeistern! - ihre Macht und ihr Übergewicht über die Männer verdankten. Das, was am Weibe Respekt und oft genug Furcht einflösst, ist seine Natur, die "natürlicher" ist als die des Mannes, seine ächte raubthierhafte listige Geschmeidigkeit, seine Tigerkralle unter dem Handschuh, seine Naivetät im Egoismus, seine Unerziehbarkeit und innerliche

Wildheit, das Unfassliche, Weite, Schweifende seiner Begierden und Tugenden….. Was, bei aller Furcht, für diese gefährliche und schöne Katze "Weib" Mitleiden macht, ist, dass es leidender, verletzbarer, liebebedürftiger und zur Enttäuschung verurtheilter erscheint als irgend ein Thier. Furcht und Mitleiden: mit diesen Gefühlen stand bisher der Mann vor dem Weibe, immer mit einem Fusse schon in der Tragödie, welche zerreisst, indem sie entzückt -. Wie? Und damit soll es nun zu Ende sein? Und die Entzauberung des Weibes ist im Werke? Die Verlangweiligung des Weibes kommt langsam herauf? Oh Europa! Europa! Man kennt das Thier mit Hörnern, welches für dich immer am anziehendsten war, von dem dir immer wieder Gefahr droht! Deine alte Fabel könnte noch einmal zur "Geschichte" werden, - noch einmal- könnte eine ungeheure Dummheit über dich Herr werden und dich davon tragen! Und unter ihr kein Gott versteckt, nein! nur eine "Idee", eine "moderne Idee"!…..

Achtes Hauptstück:

Völker und Vaterländer.

240. Ich hörte, wieder einmal zum ersten Male - Richard Wagner's Ouverture zu den Meistersingern: das ist eine prachtvolle, überladene, schwere und späte Kunst, welche den Stolz hat, zu ihrem Verständniss zwei Jahrhunderte Musik als noch lebendig vorauszusetzen: - es ehrt die Deutschen, dass sich ein solcher Stolz nicht verrechnete! Was für Säfte und Kräfte, was für Jahreszeiten und Himmelsstriche sind hier nicht gemischt! Das muthet uns bald alterthümlich, bald fremd, herb und überjung an, das ist ebenso willkürlich als pomphaft-herkömmlich, das ist nicht selten schelmisch, noch öfter derb und grob, - das hat Feuer und Muth und zugleich die schlaffe falbe Haut

von Früchten, welche zu spät reif werden. Das strömt breit und voll: und plötzlich ein Augenblick unerklärlichen Zögerns, gleichsam eine Lücke, die zwischen Ursache und Wirkung aufspringt, ein Druck, der uns träumen macht, beinahe ein Alpdruck -, aber schon breitet und weitet sich wieder der alte Strom von Behagen aus, von vielfältigstem Behagen, von altem und neuem Glück, sehr eingerechnet das Glück des Künstlers an sich selber, dessen er nicht Hehl haben will, sein erstauntes glückliches Mitwissen um die Meisterschaft seiner hier verwendeten Mittel, neuer neuerworbener unausgeprobter Kunstmittel, wie er uns zu verrathen scheint. Alles in Allem keine Schönheit, kein Süden, Nichts von südlicher feiner Helligkeit des Himmels, Nichts von Grazie, kein Tanz, kaum ein Wille zur Logik; eine gewisse Plumpheit sogar, die noch unterstrichen wird, wie als ob der Künstler uns sagen wollte: "sie gehört zu meiner Absicht"; eine schwerfällige Gewandung, etwas Willkürlich-Barbarisches und Feierliches, ein Geflirr von gelehrten und ehrwürdigen Kostbarkeiten und Spitzen; etwas Deutsches, im besten und schlimmsten Sinn des Wortes, etwas auf deutsche Art Vielfaches, Unförmliches und Unausschöpfliches; eine gewisse deutsche Mächtigkeit und Überfülle der Seele, welche keine Furcht hat, sich unter die Raffinements des Verfalls zu verstecken, - die sich dort vielleicht erst am wohlsten fühlt; ein rechtes ächtes Wahrzeichen der deutschen Seele, die zugleich jung und veraltet, übermürbe und überreich noch an Zukunft ist. Diese Art Musik drückt am besten aus, was ich von den Deutschen halte: sie sind von Vorgestern und von Übermorgen, - sie haben noch kein Heute.

241. Wir "guten Europäer": auch wir haben Stunden, wo wir uns eine herzhafte Vaterländerei, einen Plumps und Rückfall in alte Lieben und Engen gestatten - ich gab eben eine Probe davon -, Stunden nationaler Wallungen, patriotischer Beklemmungen und allerhand anderer alterthümlicher Gefühls-Überschwemmungen. Schwerfälligere Geister, als wir sind, mögen mit dem, was sich bei uns auf Stunden beschränkt und in Stunden zu Ende spielt, erst in längeren Zeiträumen fertig werden, in halben Jahren die Einen, in halben Menschenleben die Anderen, je nach der Schnelligkeit und Kraft, mit der sie verdauen und ihre "Stoffe wechseln". Ja, ich könnte mir dumpfe zögernde Rassen denken, welche auch in unserm geschwinden Europa halbe Jahrhunderte nöthig hätten, um solche atavistische Anfälle von Vaterländerei und Schollenkleberei zu überwinden und wieder zur Vernunft, will sagen zum "guten Europäerthum" zurückzukehren. Und indem ich über diese Möglichkeit ausschweife, begegnet mir's, dass ich Ohrenzeuge eines Gesprächs von zwei alten "Patrioten" werde, - sie hörten beide offenbar schlecht und sprachen darum um so lauter. "Der hält und weiss von Philosophie so viel als ein Bauer oder Corpsstudent - sagte der Eine -: der

ist noch unschuldig. Aber was liegt heute daran! Es ist das Zeitalter der Massen: die liegen vor allem Massenhaften auf dem Bauche. Und so auch in politicis. Ein Staatsmann, der ihnen einen neuen Thurm von Babel, irgend ein Ungeheuer von Reich und Macht aufthürmt, heisst ihnen ›gross‹: - was liegt daran, dass wir Vorsichtigeren und Zurückhaltenderen einstweilen noch nicht vom alten Glauben lassen, es sei allein der grosse Gedanke, der einer That und Sache Grösse giebt. Gesetzt, ein Staatsmann brächte sein Volk in die Lage, fürderhin ›grosse Politik‹ treiben zu müssen, für welche es von Natur schlecht angelegt und vorbereitet ist: so dass es nöthig hätte, einer neuen zweifelhaften Mittelmässigkeit zu Liebe seine alten und sicheren Tugenden zu opfern, - gesetzt, ein Staatsmann verurtheilte sein Volk zum ›Politisiren‹ überhaupt, während dasselbe bisher Besseres zu thun und zu denken hatte und im Grunde seiner Seele einen vorsichtigen Ekel vor der Unruhe, Leere und lärmenden Zankteufelei der eigentlich politisirenden Völker nicht los wurde: - gesetzt, ein solcher Staatsmann stachle die eingeschlafnen Leidenschaften und Begehrlichkeiten seines Volkes auf, mache ihm aus seiner bisherigen Schüchternheit und Lust am Danebenstehn einen Flecken, aus seiner Ausländerei und heimlichen Unendlichkeit eine Verschuldung, entwerthe ihm seine herzlichsten Hänge, drehe sein Gewissen um, mache seinen Geist eng, seinen Geschmack ›national‹, - wie! ein Staatsmann, der dies Alles thäte, den sein Volk in alle Zukunft hinein, falls es Zukunft hat, abbüssen müsste, ein solcher Staatsmann wäre gross?" "Unzweifelhaft! antwortete ihm der andere alte Patriot heftig: sonst hätte er es nicht gekonnt! Es war toll vielleicht, so etwas zu wollen? Aber vielleicht war alles Grosse im Anfang nur toll!" - "Missbrauch der Worte! schrie sein Unterredner dagegen: - stark! stark! stark und toll! Nicht gross!" - Die alten Männer hatten sich ersichtlich erhitzt, als sie sich dergestalt ihre "Wahrheiten" in's Gesicht schrieen; ich aber, in meinem Glück und Jenseits, erwog, wie bald über den Starken ein Stärkerer Herr werden wird; auch dass es für die geistige Verflachung eines Volkes eine Ausgleichung giebt, nämlich durch die Vertiefung eines anderen. -

242. Nenne man es nun "Civilisation" oder "Vermenschlichung" oder "Fortschritt", worin jetzt die Auszeichnung der Europäer gesucht wird; nenne man es einfach, ohne zu loben und zu tadeln, mit einer politischen Formel die demokratische Bewegung Europa's: hinter all den moralischen und politischen Vordergründen, auf welche mit solchen Formeln hingewiesen wird, vollzieht sich ein ungeheurer physiologischer Prozess, der immer mehr in Fluss geräth, - der Prozess einer Anähnlichung der Europäer, ihre wachsende Loslösung von den Bedingungen, unter denen klimatisch und ständisch gebundene Rassen entstehen, ihre zunehmende Unabhängigkeit von jedem bestimmten milieu, das Jahrhunderte lang sich mit

gleichen Forderungen in Seele und Leib einschreiben möchte, - also die langsame Heraufkunft einer wesentlich übernationalen und nomadischen Art Mensch, welche, physiologisch geredet, ein Maximum von Anpassungskunst und -kraft als ihre typische Auszeichnung besitzt. Dieser Prozess des werdenden Europäers, welcher durch grosse Rückfälle im Tempo verzögert werden kann, aber vielleicht gerade damit an Vehemenz und Tiefe gewinnt und wächst - der jetzt noch wüthende Sturm und Drang des "National-Gefühls" gehört hierher, insgleichen der eben heraufkommende Anarchismus -: dieser Prozess läuft wahrscheinlich auf Resultate hinaus, auf welche seine naiven Beförderer und Lobredner, die Apostel der "modernen Ideen", am wenigsten rechnen möchten. Die selben neuen Bedingungen, unter denen im Durchschnitt eine Ausgleichung und Vermittelmässigung des Menschen sich herausbilden wird - ein nützliches arbeitsames, vielfach brauchbares und anstelliges Heerdenthier Mensch -, sind im höchsten Grade dazu angethan, Ausnahme-Menschen der gefährlichsten und anziehendsten Qualität den Ursprung zu geben. Während nämlich jene Anpassungskraft, welche immer wechselnde Bedingungen durchprobirt und mit jedem Geschlecht, fast mit jedem Jahrzehend, eine neue Arbeit beginnt, die Mächtigkeit des Typus gar nicht möglich macht; während der Gesammt-Eindruck solcher zukünftiger Europäer wahrscheinlich der von vielfachen geschwätzigen willensarmen und äusserst anstellbaren Arbeitern sein wird, die des Herrn, des Befehlenden bedürfen wie des täglichen Brodes; während also die Demokratisirung Europa's auf die Erzeugung eines zur Sklaverei im feinsten Sinne vorbereiteten Typus hinausläuft: wird, im Einzel- und Ausnahmefall, der starke Mensch stärker und reicher gerathen müssen, als er vielleicht jemals bisher gerathen ist, - Dank der Vorurtheilslosigkeit seiner Schulung, Dank der ungeheuren Vielfältigkeit von Übung, Kunst und Maske. Ich wollte sagen: die Demokratisirung Europa's ist zugleich eine unfreiwillige Veranstaltung zur Züchtung von Tyrannen,- das Wort in jedem Sinne verstanden, auch im geistigsten.

243. Ich höre mit Vergnügen, dass unsre Sonne in rascher Bewegung gegen das Sternbild des Herkules hin begriffen ist: und ich hoffe, dass der Mensch auf dieser Erde es darin der Sonne gleich thut. Und wir voran, wir guten Europäer! -

244. Es gab eine Zeit, wo man gewohnt war, die Deutschen mit Auszeichnung "tief" zu nennen: jetzt, wo der erfolgreichste Typus des neuen Deutschthums nach ganz andern Ehren geizt und an Allem, was Tiefe hat, vielleicht die "Schneidigkeit" vermisst, ist der Zweifel beinahe zeitgemäss und patriotisch, ob man sich ehemals mit jenem Lobe nicht betrogen hat: genug, ob die deutsche Tiefe nicht im Grunde etwas Anderes

und Schlimmeres ist - und Etwas, das man, Gott sei Dank, mit Erfolg loszuwerden im Begriff steht. Machen wir also den Versuch, über die deutsche Tiefe umzulernen: man hat Nichts dazu nöthig, als ein wenig Vivisektion der deutschen Seele. - Die deutsche Seele ist vor Allem vielfach, verschiedenen Ursprungs, mehr zusammen- und übereinandergesetzt, als wirklich gebaut: das liegt an ihrer Herkunft. Ein Deutscher, der sich erdreisten wollte, zu behaupten "zwei Seelen wohnen, ach! in meiner Brust" würde sich an der Wahrheit arg vergreifen, richtiger, hinter der Wahrheit um viele Seelen zurückbleiben. Als ein Volk der ungeheuerlichsten Mischung und Zusammenrührung von Rassen, vielleicht sogar mit einem Übergewicht des vor-arischen Elementes, als "Volk der Mitte" in jedem Verstande, sind die Deutschen unfassbarer, umfänglicher, widerspruchsvoller, unbekannter, unberechenbarer, überraschender, selbst erschrecklicher, als es andere Völker sich selber sind: - sie entschlüpfen der Definition und sind damit schon die Verzweiflung der Franzosen. Es kennzeichnet die Deutschen, dass bei ihnen die Frage "was ist deutsch?" niemals ausstirbt. Kotzebue kannte seine Deutschen gewiss gut genug: "Wir sind erkannt" jubelten sie ihm zu, - aber auch Sand glaubte sie zu kennen. Jean Paul wusste, was er that, als er sich ergrimmt gegen Fichte's verlogne, aber patriotische Schmeicheleien und Übertreibungen erklärte, - aber es ist wahrscheinlich, dass Goethe anders über die Deutschen dachte, als Jean

Paul, wenn er ihm auch in Betreff Fichtens Recht gab. Was Goethe eigentlich über die Deutschen gedacht hat? - Aber er hat über viele Dinge um sich herum nie deutlich geredet und verstand sich zeitlebens auf das feine Schweigen: - wahrscheinlich hatte er gute Gründe dazu. Gewiss ist, dass es nicht "die Freiheitskriege" waren, die ihn freudiger aufblicken liessen, so wenig als die französische Revolution, - das Ereigniss, um dessentwillen er seinen Faust, ja das ganze Problem "Mensch" umgedacht hat, war das Erscheinen Napoleon's. Es giebt Worte Goethe's, in denen er, wie vom Auslande her, mit einer ungeduldigen Härte über Das abspricht, was die Deutschen sich zu ihrem Stolze rechnen: das berühmte deutsche Gemüth definirt er einmal als "Nachsicht mit fremden und eignen Schwächen". Hat er damit Unrecht? - es kennzeichnet die Deutschen, dass man über sie selten völlig Unrecht hat. Die deutsche Seele hat Gänge und Zwischengänge in sich, es giebt in ihr Höhlen, Verstecke, Burgverliesse; ihre Unordnung hat viel vom Reize des Geheimnissvollen; der Deutsche versteht sich auf die Schleichwege zum Chaos. Und wie jeglich Ding sein Gleichniss liebt, so liebt der Deutsche die Wolken und Alles, was unklar, werdend, dämmernd, feucht und verhängt ist: das Ungewisse, Unausgestaltete, Sich-Verschiebende, Wachsende jeder Art fühlt er als "tief". Der Deutsche selbst ist nicht, er wird, er "entwickelt sich". "Entwicklung" ist deshalb der eigentlich deutsche Fund und Wurf im grossen Reich philosophischer

Formeln: - ein regierender Begriff, der, im Bunde mit deutschem Bier und deutscher Musik, daran arbeitet, ganz Europa zu verdeutschen. Die Ausländer stehen erstaunt und angezogen vor den Räthseln, die ihnen die Widerspruchs-Natur im Grunde der deutschen Seele aufgiebt (welche Hegel in System gebracht, Richard Wagner zuletzt noch in Musik gesetzt hat). "Gutmüthig und tückisch" - ein solches Nebeneinander, widersinnig in Bezug auf jedes andre Volk, rechtfertigt sich leider zu oft in Deutschland: man lebe nur eine Zeit lang unter Schwaben! Die Schwerfälligkeit des deutschen Gelehrten, seine gesellschaftliche Abgeschmacktheit verträgt sich zum Erschrecken gut mit einer innewendigen Seiltänzerei und leichten Kühnheit, vor der bereits alle Götter das Fürchten gelernt haben. Will man die "deutsche Seele" ad oculos demonstrirt, so sehe man nur in den deutschen Geschmack, in deutsche Künste und Sitten hinein: welche bäurische Gleichgültigkeit gegen "Geschmack"! Wie steht da das Edelste und Gemeinste neben einander! Wie unordentlich und reich ist dieser ganze Seelen-Haushalt! Der Deutsche schleppt an seiner Seele; er schleppt an Allem, was er erlebt. Er verdaut seine Ereignisse schlecht, er wird nie damit "fertig"; die deutsche Tiefe ist oft nur eine schwere zögernde "Verdauung". Und wie alle Gewohnheits-Kranken, alle Dyspeptiker den Hang zum Bequemen haben, so liebt der Deutsche die "Offenheit" und "Biederkeit": wie bequem ist es, offen und bieder zu sein! - Es ist heute vielleicht die gefährlichste und glücklichste Verkleidung, auf die sich der Deutsche versteht, dies Zutrauliche, Entgegenkommende, die-Karten-Aufdeckende der deutschen Redlichkeit: sie ist seine eigentliche Mephistopheles-Kunst, mit ihr kann er es "noch weit bringen"! Der Deutsche lässt sich gehen, blickt dazu mit treuen blauen leeren deutschen Augen - und sofort verwechselt das Ausland ihn mit seinem Schlafrocke! - Ich wollte sagen: mag die "deutsche Tiefe" sein, was sie will, - ganz unter uns erlauben wir uns vielleicht über sie zu lachen? - wir thun gut, ihren Anschein und guten Namen auch fürderhin in Ehren zu halten und unsern alten Ruf, als Volk der Tiefe, nicht zu billig gegen preussische "Schneidigkeit" und Berliner Witz und Sand zu veräussern. Es ist für ein Volk klug, sich für tief, für ungeschickt, für gutmüthig, für redlich, für unklug gelten zu machen, gelten zu lassen: es könnte sogar - tief sein! Zuletzt: man soll seinem Namen Ehre machen, - man heisst nicht umsonst das "tiusche" Volk, das Täusche-Volk…

245. Die "gute alte" Zeit ist dahin, in Mozart hat sie sich ausgesungen: - wie glücklich wir, dass zu uns sein Rokoko noch redet, dass seine "gute Gesellschaft", sein zärtliches Schwärmen, seine Kinderlust am Chinesischen und Geschnörkelten, seine Höflichkeit des Herzens, sein Verlangen nach Zierlichem, Verliebtem, Tanzendem, Thränenseligem, sein Glaube an den Süden noch an irgend einen Rest in uns

appelliren darf! Ach, irgend wann wird es einmal damit vorbei sein! - aber wer darf zweifeln, dass es noch früher mit dem Verstehen und Schmecken Beethoven's vorbei sein wird! - der ja nur der Ausklang eines Stil-Übergangs und Stil-Bruchs war und nicht, wie Mozart, der Ausklang eines grossen Jahrhunderte langen europäischen Geschmacks. Beethoven ist das Zwischen-Begebniss einer alten mürben Seele, die beständig zerbricht, und einer zukünftigen überjungen Seele, welche beständig kommt; auf seiner Musik liegt jenes Zwielicht von ewigem Verlieren und ewigem ausschweifendem Hoffen, - das selbe Licht, in welchem Europa gebadet lag, als es mit Rousseau geträumt, als es um den Freiheitsbaum der Revolution getanzt und endlich vor Napoleon beinahe angebetet hatte. Aber wie schnell verbleicht jetzt gerade dies Gefühl, wie schwer ist heute schon das Wissen um dies Gefühl, - wie fremd klingt die Sprache jener Rousseau, Schiller, Shelley, Byron an unser Ohr, in denen zusammen das selbe Schicksal Europa's den Weg zum Wort gefunden hat, das in Beethoven zu singen wusste! - Was von deutscher Musik nachher gekommen ist, gehört in die Romantik, das heisst in eine, historisch gerechnet, noch kürzere, noch flüchtigere, noch oberflächlichere Bewegung, als es jener grosse Zwischenakt, jener Übergang Europa's von Rousseau zu Napoleon und zur Heraufkunft der Demokratie war. Weber: aber was ist uns heute Freischütz und Oberon! Oder Marschner's Hans Heiling und Vampyr! Oder selbst noch Wagner's

Tannhäuser! Das ist verklungene, wenn auch noch nicht vergessene Musik. Diese ganze Musik der Romantik war überdies nicht vornehm genug, nicht Musik genug, um auch anderswo Recht zu behalten, als im Theater und vor der Menge; sie war von vornherein Musik zweiten Ranges, die unter wirklichen Musikern wenig in Betracht kam. Anders stand es mit Felix Mendelssohn, jenem halkyonischen Meister, der um seiner leichteren reineren beglückteren Seele willen schnell verehrt und ebenso schnell vergessen wurde: als der schöne Zwischenfall der deutschen Musik. Was aber Robert Schumann angeht, der es schwer nahm und von Anfang an auch schwer genommen worden ist - es ist der Letzte, der eine Schule gegründet hat -: gilt es heute unter uns nicht als ein Glück, als ein Aufathmen, als eine Befreiung, dass gerade diese Schumann'sche Romantik überwunden ist? Schumann, in die "sächsische Schweiz" seiner Seele flüchtend, halb Wertherisch, halb Jean-Paulisch geartet, gewiss nicht Beethovenisch! gewiss nicht Byronisch! - seine Manfred-Musik ist ein Missgriff und Missverständniss bis zum Unrechte -, Schumann mit seinem Geschmack, der im Grunde ein kleiner Geschmack war, (nämlich ein gefährlicher, unter Deutschen doppelt gefährlicher Hang zur stillen Lyrik und Trunkenboldigkeit des Gefühls), beständig bei Seite gehend, sich scheu verziehend und zurückziehend, ein edler Zärtling, der in lauter anonymem Glück und Weh schwelgte, eine Art Mädchen und noli me tangere von Anbeginn: dieser

Schumann war bereits nur noch ein deutsches Ereigniss in der Musik, kein europäisches mehr, wie Beethoven es war, wie, in noch umfänglicherem Maasse, Mozart es gewesen ist, - mit ihm drohte der deutschen Musik ihre grösste Gefahr, die Stimme für die Seele Europa's zu verlieren und zu einer blossen Vaterländerei herabzusinken. -

246. - Welche Marter sind deutsch geschriebene Bücher für Den, der das dritte Ohr hat! Wie unwillig steht er neben dem langsam sich drehenden Sumpfe von Klängen ohne Klang, von Rhythmen ohne Tanz, welcher bei Deutschen ein "Buch" genannt wird! Und gar der Deutsche, der Bücher liest! Wie faul, wie widerwillig, wie schlecht liest er! Wie viele Deutsche wissen es und fordern es von sich zu wissen, dass Kunst in jedem guten Satze steckt, - Kunst, die errathen sein will, sofern der Satz verstanden sein will! Ein Missverständniss über sein Tempo zum Beispiel: und der Satz selbst ist missverstanden! Dass man über die rhythmisch entscheidenden Silben nicht im Zweifel sein darf, dass man die Brechung der allzustrengen Symmetrie als gewollt und als Reiz fühlt, dass man jedem staccato, jedem rubato ein feines geduldiges Ohr hinhält, dass man den Sinn in der Folge der Vocale und Diphthongen räth, und wie zart und reich sie in ihrem Hintereinander sich färben und umfärben können: wer unter bücherlesenden Deutschen ist gutwillig genug, solchergestalt Pflichten und Forderungen anzuerkennen

und auf so viel Kunst und Absicht in der Sprache hinzuhorchen? Man hat zuletzt eben "das Ohr nicht dafür": und so werden die stärksten Gegensätze des Stils nicht gehört, und die feinste Künstlerschaft ist wie vor Tauben verschwendet. - Dies waren meine Gedanken, als ich merkte, wie man plump und ahnungslos zwei Meister in der Kunst der Prosa mit einander verwechselte, Einen, dem die Worte zögernd und kalt herabtropfen, wie von der Decke einer feuchten Höhle - er rechnet auf ihren dumpfen Klang und Wiederklang - und einen Anderen, der seine Sprache wie einen biegsamen Degen handhabt und vom Arme bis zur Zehe hinab das gefährliche Glück der zitternden überscharfen Klinge fühlt, welche beissen, zischen, schneiden will. -

247. Wie wenig der deutsche Stil mit dem Klange und mit den Ohren zu thun hat, zeigt die Thatsache, dass gerade unsre guten Musiker schlecht schreiben. Der Deutsche liest nicht laut, nicht für's Ohr, sondern bloss mit den Augen: er hat seine Ohren dabei in's Schubfach gelegt. Der antike Mensch las, wenn er las - es geschah selten genug - sich selbst etwas vor, und zwar mit lauter Stimme; man wunderte sich, wenn jemand leise las und fragte sich insgeheim nach Gründen. Mit lauter Stimme: das will sagen, mit all den Schwellungen, Biegungen, Umschlägen des Tons und Wechseln des Tempo's, an denen die antike öffentliche Welt ihre Freude hatte. Damals waren die Gesetze des Schrift-

Stils die selben, wie die des Rede-Stils; und dessen Gesetze hiengen zum Theil von der erstaunlichen Ausbildung, den raffinirten Bedürfnissen des Ohrs und Kehlkopfs ab, zum andern Theil von der Stärke, Dauer und Macht der antiken Lunge. Eine Periode ist, im Sinne der Alten, vor Allem ein physiologisches Ganzes, insofern sie von Einem Athem zusammengefasst wird. Solche Perioden, wie sie bei Demosthenes, bei Cicero vorkommen, zwei Mal schwellend und zwei Mal absinkend und Alles innerhalb Eines Athemzugs: das sind Genüsse für antike Menschen, welche die Tugend daran, das Seltene und Schwierige im Vortrag einer solchen Periode, aus ihrer eignen Schulung zu schätzen wussten: - wir haben eigentlich kein Recht auf die grosse Periode, wir Modernen, wir Kurzathmigen in jedem Sinne! Diese Alten waren ja insgesammt in der Rede selbst Dilettanten, folglich Kenner, folglich Kritiker, - damit trieben sie ihre Redner zum Äussersten; in gleicher Weise, wie im vorigen Jahrhundert, als alle Italiäner und Italiänerinnen zu singen verstanden, bei ihnen das Gesangs-Virtuosenthum (und damit auch die Kunst der Melodik -) auf die Höhe kam. In Deutschland aber gab es (bis auf die jüngste Zeit, wo eine Art Tribünen-Beredtsamkeit schüchtern und plump genug ihre jungen Schwingen regt) eigentlich nur Eine Gattung öffentlicher und ungefähr kunstmässiger Rede: das ist die von der Kanzel herab. Der Prediger allein wusste in Deutschland, was eine Silbe, was ein Wort wiegt, inwiefern ein Satz schlägt, springt, stürzt, läuft, ausläuft, er allein hatte Gewissen in seinen Ohren, oft genug ein böses Gewissen: denn es fehlt nicht an Gründen dafür, dass gerade von einem Deutschen Tüchtigkeit in der Rede selten, fast immer zu spät erreicht wird. Das Meisterstück der deutschen Prosa ist deshalb billigerweise das Meisterstück ihres grössten Predigers: die Bibel war bisher das beste deutsche Buch. Gegen Luther's Bibel gehalten ist fast alles Übrige nur "Litteratur" - ein Ding, das nicht in Deutschland gewachsen ist und darum auch nicht in deutsche Herzen hinein wuchs und wächst: wie es die Bibel gethan hat.

248. Es giebt zwei Arten des Genie's: eins, welches vor allem zeugt und zeugen will, und ein andres, welches sich gern befruchten lässt und gebiert. Und ebenso giebt es unter den genialen Völkern solche, denen das Weibsproblem der Schwangerschaft und die geheime Aufgabe des Gestaltens, Ausreifens, Vollendens zugefallen ist - die Griechen zum Beispiel waren ein Volk dieser Art, insgleichen die Franzosen -; und andre, welche befruchten müssen und die Ursache neuer Ordnungen des Lebens werden, - gleich den Juden, den Römern und, in aller Bescheidenheit gefragt, den Deutschen? - Völker gequält und entzückt von unbekannten Fiebern und unwiderstehlich aus sich herausgedrängt, verliebt und lüstern nach fremden Rassen (nach solchen, welche sich "befruchten lassen" -

) und dabei herrschsüchtig wie Alles, was sich voller Zeugekräfte und folglich "von Gottes Gnaden" weiss. Diese zwei Arten des Genie's suchen sich, wie Mann und Weib; aber sie missverstehen auch einander, - wie Mann und Weib.

249. Jedes Volk hat seine eigne Tartüfferie, und heisst sie seine Tugenden.

- Das Beste, was man ist, kennt man nicht, - kann man nicht kennen.

250. Was Europa den Juden verdankt? - Vielerlei, Gutes und Schlimmes, und vor allem Eins, das vom Besten und Schlimmsten zugleich ist: den grossen Stil in der Moral, die Furchtbarkeit und Majestät unendlicher Forderungen, unendlicher Bedeutungen, die ganze Romantik und Erhabenheit der moralischen Fragwürdigkeiten - und folglich gerade den anziehendsten, verfänglichsten und ausgesuchtesten Theil jener Farbenspiele und Verführungen zum Leben, in deren Nachschimmer heute der Himmel unsrer europäischen Cultur, ihr Abend-Himmel, glüht, - vielleicht verglüht. Wir Artisten unter den Zuschauern und Philosophen sind dafür den Juden - dankbar.

251. Man muss es in den Kauf nehmen, wenn einem Volke, das am nationalen Nervenfieber und politischen Ehrgeize leidet, leiden will -, mancherlei Wolken und

Störungen über den Geist ziehn, kurz, kleine Anfälle von Verdummung: zum Beispiel bei den Deutschen von Heute bald die antifranzösische Dummheit, bald die antijüdische, bald die antipolnische, bald die christlich-romantische, bald die Wagnerianische, bald die teutonische, bald die preussische (man sehe sich doch diese armen Historiker, diese Sybel und Treitzschke und ihre dick verbundenen Köpfe an -), und wie sie Alle heissen mögen, diese kleinen Benebelungen des deutschen Geistes und Gewissens. Möge man mir verzeihn, dass auch ich, bei einem kurzen gewagten Aufenthalt auf sehr inficirtem Gebiete, nicht völlig von der Krankheit verschont blieb und mir, wie alle Welt, bereits Gedanken über Dinge zu machen anfieng, die mich nichts angehn: erstes Zeichen der politischen Infektion. Zum Beispiel über die Juden: man höre. - Ich bin noch keinem Deutschen begegnet, der den Juden gewogen gewesen wäre; und so unbedingt auch die Ablehnung der eigentlichen Antisemiterei von Seiten aller Vorsichtigen und Politischen sein mag, so richtet sich doch auch diese Vorsicht und Politik nicht etwa gegen die Gattung des Gefühls selber, sondern nur gegen seine gefährliche Unmässigkeit, insbesondere gegen den abgeschmackten und schandbaren Ausdruck dieses unmässigen Gefühls, - darüber darf man sich nicht täuschen. Dass Deutschland reichlich genug Juden hat, dass der deutsche Magen, das deutsche Blut Noth hat (und noch auf lange Noth haben wird), um auch nur mit diesem

Quantum "Jude" fertig zu werden - so wie der Italiäner, der Franzose, der Engländer fertig geworden sind, in Folge einer kräftigeren Verdauung -: das ist die deutliche Aussage und Sprache eines allgemeinen Instinktes, auf welchen man hören, nach welchem man handeln muss. "Keine neuen Juden mehr hinein lassen! Und namentlich nach dem Osten (auch nach Östreich) zu die Thore zusperren!" also gebietet der Instinkt eines Volkes, dessen Art noch schwach und unbestimmt ist, so dass sie leicht verwischt, leicht durch eine stärkere Rasse ausgelöscht werden könnte. Die Juden sind aber ohne allen Zweifel die stärkste, zäheste und reinste Rasse, die jetzt in Europa lebt; sie verstehen es, selbst noch unter den schlimmsten Bedingungen sich durchzusetzen (besser sogar, als unter günstigen), vermöge irgend welcher Tugenden, die man heute gern zu Lastern stempeln möchte, - Dank, vor Allem, einem resoluten Glauben, der sich vor den "modernen Ideen" nicht zu schämen braucht; sie verändern sich, wenn sie sich verändern, immer nur so, wie das russische Reich seine Eroberungen macht, - als ein Reich, das Zeit hat und nicht von Gestern ist -: nämlich nach dem Grundsatze "so langsam als möglich!" Ein Denker, der die Zukunft Europa's auf seinem Gewissen hat, wird, bei allen Entwürfen, welche er bei sich über diese Zukunft macht, mit den Juden rechnen wie mit den Russen, als den zunächst sichersten und wahrscheinlichsten Faktoren im grossen Spiel und Kampf der Kräfte. Das, was heute in Europa "Nation" genannt wird und eigentlich mehr eine res facta als nata ist (ja mitunter einer res ficta et picta zum Verwechseln ähnlich sieht -), ist in jedem Falle etwas Werdendes, Junges, Leicht-Verschiebbares, noch keine Rasse, geschweige denn ein solches aere perennius, wie es die Juden-Art ist: diese "Nationen" sollten sich doch vor jeder hitzköpfigen Concurrenz und Feindseligkeit sorgfältig in Acht nehmen! Dass die Juden, wenn sie wollten - oder, wenn man sie dazu zwänge, wie es die Antisemiten zu wollen scheinen -, jetzt schon das Übergewicht, ja ganz wörtlich die Herrschaft über Europa haben könnten, steht fest; dass sie nicht darauf hin arbeiten und Pläne machen, ebenfalls. Einstweilen wollen und wünschen sie vielmehr, sogar mit einiger Zudringlichkeit, in Europa, von Europa ein- und aufgesaugt zu werden, sie dürsten darnach, endlich irgendwo fest, erlaubt, geachtet zu sein und dem Nomadenleben, dem "ewigen Juden" ein Ziel zu setzen -; und man sollte diesen Zug und Drang (der vielleicht selbst schon eine Milderung der jüdischen Instinkte ausdrückt) wohl beachten und ihm entgegenkommen: wozu es vielleicht nützlich und billig wäre, die antisemitischen Schreihälse des Landes zu verweisen. Mit aller Vorsicht entgegenkommen, mit Auswahl; ungefähr so wie der englische Adel es thut. Es liegt auf der Hand, dass am unbedenklichsten noch sich die stärkeren und bereits fester geprägten Typen des neuen Deutschthums mit ihnen einlassen könnten, zum Beispiel der adelige Offizier aus der Mark: es wäre von vielfachem Interesse, zu sehen, ob sich nicht zu der erblichen Kunst des Befehlens und Gehorchens - in Beidem ist das bezeichnete Land heute klassisch - das Genie des Geldes und der Geduld (und vor allem etwas Geist und Geistigkeit, woran es reichlich an der bezeichneten Stelle fehlt -) hinzuthun, hinzuzüchten liesse. Doch hier ziemt es sich, meine heitere Deutschthümelei und Festrede abzubrechen: denn ich rühre bereits an meinen Ernst, an das "europäische Problem", wie ich es verstehe, an die Züchtung einer neuen über Europa, regierenden Kaste. -

252. Das ist keine philosophische Rasse - diese Engländer: Bacon bedeutet einen Angriff auf den philosophischen Geist überhaupt, Hobbes, Hume und Locke eine Erniedrigung und Werth-Minderung des Begriffs "Philosoph" für mehr als ein Jahrhundert. Gegen Hume erhob und hob sich Kant; Locke war es, von dem Schelling sagen durfte: "je méprise Locke"; im Kampfe mit der englisch-mechanistischen Welt-Vertölpelung waren Hegel und Schopenhauer (mit Goethe) einmüthig, jene beiden feindlichen Brüder-Genies in der Philosophie, welche nach den entgegengesetzten Polen des deutschen Geistes auseinander strebten und sich dabei Unrecht thaten, wie sich eben nur Brüder Unrecht thun. - Woran es in England fehlt und immer gefehlt hat, das wusste jener Halb-Schauspieler und Rhetor gut genug, der abgeschmackte Wirrkopf Carlyle, welcher es unter

leidenschaftlichen Fratzen zu verbergen suchte, was er von sich selbst wusste: nämlich woran es in Carlyle fehlte - an eigentlicher Macht der Geistigkeit, an eigentlicher Tiefe des geistigen Blicks, kurz, an Philosophie. - Es kennzeichnet eine solche unphilosophische Rasse, dass sie streng zum Christenthume hält: sie braucht seine Zucht zur "Moralisirung" und Veranmenschlichung. Der Engländer, düsterer, sinnlicher, willensstärker und brutaler als der Deutsche - ist eben deshalb, als der Gemeinere von Beiden, auch frömmer als der Deutsche: er hat das Christenthum eben noch nöthiger. Für feinere Nüstern hat selbst dieses englische Christenthum noch einen ächt englischen Nebengeruch von Spleen und alkoholischer Ausschweifung, gegen welche es aus guten Gründen als Heilmittel gebraucht wird, - das feinere Gift nämlich gegen das gröbere: eine feinere Vergiftung ist in der That bei plumpen Völkern schon ein Fortschritt, eine Stufe zur Vergeistigung. Die englische Plumpheit und Bauern-Ernsthaftigkeit wird durch die christliche Gebärdensprache und durch Beten und Psalmensingen noch am erträglichsten verkleidet, richtiger: ausgelegt und umgedeutet; und für jenes Vieh von Trunkenbolden und Ausschweifenden, welches ehemals unter der Gewalt des Methodismus und neuerdings wieder als "Heilsarmee" moralisch grunzen lernt, mag wirklich ein Busskrampf die verhältnissmässig höchste Leistung von "Humanität" sein, zu der es gesteigert werden kann: so viel darf man billig zugestehn. Was aber auch noch am humansten Engländer beleidigt, das ist sein Mangel an Musik, im Gleichniss (und ohne Gleichniss -) zu reden: er hat in den Bewegungen seiner Seele und seines Leibes keinen Takt und Tanz, ja noch nicht einmal die Begierde nach Takt und Tanz, nach "Musik". Man höre ihn sprechen; man sehe die schönsten Engländerinnen gehn - es giebt in keinem Lande der Erde schönere Tauben und Schwäne, - endlich: man höre sie singen! Aber ich verlange zu viel…..

253. Es giebt Wahrheiten, die am besten von mittelmässigen Köpfen erkannt werden, weil sie ihnen am gemässesten sind, es giebt Wahrheiten, die nur für mittelmässige Geister Reize und Verführungskräfte besitzen - - auf diesen vielleicht unangenehmen Satz wird man gerade jetzt hingestossen, seitdem der Geist achtbarer, aber mittelmässiger Engländer - ich nenne Darwin, John Stuart Mill und Herbert Spencer - in der mittleren Region des europäischen Geschmacks zum Übergewicht zu gelangen anhebt. In der That, wer möchte die Nützlichkeit davon anzweifeln, dass zeitweilig solche Geister herrschen? Es wäre ein Irrthum, gerade die hochgearteten und abseits fliegenden Geister für besonders geschickt zu halten, viele kleine gemeine Thatsachen festzustellen, zu sammeln und in Schlüsse zu drängen: - sie sind vielmehr, als Ausnahmen, von vornherein in keiner günstigen Stellung zu den "Regeln". Zuletzt haben sie

mehr zu thun, als nur zu erkennen - nämlich etwas Neues zu sein, etwas Neues zu bedeuten, neue Werthe darzustellen! Die Kluft zwischen Wissen und Können ist vielleicht grösser, auch unheimlicher als man denkt: der Könnende im grossen Stil, der Schaffende wird möglicherweise ein Unwissender sein müssen, - während andererseits zu wissenschaftlichen Entdeckungen nach der Art Darwin's eine gewisse Enge, Dürre und fleissige Sorglichkeit, kurz, etwas Englisches nicht übel disponiren mag. - Vergesse man es zuletzt den Engländern nicht, dass sie schon Ein Mal mit ihrer tiefen Durchschnittlichkeit eine Gesammt-Depression des europäischen Geistes verursacht haben: Das, was man "die modernen Ideen" oder "die Ideen des achtzehnten Jahrhunderts" oder auch "die französischen Ideen" nennt - Das also, wogegen sich der deutsche Geist mit tiefem Ekel erhoben hat -, war englischen Ursprungs, daran ist nicht zu zweifeln. Die Franzosen sind nur die Affen und Schauspieler dieser Ideen gewesen, auch ihre besten Soldaten, insgleichen leider ihre ersten und gründlichsten Opfer: denn an der verdammlichen Anglomanie der "modernen Ideen" ist zuletzt die âme française so dünn geworden und abgemagert, dass man sich ihres sechszehnten und siebzehnten Jahrhunderts, ihrer tiefen leidenschaftlichen Kraft, ihrer erfinderischen Vornehmheit heute fast mit Unglauben erinnert. Man muss aber diesen Satz historischer Billigkeit mit den Zähnen festhalten und gegen den Augenblick und

Augenschein vertheidigen: die europäische noblesse - des Gefühls, des Geschmacks, der Sitte, kurz, das Wort in jedem hohen Sinne genommen - ist Frankreich's Werk und Erfindung, die europäische Gemeinheit, der Plebejismus der modernen Ideen -Englands.-

254. Auch jetzt noch ist Frankreich der Sitz der geistigsten und raffinirtesten Cultur Europa's und die hohe Schule des Geschmacks: aber man muss dies "Frankreich des Geschmacks" zu finden wissen. Wer zu ihm gehört, hält sich gut verborgen: - es mag eine kleine Zahl sein, in denen es leibt und lebt, dazu vielleicht Menschen, welche nicht auf den kräftigsten Beinen stehn, zum Theil Fatalisten, Verdüsterte, Kranke, zum Theil Verzärtelte und Verkünstelte, solche, welche den Ehrgeiz haben, sich zu verbergen. Etwas ist Allen gemein: sie halten sich die Ohren zu vor der rasenden Dummheit und dem lärmenden Maulwerk des demokratischen bourgeois. In der That wälzt sich heut im Vordergrunde ein verdummtes und vergröbertes Frankreich, - es hat neuerdings, bei dem Leichenbegängniss Victor Hugo's, eine wahre Orgie des Ungeschmacks und zugleich der Selbstbewunderung gefeiert. Auch etwas Anderes ist ihnen gemeinsam: ein guter Wille, sich der geistigen Germanisirung zu erwehren - und ein noch besseres Unvermögen dazu! Vielleicht ist jetzt schon Schopenhauer in diesem Frankreich des Geistes, welches auch ein Frankreich des Pessimismus ist, mehr

zu Hause und heimischer geworden, als er es je in Deutschland war; nicht zu reden von Heinrich Heine, der den feineren und anspruchsvolleren Lyrikern von Paris lange schon in Fleisch und Blut übergegangen ist, oder von Hegel, der heute in Gestalt Taine's - das heisst des ersten lebenden Historikers - einen beinahe tyrannischen Einfluss ausübt. Was aber Richard Wagner betrifft: je mehr sich die französische Musik nach den wirklichen Bedürfnissen der âme moderne gestalten lernt, um so mehr wird sie "wagnerisiren", das darf man vorhersagen, - sie thut es jetzt schon genug! Es ist dennoch dreierlei, was auch heute noch die Franzosen mit Stolz als ihr Erb und Eigen und als unverlornes Merkmal einer alten Cultur-Überlegenheit über Europa aufweisen können, trotz aller freiwilligen oder unfreiwilligen Germanisirung und Verpöbelung des Geschmacks: einmal die Fähigkeit zu artistischen Leidenschaften, zu Hingebungen an die "Form", für welche das Wort l'art pour l'art, neben tausend anderen, erfunden ist: - dergleichen hat in Frankreich seit drei Jahrhunderten nicht gefehlt und immer wieder, Dank der Ehrfurcht vor der "kleinen Zahl", eine Art Kammermusik der Litteratur ermöglicht, welche im übrigen Europa sich suchen lässt -. Das Zweite, worauf die Franzosen eine Überlegenheit über Europa begründen können, ist ihre alte vielfache moralistische Cultur, welche macht, dass man im Durchschnitt selbst bei kleinen romanciers der Zeitungen und zufälligen boulevardiers de Paris eine psychologische Reizbarkeit und Neugierde findet, von der man zum Beispiel in Deutschland keinen Begriff (geschweige denn die Sache!) hat. Den Deutschen fehlen dazu ein paar Jahrhunderte moralistischer Art, welche, wie gesagt, Frankreich sich nicht erspart hat; wer die Deutschen darum "naiv" nennt, macht ihnen aus einem Mangel ein Lob zurecht. (Als Gegensatz zu der deutschen Unerfahrenheit und Unschuld in voluptate psychologica, die mit der Langweiligkeit des deutschen Verkehrs nicht gar zu fern verwandt ist, - und als gelungenster Ausdruck einer ächt französischen Neugierde und Erfindungsgabe für dieses Reich zarter Schauder mag Henri Beyle gelten, jener merkwürdige vorwegnehmende und vorauslaufende Mensch, der mit einem Napoleonischen Tempo durch sein Europa, durch mehrere Jahrhunderte der europäischen Seele lief, als ein Ausspürer und Entdecker dieser Seele: - es hat zweier Geschlechter bedurft, um ihn irgendwie einzuholen, um einige der Räthsel nachzurathen, die ihn quälten und entzückten, diesen wunderlichen Epicureer und Fragezeichen-Menschen, der Frankreichs letzter grosser Psycholog war -). Es giebt noch einen dritten Anspruch auf Überlegenheit: im Wesen der Franzosen ist eine halbwegs gelungene Synthesis des Nordens und Südens gegeben, welche sie viele Dinge begreifen macht und andre Dinge thun heisst, die ein Engländer nie begreifen wird; ihr dem Süden periodisch zugewandtes und abgewandtes Temperament, in dem von Zeit zu Zeit das provençalische und ligurische Blut überschäumt, bewahrt sie vor dem schauerlichen nordischen Grau in Grau und der sonnenlosen Begriffs-Gespensterei und Blutarmuth, - unsrer deutschen Krankheit des Geschmacks, gegen deren Übermaass man sich augenblicklich mit grosser Entschlossenheit Blut und Eisen, will sagen: die "grosse Politik" verordnet hat (gemäss einer gefährlichen Heilkunst, welche mich warten und warten, aber bis jetzt noch nicht hoffen lehrt -). Auch jetzt noch giebt es in Frankreich ein Vorverständniss und ein Entgegenkommen für jene seltneren und selten befriedigten Menschen, welche zu umfänglich sind, um in irgend einer Vaterländerei ihr Genüge zu finden und im Norden den Süden, im Süden den Norden zu lieben wissen, - für die geborenen Mittelländler, die "guten Europäer". - Für sie hat Bizet Musik gemacht, dieses letzte Genie, welches eine neue Schönheit und Verführung gesehn, - der ein Stück Süden der Musik entdeckt hat.

255. Gegen die deutsche Musik halte ich mancherlei Vorsicht für geboten. Gesetzt, dass Einer den Süden liebt, wie ich ihn liebe, als eine grosse Schule der Genesung, im Geistigsten und Sinnlichsten, als eine unbändige Sonnenfülle und Sonnen-Verklärung, welche sich über ein selbstherrliches, an sich glaubendes Dasein breitet: nun, ein Solcher wird sich etwas vor der deutschen Musik in Acht nehmen lernen, weil sie, indem sie seinen Geschmack zurück verdirbt,

ihm die Gesundheit mit zurück verdirbt. Ein solcher Südländer, nicht der Abkunft, sondern dem Glauben nach, muss, falls er von der Zukunft der Musik träumt, auch von einer Erlösung der Musik vom Norden träumen und das Vorspiel einer tieferen, mächtigeren, vielleicht böseren und geheimnissvolleren Musik in seinen Ohren haben, einer überdeutschen Musik, welche vor dem Anblick des blauen wollüstigen Meers und der mittelländischen Himmels-Helle nicht verklingt, vergilbt, verblasst, wie es alle deutsche Musik thut, einer übereuropäischen Musik, die noch vor den braunen Sonnen-Untergängen der Wüste Recht behält, deren Seele mit der Palme verwandt ist und unter grossen schönen einsamen Raubthieren heimisch zu sein und zu schweifen versteht….. Ich könnte mir eine Musik denken, deren seltenster Zauber darin bestünde, dass sie von Gut und Böse nichts mehr wüsste, nur dass vielleicht irgend ein Schiffer-Heimweh, irgend welche goldne Schatten und zärtliche Schwächen hier und da über sie hinwegliefen: eine Kunst, welche von grosser Ferne her die Farben einer untergehenden, fast unverständlich gewordenen moralischen Welt zu sich flüchten sähe, und die gastfreundlich und tief genug zum Empfang solcher späten Flüchtlinge wäre. -

256. Dank der krankhaften Entfremdung, welche der Nationalitäts-Wahnsinn zwischen die Völker Europa's gelegt hat und noch legt, Dank ebenfalls den Politikern

des kurzen Blicks und der raschen Hand, die heute mit seiner Hülfe obenauf sind und gar nicht ahnen, wie sehr die auseinanderlösende Politik, welche sie treiben, nothwendig nur Zwischenakts-Politik sein kann, - Dank Alledem und manchem heute ganz Unaussprechbaren werden jetzt die unzweideutigsten Anzeichen übersehn oder willkürlich und lügenhaft umgedeutet, in denen sich ausspricht, dass Europa Eins werden will. Bei allen tieferen und umfänglicheren Menschen dieses Jahrhunderts war es die eigentliche Gesammt-Richtung in der geheimnissvollen Arbeit ihrer Seele, den Weg zu jener neuen Synthesis vorzubereiten und versuchsweise den Europäer der Zukunft vorwegzunehmen: nur mit ihren Vordergründen, oder in schwächeren Stunden, etwa im Alter, gehörten sie zu den "Vaterländern", - sie ruhten sich nur von sich selber aus, wenn sie "Patrioten" wurden. Ich denke an Menschen wie Napoleon, Goethe, Beethoven, Stendhal, Heinrich Heine, Schopenhauer: man verarge mir es nicht, wenn ich auch Richard Wagner zu ihnen rechne, über den man sich nicht durch seine eignen Missverständnisse verführen lassen darf, - Genies seiner Art haben selten das Recht, sich selbst zu verstehen. Noch weniger freilich durch den ungesitteten Lärm, mit dem man sich jetzt in Frankreich gegen Richard Wagner sperrt und wehrt: - die Thatsache bleibt nichtsdestoweniger bestehen, dass die französische Spät-Romantik der Vierziger Jahre und Richard Wagner auf das Engste und Innigste zu einander, gehören. Sie sind sich in allen

Höhen und Tiefen ihrer Bedürfnisse verwandt, grundverwandt: Europa ist es, das Eine Europa, dessen Seele sich durch ihre vielfältige und ungestüme Kunst hinaus, hinauf drängt und sehnt - wohin? in ein neues Licht? nach einer neuen Sonne? Aber wer möchte genau aussprechen, was alle diese Meister neuer Sprachmittel nicht deutlich auszusprechen wussten? Gewiss ist, dass der gleiche Sturm und Drang sie quälte, dass sie auf gleiche Weise suchten, diese letzten grossen Suchenden! Allesammt beherrscht von der Litteratur bis in ihre Augen und Ohren - die ersten Künstler von weltlitterarischer Bildung - meistens sogar selber Schreibende, Dichtende, Vermittler und Vermischer der Künste und der Sinne (Wagner gehört als Musiker unter die Maler, als Dichter unter die Musiker, als Künstler überhaupt unter die Schauspieler); allesammt Fanatiker des Ausdrucks "um jeden Preis" - ich hebe Delacroix hervor, den Nächstverwandten Wagner's -, allesammt grosse Entdecker im Reiche des Erhabenen, auch des Hässlichen und Grässlichen, noch grössere Entdecker im Effekte, in der Schaustellung, in der Kunst der Schauläden, allesammt Talente weit über ihr Genie hinaus -, Virtuosen durch und durch, mit unheimlichen Zugängen zu Allem, was verführt, lockt, zwingt, umwirft, geborene Feinde der Logik und der geraden Linien, begehrlich nach dem Fremden, dem Exotischen, dem Ungeheuren, dem Krummen, dem Sich-Widersprechenden; als Menschen Tantalusse des

Willens, heraufgekommene Plebejer, welche sich im Leben und Schaffen eines vornehmen tempo, eines lento unfähig wussten, - man denke zum Beispiel an Balzac - zügellose Arbeiter, beinahe Selbst-Zerstörer durch Arbeit; Antinomisten und Aufrührer in den Sitten, Ehrgeizige und Unersättliche ohne Gleichgewicht und Genuss; allesammt zuletzt an dem christlichen Kreuze zerbrechend und niedersinkend (und das mit Fug und Recht: denn wer von ihnen wäre tief und ursprünglich genug zu einer Philosophie des Antichrist gewesen? -) im Ganzen eine verwegen-wagende, prachtvoll-gewaltsame, hochfliegende und hoch emporreissende Art höherer Menschen, welche ihrem Jahrhundert - und es ist das Jahrhundert der Menge! - den Begriff "höherer Mensch" erst zu lehren hatte Mögen die deutschen Freunde Richard Wagner's darüber mit sich zu Rathe gehn, ob es in der Wagnerischen Kunst etwas schlechthin Deutsches giebt, oder ob nicht gerade deren Auszeichnung ist, aus überdeutschen Quellen und Antrieben zu kommen: wobei nicht unterschätzt werden mag, wie zur Ausbildung seines Typus gerade Paris unentbehrlich war, nach dem ihn in der entscheidensten Zeit die Tiefe seiner Instinkte verlangen hiess, und wie die ganze Art seines Auftretens, seines Selbst-Apostolats erst Angesichts des französischen Socialisten-Vorbilds sich vollenden konnte. Vielleicht wird man, bei einer feineren Vergleichung, zu Ehren der deutschen Natur Richard Wagner's finden, dass er es in Allem stärker, verwegener, härter, höher getrieben hat, als es ein Franzose des neunzehnten Jahrhunderts treiben könnte, - Dank dem Umstande, dass wir Deutschen der Barbarei noch näher stehen als die Franzosen -; vielleicht ist sogar das Merkwürdigste, was Richard Wagner geschaffen hat, der ganzen so späten lateinischen Rasse für immer und nicht nur für heute unzugänglich, unnachfühlbar, unnachahmbar: die Gestalt des Siegfried, jenes sehr freien Menschen, der in der That bei weitem zu frei, zu hart, zu wohlgemuth, zu gesund, zu antikatholisch für den Geschmack alter und mürber Culturvölker sein mag. Er mag sogar eine Sünde wider die Romantik gewesen sein, dieser antiromanische Siegfried: nun, Wagner hat diese Sünde reichlich quitt gemacht, in seinen alten trüben Tagen, als er - einen Geschmack vorwegnehmend, der inzwischen Politik geworden ist - mit der ihm eignen religiösen Vehemenz den Weg nach Rom, wenn nicht zu gehn, so doch zu predigen anfieng. - Damit man mich, mit diesen letzten Worten, nicht missverstehe, will ich einige kräftige Reime zu Hülfe nehmen, welche auch weniger feinen Ohren es verrathen werden, was ich will, - was ich gegen den "letzten Wagner" und seine Parsifal-Musik will.

- Ist das noch deutsch? -

Aus deutschem Herzen kam dies schwüle Kreischen?

Und deutschen Leibs ist dies Sich-selbst-

Entfleischen?
Deutsch ist dies Priester-Händespreitzen,
Dies weihrauch-düftelnde Sinne-Reizen?
Und deutsch dies Stocken, Stürzen, Taumeln,
Dies ungewisse Bimbambaumeln?
Dies Nonnen-Äugeln, Ave-Glocken-Bimmeln,
Dies ganze falsch verzückte Himmel-Überhimmeln?

- Ist Das noch deutsch? -

Erwägt! Noch steht ihr an der Pforte: - Denn, was ihr hört, ist Rom, - Rom's Glaube ohne Worte!

Neuntes Hauptstück:

Was ist vornehm?

257. Jede Erhöhung des Typus "Mensch" war bisher das Werk einer aristokratischen Gesellschaft - und so wird es immer wieder sein: als einer Gesellschaft, welche an eine lange Leiter der Rangordnung und Werthverschiedenheit von Mensch und Mensch glaubt und Sklaverei in irgend einem Sinne nöthig hat. Ohne das Pathos der Distanz, wie es aus dem eingefleischten Unterschied der Stände, aus dem beständigen Ausblick und Herabblick der herrschenden Kaste auf Unterthänige und Werkzeuge und aus ihrer ebenso

beständigen Übung im Gehorchen und Befehlen, Nieder- und Fernhalten erwächst, könnte auch jenes andre geheimnissvollere Pathos gar nicht erwachsen, jenes Verlangen nach immer neuer Distanz-Erweiterung innerhalb der Seele selbst, die Herausbildung immer höherer, seltnerer, fernerer, weitgespannterer, umfänglicherer Zustände, kurz eben die Erhöhung des Typus "Mensch", die fortgesetzte "Selbst-Überwindung des Menschen", um eine moralische Formel in einem übermoralischen Sinne zu nehmen. Freilich: man darf sich über die Entstehungsgeschichte einer aristokratischen Gesellschaft (also der Voraussetzung jener Erhöhung des Typus "Mensch" -) keinen humanitären Täuschungen hingeben: die Wahrheit ist hart. Sagen wir es uns ohne Schonung, wie bisher jede höhere Cultur auf Erden angefangen hat! Menschen mit einer noch natürlichen Natur, Barbaren in jedem furcht baren Verstande des Wortes, Raubmenschen, noch im Besitz ungebrochner Willenskräfte und Macht-Begierden, warfen sich auf schwächere, gesittetere, friedlichere, vielleicht handeltreibende oder viehzüchtende Rassen, oder auf alte mürbe Culturen, in denen eben die letzte Lebenskraft in glänzenden Feuerwerken von Geist und Verderbniss verflackerte. Die vornehme Kaste war im Anfang immer die Barbaren-Kaste: ihr Übergewicht lag nicht vorerst in der physischen Kraft, sondern in der seelischen, - es waren die ganzeren Menschen (was auf jeder Stufe auch so viel mit bedeutet als "die ganzeren Bestien").

258. Corruption, als der Ausdruck davon, dass innerhalb der Instinkte Anarchie droht, und dass der Grundbau der Affekte, der "Leben" heisst, erschüttert ist: Corruption ist, je nach dem Lebensgebilde, an dem sie sich zeigt, etwas Grundverschiedenes. Wenn zum Beispiel eine Aristokratie, wie die Frankreichs am Anfange der Revolution, mit einem sublimen Ekel ihre Privilegien wegwirft und sich selbst einer Ausschweifung ihres moralischen Gefühls zum Opfer bringt, so ist dies Corruption: - es war eigentlich nur der Abschlussakt jener Jahrhunderte dauernden Corruption, vermöge deren sie Schritt für Schritt ihre herrschaftlichen Befugnisse abgegeben und sich zur Funktion des Königthums (zuletzt gar zu dessen Putz und Prunkstück) herabgesetzt hatte. Das Wesentliche an einer guten und gesunden Aristokratie ist aber, dass sie sich nicht als Funktion (sei es des Königthums, sei es des Gemeinwesens), sondern als dessen Sinn und höchste Rechtfertigung fühlt, - dass sie deshalb mit gutem Gewissen das Opfer einer Unzahl Menschen hinnimmt, welche um ihretwillen zu unvollständigen Menschen, zu Sklaven, zu Werkzeugen herabgedrückt und vermindert werden müssen. Ihr Grundglaube muss eben sein, dass die Gesellschaft nicht um der Gesellschaft willen dasein dürfe, sondern nur als Unterbau und Gerüst, an dem sich eine ausgesuchte Art

Wesen zu ihrer höheren Aufgabe und überhaupt zu einem höheren Sein emporzuheben vermag: vergleichbar jenen sonnensüchtigen Kletterpflanzen auf Java - man nennt sie Sipo Matador -, welche mit ihren Armen einen Eichbaum so lange und oft umklammern, bis sie endlich, hoch über ihm, aber auf ihn gestützt, in freiem Lichte ihre Krone entfalten und ihr Glück zur Schau tragen können. -

259. Sich gegenseitig der Verletzung, der Gewalt, der Ausbeutung enthalten, seinen Willen dem des Andern gleich setzen: dies kann in einem gewissen groben Sinne zwischen Individuen zur guten Sitte werden, wenn die Bedingungen dazu gegeben sind (nämlich deren thatsächliche Ähnlichkeit in Kraftmengen und Werthmaassen und ihre Zusammengehörigkeit innerhalb Eines Körpers). Sobald man aber dies Princip weiter nehmen wollte und womöglich gar als Grundprincip der Gesellschaft, so würde es sich sofort erweisen als Das, was es ist: als Wille zur Verneinung des Lebens, als Auflösungs- und Verfalls-Princip. Hier muss man gründlich auf den Grund denken und sich aller empfindsamen Schwächlichkeit erwehren: Leben selbst ist wesentlich Aneignung, Verletzung, Überwältigung des Fremden und Schwächeren, Unterdrückung, Härte, Aufzwängung eigner Formen, Einverleibung und mindestens, mildestens, Ausbeutung, - aber wozu sollte man immer gerade solche Worte gebrauchen, denen von Alters her eine

verleumderische Absicht eingeprägt ist? Auch jener Körper, innerhalb dessen, wie vorher angenommen wurde, die Einzelnen sich als gleich behandeln - es geschieht in jeder gesunden Aristokratie -, muss selber, falls er ein lebendiger und nicht ein absterbender Körper ist, alles Das gegen andre Körper thun, wessen sich die Einzelnen in ihm gegen einander enthalten: er wird der leibhafte Wille zur Macht sein müssen, er wird wachsen, um sich greifen, an sich ziehn, Übergewicht gewinnen wollen, - nicht aus irgend einer Moralität oder Immoralität heraus, sondern weil erlebt, und weil Leben eben Wille zur Macht ist. In keinem Punkte ist aber das gemeine Bewusstsein der Europäer widerwilliger gegen Belehrung, als hier; man schwärmt jetzt überall, unter wissenschaftlichen Verkleidungen sogar, von kommenden Zuständen der Gesellschaft, denen "der ausbeuterische Charakter" abgehn soll: - das klingt in meinen Ohren, als ob man ein Leben zu erfinden verspräche, welches sich aller organischen Funktionen enthielte. Die "Ausbeutung" gehört nicht einer verderbten oder unvollkommnen und primitiven Gesellschaft an: sie gehört in's Wesen des Lebendigen, als organische Grundfunktion, sie ist eine Folge des eigentlichen Willens zur Macht, der eben der Wille des Lebens ist. - Gesetzt, dies ist als Theorie eine Neuerung, - als Realität ist es das Ur-Faktum aller Geschichte: man sei doch so weit gegen sich ehrlich! -

260. Bei einer Wanderung durch die vielen feineren und gröberen Moralen, welche bisher auf Erden geherrscht haben oder noch herrschen, fand ich gewisse Züge regelmässig mit einander wiederkehrend und aneinander geknüpft: bis sich mir endlich zwei Grundtypen verriethen, und ein Grundunterschied heraussprang. Es giebt Herren-Moral und Sklaven-Moral; - ich füge sofort hinzu, dass in allen höheren und gemischteren Culturen auch Versuche der Vermittlung beider Moralen zum Vorschein kommen, noch öfter das Durcheinander derselben und gegenseitige Missverstehen, ja bisweilen ihr hartes Nebeneinander - sogar im selben Menschen, innerhalb Einer Seele. Die moralischen Werthunterscheidungen sind entweder unter einer herrschenden Art entstanden, welche sich ihres Unterschieds gegen die beherrschte mit Wohlgefühl bewusst wurde, - oder unter den Beherrschten, den Sklaven und Abhängigen jeden Grades. Im ersten Falle, wenn die Herrschenden es sind, die den Begriff gut- bestimmen, sind es die erhobenen stolzen Zustände der Seele, welche als das Auszeichnende und die Rangordnung Bestimmende empfunden werden. Der vornehme Mensch trennt die Wesen von sich ab, an denen das Gegentheil solcher gehobener stolzer Zustände zum Ausdruck kommt: er verachtet sie. Man bemerke sofort, dass in dieser ersten Art Moral der Gegensatz "gut" und "schlecht" so viel bedeutet wie "vornehm" und "verächtlich": - der Gegensatz "gut" und "böse" ist anderer Herkunft.

Verachtet wird der Feige, der Ängstliche, der Kleinliche, der an die enge Nützlichkeit Denkende; ebenso der Misstrauische mit seinem unfreien Blicke, der Sich-Erniedrigende, die Hunde-Art von Mensch, welche sich misshandeln lässt, der bettelnde Schmeichler, vor Allem der Lügner: - es ist ein Grundglaube aller Aristokraten, dass das gemeine Volk lügnerisch ist. "Wir Wahrhaftigen" - so nannten sich im alten Griechenland die Adeligen. Es liegt auf der Hand, dass die moralischen Werthbezeichnungen überall zuerst auf Menschen und erst abgeleitet und spät auf Handlungen gelegt worden sind: weshalb es ein arger Fehlgriff ist, wenn Moral-Historiker von Fragen den Ausgang nehmen wie "warum ist die mitleidige Handlung gelobt worden?" Die vornehme Art Mensch fühlt sich als werthbestimmend, sie hat nicht nöthig, sich gutheissen zu lassen, sie urtheilt "was mir schädlich ist, das ist an sich schädlich", sie weiss sich als Das, was überhaupt erst Ehre den Dingen verleiht, sie ist wertheschaffend. Alles, was sie an sich kennt, ehrt sie: eine solche Moral ist Selbstverherrlichung. Im Vordergrunde steht das Gefühl der Fülle, der Macht, die überströmen will, das Glück der hohen Spannung, das Bewusstsein eines Reichthums, der schenken und abgeben möchte: - auch der vornehme Mensch hilft dem Unglücklichen, aber nicht oder fast nicht aus Mitleid, sondern mehr aus einem Drang, den der Überfluss von Macht erzeugt. Der vornehme Mensch ehrt in sich den Mächtigen, auch Den, welcher Macht über sich selbst hat, der zu reden und zu schweigen versteht, der mit Lust Strenge und Härte gegen sich übt und Ehrerbietung vor allem Strengen und Härten hat. "Ein hartes Herz legte Wotan mir in die Brust" heisst es in einer alten skandinavischen Saga: so ist es aus der Seele eines stolzen Wikingers heraus mit Recht gedichtet. Eine solche Art Mensch ist eben stolz darauf, nicht zum Mitleiden gemacht zu sein: weshalb der Held der Saga warnend hinzufügt "wer jung schon kein hartes Herz hat, dem wird es niemals hart". Vornehme und Tapfere, welche so denken, sind am entferntesten von jener Moral, welche gerade im Mitleiden oder im Handeln für Andere oder im désintéressement das Abzeichen des Moralischen sieht; der Glaube an sich selbst, der Stolz auf sich selbst, eine Grundfeindschaft und Ironie gegen "Selbstlosigkeit" gehört eben so bestimmt zur vornehmen Moral wie eine leichte Geringschätzung und Vorsicht vor den Mitgefühlen und dem "warmen Herzen". - Die Mächtigen sind es, welche zu ehren verstehen, es ist ihre Kunst, ihr Reich der Erfindung. Die tiefe Ehrfurcht vor dem Alter und vor dem Herkommen - das ganze Recht steht auf dieser doppelten Ehrfurcht -, der Glaube und das Vorurtheil zu Gunsten der Vorfahren und zu Ungunsten der Kommenden ist typisch in der Moral der Mächtigen; und wenn umgekehrt die Menschen der "modernen Ideen" beinahe instinktiv an den "Fortschritt" und die "Zukunft" glauben und der Achtung vor dem Alter immer mehr ermangeln, so verräth sich damit genugsam schon die unvornehme Herkunft dieser "Ideen". Am meisten ist aber eine Moral der Herrschenden dem gegenwärtigen Geschmacke fremd und peinlich in der Strenge ihres Grundsatzes, dass man nur gegen Seinesgleichen Pflichten habe; dass man gegen die Wesen niedrigeren Ranges, gegen alles Fremde nach Gutdünken oder "wie es das Herz will" handeln dürfe und jedenfalls "jenseits von Gut und Böse" -: hierhin mag Mitleiden und dergleichen gehören. Die Fähigkeit und Pflicht zu langer Dankbarkeit und langer Rache - beides nur innerhalb seines Gleichen -, die Feinheit in der Wiedervergeltung, das Begriffs-Raffinement in der Freundschaft, eine gewisse Nothwendigkeit, Feinde zu haben (gleichsam als Abzugsgräben für die Affekte Neid Streitsucht Übermuth, - im Grunde, um gut freund sein zu können): Alles das sind typische Merkmale der vornehmen Moral, welche, wie angedeutet, nicht die Moral der "modernen Ideen" ist und deshalb heute schwer nachzufühlen, auch schwer auszugraben und aufzudecken ist. - Es steht anders mit dem zweiten Typus der Moral, der Sklaven-Moral. Gesetzt, dass die Vergewaltigten, Gedrückten, Leidenden, Unfreien, Ihrer-selbst-Ungewissen und Müden moralisiren: was wird das Gleichartige ihrer moralischen Werthschätzungen sein? Wahrscheinlich wird ein pessimistischer Argwohn gegen die ganze Lage des Menschen zum Ausdruck kommen, vielleicht eine Verurtheilung des Menschen mitsammt seiner Lage.

Der Blick des Sklaven ist abgünstig für die Tugenden des Mächtigen: er hat Skepsis und Misstrauen, er hat Feinheit des Misstrauens gegen alles "Gute", was dort geehrt wird -, er möchte sich überreden, dass das Glück selbst dort nicht ächt sei. Umgekehrt werden die Eigenschaften hervorgezogen und mit Licht übergossen, welche dazu dienen, Leidenden das Dasein zu erleichtern: hier kommt das Mitleiden, die gefällige hülfbereite Hand, das warme Herz, die Geduld, der Fleiss, die Demuth, die Freundlichkeit zu Ehren -, denn das sind hier die nützlichsten Eigenschaften und beinahe die einzigen Mittel, den Druck des Daseins auszuhalten. Die Sklaven-Moral ist wesentlich Nützlichkeits-Moral. Hier ist der Herd für die Entstehung jenes berühmten Gegensatzes "gut" und "böse": - in's Böse wird die Macht und Gefährlichkeit hinein empfunden, eine gewisse Furchtbarkeit, Feinheit und Stärke, welche die Verachtung nicht aufkommen lässt. Nach der Sklaven-Moral erregt also der "Böse" Furcht; nach der Herren Moral ist es gerade der "Gute", der Furcht erregt und erregen will, während der "schlechte" Mensch als der verächtliche empfunden wird. Der Gegensatz kommt auf seine Spitze, wenn sich, gemäss der Sklavenmoral-Consequenz, zuletzt nun auch an den "Guten" dieser Moral ein Hauch von Geringschätzung hängt - sie mag leicht und wohlwollend sein -, weil der Gute innerhalb der Sklaven-Denkweise jedenfalls der ungefährliche Mensch sein muss: er ist gutmüthig, leicht zu betrügen, ein bischen dumm vielleicht, un bonhomme. überall, wo die Sklaven-Moral zum Übergewicht kommt, zeigt die Sprache eine Neigung, die Worte "gut" und "dumm" einander anzunähern. - Ein letzter Grundunterschied: das Verlangen nach Freiheit, der Instinkt für das Glück und die Feinheiten des Freiheits-Gefühls gehört ebenso nothwendig zur Sklaven-Moral und -Moralität, als die Kunst und Schwärmerei in der Ehrfurcht, in der Hingebung das regelmässige Symptom einer aristokratischen Denk- und Werthungsweise ist. - Hieraus lässt sich ohne Weiteres verstehn, warum die Liebe als Passion - es ist unsre europäische Spezialität - schlechterdings vornehmer Abkunft sein muss: bekanntlich gehört ihre Erfindung den provençalischen Ritter-Dichtern zu, jenen prachtvollen erfinderischen Menschen des "gai saber", denen Europa so Vieles und beinahe sich selbst verdankt. -

261. Zu den Dingen, welche einem vornehmen Menschen vielleicht am schwersten zu begreifen sind, gehört die Eitelkeit: er wird versucht sein, sie noch dort zu leugnen, wo eine andre Art Mensch sie mit beiden Händen zu fassen meint. Das Problem ist für ihn, sich Wesen vorzustellen, die eine gute Meinung über sich zu erwecken suchen, welche sie selbst von sich nicht haben - und also auch nicht "verdienen" -, und die doch hinterdrein an diese gute Meinung selber glauben. Das erscheint ihm zur Hälfte so geschmacklos und

unehrerbietig vor sich selbst, zur andren Hälfte so barock-unvernünftig, dass er die Eitelkeit gern als Ausnahme fassen möchte und sie in den meisten Fällen, wo man von ihr redet, anzweifelt. Er wird zum Beispiel sagen: "ich kann mich über meinen Werth irren und andererseits doch verlangen, dass mein Werth gerade so, wie ich ihn ansetze, auch von Andern anerkannt werde, - aber das ist keine Eitelkeit (sondern Dünkel oder, in den häufigeren Fällen, Das, was `Demuth`, auch `Bescheidenheit` genannt wird)." Oder auch: "ich kann mich aus vielen Gründen über die gute Meinung Anderer freuen, vielleicht weil ich sie ehre und liebe und mich an jeder ihrer Freuden erfreue, vielleicht auch weil ihre gute Meinung den Glauben an meine eigne gute Meinung bei mir unterschreibt und kräftigt, vielleicht weil die gute Meinung Anderer, selbst in Fällen, wo ich sie nicht theile, mir doch nützt oder Nutzen verspricht, - aber das ist Alles nicht Eitelkeit." Der vornehme Mensch muss es sich erst mit Zwang, namentlich mit Hülfe der Historie, vorstellig machen, dass, seit unvordenklichen Zeiten, in allen irgendwie abhängigen Volksschichten der gemeine Mensch nur Das war, was er galt: - gar nicht daran gewöhnt, Werthe selbst anzusetzen, mass er auch sich keinen andern Werth bei, als seine Herren ihm beimassen (es ist das eigentliche Herrenrecht, Werthe zu schaffen). Mag man es als die Folge eines ungeheuren Atavismus begreifen, dass der gewöhnliche Mensch auch jetzt noch immer erst auf eine Meinung über sich wartet und sich dann derselben instinktiv unterwirft: aber durchaus nicht bloss einer "guten" Meinung, sondern auch einer schlechten und unbilligen (man denke zum Beispiel an den grössten Theil der Selbstschätzungen und Selbstunterschätzungen, welche gläubige Frauen ihren Beichtvätern ablernen, und überhaupt der gläubige Christ seiner Kirche ablernt). Thatsächlich wird nun, gemäss dem langsamen Heraufkommen der demokratischen Ordnung der Dinge (und seiner Ursache, der Blutvermischung von Herren und Sklaven), der ursprünglich vornehme und seltne Drang, sich selbst von sich aus einen Werth zuzuschreiben und von sich "gut zu denken", mehr und mehr ermuthigt und ausgebreitet werden: aber er hat jeder Zeit einen ältern, breiteren und gründlicher einverleibten Hang gegen sich, - und im Phänomene der "Eitelkeit" wird dieser ältere Hang Herr über den jüngeren. Der Eitle freut sich über jede gute Meinung, die er über sich hört (ganz abseits von allen Gesichtspunkten ihrer Nützlichkeit, und ebenso abgesehn von wahr und falsch), ebenso wie er an jeder schlechten Meinung leidet: denn er unterwirft sich beiden, er fühlt sich ihnen unterworfen, aus jenem ältesten Instinkte der Unterwerfung, der an ihm ausbricht. - Es ist "der Sklave" im Blute des Eitlen, ein Rest von der Verschmitztheit des Sklaven - und wie viel "Sklave" ist zum Beispiel jetzt noch im Weibe rückständig! welcher zu guten Meinungen über sich zu verführen sucht; es ist ebenfalls der Sklave, der vor diesen Meinungen nachher sofort selbst niederfällt, wie als ob er sie nicht hervorgerufen hätte. - Und nochmals gesagt: Eitelkeit ist ein Atavismus.

262. Eine Art entsteht, ein Typus wird fest und stark unter dem langen Kampfe mit wesentlich gleichen ungünstigen Bedingungen. Umgekehrt weiss man aus den Erfahrungen der Züchter, dass Arten, denen eine überreichliche Ernährung und überhaupt ein Mehr von Schutz und Sorgfalt zu Theil wird, alsbald in der stärksten Weise zur Variation des Typus neigen und reich an Wundern und Monstrositäten (auch an monströsen Lastern) sind. Nun sehe man einmal ein aristokratisches Gemeinwesen, etwa eine alte griechische Polis oder Venedig, als eine, sei es freiwillige, sei es unfreiwillige Veranstaltung zum Zweck der Züchtung an: es sind da Menschen bei einander und auf sich angewiesen, welche ihre Art durchsetzen wollen, meistens, weil sie sich durchsetzen müssen oder in furchtbarer Weise Gefahr laufen, ausgerottet zu werden. Hier fehlt jene Gunst, jenes Übermaass, jener Schutz, unter denen die Variation begünstigt ist; die Art hat sich als Art nöthig, als Etwas, das sich gerade vermöge seiner Härte, Gleichförmigkeit, Einfachheit der Form überhaupt durchsetzen und dauerhaft machen kann, im beständigen Kampfe mit den Nachbarn oder mit den aufständischen oder Aufstand drohenden Unterdrückten. Die mannichfaltigste Erfahrung lehrt

sie, welchen Eigenschaften vornehmlich sie es verdankt, dass sie, allen Göttern und Menschen zum Trotz, noch da ist, dass sie noch immer obgesiegt hat: diese Eigenschaften nennt sie Tugenden, diese Tugenden allein züchtet sie gross. Sie thut es mit Härte, ja sie will die Härte; jede aristokratische Moral ist unduldsam, in der Erziehung der Jugend, in der Verfügung über die Weiber, in den Ehesitten, im Verhältnisse von Alt und jung, in den Strafgesetzen (welche allein die Abartenden in's Auge fassen): - sie rechnet die Unduldsamkeit selbst unter die Tugenden, unter dem Namen "Gerechtigkeit". Ein Typus mit wenigen, aber sehr starken Zügen, eine Art strenger kriegerischer klug-schweigsamer, geschlossener und verschlossener Menschen (und als solche vom feinsten Gefühle für die Zauber und nuances der Societät) wird auf diese Weise über den Wechsel der Geschlechter hinaus festgestellt; der beständige Kampf mit immer gleichen ungünstigen Bedingungen ist, wie gesagt, die Ursache davon, dass ein Typus fest und hart wird. Endlich aber entsteht einmal eine Glückslage, die ungeheure Spannung lässt nach; es giebt vielleicht keine Feinde mehr unter den Nachbarn, und die Mittel zum Leben, selbst zum Genusse des Lebens sind überreichlich da. Mit Einem Schlage reisst das Band und der Zwang der alten Zucht: sie fühlt sich nicht mehr als nothwendig, als Dasein-bedingend, - wollte sie fortbestehn, so könnte sie es nur als eine Form des Luxus, als archaisirender Geschmack. Die Variation, sei es als Abartung (in's Höhere, Feinere, Seltnere), sei es als Entartung und Monstrosität, ist plötzlich in der grössten Fülle und Pracht auf dem Schauplatz, der Einzelne wagt einzeln zu sein und sich abzuheben. An diesen Wendepunkten der Geschichte zeigt sich neben einander und oft in einander verwickelt und verstrickt ein herrliches vielfaches urwaldhaftes Heraufwachsen und Emporstreben, eine Art tropisches Tempo im Wetteifer des Wachsthums und ein ungeheures Zugrundegehen und Sich-zu-Grunde-Richten, Dank den wild gegeneinander gewendeten, gleichsam explodirenden Egoismen, welche "um Sonne und Licht" mit einander ringen und keine Grenze, keine Zügelung, keine Schonung mehr aus der bisherigen Moral zu entnehmen wissen. Diese Moral selbst war es, welche die Kraft in's Ungeheure aufgehäuft, die den Bogen auf so bedrohliche Weise gespannt hat - - jetzt ist, jetzt wird sie "überlebt". Der gefährliche und unheimliche Punkt ist erreicht, wo das grössere, vielfachere, umfänglichere Leben über die alte Moral hinweg lebt; das "Individuum" steht da, genöthigt zu einer eigenen Gesetzgebung, zu eigenen Künsten und Listen der Selbst-Erhaltung, Selbst-Erhöhung, Selbst-Erlösung. Lauter neue Wozu's, lauter neue Womit's, keine gemeinsamen Formeln mehr, Missverständniss und Missachtung mit einander im Bunde, der Verfall, Verderb und die höchsten Begierden schauerlich verknotet, das Genie der Rasse aus allen Füllhörnern des Guten und Schlimmen überquellend, ein verhängnissvolles Zugleich von Frühling und Herbst, voll neuer Reize und Schleier, die, der jungen, noch unausgeschöpften, noch unermüdeten Verderbniss zu eigen sind. Wieder ist die Gefahr da, die Mutter der Moral, die grosse Gefahr, dies Mal in's Individuum verlegt, in den Nächsten und Freund, auf die Gasse, in's eigne Kind, in's eigne Herz, in alles Eigenste und Geheimste von Wunsch und Wille: was werden jetzt die Moral-Philosophen zu predigen haben, die um diese Zeit heraufkommen? Sie entdecken, diese scharfen Beobachter und Eckensteher, dass es schnell zum Ende geht, dass Alles um sie verdirbt und verderben macht, dass Nichts bis übermorgen steht, Eine Art Mensch ausgenommen, die unheilbar Mittelmässigen. Die Mittelmässigen allein haben Aussicht, sich fortzusetzen, sich fortzupflanzen, - sie sind die Menschen der Zukunft, die einzig überlebenden; "seid wie sie! werdet mittelmässig!" heisst nunmehr die alleinige Moral, die noch Sinn hat, die noch Ohren findet. - Aber sie ist schwer zu predigen, diese Moral der Mittelmässigkeit! - sie darf es ja niemals eingestehn, was sie ist und was sie will! sie muss von Maass und Würde und Pflicht und Nächstenliebe reden, - sie wird noth haben, die Ironie zu verbergen! -

263. Es giebt einen Instinkt für den Rang, welcher, mehr als Alles, schon das Anzeichen eines hohen Ranges ist; es giebt eine Lust an den Nuancen der Ehrfurcht, die auf vornehme Abkunft und

Gewohnheiten rathen lässt. Die Feinheit, Güte und Höhe einer Seele wird gefährlich auf die Probe gestellt, wenn Etwas an ihr vorüber geht, das ersten Ranges ist, aber noch nicht von den Schaudern der Autorität vor zudringlichen Griffen und Plumpheiten gehütet wird: Etwas, das, unabgezeichnet, unentdeckt, versuchend, vielleicht willkürlich verhüllt und verkleidet, wie ein lebendiger Prüfstein seines Weges geht. Zu wessen Aufgabe und Übung es gehört, Seelen auszuforschen, der wird sich in mancherlei Formen gerade dieser Kunst bedienen, um den letzten Werth einer Seele, die unverrückbare eingeborne Rangordnung, zu der sie gehört, festzustellen: er wird sie auf ihren Instinkt der Ehrfurcht hin auf die Probe stellen. Différence engendre haine: die Gemeinheit mancher Natur sprützt plötzlich wie schmutziges Wasser hervor, wenn irgend ein heiliges Gefäss, irgend eine Kostbarkeit aus verschlossenen Schreinen, irgend ein Buch mit den Zeichen des grossen Schicksals vorübergetragen wird; und andrerseits giebt es ein unwillkürliches Verstummen, ein Zögern des Auges, ein Stillewerden aller Gebärden, woran sich ausspricht, dass eine Seele die Nähe des Verehrungswürdigsten fühlt. Die Art, mit der im Ganzen bisher die Ehrfurcht vor der Bibel in Europa aufrecht erhalten wird, ist vielleicht das beste Stück Zucht und Verfeinerung der Sitte, das Europa dem Christenthume verdankt: solche Bücher der Tiefe und der letzten Bedeutsamkeit brauchen zu ihrem Schutz eine von Aussen kommende Tyrannei von

Autorität, um jene Jahrtausende von Dauer zu gewinnen, welche nöthig sind, sie auszuschöpfen und auszurathen. Es ist Viel erreicht, wenn der grossen Menge (den Flachen und Geschwind-Därmen aller Art) jenes Gefühl endlich angezüchtet ist, dass sie nicht an Alles rühren dürfe; dass es heilige Erlebnisse giebt, vor denen sie die Schuhe auszuziehn und die unsaubere Hand fern zu halten hat, - es ist beinahe ihre höchste Steigerung zur Menschlichkeit. Umgekehrt wirkt an den sogenannten Gebildeten, den Gläubigen der "modernen Ideen", vielleicht Nichts so ekelerregend, als ihr Mangel an Scham, ihre bequeme Frechheit des Auges und der Hand, mit der von ihnen an Alles gerührt, geleckt, getastet wird; und es ist möglich, dass sich heut im Volke, im niedern Volke, namentlich unter Bauern, immer noch mehr relative Vornehmheit des Geschmacks und Takt der Ehrfurcht vorfindet, als bei der zeitunglesenden Halbwelt des Geistes, den Gebildeten.

264. Es ist aus der Seele eines Menschen nicht wegzuwischen, was seine Vorfahren am liebsten und beständigsten gethan haben: ob sie etwa emsige Sparer waren und Zubehör eines Schreibtisches und Geldkastens, bescheiden und bürgerlich in ihren Begierden, bescheiden auch in ihren Tugenden; oder ob sie an's Befehlen von früh bis spät gewöhnt lebten, rauhen Vergnügungen hold und daneben vielleicht noch rauheren Pflichten und Verantwortungen; oder ob sie

endlich alte Vorrechte der Geburt und des Besitzes irgendwann einmal geopfert haben, um ganz ihrem Glauben - ihrem "Gotte" - zu leben, als die Menschen eines unerbittlichen und zarten Gewissens, welches vor jeder Vermittlung erröthet. Es ist gar nicht möglich, dass ein Mensch nicht die Eigenschaften und Vorlieben seiner Eltern und Altvordern im Leibe habe: was auch der Augenschein dagegen sagen mag. Dies ist das Problem der Rasse. Gesetzt, man kennt Einiges von den Eltern, so ist ein Schluss auf das Kind erlaubt: irgend eine widrige Unenthaltsamkeit, irgend ein Winkel-Neid, eine plumpe Sich-Rechtgeberei - wie diese Drei zusammen zu allen Zeiten den eigentlichen Pöbel-Typus ausgemacht haben - dergleichen muss auf das Kind so sicher übergehn, wie verderbtes Blut; und mit Hülfe der besten Erziehung und Bildung wird man eben nur erreichen, über eine solche Vererbung zu täuschen. - Und was will heute Erziehung und Bildung Anderes! In unsrem sehr volksthümlichen, will sagen pöbelhaften Zeitalter muss "Erziehung" und "Bildung" wesentlich die Kunst, zu täuschen, sein, - über die Herkunft, den vererbten Pöbel in Leib und Seele hinweg zu täuschen. Ein Erzieher, der heute vor Allem Wahrhaftigkeit predigte und seinen Züchtlingen beständig zuriefe "seid wahr! seid natürlich! gebt euch, wie ihr seid!" - selbst ein solcher tugendhafter und treuherziger Esel würde nach einiger Zeit zu jener furca des Horaz greifen lernen, um naturam expellere: mit welchem Erfolge? "Pöbel" usque recurret. -

265. Auf die Gefahr hin, unschuldige Ohren missvergnügt zu machen, stelle ich hin: der Egoismus gehört zum Wesen der vornehmen Seele, ich meine jenen unverrückbaren Glauben, dass einem Wesen, wie "wir sind", andre Wesen von Natur unterthan sein müssen und sich ihm zu opfern haben. Die vornehme Seele nimmt diesen Thatbestand ihres Egoismus ohne jedes Fragezeichen hin, auch ohne ein Gefühl von Härte Zwang, Willkür darin, vielmehr wie Etwas, das im Urgesetz der Dinge begründet sein mag: - suchte sie nach einem Namen dafür, so würde sie sagen "es ist die Gerechtigkeit selbst". Sie gesteht sich, unter Umständen, die sie anfangs zögern lassen, zu, dass es mit ihr Gleichberechtigte giebt; sobald sie über diese Frage des Rangs im Reinen ist, bewegt sie sich unter diesen Gleichen und Gleichberechtigten mit der gleichen Sicherheit in Scham und zarter Ehrfurcht, welche sie im Verkehre mit sich selbst hat, - gemäss einer eingebornen himmlischen Mechanik, auf welche sich alle Sterne verstehn. Es ist ein Stück ihres Egoismus mehr, diese Feinheit und Selbstbeschränkung im Verkehre mit ihres Gleichen - jeder Stern ist ein solcher Egoist -: sie ehrt sich in ihnen und in den Rechten, welche sie an dieselben abgiebt, sie zweifelt nicht, dass der Austausch von Ehren und Rechten als Wesen alles Verkehrs ebenfalls zum naturgemässen Zustand der Dinge gehört. Die vornehme Seele giebt, wie sie nimmt, aus dem leidenschaftlichen und reizbaren Instinkte der Vergeltung heraus, welcher auf

ihrem Grunde liegt. Der Begriff "Gnade" hat inter pares keinen Sinn und Wohlgeruch; es mag eine sublime Art geben, Geschenke von Oben her gleichsam über sich ergehen zu lassen und wie Tropfen durstig aufzutrinken: aber für diese Kunst und Gebärde hat die vornehme Seele kein Geschick. Ihr Egoismus hindert sie hier: sie blickt ungern überhaupt nach "Oben", - sondern entweder vor sich, horizontal und langsam, oder hinab: - sie weiss sich in der Höhe.-

266. "Wahrhaft hochachten kann man nur, wer sich nicht selbst *sucht*". - Goethe an Rath Schlosser.

267. Es giebt ein Sprüchwort bei den Chinesen, das die Mütter schon ihre Kinder lehren: siao-sin "mache dein Herz klein!" Dies ist der eigentliche Grundhang in späten Civilisationen: ich zweifle nicht, dass ein antiker Grieche auch an uns Europäern von Heute zuerst die Selbstverkleinerung herauserkennen würde, - damit allein schon giengen wir ihm "wider den Geschmack". -

268. Was ist zuletzt die Gemeinheit? - Worte sind Tonzeichen für Begriffe; Begriffe aber sind mehr oder weniger bestimmte Bildzeichen für oft wiederkehrende und zusammen kommende Empfindungen, für Empfindungs-Gruppen. Es genügt noch nicht, um sich einander zu verstehen, dass man die selben Worte gebraucht: man muss die selben Worte auch für die

selbe Gattung innerer Erlebnisse gebrauchen, man muss zuletzt seine Erfahrung mit einander gemein haben. Deshalb verstehen sich die Menschen Eines Volkes besser unter einander, als Zugehörige verschiedener Völker, selbst wenn sie sich der gleichen Sprache bedienen; oder vielmehr, wenn Menschen lange unter ähnlichen Bedingungen (des Klima's, des Bodens, der Gefahr, der Bedürfnisse, der Arbeit) zusammen gelebt haben, so entsteht daraus Etwas, das "sich versteht", ein Volk. In allen Seelen hat eine gleiche Anzahl oft wiederkehrender Erlebnisse die Oberhand gewonnen über seltner kommende: auf sie hin versteht man sich, schnell und immer schneller - die Geschichte der Sprache ist die Geschichte eines Abkürzungs-Prozesses -; auf dies schnelle Verstehen hin verbindet man sich, enger und immer enger. Je grösser die Gefährlichkeit, um so grösser ist das Bedürfniss, schnell und leicht über Das, was noth thut, übereinzukommen; sich in der Gefahr nicht misszuverstehn, das ist es, was die Menschen zum Verkehre schlechterdings nicht entbehren können. Noch bei jeder Freundschaft oder Liebschaft macht man diese Probe: Nichts derart hat Dauer, sobald man dahinter kommt, dass Einer von Beiden bei gleichen Worten anders fühlt, meint, wittert, wünscht, fürchtet, als der Andere. (Die Furcht vor dem "ewigen Missverständniss": das ist jener wohlwollende Genius, der Personen verschiedenen Geschlechts so oft von übereilten Verbindungen abhält, zu denen Sinne und Herz rathen - und nicht irgend ein

Schopenhauerischer "Genius der Gattung" -!) Welche Gruppen von Empfindungen innerhalb einer Seele am schnellsten wach werden, das Wort ergreifen, den Befehl geben, das entscheidet über die gesammte Rangordnung ihrer Werthe, das bestimmt zuletzt ihre Gütertafel. Die Werthschätzungen eines Menschen verrathen etwas vom Aufbau seiner Seele, und worin sie ihre Lebensbedingungen, ihre eigentliche Noth sieht. Gesetzt nun, dass die Noth von jeher nur solche Menschen einander angenähert hat, welche mit ähnlichen Zeichen ähnliche Bedürfnisse, ähnliche Erlebnisse andeuten konnten, so ergiebt sich im Ganzen, dass die leichte Mittheilbarkeit der Noth, das heisst im letzten Grunde das Erleben von nur durchschnittlichen und gemeinen Erlebnissen, unter allen Gewalten, welche über den Menschen bisher verfügt haben, die gewaltigste gewesen sein muss. Die ähnlicheren, die gewöhnlicheren Menschen waren und sind immer im Vortheile, die Ausgesuchteren, Feineren, Seltsameren, schwerer Verständlichen bleiben leicht allein, unterliegen, bei ihrer Vereinzelung, den Unfällen und pflanzen sich selten fort. Man muss ungeheure Gegenkräfte anrufen, um diesen natürlichen, allzunatürlichen progressus in simile, die Fortbildung des Menschen in's Ähnliche, Gewöhnliche, Durchschnittliche, Heerdenhafte - in's Gemeine! - zu kreuzen.

269. Je mehr ein Psycholog - ein geborner, ein unvermeidlicher Psycholog und Seelen-Errather - sich den ausgesuchteren Fällen und Menschen zukehrt, um so grösser wird seine Gefahr, am Mitleiden zu ersticken: er hat Härte und Heiterkeit nöthig, mehr als ein andrer Mensch. Die Verderbniss, das Zugrundegehen der höheren Menschen, der fremder gearteten Seelen ist nämlich die Regel: es ist schrecklich, eine solche Regel immer vor Augen zu haben. Die vielfache Marter des Psychologen, der dieses Zugrundegehen entdeckt hat, der diese gesammte innere "Heillosigkeit" des höheren Menschen, dieses ewige "Zu spät!" in jedem Sinne, erst einmal und dann fast immer wieder entdeckt, durch die ganze Geschichte hindurch, - kann vielleicht eines Tages zur Ursache davon werden, dass er mit Erbitterung sich gegen sein eignes Loos wendet und einen Versuch der Selbst-Zerstörung macht, - dass er selbst "verdirbt". Man wird fast bei jedem Psychologen eine verrätherische Vorneigung und Lust am Umgange mit alltäglichen und wohlgeordneten Menschen wahrnehmen: daran verräth sich, dass er immer einer Heilung bedarf, dass er eine Art Flucht und Vergessen braucht, weg von dem, was ihm seine Einblicke und Einschnitte, was ihm sein "Handwerk" auf's Gewissen gelegt hat. Die Furcht vor seinem Gedächtniss ist ihm eigen. Er kommt vor dem Urtheile Anderer leicht zum Verstummen: er hört mit einem unbewegten Gesichte zu, wie dort verehrt, bewundert, geliebt, verklärt wird,

wo er gesehen hat, - oder er verbirgt noch sein Verstummen, indem er irgend einer Vordergrunds-Meinung ausdrücklich zustimmt. Vielleicht geht die Paradoxie seiner Lage so weit in's Schauerliche, dass die Menge, die Gebildeten, die Schwärmer gerade dort, wo er das grosse Mitleiden neben der grossen Verachtung gelernt hat, ihrerseits die grosse Verehrung lernen, - die Verehrung für "grosse Männer" und Wunderthiere, um derentwillen man das Vaterland, die Erde, die Würde der Menschheit, sich selber segnet und in Ehren hält, auf welche man die Jugend hinweist, hinerzieht…. Und wer weiss, ob sich nicht bisher in allen grossen Fällen eben das Gleiche begab: dass die Menge einen Gott anbetete, - und dass der "Gott" nur ein armes Opferthier war! Der Erfolg war immer der grösste Lügner, und das "Werk" selbst ist ein Erfolg; der grosse Staatsmann, der Eroberer, der Entdecker ist in seine Schöpfungen verkleidet, bis in's Unerkennbare; das "Werk", das des Künstlers, des Philosophen, erfindet erst Den, welcher es geschaffen hat, geschaffen haben soll; die "grossen Männer", wie sie verehrt werden, sind kleine schlechte Dichtungen hinterdrein; in der Welt der geschichtlichen Werthe herrscht die Falschmünzerei. Diese grossen Dichter zum Beispiel, diese Byron, Musset, Poe, Leopardi, Kleist, Gogol, - so wie sie nun einmal sind, vielleicht sein müssen: Menschen der Augenblicke, begeistert, sinnlich, kindsköpfisch, im Misstrauen und Vertrauen leichtfertig und plötzlich; mit Seelen, an denen gewöhnlich irgend ein Bruch verhehlt werden soll; oft mit ihren Werken Rache nehmend für eine innere Besudelung, oft mit ihren Aufflügen Vergessenheit suchend vor einem allzutreuen Gedächtniss, oft in den Schlamm verirrt und beinahe verliebt, bis sie den Irrlichtern um die Sümpfe herum gleich werden und sich zu Sternen verstellen - das Volk nennt sie dann wohl Idealisten -, oft mit einem langen Ekel kämpfend, mit einem wiederkehrenden Gespenst von Unglauben, der kalt macht und sie zwingt, nach gloria zu schmachten und den "Glauben an sich" aus den Händen berauschter Schmeichler zu fressen: - welche Marter sind diese grossen Künstler und überhaupt die höheren Menschen für Den, der sie einmal errathen hat! Es ist so begreiflich, dass sie gerade vom Weibe - welches hellseherisch ist in der Welt des Leidens und leider auch weit über seine Kräfte hinaus hülf- und rettungssüchtig - so leicht jene Ausbrüche unbegrenzten hingebendsten Mitleids erfahren, welche die Menge, vor Allem die verehrende Menge, nicht versteht und mit neugierigen und selbstgefälligen Deutungen überhäuft. Dieses Mitleiden täuscht sich regelmässig über seine Kraft; das Weib möchte glauben, dass Liebe Alles vermag, - es ist sein eigentlicher Glaube. Ach, der Wissende des Herzens erräth, wie arm, dumm, hülflos, anmaaslich, fehlgreifend, leichter zerstörend als rettend auch die beste tiefste Liebe ist! - Es ist möglich, dass unter der heiligen Fabel und Verkleidung von Jesu Leben einer der schmerzlichsten Fälle vom Martyrium des Wissens um die Liebe verborgen liegt: das Martyrium des unschuldigsten und begehrendsten Herzens, das an keiner Menschen-Liebe je genug hatte, das Liebe, Geliebt-werden und Nichts ausserdem verlangte, mit Härte, mit Wahnsinn, mit furchtbaren Ausbrüchen gegen Die, welche ihm Liebe verweigerten; die Geschichte eines armen Ungesättigten und Unersättlichen in der Liebe, der die Hölle erfinden musste, um Die dorthin zu schicken, welche ihn nicht lieben wollten, - und der endlich, wissend geworden über menschliche Liebe, einen Gott erfinden musste, der ganz Liebe, ganz Lieben- können ist, - der sich der Menschen-Liebe erbarmt, weil sie gar so armselig, so unwissend ist! Wer so fühlt, wer dergestalt um die Liebe weiss -, sucht den Tod. - Aber warum solchen schmerzlichen Dingen nachhängen? Gesetzt, dass man es nicht muss. -

270. Der geistige Hochmuth und Ekel jedes Menschen, der tief gelitten hat - es bestimmt beinahe die Rangordnung, wie tief Menschen leiden können -, seine schaudernde Gewissheit, von der er ganz durchtränkt und gefärbt ist, vermöge seines Leidens mehr zu wissen, als die Klügsten und Weisesten wissen können, in vielen fernen entsetzlichen Welten bekannt und einmal "zu Hause" gewesen zu sein, von denen "ihr nichts wisst!"....... dieser geistige schweigende Hochmuth des Leidenden, dieser Stolz des Auserwählten der Erkenntniss, des "Eingeweihten", des

beinahe Geopferten findet alle Formen von Verkleidung nöthig, um sich vor der Berührung mit zudringlichen und mitleidigen Händen und überhaupt vor Allem, was nicht Seinesgleichen im Schmerz ist, zu schützen. Das tiefe Leiden macht vornehm; es trennt. Eine der feinsten Verkleidungs-Formen ist der Epicureismus und eine gewisse fürderhin zur Schau getragene Tapferkeit des Geschmacks, welche das Leiden leichtfertig nimmt und sich gegen alles Traurige und Tiefe zur Wehre setzt. Es giebt "heitere Menschen", welche sich der Heiterkeit bedienen, weil sie um ihretwillen missverstanden werden: - sie wollen missverstanden sein. Es giebt "wissenschaftliche Menschen", welche sich der Wissenschaft bedienen, weil dieselbe einen heiteren Anschein giebt, und weil Wissenschaftlichkeit darauf schliessen lässt, dass der Mensch oberflächlich ist: - sie wollen zu einem falschen Schlusse verführen. Es giebt freie freche Geister, welche verbergen und verleugnen möchten, dass sie zerbrochene stolze unheilbare Herzen sind; und bisweilen ist die Narrheit selbst die Maske für ein unseliges allzugewisses Wissen. - Woraus sich ergiebt, dass es zur feineren Menschlichkeit gehört, Ehrfurcht "vor der Maske" zu haben und nicht an falscher Stelle Psychologie und Neugierde zu treiben.

271. Was am tiefsten zwei Menschen trennt, das ist ein verschiedener Sinn und Grad der Reinlichkeit. Was hilft alle Bravheit und gegenseitige Nützlichkeit, was

hilft aller guter Wille für einander: zuletzt bleibt es dabei - sie "können sich nicht riechen!" Der höchste Instinkt der Reinlichkeit stellt den mit ihm Behafteten in die wunderlichste und gefährlichste Vereinsamung, als einen Heiligen: denn eben das ist Heiligkeit - die höchste Vergeistigung des genannten Instinktes. Irgend ein Mitwissen um eine unbeschreibliche Fülle im Glück des Bades, irgend eine Brunst und Durstigkeit, welche die Seele beständig aus der Nacht in den Morgen und aus dem Trüben, der "Trübsal", in's Helle, Glänzende, Tiefe, Feine treibt -: eben so sehr als ein solcher Hang auszeichnet - es ist ein vornehmer Hang -, trennt er auch. - Das Mitleiden des Heiligen ist das Mitleiden mit dem Schmutz des Menschlichen, Allzumenschlichen. Und es giebt Grade und Höhen, wo das Mitleiden selbst von ihm als Verunreinigung, als Schmutz gefühlt wird......

272. Zeichen der Vornehmheit: nie daran denken, unsre Pflichten zu Pflichten für Jedermann herabzusetzen; die eigne Verantwortlichkeit
nicht abgeben wollen, nicht theilen wollen; seine Vorrechte und deren Ausübung unter seine Pflichten rechnen.

273. Ein Mensch, der nach Grossem strebt, betrachtet Jedermann, dem er auf seiner Bahn begegnet, entweder als Mittel oder als Verzögerung und Hemmniss - oder

als zeitweiliges Ruhebett. Seine ihm eigenthümliche hochgeartete Güte gegen Mitmenschen ist erst möglich, wenn er auf seiner Höhe ist und herrscht. Die Ungeduld und sein Bewusstsein, bis dahin immer zur Komödie verurtheilt zu sein - denn selbst der Krieg ist eine Komödie und verbirgt, wie jedes Mittel den Zweck verbirgt -, verdirbt ihm jeden Umgang: diese Art Mensch kennt die Einsamkeit und was sie vom Giftigsten an sich hat.

274. Das Problem der Wartenden. - Es sind Glücksfälle dazu nöthig und vielerlei Unberechenbares, dass ein höherer Mensch, in dem die Lösung eines Problems schläft, noch zur rechten Zeit zum Handeln kommt - "zum Ausbruch", wie man sagen könnte. Es geschieht durchschnittlich nicht, und in allen Winkeln der Erde sitzen Wartende, die es kaum wissen, in wiefern sie warten, noch weniger aber, dass sie umsonst warten. Mitunter auch kommt der Weckruf zu spät, jener Zufall, der die "Erlaubniss" zum Handeln giebt, - dann, wenn bereits die beste Jugend und Kraft zum Handeln durch Stillsitzen verbraucht ist; und wie Mancher fand, eben als er "aufsprang", mit Schrecken seine Glieder eingeschlafen und seinen Geist schon zu schwer! "Es ist zu spät" - sagte er sich, ungläubig über sich geworden und nunmehr für immer unnütz. - Sollte, im Reiche des Genie's, der "Raffael ohne Hände", das Wort im weitesten Sinn verstanden, vielleicht nicht die Ausnahme, sondern die Regel sein? - Das Genie ist

vielleicht gar nicht so selten: aber die fünfhundert Hände, die es nöthig hat, um den kairós, "die rechte Zeit" - zu tyrannisiren, um den Zufall am Schopf zu fassen!

275. Wer das Hohe eines Menschen nicht sehen will, blickt um so schärfer nach dem, was niedrig und Vordergrund an ihm ist - und verräth sich selbst damit.

276. Bei aller Art von Verletzung und Verlust ist die niedere und gröbere Seele besser daran, als die vornehmere: die Gefahren der letzteren müssen grösser sein, ihre Wahrscheinlichkeit, dass sie verunglückt und zu Grunde geht, ist sogar, bei der Vielfachheit ihrer Lebensbedingungen, ungeheuer. - Bei einer Eidechse wächst ein Finger nach, der ihr verloren gieng: nicht so beim Menschen. -

277. - Schlimm genug! Wieder die alte Geschichte! Wenn man sich sein Haus fertig gebaut hat, merkt man, unversehens Etwas dabei gelernt zu haben, das man schlechterdings hätte wissen müssen, bevor man zu bauen - anfieng. Das ewige leidige "Zu spät!" - Die Melancholie alles Fertigen!.....

278. - Wanderer, wer bist du? Ich sehe dich deines Weges gehn, ohne Hohn, ohne Liebe, mit unerrathbaren Augen; feucht und traurig wie ein Senkblei, das ungesättigt aus jeder Tiefe wieder an's Licht gekommen

- was suchte es da unten? -, mit einer Brust, die nicht seufzt, mit einer Lippe, die ihren Ekel verbirgt, mit einer Hand, die nur noch langsam greift: wer bist du? was thatest du? Ruhe dich hier aus: diese Stelle ist gastfreundlich für Jedermann, - erhole dich! Und wer du auch sein magst: was gefällt dir jetzt? Was dient dir zur Erholung? Nenne es nur: was ich habe, biete ich dir an! - "Zur Erholung? Zur Erholung? Oh du Neugieriger, was sprichst du da! Aber gieb mir, ich bitte - -" Was? Was? sprich es aus! - "Eine Maske mehr! Eine zweite Maske!".....

279. Die Menschen der tiefen Traurigkeit verrathen sich, wenn sie glücklich sind: sie haben eine Art, das Glück zu fassen, wie als ob sie es erdrücken und ersticken möchten, aus Eifersucht, - ach, sie wissen zu gut, dass es ihnen davonläuft!

280. "Schlimm! Schlimm! Wie? geht er nicht - zurück?" - Ja! Aber ihr versteht ihn schlecht, wenn ihr darüber klagt. Er geht zurück, wie jeder, der einen grossen Sprung thun will. - -

281.- "Wird man es mir glauben? aber ich verlange, dass man mir es glaubt: ich habe immer nur schlecht an mich, über mich gedacht, nur in ganz seltnen Fällen, nur gezwungen, immer ohne Lust `zur Sache`, bereit, von `Mir` abzuschweifen, immer ohne Glauben an das Ergebniss, Dank einem unbezwinglichen Misstrauen gegen die Möglichkeit der Selbst-Erkenntniss, das mich so weit geführt hat, selbst am Begriff `unmittelbare Erkenntniss`, welchen sich die Theoretiker erlauben, eine contradictio in adjecto zu empfinden: - diese ganze Thatsache ist beinahe das Sicherste, was ich über mich weiss. Es muss eine Art Widerwillen in mir geben, etwas Bestimmtes über mich zu glauben. - Steckt darin vielleicht ein Räthsel? Wahrscheinlich; aber glücklicherweise keins für meine eigenen Zähne. - Vielleicht verräth es die species, zu der ich gehöre? - Aber nicht mir: wie es mir selbst erwünscht genug ist."

282. "Aber was ist dir begegnet?" - "Ich weiss es nicht, sagte er zögernd; vielleicht sind mir die Harpyien über den Tisch geflogen." - Es kommt heute bisweilen vor, dass ein milder mässiger zurückhaltender Mensch plötzlich rasend wird, die Teller zerschlägt, den Tisch umwirft, schreit, tobt, alle Welt beleidigt - und endlich bei Seite geht, beschämt, wüthend über sich, - wohin? wozu? Um abseits zu verhungern? Um an seiner Erinnerung zu ersticken? - Wer die Begierden einer hohen wählerischen Seele hat und nur selten seinen Tisch gedeckt, seine Nahrung bereit findet, dessen Gefahr wird zu allen Zeiten gross sein: heute aber ist sie ausserordentlich. In ein lärmendes und pöbelhaftes Zeitalter hineingeworfen, mit dem er nicht aus Einer Schüssel essen mag, kann er leicht vor Hunger und Durst, oder, falls er endlich dennoch "zugreift" - vor plötzlichem Ekel zu Grunde gehn. - Wir haben

wahrscheinlich Alle schon an Tischen gesessen, wo wir nicht hingehörten; und gerade die Geistigsten von uns, die am schwersten zu ernähren sind, kennen jene gefährliche dyspepsia, welche aus einer plötzlichen Einsicht und Enttäuschung über unsre Kost und Tischnachbarschaft entsteht, - den Nachtisch-Ekel.

283. Es ist eine feine und zugleich vornehme Selbstbeherrschung, gesetzt, dass man überhaupt loben will, immer nur da zu loben, wo man nicht übereinstimmt: - im andern Falle würde man ja sich selbst loben, was wider den guten Geschmack geht - freilich eine Selbstbeherrschung, die einen artigen Anlass und Anstoss bietet, um beständig missverstanden zu werden. Man muss, um sich diesen wirklichen Luxus von Geschmack und Moralität gestatten zu dürfen, nicht unter Tölpeln des Geistes leben, vielmehr unter Menschen, bei denen Missverständnisse und Fehlgriffe noch durch ihre Feinheit belustigen, - oder man wird es theuer büssen müssen! - "Er lobt mich: also giebt er mir Recht" - diese Eselei von Schlussfolgerung verdirbt uns Einsiedlern das halbe Leben, denn es bringt die Esel in unsre Nachbarschaft und Freundschaft.

284. Mit einer ungeheuren und stolzen Gelassenheit leben; immer jenseits -. Seine Affekte, sein Für und Wider willkürlich haben und nicht haben, sich auf sie herablassen, für Stunden; sich auf sie setzen, wie auf

Pferde, oft wie auf Esel: - man muss nämlich ihre Dummheit so gut wie ihr Feuer zu nützen wissen. Seine dreihundert Vordergründe sich bewahren; auch die schwarze Brille: denn es giebt Fälle, wo uns Niemand in die Augen, noch weniger in unsre "Gründe" sehn darf. Und jenes spitzbübische und heitre Laster sich zur Gesellschaft wählen, die Höflichkeit. Und Herr seiner vier Tugenden bleiben, des Muthes, der Einsicht, des Mitgefühls, der Einsamkeit. Denn die Einsamkeit ist bei uns eine Tugend, als ein sublimer Hang und Drang der Reinlichkeit, welcher erräth, wie es bei Berührung von Mensch und Mensch - "in Gesellschaft" - unvermeidlich-unreinlich zugehn muss. Jede Gemeinschaft macht, irgendwie, irgendwo, irgendwann - "gemein".

285. Die grössten Ereignisse und Gedanken - aber die grössten Gedanken sind die grössten Ereignisse - werden am spätesten begriffen: die Geschlechter, welche mit ihnen gleichzeitig sind, erleben solche Ereignisse nicht, - sie leben daran vorbei. Es geschieht da Etwas, wie im Reich der Sterne. Das Licht der fernsten Sterne kommt am spätesten zu den Menschen; und bevor es nicht angekommen ist, leugnet der Mensch, dass es dort - Sterne giebt. "Wie viel Jahrhunderte braucht ein Geist, um begriffen zu werden?" - das ist auch ein Maassstab, damit schafft man auch eine Rangordnung und Etikette, wie sie noth thut: für Geist und Stern. -

286. "Hier ist die Aussicht frei, der Geist erhoben". - Es giebt aber eine umgekehrte Art von Menschen, welche auch auf der Höhe ist und auch die Aussicht frei hat - aber hinab blickt.

287. - Was ist vornehm? Was bedeutet uns heute noch das Wort "vornehm"? Woran verräth sich, woran erkennt man, unter diesem schweren verhängten Himmel der beginnenden Pöbelherrschaft, durch den Alles undurchsichtig und bleiern wird, den vornehmen Menschen? - Es sind nicht die Handlungen, die ihn beweisen, - Handlungen sind immer vieldeutig, immer unergründlich -; es sind auch die "Werke" nicht. Man findet heute unter Künstlern und Gelehrten genug von Solchen, welche durch ihre Werke verrathen, wie eine tiefe Begierde nach dem Vornehmen hin sie treibt: aber gerade dies Bedürfniss nach dem Vornehmen ist von Grund aus verschieden von den Bedürfnissen der vornehmen Seele selbst, und geradezu das beredte und gefährliche Merkmal ihres Mangels. Es sind nicht die Werke, es ist der Glaube, der hier entscheidet, der hier die Rangordnung feststellt, um eine alte religiöse Formel in einem neuen und tieferen Verstande wieder aufzunehmen: irgend eine Grundgewissheit, welche eine vornehme Seele über sich selbst hat, Etwas, das sich nicht suchen, nicht finden und vielleicht auch nicht verlieren lässt.- Die vornehme Seele hat Ehrfurcht vor sich.-

288. Es giebt Menschen, welche auf eine unvermeidliche Weise Geist haben, sie mögen sich drehen und wenden, wie sie wollen, und die Hände vor die verrätherischen Augen halten (- als ob die Hand kein Verräther wäre! -): schliesslich kommt es immer heraus, dass sie Etwas haben, das sie verbergen, nämlich Geist. Eins der feinsten Mittel, um wenigstens so lange als möglich zu täuschen und sich mit Erfolg dümmer zu stellen als man ist - was im gemeinen Leben oft so wünschenswerth ist wie ein Regenschirm -, heisst Begeisterung: hinzugerechnet, was hinzu gehört, zum Beispiel Tugend. Denn, wie Galiani sagt, der es wissen musste -: vertu est enthousiasme.

289. Man hört den Schriften eines Einsiedlers immer auch Etwas von dem Wiederhall der Öde, Etwas von dem Flüstertone und dem scheuen Umsichblicken der Einsamkeit an; aus seinen stärksten Worten, aus seinem Schrei selbst klingt noch eine neue und gefährlichere Art des Schweigens, Verschweigens heraus. Wer Jahraus, Jahrein und Tags und Nachts allein mit seiner Seele im vertraulichen Zwiste und Zwiegespräche zusammengesessen hat, wer in seiner Höhle - sie kann ein Labyrinth, aber auch ein Goldschacht sein - zum Höhlenbär oder Schatzgräber oder Schatzwächter und Drachen wurde: dessen Begriffe selber erhalten zuletzt eine eigne Zwielicht-Farbe, einen Geruch ebenso sehr der Tiefe als des Moders, etwas Unmittheilsames und Widerwilliges, das jeden Vorübergehenden kalt anbläst.

Der Einsiedler glaubt nicht daran, dass jemals ein Philosoph - gesetzt, dass ein Philosoph immer vorerst ein Einsiedler war - seine eigentlichen und letzten Meinungen in Büchern ausgedrückt habe: schreibt man nicht gerade Bücher, um zu verbergen, was man bei sich birgt? - ja er wird zweifeln, ob ein Philosoph "letzte und eigentliche" Meinungen überhaupt haben könne, ob bei ihm nicht hinter jeder Höhle noch eine tiefere Höhle liege, liegen müsse - eine umfänglichere fremdere reichere Welt über einer Oberfläche, ein Abgrund hinter jedem Grunde, unter jeder "Begründung". Jede Philosophie ist eine Vordergrunds-Philosophie - das ist ein Einsiedler-Urtheil: "es ist etwas Willkürliches daran, dass er hier stehen blieb, zurückblickte, sich umblickte, dass er hier nicht mehr tiefer grub und den Spaten weglegte, - es ist auch etwas Misstrauisches daran." Jede Philosophie verbirgt auch eine Philosophie; jede Meinung ist auch ein Versteck, jedes Wort auch eine Maske.

290. Jeder tiefe Denker fürchtet mehr das Verstanden-werden, als das Missverstanden-werden. Am Letzteren leidet vielleicht seine Eitelkeit; am Ersteren aber sein Herz, sein Mitgefühl, welches immer spricht: "ach, warum wollt ihres auch so schwer haben, wie ich?"

291. Der Mensch, ein vielfaches, verlogenes, künstliches und undurchsichtiges Thier, den andern Thieren weniger durch Kraft als durch List und

Klugheit unheimlich, hat das gute Gewissen erfunden, um seine Seele einmal als einfach zu geniessen; und die ganze Moral ist eine beherzte lange Fälschung, vermöge deren überhaupt ein Genuss im Anblick der Seele möglich wird. Unter diesem Gesichtspunkte gehört vielleicht viel Mehr in den Begriff "Kunst" hinein, als man gemeinhin glaubt.

292. Ein Philosoph: das ist ein Mensch, der beständig ausserordentliche Dinge erlebt, sieht, hört, argwöhnt, hofft, träumt; der von seinen eignen Gedanken wie von Aussen her, wie von Oben und Unten her, als von seiner Art Ereignissen und Blitzschlägen getroffen wird; der selbst vielleicht ein Gewitter ist, welches mit neuen Blitzen schwanger geht; ein verhängnissvoller Mensch, um den herum es immer grollt und brummt und klafft und unheimlich zugeht. Ein Philosoph: ach, ein Wesen, das oft von sich davon läuft, oft vor sich Furcht hat, - aber zu neugierig ist, um nicht immer wieder zu sich zu kommen......

293. Ein Mann, der sagt: "das gefällt mir, das nehme ich zu eigen und will es schützen und gegen Jedermann vertheidigen"; ein Mann, der eine Sache führen, einen Entschluss durchführen, einem Gedanken Treue wahren, ein Weib festhalten, einen Verwegenen strafen und niederwerfen kann; ein Mann, der seinen Zorn und sein Schwert hat, und dem die Schwachen, Leidenden, Bedrängten, auch die Thiere gern zufallen und von

Natur zugehören, kurz ein Mann, der von Natur Herr ist, - wenn ein solcher Mann Mitleiden hat, nun! dies Mitleiden hat Werth! Aber was liegt am Mitleiden Derer, welche leiden! Oder Derer, welche gar Mitleiden predigen! Es giebt heute fast überall in Europa eine krankhafte Empfindlichkeit und Reizbarkeit für Schmerz, insgleichen eine widrige Unenthaltsamkeit in der Klage, eine Verzärtlichung, welche sich mit Religion und philosophischem Krimskrams zu etwas Höherem aufputzen möchte, - es giebt einen förmlichen Cultus des Leidens. Die Unmännlichkeit dessen, was in solchen Schwärmerkreisen "Mitleid" getauft wird, springt, wie ich meine, immer zuerst in die Augen. - Man muss diese neueste Art des schlechten Geschmacks kräftig und gründlich in den Bann thun; und ich wünsche endlich, dass man das gute Amulet "gai saber" sich dagegen um Herz und Hals lege, - "fröhliche Wissenschaft", um es den Deutschen zu verdeutlichen.

294. Das olympische Laster. - Jenem Philosophen zum Trotz, der als ächter Engländer dem Lachen bei allen denkenden Köpfen eine üble Nachrede zu schaffen suchte - "das Lachen ist ein arges Gebreste der menschlichen Natur, welches jeder denkende Kopf zu überwinden bestrebt sein wird" (Hobbes) -, würde ich mir sogar eine Rangordnung der Philosophen erlauben, je nach dem Range ihres Lachens - bis hinauf zu denen, die des goldnen Gelächters fähig sind. Und gesetzt,

dass auch Götter philosophiren, wozu mich mancher Schluss schon gedrängt hat -, so zweifle ich nicht, dass sie dabei auch auf eine übermenschliche und neue Weise zu lachen wissen - und auf Unkosten aller ernsten Dinge! Götter sind spottlustig: es scheint, sie können selbst bei heiligen Handlungen das Lachen nicht lassen.

295. Das Genie des Herzens, wie es jener grosse Verborgene hat, der Versucher-Gott und geborene Rattenfänger der Gewissen, dessen Stimme bis in die Unterwelt jeder Seele hinabzusteigen weiss, welcher nicht ein Wort sagt, nicht einen Blick blickt, in dem nicht eine Rücksicht und Falte der Lockung läge, zu dessen Meisterschaft es gehört, dass er zu scheinen versteht - und nicht Das, was er ist, sondern was Denen, die ihm folgen, ein Zwang mehr ist, um sich immer näher an ihn zu drängen, um ihm immer innerlicher und gründlicher zu folgen: - das Genie des Herzens, das alles Laute und Selbstgefällige verstummen macht und horchen lehrt, das die rauhen Seelen glättet und ihnen ein neues Verlangen zu kosten giebt, - still zu liegen wie ein Spiegel, dass sich der tiefe Himmel auf ihnen spiegele -; das Genie des Herzens, das die tölpische und überrasche Hand zögern und zierlicher greifen lehrt; das den verborgenen und vergessenen Schatz, den Tropfen Güte und süsser Geistigkeit unter trübem dickem Eise erräth und eine Wünschelruthe für jedes Korn Goldes ist, welches lange im Kerker vielen

Schlamms und Sandes begraben lag; das Genie des Herzens, von dessen Berührung jeder reicher fortgeht, nicht begnadet und überrascht, nicht wie von fremdem Gute beglückt und bedrückt, sondern reicher an sich selber, sich neuer als zuvor, aufgebrochen, von einem Thauwinde angeweht und ausgehorcht, unsicherer vielleicht, zärtlicher zerbrechlicher zerbrochener, aber voll Hoffnungen, die noch keinen Namen haben, voll neuen Willens und Strömens, voll neuen Unwillens und Zurückströmens...... aber was thue ich, meine Freunde? Von wem rede ich zu euch? Vergass ich mich soweit, dass ich euch nicht einmal seinen Namen nannte? es sei denn, dass ihr nicht schon von selbst erriethet, wer dieser fragwürdige Geist und Gott ist, der in solcher Weise gelobt sein will. Wie es nämlich einem jeden ergeht, der von Kindesbeinen an immer unterwegs und in der Fremde war, so sind auch mir manche seltsame und nicht ungefährliche Geister über den Weg gelaufen, vor Allem aber der, von dem ich eben sprach, und dieser immer wieder, kein Geringerer nämlich, als der Gott Dionysos, jener grosse Zweideutige und Versucher Gott, dem ich einstmals, wie ihr wisst, in aller Heimlichkeit und Ehrfurcht meine Erstlinge dargebracht habe - als der Letzte, wie mir scheint, der ihm ein Opfer dargebracht hat: denn ich fand Keinen, der es verstanden hätte, was ich damals that. Inzwischen lernte ich Vieles, Allzuvieles über die Philosophie dieses Gottes hinzu, und, wie gesagt, von Mund zu Mund, - ich, der letzte jünger und

Eingeweihte des Gottes Dionysos: und ich dürfte wohl endlich einmal damit anfangen, euch, meinen Freunden, ein Wenig, so weit es mir erlaubt ist, von dieser Philosophie zu kosten zu geben? Mit halber Stimme, wie billig: denn es handelt sich dabei um mancherlei Heimliches, Neues, Fremdes, Wunderliches, Unheimliches. Schon dass Dionysos ein Philosoph ist, und dass also auch Götter philosophiren, scheint mir eine Neuigkeit, welche nicht unverfänglich ist und die vielleicht gerade unter Philosophen Misstrauen erregen möchte, - unter euch, meine Freunde, hat sie schon weniger gegen sich, es sei denn, dass sie zu spät und nicht zur rechten Stunde kommt: denn ihr glaubt heute ungern, wie man mir verrathen hat, an Gott und Götter. Vielleicht auch, dass ich in der Freimüthigkeit meiner Erzählung weiter gehn muss, als den strengen Gewohnheiten eurer Ohren immer liebsam ist? Gewisslich gieng der genannte Gott bei dergleichen Zwiegesprächen weiter, sehr viel weiter, und war immer um viele Schritt mir voraus.... ja ich würde, falls es erlaubt wäre, ihm nach Menschenbrauch schöne feierliche Prunk- und Tugendnamen beizulegen, viel Rühmens von seinem Forscher- und Entdecker-Muthe, von seiner gewagten Redlichkeit, Wahrhaftigkeit und Liebe zur Weisheit zu machen haben. Aber mit all diesem ehrwürdigen Plunder und Prunk weiss ein solcher Gott nichts anzufangen. "Behalte dies, würde er sagen, für dich und deines Gleichen und wer sonst es nöthig hat! Ich - habe keinen Grund, meine Blösse zu decken!" - Man erräth: es fehlt dieser Art von Gottheit und Philosophen vielleicht an Scham? - So sagte er einmal: "unter Umständen liebe ich den Menschen - und dabei spielte er auf Ariadne an, die zugegen war -: der Mensch ist mir ein angenehmes tapferes erfinderisches Thier, das auf Erden nicht seines Gleichen hat, es findet sich in allen Labyrinthen noch zurecht. Ich bin ihm gut: ich denke oft darüber nach, wie ich ihn noch vorwärts bringe und ihn stärker, böser und tiefer mache, als er ist." - "Stärker, böser und tiefer?" fragte ich erschreckt. "Ja, sagte er noch Ein Mal, stärker, böser und tiefer; auch schöner" - und dazu lächelte der Versucher-Gott mit seinem halkyonischen Lächeln, wie als ob er eben eine bezaubernde Artigkeit gesagt habe. Man sieht hier zugleich: es fehlt dieser Gottheit nicht nur an Scham -; und es giebt überhaupt gute Gründe dafür, zu muthmaassen, dass in einigen Stücken die Götter insgesammt bei uns Menschen in die Schule gehn könnten. Wir Menschen sind - menschlicher…

296. Ach, was seid ihr doch, ihr meine geschriebenen und gemalten Gedanken! Es ist nicht lange her, da wart ihr noch so bunt, jung und boshaft, voller Stacheln und geheimer Würzen, dass ihr mich niesen und lachen machtet - und jetzt? Schon habt ihr eure Neuheit ausgezogen, und einige von euch sind, ich fürchte es, bereit, zu Wahrheiten zu werden: so unsterblich sehn sie bereits aus, so herzbrechend rechtschaffen, so

langweilig! Und war es jemals anders? Welche Sachen schreiben und malen wir denn ab, wir Mandarinen mit chnesischem Pinsel, wir Verewiger der Dinge, welche sich schreiben lassen, was vermögen wir denn allein abzumalen? Ach, immer nur Das, was eben welk werden will und anfängt, sich zu verriechen! Ach, immer nur abziehende und erschöpfte Gewitter und gelbe späte Gefühle! Ach, immer nur Vögel, die sich müde flogen und verflogen und sich nun mit der Hand haschen lassen, - mit unserer Hand! Wir verewigen, was nicht mehr lange leben und fliegen kann, müde und mürbe Dinge allein! Und nur euer Nachmittag ist es, ihr meine geschriebenen und gemalten Gedanken, für den allein ich Farben habe, viel Farben vielleicht, viel bunte Zärtlichkeiten und fünfzig Gelbs und Brauns und Grüns und Roths: - aber Niemand erräth mir daraus, wie ihr in eurem Morgen aussahet, ihr plötzlichen Funken und Wunder meiner Einsamkeit, ihr meine alten geliebten - - schlimmen Gedanken!

Aus hohen Bergen.

Nachgesang.

  Oh Lebens Mittag! Feierliche Zeit!
Oh Sommergarten!
Unruhig Glück im Stehn und Spähn und Warten: -
Der Freunde harr' ich, Tag und Nacht bereit,
Wo bleibt ihr Freunde? Kommt! 's ist Zeit! 's ist Zeit!

  War's nicht für euch, dass sich des Gletschers Grau
Heut schmückt mit Rosen?
Euch sucht der Bach, sehnsüchtig drängen, stossen
Sich Wind und Wolke höher heut in's Blau,
Nach euch zu spähn aus fernster Vogel-Schau.

  Im Höchsten ward für euch mein Tisch gedeckt -
Wer wohnt den Sternen
So nahe, wer des Abgrunds grausten Fernen?
Mein Reich - welch Reich hat weiter sich gereckt?
Und meinen Honig - wer hat ihn geschmeckt?….

  - Da *seid* ihr, Freunde! - Weh, doch *ich* bin's nicht,
Zu dem ihr wolltet?

Ihr zögert, staunt - ach, dass ihr lieber grolltet!
Ich - bin's nicht mehr? Vertauscht Hand, Schritt,

 Gesicht?
Und was ich bin, euch Freunden - bin ich's nicht?

 Ein Andrer ward ich? Und mir selber fremd?
Mir selbst entsprungen?
Ein Ringer, der zu oft sich selbst bezwungen?
Zu oft sich gegen eigne Kraft gestemmt,
Durch eignen Sieg verwundet und gehemmt?

Ich suchte, wo der Wind am schärfsten weht?
Ich lernte wohnen,
Wo Niemand wohnt, in öden Eisbär-Zonen,
Verlernte Mensch und Gott, Fluch und Gebet?
Ward zum Gespenst, das über Gletscher geht?

- Ihr alten Freunde! Seht! Nun blickt ihr bleich,
Voll Lieb' und Grausen!
Nein, geht! Zürnt nicht! Hier - könntet *ihr* nicht hausen:
Hier zwischen fernstem Eis- und Felsenreich -
Hier muss man Jäger sein und gemsengleich.

Ein *schlimmer* Jäger ward ich! - Seht, wie steil
Gespannt mein Bogen!
Der Stärkste war's, der solchen Zug gezogen—:

Doch wehe nun! Gefährlich ist *der* Pfeil,
Wie *kein* Pfeil, - fort von hier! Zu eurem Heil!…..

Ihr wendet euch? - Oh Herz, du trugst genung,
Stark blieb dein Hoffen:
Halt *neuen* Freunden deine Thüren offen!
Die alten lass! Lass die Erinnerung!
Warst einst du jung, jetzt - bist du besser jung!

Was je uns knüpfte, Einer Hoffnung Band, -
Wer liest die Zeichen,
Die Liebe einst hineinschrieb, noch, die bleichen?
Dem Pergament vergleich ich's, das die Hand
zu fassen *scheut*, - ihm gleich verbräunt, verbrannt.

Nicht Freunde mehr, das sind - wie nenn' ich's doch? -
Nur Freunds-Gespenster!
Das klopft mir wohl noch Nachts an Herz und Fenster,
Das sieht mich an und spricht: "wir *waren's* doch?"—
Oh welkes Wort, das einst wie Rosen roch!

Oh Jugend-Sehnen, das sich missverstand!
Die *ich* ersehnte,
Die ich mir selbst verwandt-verwandelt wähnte,
Dass *alt* sie wurden, hat sie weggebannt:
Nur wer sich wandelt, bleibt mit mir verwandt.

Oh Lebens Mittag! Zweite Jugendzeit!
Oh Sommergarten!
Unruhig Glück im Stehn und Spähn und Warten!
Der Freunde harr' ich, Tag und Nacht bereit,
Der *neuen* Freunde! Kommt! 's ist Zeit! 's ist Zeit!

Dies Lied ist aus, - der Sehnsucht süsser Schrei
Erstarb im Munde:

Ein Zaubrer that's, der Freund zur rechten Stunde,
Der Mittags-Freund - nein! fragt nicht, wer es sei -
Um Mittag war's, da wurde Eins zu Zwei…

  Nun feiern wir, vereinten Siegs gewiss,
Das Fest der Feste:
Freund *Zarathustra* kam, der Gast der Gäste!
Nun lacht die Welt, der grause Vorhang riss,
Die Hochzeit kam für Licht und Finsterniss…

Table of content :

English version by Helen Zimmern

Preface pag. 5

Chapter 1   Prejudices of Philosophers pag. 9

Chapter 2   The Free Spirit pag. 40

Chapter 3   The Religious Mood pag. 67

Chapter 4   Apophthegms and Interludes pag. 92

Chapter 5   The Natural History Of Morals pag. 109

Chapter 6   We Scholars pag. 139

Chapter 7   Our Virtues pag. 166

Chapter 8   Peoples and Countries pag. 200

Chapter 9   What Is Noble ? pag. 233

From The Heights pag. 266

German original text / Inhalt

Vorrede   pag.   284

1. Hauptstück: Von den Vorurtheilen der Philosophen.   pag. 288

2. Hauptstück: Der freie Geist.   pag. 321

3. Hauptstück: Das religiöse Wesen.   pag. 351

4. Hauptstück: Sprüche und Zwischenspiele.   pag. 377

5. Hauptstück: Zur Naturgeschichte der Moral.   pag. 394

6. Hauptstück: Wir Gelehrten.   pag. 425

7. Hauptstück: Unsere Tugenden.   pag. 453

8. Hauptstück: Völker und Vaterländer.   pag. 489

9. Hauptstück: Was ist vornehm?   pag. 524

Aus hohen Bergen. Nachgesang. pag. 570

Contino Publishers Ltd.
Dorking, UK

page intentionally left blank

www.ingramcontent.com/pod-product-compliance
Lightning Source LLC
Chambersburg PA
CBHW081201170426
43197CB00018B/2886